Also by Robert Smith Thompson

Pledge to Destiny: Charles DeGaulle and the Rise of the Free French
A Time for War: Franklin D. Roosevelt and the Path to Pearl Harbor

The Missiles of October

The Declassified Story of John F. Kennedy and the Cuban Missile Crisis

Robert Smith Thompson

Simon & Schuster

New York · London · Toronto · Sydney · Tokyo · Singapore

SIMON & SCHUSTER
Simon & Schuster Building
Rockefeller Center
1230 Avenue of the Americas
New York, New York 10020

Designed by Irving Perkins Associates
Manufactured in the United States of America

10 9 8 7 6 5 4 3 2 1

Library of Congress Cataloging-in-Publication Data
Thompson, Robert Smith.
The missiles of October: the declassified story of John F.
Kennedy and the Cuban missile crisis/Robert Smith Thompson.
p. cm.
Includes bibliographical references and index.
1. Cuban Missile Crisis, Oct. 1962.   2. Kennedy, John F. (John
Fitzgerald), 1917–1963.   I. Title.
E841.T52   1992
973.922—dc20   92–20238
CIP

ISBN: 0-671-76806-9

FOR JUDY,
Now and always

Acknowledgments

To Sandra Taylor, Francisco Wong, and James Holt, who have read the manuscript and saved me from at least a few egregious errors, my thanks.

My thanks also to the always helpful archivists, June Payne and Jim Cedrone at the Kennedy Library, Mary M. Huth at the Rush Rhees Library of the University of Rochester, Marilyn Kann at the Hoover Institution, and David Wallace, John Stier, and John Ruthroth at the National Security Archive.

And my thanks, finally, to those with the wisdom to create the National Security Archive—journalist Scott Armstrong, the MacArthur Foundation, and others. A nongovernmental organization in Washington, the Archive houses invaluable collections on the Iran-Contra scandal, Afghanistan, the Philippines, U.S. intelligence agencies, as well as the Cuban missile crisis. These collections have not come cheaply. Over and over the Archive has had to incur the substantial legal costs of invoking the Freedom of Information Act. The Archive deserves our plaudits and our support. Its files are essential to the upholding of the public's right to know—and thus to the preservation of American democracy.

I also owe many thanks to my agent, Russell Galen, and to two fine editors, Paul Aron and Rebecca Saletan.

Contents

Part IV. Endgame

From an oral interview conducted on October 13, 1987, at the John F. Kennedy School of Government, Harvard University:

Q: Mr. Mikoyan [Sergo, son of Anastas Mikoyan, Deputy Premier of the Soviet Union at the time of the Cuban missile crisis], why did the Soviet Union deploy MRBMs [Medium Range Ballistic Missiles] in Cuba?

A: In the spring of 1962, we in Moscow were absolutely convinced that a second Bay of Pigs was at hand, that a new military invasion of Cuba was at hand—but this time with all the American military might, not only with proxy troops.

Prologue

As Rudolph Anderson, a U.S. Air Force major on loan to the Central Intelligence Agency, took off from Florida's McCoy Air Force Base early in the morning of October 15, 1962, he saw the first orange streaks of the Atlantic sunrise, off to his left and far to the east. His aircraft was a U-2, a lightweight, high-flying spy plane, and as he reached the northern shoreline of Cuba, he was at seventy thousand feet, and he banked toward the southwest. The time was just before 7:00 A.M., a moment the CIA had selected with care. At that hour, in the middle of October, the sun would have risen just enough that shadows on the ground in Cuba would be long and sharp: for CIA photoanalysts, objects captured by U-2 cameras would stand out in clear silhouettes.

As Anderson started to cross the western tip of Cuba, the eastern side of his airplane was bathed by the rays of the sun. He activated the cameras, positioned in the belly of his plane. Moments later he had crossed over Cuba, and began a circuitous route back to Florida. By midmorning, the pictures he had taken were processed and winging their way to CIA headquarters in northern Virginia, just across the Potomac River from the District of Columbia.

The sky over Washington that day was cloudy, and by late afternoon, the temperature hovered close to eighty degrees, warm for the middle of October. The day was a Monday, and as the government's hordes of bureaucrats filed into the city to take their places at their various desks, the week coming up seemed to be just like any other week in the nation's capital, except that it was unseasonably muggy. In the course of the day, a State Department official told reporters that "Red China" was a potential enemy; former President Eisenhower, campaigning for the Republicans in Boston, assailed present President Kennedy's "dreary foreign record of the past twenty-one months"; and Herblock, cartoonist for *The Washington Post*, was inking in his drawing for the next morning's edition, a potbellied Fidel Castro, complete with fatigues, beard, and cigar all sketched in miniature, as the Cuban leader stomped on the head of a man labeled John Q. Public. This Monday in October was a slow news day.

Indeed, about the only excitement in the offing was going to be on television that evening, the fourth game of baseball's World Series. And as Washingtonians at 5:00 P.M. waited for buses to return them to their apartments up Connecticut Avenue, or joined the traffic jams that crept out toward the suburbs in Virginia and Maryland, they looked forward to seeing Willie Mays and the San Francisco Giants face off against Whitey Ford and the New York Yankees. They reckoned on nothing more dramatic than that.

At about 7:00 P.M., however, unknown of course to the commuters, a telephone rang in an apartment of The Towers, an elegant complex that looked out upon the Washington Cathedral. Roswell Gilpatric, who had been dressing for dinner, picked up a special receiver. A slender six-footer, aged fifty-six, Gilpatric had a boyish look and blue eyes that sometimes looked shy. Or at least they masked his importance. He had graduated high in his classes at Yale College and Yale Law School; he had been a partner in the Manhattan legal firm of Cravath, Swaine & Moore; he owned homes in New York and the Maryland Eastern Shore as well as in the District of Columbia; he had held a series of high-ranking posts in the Pentagon; and now he was the Deputy Secretary of Defense. The department's secretary, Robert S. McNamara, was the cold-blooded and impersonal administrator; its deputy secretary, Gilpatric, was the diplomat, the unruffler of people's feelings, or, as one of the papers had put it, the "Humanizer." When McNamara was unavailable—on the evening of October 15, 1962, he was a guest at the Virginia estate of Attorney General Robert F. Kennedy—Gilpatric was the man in charge.

His telephone call was from Room 3C320 in the Pentagon, from Joseph F. Carroll, an Air Force lieutenant general and the director of the Defense Intelligence Agency. He had been studying that morning's U-2 photographs taken from over Cuba, he told Gilpatric, and he had detected something alarming. He wanted Gilpatric to see the pictures right away, and he was going to send two analysts up to Gilpatric's apartment.

The photoanalysts found Gilpatric in his bedroom, knotting his black tie. Laying out large glossy prints of several pictures, snapshots from over the western end of Cuba, they pointed out a trapezoidal clearing in a forest, clusters of military vehicles and tents, some long sheds, and, on the ground, the beginnings of what looked like missile ramps; the pattern of these objects, they told Gilpatric, resembled that of certain missile sites in the Soviet Union. It looked as if the Soviets were placing medium-range ballistic missiles in Cuba.

Gilpatric made a quick decision. He was due shortly at Fort McNair, down at the confluence of the Potomac and Anacostia Rivers, there to dine at the quarters of General Maxwell Taylor, Chairman of the Joint Chiefs of Staff; if Gilpatric missed the dinner, he might cause a stir. So he told the analysts to meet with him and the "boss," McNamara, at 7:30 A.M. the next day. A limousine whisked Gilpatric down through Georgetown and out through the Mall to General Taylor's residence.

A Kennedy-style general, cool, controlled, and cultured, or cultured at least to the extent that he had authored a book, on warfare, Maxwell Taylor had impressed the Kennedy's and the President had skipped him over several echelons of higher-ranking brass to become the Chairman of the Joint Chiefs. So Taylor's dinner parties were important social occasions. As the wives noticed, each of the major guests, Gilpatric, General Carroll, General Marshall Carter of the Central Intelligence Agency, and State Department Deputy Undersecretary U. Alexis Johnson, all kept leaving the table to talk on the telephone, and returning with anxious looks on their faces. Each of them, obviously, could hardly wait for the party to end.

Such, too, was the mood of McGeorge Bundy, hosting another dinner party in his home at 5225 Partridge Lane in the northwestern corner of the city. Steely-eyed and driving, Bundy had been the brilliant dean at Harvard and now was the equally brilliant National Security Adviser in the White House. But now even Bundy seemed shaken—at 8:30 P.M., he accepted a telephone call from Ray Cline, an official down at the CIA, and heard the news about Cuba. Over coffee and cognac, he wrestled with a question in silence. Should he notify President Kennedy, then and there?

With the congressional elections just over two weeks away, John F. Kennedy had been out of town, campaigning for the Democrats in Niagara Falls and Manhattan, and had returned that day looking tired. He would need a good night of sleep. Bundy decided he would tell the President in the morning.

The next day, October 16, 1962, Bundy arrived at his office in the White House basement even earlier than usual, and closeting himself with the same photoanalysts who had visited Gilpatric, he studied the pictures of Cuba. At 8:00 A.M. he took the elevator to the presidential living quarters, and showed the photos to Kennedy. Appalled, JFK told Bundy to call a meeting of about a dozen foreign policy and defense officials, a meeting to be convened in the White House at 11:45 A.M. that day, and to be conducted in the strictest secrecy.

Shortly before noon, sleek black official limousines, one by one and pulling in through different entrances, reached the White House complex, and the occupants of the automobiles went inside. The Cuban missile crisis had begun.

For the last three decades, the Cuban missile crisis has raised some troubling questions. Why did the Soviets place the missiles in Cuba? High American officials at the time believed, or said they believed, that the Soviets were trying to cow America into defeat; yet the Soviets then and now claimed they were trying to forestall a full-scale U.S. invasion of Cuba. Did President Kennedy, on the morning of October 16, 1962, have no prior knowledge of the presence of the missiles in Cuba? In his memoir of the Cuban missile crisis, the President's brother, Robert F. Kennedy, indicated that JFK had known nothing of the missiles before that morning; yet several times before the missile crisis erupted, Kenneth B. Keating, a white-maned Republican senator from Rochester, New York, charged that the

Soviets were putting missiles on Cuba, and in 1964 he claimed that his information had been "either furnished or confirmed by government sources." (In the Keating papers, available at the University of Rochester, almost all materials from September and early October, 1962, are missing.) What brought the Cuban missile crisis to an end? Secretary of State Dean Rusk claimed that we and the Soviets had stood eyeball to eyeball, and that they had blinked first; yet, as now-declassified documents show, President Kennedy offered the Soviets a pledge not only to refrain from an invasion of Cuba but also to remove from Turkey American missiles that Moscow said it found frightening. And President Kennedy kept the latter concession secret from most of his top advisers, especially those from the military. And what was the outcome of the Cuban missile crisis? Was America's power enhanced? Or were critical vulnerabilities, including those of President Kennedy himself, revealed?

A veritable mountain of declassified materials enables us to look at these questions anew. But the documents alone do not convey a sense of what the Cuban missile crisis was all about. We need historical perspective, back at least to the end of the Second World War. For the Cuban missile crisis actually was the climax of two massive and parallel efforts, the one on the part of U.S. foreign policymakers in general and the other on the part of the family of the tycoon named Joseph P. Kennedy, to become masters of the world. And the Cuban missile crisis illustrated more vividly than had any previous event that such efforts at control were illusory.

Part I
Threat

CHAPTER 1

The Cold Warriors

1 Our starting place is an island called Tinian. Our starting date is August 16, 1945, at just before 2:30 A.M.

A bit northeast of Guam, off the Philippines in the far Pacific, Tinian, smaller than Guam, was—as if this were possible— even more desolate. The Marines had just captured the place from Japan, and U.S. military engineers had improved the four already existing airstrips. On Tinian Island, just about everything centered around those airstrips, the beaches, the palm trees, the Quonset huts, the mess halls, the movie theater, and, of course, the sleek and silvery B-29s, heavily guarded and, when not up in the air and dropping bombs, parked on the aprons that skirted the runways. But three of those B-29s had yet to fly as far as Japan. They formed a special contingent, the 509th Composite Group of the Army Air Corps, and they had been confined to bombing Japanese stragglers on nearby Reta Island. Over Reta nonetheless they had honed their timing to perfection; their mission, top secret, was rumored to be of the highest importance.

Some of the men on Tinian Island had their suspicions. Wrote one soldier-satirist:

> Into the air the secret rose,
> Where they're going nobody knows.
> Tomorrow they'll return again.

But we'll never know where they've been.
Don't ask us about results or such.
Unless you want to get into Dutch.
But take it from one who knows the score—
The 509th is winning the war.

Indeed: now, at last, in the small hours of the morning of August 6, 1945, the three bombers, to be accompanied by three weather scout planes, were being prepared for the flight to Japan. Off on the aprons, all night long, mechanics had been at work, oiling, greasing, checking the weldings and the times on the dials, making certain that the engines were in perfect tune. One of these bombers must have been the most thoroughly checked-over airplane in the world; it certainly was going to be the most famous, or infamous, airplane in the world. It was named the *Enola Gay.*

Even while the *Enola Gay* was still on the apron, floodlights cut through the darkness. The lights were ten or twelve in number, and all of them were illuminating the *Enola Gay;* interspersed among the floodlights were a hundred or more persons, military police, security agents, officers, scientists, and cinematographers. The film crews had been sent out by the U.S. government for, back in Washington, those members of officialdom who were in the know wanted this moment recorded for posterity. So as a military truck bearing the flight crew roared down the tarmac and pulled to a stop by the apron, the commander stepped down—and found himself besieged by cameras.

The commander was Colonel Paul W. Tibbetts, reputed to be the best pilot in the U.S. Army Air Corps. Tibbetts had been tipped off about possible publicity but this, he later declared, was "full-scale Hollywood premiere treatment. I expected to see MGM's lion walk on to the apron or Warner's logo light up the sky." As another of the pilots climbed down from the truck, a photographer yelled at him: "You're gonna be famous—so smile!" As the rest of the crew clambered down one by one, they blinked into the lights, eventually smiled or waved, then mounted the steps to the airplane. Twelve men were in the flight crew. In his pocket Tibbetts carried twelve cyanide capsules.

Up in the nose of the bomber, Tibbetts slid open a side window and waved down. Newsreel cameras caught his every gesture. He grinned, but then he yelled, "Okay, fellows, cut those lights. We gotta be going."

Gradually the camera lights dimmed and went out. Even in the darkness, however, a *New York Times* reporter was able to scribble on a notepad: "Started engines at 2:27 A.M."

Up in the cockpit, Commander Tibbetts gave a nod and the propellers began to turn. In a moment or so, the *Enola Gay* glided into motion, starting to roll out onto the first of the four parallel runways on Tinian Island. The copilot turned the radio on. "This is Dimples 82 to North Tinian Tower," he said, "ready for taxi out and takeoff instructions." A voice responded: "Tower to Dimples 82, clear to taxi. Takeoff on Runway A for Able." Led by a jeep, the bomber moved on out; and for a few moments the jeep's headlights illuminated the fire trucks and ambulances, parked at fifty-foot intervals, all the way down both sides of the runway. Then, flashing its lights, the jeep finally pulled off the strip. At 2:35 A.M., the big bomber was positioned at the takeoff end of the runway.

In another exchange of messages, the bomber asked clearance for departure. The tower immediately granted permission.

Checking the instrument panel, Commander Tibbetts realized that with twelve men aboard and with seven thousand tons of gasoline in the tanks, the bomber was far more heavily laden than usual. So he made a quick, and secret, decision. He would delay actual lift-off until the last possible moment.

At 2:45 A.M., the *Enola Gay* moved forward, slowly at first and then with a gathering speed. The copilot, Captain Robert A. Lewis, was nervous: at about the two-thirds mark on the runway, the bomber was still on the ground. Lewis made a motion toward the control column. "No! Leave it!" Tibbetts barked. Lewis obeyed, pulling his hand back; and as he did so he could make out, in the illumination of the bomber's own front lights, the edge of the cliff that marked the end of this, this first of the four runways on Tinian Island. Only the sea lay beyond—they were practically upon the edge of the sea—and in that moment Commander Tibbetts eased his wheel back, and the airplane ascended.

Five hours later, as the *Enola Gay* was lumbering close to the Japanese coast, Tibbetts spoke on the intercom, announcing that the airplane was carrying "the world's first atomic bomb." Soon thereafter, he ordered his men to put on their goggles; and then, as the airship trembled, a flash of light suffused the crew, and a huge, purplish cloud rose high in the atmosphere. "Even though we had expected something terrific," copilot Lewis later remembered, "what we saw made us feel that we were Buck Rogers's twenty-fifth-century warriors."

For the *Enola Gay* had just bombed Hiroshima. A few days later a bomber dropped another atomic bomb on Nagasaki, and the Second World War was over: Japan surrendered.

President Harry S Truman received news of the bombing with glee, calling it "the greatest thing in history." Truman at the time was aboard the cruiser *Augusta*, leaving Germany after an unsuccessful summit meeting with Josef Stalin at Potsdam, just outside Berlin—Stalin had made clear that he had no intention of willingly releasing his grip on Poland. But when word of Hiroshima reached the *Augusta*, Stalin's obstreperousness seemed trivial. According to the *Augusta*'s logbook, Truman "jumped up from his seat" on deck, strode over to James F. Byrnes, his shrewd little secretary of state from South Carolina, and exclaimed, "It's time for us to get on home!" Then he raced down to the wardroom and said to the officers, "Keep your seats, gentlemen. We have just dropped a bomb on Japan which has more power than twenty thousand tons of TNT. It was an overwhelming success. We won the gamble!" The officers rose anyway, and they cheered and clapped.

Four years before Hiroshima and Nagasaki, Henry Luce, publisher of *Time* and *Life*, had proclaimed the advent of the "American century." Now, as President Truman and his advisers steamed back across the Atlantic, Luce's prophecy seemed true. In the words of a recent historian, the United States in the summer of 1945 possessed the "prime weapon of *de*struction—the atomic bomb—and the prime weapon of *re*construction—such wealth as no nation hitherto had possessed." Or, as another recent historian has put it, "We thought we could do anything."

Back in Moscow, Josef Stalin found the bomb—and the new American attitude—disturbing, confirming his worst fears and suspicions. Russia, in his eyes, had just saved the West from Nazi barbarism, and now the Americans were repaying the debt with rejection and ingratitude.

Embittered, Stalin looked with narrowed eyes at enemies abroad and rivals at home, and he set out to give his dictatorship its culminating twists, a reign of terror and a personality cult in the Soviet Union, and tight control over the eastern European satellites. The Americans protested these policies, but he attributed the protests to arrogance. Americans, in his view, thought they owned the world.

Such certainly was the mood in Washington, late in the summer and early in the autumn of 1945. Those few months now seem so quaint: every day just after 6:00 A.M., Harry Truman, much to the despair of the Secret Service, would set out for a brisk walk, up through Lafayette Square, around the mansions that faced onto Dupont Circle, then down to the Washington Monument, and up, finally, to his day's work in the Oval Office. Wearing a double-breasted gray suit and a polka-dot bow tie, with his gray hair slicked down and his eyes appearing enlarged through the thick lenses of his steel-rimmed glasses, he would trade jokes with reporters, give a wave to an astonished tourist, and stop to shake the hand of a street sweeper. With his background in the corruption and parochialism of the Kansas City Democratic political machine, Truman had seemed a joke as President. Yet here he was, back from Europe full of vigor and peppery retorts, and ready to do whatever he could to advance what he saw as the national interests of the United States of America.

Problems did emerge abroad, even before the turn of the year. In Poland, Hungary, and Bulgaria, intelligence reports were showing, the Soviets were imposing a reign of terror. In Iran, contrary to a wartime U.S.-British-Soviet understanding, Stalin was keeping his troops in the northern part of the country, even after Washington and London had withdrawn their forces from the rest of that state. And in China, the prewar civil conflict between the government loyalists of Chiang Kai-shek and the Communist guerrillas of Mao Tse-tung had reemerged with a vengeance.

Yet China's Communists were hardly pro-Russian. The Soviets produced documents that showed a historic Russian interest in the upper provinces of Iran. And in the eastern reaches of Europe, the United States was proffering foreign aid to local

politicians, clearly in the hope that such personages would distance themselves from Moscow. So, as revelers gathered in New
York's Times Square for the New Year's orgy at the end of 1945,
the national interests President Truman had resolved to protect
were not in danger.

Yet, as from the depths, a national clamor was arising. We
were bringing the boys back home, and sometimes they had no
jobs; civilians who had had to deal with rationings, and thus had
substantial savings, started to consume as if there were no
tomorrow, and prices took off as if on a rocket; and the labor
unions, restrained in their wartime demands on management
for reasons patriotic, now burst forth in strikes. The American
mood, as Dean Acheson, at the time Assistant Secretary of
State, discovered, was turning ugly. Tall, elegant in dress, and
mustachioed in the manner of a British grenadier, Acheson gave
a speech late in November 1945 to a rally in Madison Square
Garden. He expressed sympathy for the Soviets' security aims—
and amidst the catcalls and the boos, he found a policeman
touching him on the arm, showing him a quiet way out to his
car.

Echoing public sentiment, George F. Kennan, the U.S. chargé
d'affaires in Moscow, in response to questions from the government in Washington, sent back a cable known to history as the
"long telegram." A brilliant misfit at Princeton and later a
Soviet expert in the Foreign Service, Kennan had come to loathe
the Soviets, and his sentiments found their way into his message:

[The] U.S.S.R. still lives in antagonistic "capitalistic encirclement"
with which in the long run there can be no permanent peaceful coexistence. . . . At bottom of [this] neurotic view of world affairs is traditional
and instinctive Russian sense of insecurity. [The Russian rulers] have
always feared foreign penetration, feared direct contact between Western world and their own, feared what would happen if [the people]
learned truth about world without or if foreigners learned truth about
world within. And they have learned to seek security only in patient
but *deadly struggle for total destruction of rival power, never in com-
pacts and compromises within it* [emphasis added] . . . . [W]e have here
a police force committed fanatically to the belief that with U.S. there
can be no permanent modus vivendi, that it is desirable and necessary

that the internal harmony of our society be disrupted, our traditional way of life be destroyed, the international authority of our state be broken, if Soviet power is to be secure. . . .

Gauged against Western world as a whole, Soviets are still by far the weaker force. Thus, their success will really depend on degree of cohesion, firmness and vigor which Western world can muster. . . .

Kennan later regretted these words, admitting that his telegram had read like a primer published by "the Daughters of the American Revolution, designed to arouse the citizenry to the dangers of the Communist conspiracy." Kennan nonetheless had done the deed; and when the ill-fated Defense Secretary James V. Forrestal (he was soon to commit suicide) got wind of Kennan's cable, he obtained a copy, required his staff and top officers to read it, and directed the Pentagon to publish and distribute scores of the message all around Washington. Like a missionary passing out Bibles, Forrestal was preaching the good news that the Soviets were bad.

They certainly sounded bad. In February, 1946—at just about the time Kennan's cable was flashing to Washington—Marshal Stalin spoke in the Bolshoi Theater, conceding that during World War II, the Soviets and the West had fought for a common cause, but making frequent references to the "hostile" international system and to the American-designed "capitalist encirclement." War, Stalin warned, just might be in the offing. The reaction in America was nearly hysterical. While Stalin may have made the speech "for purely Russian reasons," said *Time*, it was still "the most warlike pronouncement uttered by any top-rank statesman since V-J Day."

Truman responded to Stalin's speech by inviting Winston S. Churchill (voted out of Britain's prime ministership while he was attending the Potsdam Conference) to give an address in America. After they had ridden by train from Washington to Fulton, Missouri, Truman's home state, and with President Truman sitting prominently on a newly built wooden platform, Churchill lashed out at Stalin: "From Stettin in the Baltic to Trieste in the Adriatic," Churchill said with his ever-present lisp, "an iron curtain has descended across the continent!"

Not to be outdone, Stalin raged back with another speech, declaring this time that he had no intention of exchanging the "lordship of Hitler for the lordship of Churchill." East and West were going to war with words. And soon the war was to be with more than words.

Friday, February 21, 1947, was a cold and overcast day in Washington, and in the State Department the grayness of the sky was reflected in the grayness of the mood. The State Department that day was starting to move from the marble Victorian pile just west of the White House (now the Old Executive Office Building) to a new building in Foggy Bottom just above the Potomac River. The new place, James Reston wrote in *The New York Times*, possessed "about as much character as a chewing gum factory in Los Angeles," and the diplomatic officials agreed. The department had outgrown the old building, and the Foreign Service officers knew they would miss its high-ceilinged offices and, in the echoing corridors, the black-and-white squares along the marble floors, floors now cluttered with file cabinets and packing boxes. The day, unfortunately, was one for lifting and hauling, not for carrying out America's foreign policy.

Into the chaos of crates and moving vans, however, an official from the British embassy walked into the Department. He wanted to see General George C. Marshall, who recently had replaced James F. Byrnes as secretary of state, but Marshall was out of town, en route to give a speech up in Princeton, and so the Britisher called on the undersecretary of state, Dean G. Acheson. A tall, imperious Washington lawyer, Acheson was nearing the department's pinnacle of power, and in the "blue piece of paper" borne by the British visitor, he sensed his own chance to attain the highest level, as well as President Truman's chance to win reelection. A "blue piece of paper" was diplomatic parlance for a message of extreme importance: the British wanted nothing less than for the United States to assume Britain's traditional role as the protector of Turkey and Greece.

President Truman's prestige was low ("To err is Truman," a newsman had quipped) but the British request, Acheson sensed, would allow HST to do what Americans liked most in their Chiefs of State—stand tall overseas. And if Acheson, although only the undersecretary, could be the one to help Truman design the policy, Acheson could speed to the top of the State

Department. For reasons of career and conviction alike, Acheson had become a convert to containment.

Standing tall overseas was indeed smart politics, for despite their postwar prosperity, Americans had been growing restive. The Soviets, according to the news reports, were exhausting economically their zone in Germany. The Soviets in the Security Council of the United Nations, in July 1946, vetoed the Baruch Plan, a scheme that would have given the U.N. control over atomic weaponry (although only after the Soviet Union had turned its own fissionable materials over to the U.N. and submitted to that body's inspection would the U.S. give up its own atomic bomb monopoly). The Soviets, in August 1946, began demanding steaming rights to the Mediterranean through the Dardanelles, and Turkey protested to the Western powers (although twice during World War II, in 1943 at Tehran and in 1944 at Moscow, Churchill had promised Stalin precisely such access). In late 1946 and early 1947, General George C. Marshall (before becoming secretary of state) flew to China in an effort to persuade the Communists and the Nationalists to cease their civil war, and after he had returned, his mission a failure, the Communists kept gaining ground (although the Soviets had given them precious little help). And at the same time, another civil war had erupted, in Greece, a vicious conflict that pitted the British-supported forces of the Monarchy against a united front that included Communists, and the U.S. press portrayed the Communists as the instigators of the fight (although because they were nationalists and admired the independent-minded Yugoslav leader, Tito, Stalin despised the Greek Communists and withheld meaningful aid).

Whatever the truth, the American public saw the Soviet Union as bent on world conquest, and excoriated Truman for his failure, apparently, to hold back the tide. Enter Undersecretary of State Dean Acheson and the "blue piece of paper": persuading Truman to address the Congress, he then wrote a speech for the President intended to "scare hell out of the American people."

At 1 P.M., March 12, 1947, President Harry S Truman addressed a Joint Session of Congress, his thick glasses glinting from behind the rostrum of the House of Representatives. In phrases that echoed those of Truman's predecessor when on December 8, 1941, President Franklin D. Roosevelt had asked Congress to declare war on Japan, Truman divided the world between "free peoples" and regimes that relied on "terror and oppression . . . the suppression of personal freedoms." Asking Congress for $400 million, he then went on to state that "it must be the policy of the United States to support free peoples who are resisting attempted subjugation by armed minorities or by outside pressures." In this Truman Doctrine, the United States had the responsibility—to itself and to the "free world" alike—to contain the power of the Soviet Union.

One member of Congress who heard Truman's speech was Arkansas's J. William Fulbright. "More by far than any other factor," Fulbright wrote some years later, "the anti-communism of the Truman Doctrine has been the guiding spirit of American foreign policy. . . ."

Another member of Congress in the audience that day was a young man from Massachusetts who just had taken his House seat. His name was John F. Kennedy.

2   About a year and a half before, in the autumn of 1945 and soon after John F. Kennedy had left the U.S. Navy, the Kennedy family held a reunion in their big house that overlooked Hyannis Port on the south shore of Cape Cod. During a luncheon, JFK's maternal grandfather, John Francis "Honey Fitz" Fitzgerald, rose to propose a toast. A bouncy, dapper little man, Honey Fitz had been mayor of Boston and wealthy besides, and he had married off his daughter, Rose, to another political and wealthy Bostonian, Joseph P. Kennedy, who had seemed well on his way to becoming a multimillionaire. Honey Fitz had wanted to found a dynasty, and now, at Hyannis Port, he wanted to launch that dynasty on its quest for national power. Raising a glass, he said: "To the future President of the United States, my grandson, John Fitzgerald Kennedy."

The Kennedy's and their allies, such as Honey Fitz, had long since embarked on the quest for wealth and power. Born in 1858 on Noddle's Island, a cluster of wharves and tenements out in the chills of the Boston Harbor, P. J. Kennedy, a good-looking, sandy-haired fellow, had become an East Boston saloonkeeper, a politically significant fact: saloonkeepers had had the power to listen to troubles, lend out money, put up bail, mediate disputes, provide liquor at weddings and wakes, and thus cause others to be in debt to him throughout the Irish-American wards. So P. J. Kennedy had become a politician, of the smoke-filled-room variety; and by the end of the nineteenth century, he, along with three others, Joe Corbett of Charlestown, "Smiling Jim" Donovan of the South End, and mayor-to-be "Honey Fitz" Fitzgerald, had emerged as the the bosses of Boston.

His power had been based on his ability to deliver the votes, by any means whatever. For, like the other chieftains of the Boston Irish, his credo had been, "Win at all costs." He had ingrained this code in his son. The son, born in 1887, had been named Joseph P. Kennedy.

Young Joe Kennedy was practically a street tough, solid and muscular, a boss in the youth gangs in the alleys of East Boston. He was a jock, too, and after his parents sent him to Boston Latin for high school—a brazen step in itself, since the institution was the citadel of the city's Anglo elite—he became an all-city batting champion. Moving over the Charles River to Harvard, he kept up with his baseball, although without his high school success. In fact, he did not play until the last inning of the last game of his senior year, and then only through the intervention of his father. The Harvard captain, "Chick" McLaughlin, had been reluctant to put Kennedy in the lineup; but he also had been hoping, after graduation, to get a city license to start up a movie theater. The license had seemed a sure thing. Just before that last game, however, he had had a visit from a pair of East Boston wardheelers. They had been blunt. "Either you put Joe in the game," they had stated, "or no license."

Joe went in the game, at first base, and after he had made the final put-out, he had kept the winning game ball. He won his Harvard letter in baseball—and learned a thing or two about how a father, blessed with power and money, can control his son's fate.

For then, staked by his father, Joe Kennedy became a slum landlord: taking over delapidated tenements, many of them in his native East Boston, he raised rents, forced tenants out, had the buildings cleaned and painted, then resold at a profit. He had destroyed many families, Irish and Italian, but he possessed $25,000, a sum he plowed back into a new business. During the First World War, he maneuvered himself into the management of Boston's Fore River shipyard, and realized that, there, the workers had no place on site to eat—so he invested in a Victory lunchroom, charged high prices, forbade competition, and made another bundle. The war over, he became a Boston stockbroker; on the basis of inside knowledge, he bought fifteen thousand shares of Pond Creek Coal Company stock, paper that Henry Ford intended to buy, and after he leaked word of Ford's plan, and the Pond Creek shares took off toward the stratosphere, he sold. His dealings had been shady but, after paying off the mortgage of a large house he had bought in Brookline, he had a net worth of $210,000.

Next he turned to stockpooling, a practice more than shady and eventually outlawed: a broker would buy many shares of a particular stock, driving up the price and attracting investments from the gullible; when the shares hit a price the broker and his comrades had already arranged, the broker would sell, and the stock value would plummet.

Kennedy was a master of the scam. Thousands of people in Boston and elsewhere lost their shirts. But Kennedy now was rich, rich beyond the dreams of any of his forebears.

Not even wealth of that magnitude was enough. Hard evidence of what he did in the 1920s is buried in the vaults of the Kennedy Library in Boston, unavailable to researchers. But was he a bootlegger? From congressional testimony in the 1970s, we have a statement by Frank Costello of the Luciano crime family—a former bootlegger himself—that "I helped Joe Kennedy get rich."

When Prohibition ended, on December 5, 1933, Joe Kennedy just happened to own Somerset Importers, a Boston area firm the warehouses of which just happened to be stacked to the rafters with cases of gin and scotch. In 1946, fearing that the liquor business might taint the candidacy of his son John for Congress, Joe sold Somerset Importers—for $8 million. Much of the money went into the congressional campaign.

He had shown his children no mercy. Whether at the white clapboard house at Hyannis Port, or at the brick Georgian mansion in Bronxville, or at the Spanish-style residence in West

Palm Beach—all of them bought with the proceeds of illegal booze—Joe Kennedy's pattern remained the same: he ran the household, and he ran it to raise the kind of children who one day would rule the world. How else can we interpret the evidence? The children, a historian of the Kennedy family has written, "were expected at meals five minutes ahead of time, and if one was late, he or she got hell. When Father Joe spoke to a child at meals, he expected to receive an intelligent answer back, no small talk or wisecracks. Activities and competitions were planned for each day, and all children were compelled to adhere to the schedule and to excel in the given competitions. Tensions among the perpetually driven children ran high, and fights among them were frequent and vicious. The Kennedy children were never allowed to relax and be themselves. They were never allowed to grow up at their own individual paces and in their own special ways. . . . No Kennedy child, especially a son, would ever dream of refusing to to enter a competition his father cared about. . . ."

Soon after the end of World War II, a congressional seat came open. The district in question was the Massachusetts Eleventh, a political mishmash that embraced Harvard, the Massachusetts Institute of Technology, and the elegant academic homes along Cambridge's Brattle Street, but also seedy Central Square, the working-class quarters in Charlestown and Somerville, and East Boston, by late 1945 more Italian than Irish. The incumbent congressman, James Michael Curley, had managed to hold it all together, winning reelection after reelection. But, before going to Congress, he had been mayor of Boston and, in late 1945, he decided to run for city hall again. Joe Kennedy must have been overjoyed: although he hated Curley's guts, he secretly gave the once and future mayor enough money to ensure the gentleman's departure from the halls of Congress. Curley got the job downtown, and the congressional seat came open.

A flock of hopefuls filed for the primary election. One of them was John F. Kennedy.

It was not, according to Joseph P. Kennedy, supposed to have been that way. The congressional seat, and the subsequent career that was to have to rocketed to the very top of the world, were to have gone to Joseph P. Kennedy, Jr., the oldest of the

Kennedy brood. But Joe junior had died in an air attack aimed at Germany.

So, in late 1945 and early 1946, young Jack Kennedy launched the congressional campaign his older brother, Joe junior, had been scheduled to run. John's father gave him no choice but to do so. "I got Jack into politics," Joseph Kennedy boasted later. "I was the one. I told him Joe was dead and that it was therefore his responsibility to run for Congress. He didn't want to. He felt he didn't have the ability and he still feels that way [this was in 1957]. But I told him he had to."

John F. Kennedy in 1945 must have seemed a most unlikely candidate for Congress. He was physically frail, suffering from both an adrenal deficiency and a spinal curvature; he was bookish, in a dreamy sort of way; and he knew virtually nothing of the district in which he was going to run. For the typical young congressional aspirant, knowledge of the district is the key to success: you go to law school and make friends with other young lawyers who will work in the district; you practice law and serve clients who live in the district; you run for the state legislature and do favors for powerful persons who can control the district; you give speeches before clubs in the district; you learn the names and histories of voters throughout the district. And *then* you run for Congress.

John F. Kennedy had done none of these things; he had not even held a job. As Joseph P. Kennedy had conquered the world of finance, nonetheless, he set out to mold his son into a successful candidate for Congress. In doing so, Joseph Kennedy possessed three resources (besides the money, of course). First, John had written, or sort of written, a book, *Why England Slept*, that just before the war had been a best-seller. We now know that the book, based on John Kennedy's senior thesis at Harvard, was largely a compilation of papers his father had accumulated while serving as ambassador to Britain; that Joseph Kennedy had bought enough copies to make sure of best-sellerdom; that Harold Lasky, professor at the London School of Economics and an acquaintance of the Kennedys, wrote to Joseph, "I don't honestly think any publisher would have looked at that book of Jack's if he had not been your son, and you had not been the ambassador." Second, John had been a war hero, supposedly; after his patrol boat, the PT-109, was sunk beneath him, he had hauled his chief engineer through water to safety;

John certainly received a medal for heroism, the citation being signed by then Navy Undersecretary James V. Forrestal, a friend of Joseph P. Kennedy. Actually, the sinking had been John's own fault, for he had managed to steer the PT boat right into the path of an oncoming Japanese destroyer. Yet according to a *New Yorker* article by John Hersey, an employee of press magnate Henry Luce, who was a friend of Joseph P. Kennedy, John's "exploit" was about the greatest of World War II. And to make sure that Democratic voters in the Massachusetts Eleventh—people who were not exactly *New Yorker* readers—got the message, Joseph Kennedy, through the intervention of his faithful friend Arthur Krock of *The New York Times*, persuaded *Reader's Digest* to condense the piece; copies of the *Reader's Digest* version reached every mailbox in the district. And third, Joseph Kennedy had his energetic and numerous family members, as well as the undeniable charm of John himself.

All these resources Joseph Kennedy fairly hurled at the open Massachusetts House district. John F. Kennedy appeared everywhere, spoke everywhere, shook hands everywhere. His mother pitched in: speaking to Italian women over in East Boston, she would make mention of her large brood of children; taking tea with society women down in Back Bay, she would sport her large diamonds and a mink stole. The rest of the family helped out, too, honing particular appeals for particular groups, and flooding the district with leaflets. Joseph Kennedy was the campaign manager, but from behind the scenes, and he pumped a fortune into the district, although just how much we probably shall never know.

But at whatever the cost, the Kennedys won the congressional seat, and it was theirs to control for as long as they wished. The next step was the U.S. Senate—and to win a seat in the upper chamber, John F. Kennedy had to make sure that he represented Democratic Party views. He endorsed the Truman Doctrine wholeheartedly.

3   Not everyone did so. Following events in the study of his northwest Washington home, Walter Lippmann was horrified. Tall, dark-haired, hawk-nosed, and always impeccably turned out, Lippmann, the nation's foremost columnist, prided himself on his aloofness from the fashions—and passions—of the day; and as Truman's doctrine of containment spread in popularity, Lippmann stood out in resistance. In a series of 1947 newspaper articles, pieces he gathered into a book he called *The Cold War*, he challenged containment as a "strategic monstrosity," a doctrine that failed to distinguish vital from not-so-vital national interests, and that would condemn the United States forever to be "recruiting, subsidizing, and supporting a heterogeneous array of satellites, clients, dependents, and puppets." In Lippmann's eyes, President Truman, Dean Acheson, and others in the administration had forgotten their primary responsibility—diplomacy. "For a diplomat to think that rival and unfriendly powers cannot be brought to a settlement," Lippmann wrote, "is to forget what diplomacy is about."

Lippmann, however, could not slow the rush toward Cold War. Indeed, the rush was turning into a stampede.

In 1947, Congress established: the National Security Council, a White House organ designed to give the President disinterested defense and foreign policy advice; the National Security Agency, set up in Fort Meade, Maryland, to break codes of foreign countries, hostile and friendly; and the CIA, organized at first to coordinate the government's intelligence gathering. Within a year, however, President Truman had issued a secret order, authorizing the CIA to engage in "sabotage" and "subversion," and to carry out its operations so that "if uncovered the U.S. government [can] plausibly disclaim any responsibility."

In June 1947, furthermore, Secretary of State Marshall, as tight-lipped and erect as when he had been a soldier, spoke at the Harvard commencement, announcing a vast American plan for rescuing the European economies. Although the Marshall Plan, as the operation came to be called, bore the marks of the usual influence-peddling—the tobacco lobby was able to have the government buy and ship over forty tons of cigarettes, and Coca-Cola was able to market 50 million bottles a day—it did pump billions of dollars into Europe. At a price, of course: recipient nations had to join an American-run international organization, the Organization of European Economic Cooperation, and in effect allow it to run their economies. So, even though the U.S. offered the Soviet Union an invitation to join, Stalin declined. To him, the OEEC promised to be nothing less than an instrument by which the U.S. could overturn communism in Russia.

In March 1948, alarmed by the interest the leaders of Czechoslovakia had shown in joining the Marshall Plan, Stalin sent the Red Army into Prague to overthrow the government. As portrayed in American newsreels, the fall of Czechoslovakia might be prelude to the fall of Italy, France, and Britain.

Then, in June 1948, U.S. authorities in Europe introduced a strong new currency, one intended to give sustenance to a united and perhaps independent West Germany—and the Soviets responded by cutting rail and road traffic to West Berlin. The Berlin blockade had started, and behind a locked door on the fifth floor of the new State Department, a wall screen reflected cables as they flashed in from General Lucius Clay, the U.S. military commander in Germany. A couple of months before, one of these cables from Clay had warned Washington that war "may come with dramatic suddenness"; Clay had sent the warning, we now know, not because he had feared the Soviets but rather he had hoped to frighten Congress into upping the military budget. Clay's cables now were equally hysterical and perhaps equally motivated. He wanted to break the blockade then and there by launching a massive armored assault on the Soviet positions. President Truman held back, choosing instead to airlift supplies to Berlin. And in May 1949, the Soviets lifted the blockade.

The blockade nonetheless had come as a shock, and the Truman administration soon oversaw the creation of the North Atlantic Treaty Organization, NATO (which embraced two countries not exactly on the North Atlantic, Turkey and Greece) and engineered the signing of a peace treaty with Japan. Both alliances were intended to tighten the ring around the Russians.

Truman nonetheless faced political danger. Early in February 1950, a beefy, burly, dark-haired senator from Wisconsin went to the lectern of a women's club in Wheeling, West Virginia. His name was Joe McCarthy.

Using a figure that had appeared in a letter written on July 26,

1946, by then–Secretary of State James F. Byrnes to a Chicago congressman, McCarthy declared:

> while I cannot take the time to name all the men in the State Department who have been named as active members of the Communist Party and members of a spy ring, I have here in my hand a list of 205—a list of names that were made known to the secretary of state as being members of the Communist Party and who nevertheless are still working and shaping policy in the State Department.

As these words spewed across the front pages of the nation's newspapers, McCarthyism was launched—asking rhetorically who, in 1949, had "lost China," and answering "Truman and Acheson," Senator McCarthy and his Republican cohorts had found the best of all cudgels with which to beat the administration: they were calling Truman a traitor.

The Red Scare he himself had helped to launch now having come back to haunt him, President Truman cast about for ways to deflect the charge. One of the ways was a document, highly classified, entitled NSC [National Security Council]-68. Even more than the Truman Doctrine, NSC-68 was a blueprint for future American foreign policy.

Approved by President Truman, overseen by Secretary Acheson, and actually drafted in what he called "Hemingway sentences" by Paul H. Nitze, a handsome, well-groomed sometime Wall Street banker and sometime State Department official, NSC-68 reflected HST's wish to win the Cold War. It portrayed the Soviets as bogeymen: (1) the Kremlin's bosses, it said, were driven by a "fanatic faith," communism, that sought "to impose its absolute authority over the rest of the world"; (2) since conflict between America and Russia therefore was "endemic," every person in the world faced the "ever-present possibility of annihilation"; (3) the "inescapably militant" Soviet dictatorship nevertheless could be checked, simply because its weakest link was its "relations with the Soviet people"; (4) and once the United States had shown that it could contain the power of communism, it would "foster the seeds of destruction within the Soviet system." NSC-68 was not declassified until 1975. It had aimed nonetheless at the destruction of the Soviet system. Judiciously, administration officials leaked bits and pieces of NSC-68 to the press, creating for the public the picture of a Soviet bogeyman.

More concretely, NSC-68 meant that the United States had to be able to haul or lift troops to far-flung points of the globe, to blunt tank attacks with tanks, to control the skies from the Baltic to the Sea of Japan, to be eternally ready to fight a total war. The cost of such readiness, Nitze estimated, would be from $40 billion to $50 billion, three times the 1950 defense budget. The cost, however, Nitze believed, was worth it because, he wrote,

> The grim oligarchy of the Kremlin . . . is seeking to demonstrate to the Free World that force and the will to use it are on the side of the Kremlin. . . . The implacable purpose of the slave state is to eliminate the challenge of freedom.

The problem with NSC-68, reckoned its drafters, lay in the Congress. The "yahoos" on Capitol Hill, to use one of Acheson's politer epithets, even with their Red-baiting and anti-Communist clamorings, were too dumb to comprehend the danger from Russia. President Truman, to be sure, had a more subtle grasp of Congress than did Acheson: as HST knew from experience, the overriding concern of the Congress was with the mood of the voters back home. And that was the trouble with NSC-68. The voters were feeling anti-Communist but cheap; they wanted Truman to stand tall abroad *and* keep taxes down at home.

So NSC-68 might have ended up on a dusty shelf in a State Department vault, Truman having been unable to sell the public on a huge defense budget. But in June 1950, North Korea invaded the south, and everything changed.

The weather in Washington that June had been steamy, the papers were full of McCarthy's venom, and President Truman's schedule for a few days was free: HST decided to fly to his home in Independence, Missouri, for a few days' respite. He got little rest. Even while his airplane was high over the Mississippi

Valley, starting the last leg of its route to Kansas City, the cables began to reach Washington: a war had broken out in Korea. The date was June 24, 1950.

As was customary in Washington in times of crisis, a duty officer, in this instance in the State Department's Far Eastern Bureau, called around town to notify those who had to be notified, whether they were in the government or out. One such call went to columnist Joseph Alsop. An Ivy Leaguer who also was a distant cousin of Franklin D. Roosevelt, Alsop (described by another Washington reporter as "rotund but profound") was an integral part of the Georgetown social whirl. On the particular night of June 24, 1950, he was entertaining several prominent guests: Justice Felix Frankfurter (who seemed as much a part of political Washington as he did of the Supreme Court); Secretary of the Army Frank Pace; Undersecretary of the Air Force John McCone (in private life a California industrialist); and Assistant Secretary of State for Far Eastern Affairs Dean Rusk. They had gone outside and "the night was marvelously beautiful," Alsop was to remember. "The talk on the terrace under the stars was growing lively."

But a servant came out, announcing a phone call for a "Mr. Rush." Deciding he was "Mr. Rush," Rusk went inside. He was a big man, already balding, with good skin color, but when he returned he was "as white as a sheet." After a brief discussion he left for the State Department. The rest of the assemblage, according to Alsop, "settled down to argue whether *this was it.*"

Another telephone call went to Secretary of State Dean Acheson, who was relaxing on his Maryland farm. Having spent the afternoon gardening, he had had a good dinner and had turned into bed to read. Just after 10:00 P.M., however, his bedside telephone rang, and he learned of the attack in Korea. Without delay, he placed a call to Independence, Missouri. "Mr. President," he said, "I have very serious news. The North Koreans have invaded South Korea."

Arriving in Washington early the next evening, Truman met with advisers in Blair House (across Pennsylvania Avenue from the White House, Blair House was the Truman's official residence while the Executive Mansion was undergoing repairs) and considered their courses of action. They did not deliberate long: within days the United States, under the auspices of the United Nations, intervened militarily on the Korean peninsula.

Truman's reputation soared, at first, for he had stood tall against Stalin, or at least against North Korea's Dear Leader, Kim Il Sung. Soon, however, his public repute plummeted again: reports of battlefield shortages reached the papers; Ohio's Republican Senator Robert A. Taft charged that Truman's own weakness had invited the attack; Senator McCarthy's attacks on Truman were finding ever-widening audiences; the Chinese themselves intervened in the war (after General Douglas MacArthur and the largely American army had broken the North Korean lines and had pushed high toward the Yalu River) and by dint of sheer numbers pushed the U.S. forces southward again; the war began to settle into stalemate; President Truman fired General MacArthur for insubordination (contrary to Truman's wishes, MacArthur had indicated that he would attack China); and the war, by the presidential election year of 1952, was going nowhere.

The Democrats already had lost control of the Congress. Now they stood to lose control of the White House.

The Republicans took full advantage of the Democrats' plight. They nominated Dwight D. Eisenhower to run for President (he promised to "go to Korea," although he failed to say how such a trip would resolve the conflict); they nominated Richard M. Nixon for Vice President (who attacked the Democratic candidate, Illinois Governor Adlai E. Stevenson, as a graduate of "Dean Acheson's cowardly College of Communist Containment"); and in one plank of their party platform (written by New York attorney John Foster Dulles), they accused the Truman administration of having practiced "appeasement." Come the November elections, they swept into power.

Yet in all the hubbub and turmoil of a change of government, most of what Truman and Acheson had created remained. In brutalizing the nations of Eastern Europe, the Soviets bore great responsibility for the coming of the Cold War—yet Soviet behavior hardly had taken place in a vacuum. Truman's policies had augmented Soviet fears, and those fears endured beyond the 1952 elections. Furthermore, even with Eisenhower as President, NSC-68, and its portrayal of godless communism ever on the march, remained the guiding beacon of American foreign policy. And with the Korean War, finally, the United States possessed a vast array of new defense commitments, to South Korea, Taiwan, and indeed Indochina. Above all the U.S. had taken upon itself the commitment to ensure that, virtually everywhere in the world, forces that would disrupt the status quo would not endure.

4   Nor were the forces that stood in the way of John F. Kennedy's drive to the presidency to endure. According to Joseph P. Kennedy, and, increasingly, to his son John, opponents existed simply to be crushed, as Washingtonians soon learned to their dismay. House freshmen were expected to be meek, humble, and deferential to the leadership. Not so with Jack Kennedy. Hardly had he arrived in Washington than he offended John McCormack, another Massachusetts member and soon-to-be Speaker, by popping in late at the session's first Democratic caucus; and then he made a practice of popping in late, usually dressed in a sports jacket, unpressed khakis, and sneakers, during the House debates. He offended thereby another House freshman, one from California, Richard M. Nixon. Flaunting his wealth, Kennedy took up residence in a three-story house in Georgetown, at 1528 31st Street. There, with little attempt at secrecy, he resumed a wartime affair with Inga Arvad, a beautiful Dane who had served in naval intelligence. She had been, allegedly, a Nazi sympathizer—and the FBI began tracking the goings-on of freshman U.S. Representative John F. Kennedy.

Yet as if thumbing his nose at the FBI, Kennedy soon announced his candidacy for the Senate. The year was 1951, and Kennedy's opponent was Massachusetts's incumbent Republican Senator, Henry Cabot Lodge. Wellborn, elegant, and rich, Lodge was the grandson of the famous Massachusetts senator of his same name, and he practically had inherited his seat: up to 1951, he had been politically invincible, representing precisely the kind of challenge Jack Kennedy had been taught to crave.

In quest of a new win, Kennedy and his family went all out, for their goal was that of burying Lodge, and they organized a polical machine potent in Massachusetts even now. The Kennedy campaign for Senate in 1952, commented Lawrence O'Brien, the savvy Kennedy operator from Springfield, Massachusetts, was "the most nearly perfect [one] I've ever seen." The "key to the Kennedy organization in 1952," O'Brien wrote in his memoirs, "was the network of 300 local campaign directors we recruited, the Kennedy secretaries, as we called them. The title was significant. We would have called them the Kennedy chairmen, but that might have offended the local party chairmen. . . . I had the primary responsibility for selecting these men, and I was looking for fresh faces. . . . Once we had our secretaries, we had to be sure they carried out the program of political activity we envisioned. To that end, I wrote a . . . detailed version of the O'Brien Manual—containing instructions on telephone campaigns, voter registration, press relations, and so on." O'Brien also encouraged the Kennedy secretaries to organize teas around the state; Kennedy himself, along with his ever popular mother and sisters, attended those receptions, shaking hands for hours.

O'Brien's description, however, failed to convey the campaign's intensity. But we do have images of Jack Kennedy himself: sleeping in a hotel room so crummy that its only illumination was a naked light bulb over the bed; shaving over a corroded basin in the men's room of a small-town bowling alley; racing a locomotive to a railway crossing because he was desperate to get to a Knights of Columbus speaking engagement. We have Robert F. Kennedy, twenty-six years old, just out of the University of Virginia Law School, shy and awkward, but emerging, in the words of Kenneth O'Donnell, into a "tough, cocky, ruthless field general." And, of course, we have Joe Kennedy, making a $500,000 loan to the nearly bankrupt *Boston Post*, which proceeded to endorse John F. Kennedy for the Senate.

Despite the Eisenhower landslide of November 1952, Kennedy defeated Lodge by seventy thousand votes. For the Kennedys had launched, as a Joe Kennedy biographer put it, the "most methodical, most scientific, most thoroughly detailed, intricate, disciplined and smoothly working campaign . . . in Massachusetts history." John F. Kennedy had won, at all cost.

Including the truth. A frequent guest at the Kennedy's Hyannis Port estate had been Wisconsin's junior senator, Joe McCarthy: like many Irish Catholics from Boston, the Kennedys had seen McCarthy almost as a hero. So virulent was John Kennedy's McCarthyism, in fact, that his campaign literature had portrayed him as a staunch opponent of "atheistic communism"; and the *Chicago Tribune* (influenced by his father, no doubt) had lauded him as a "fighting conservative." But did the Kennedy's fess up to the McCarthy connection? No. Thinking ahead, they kept the friendship quiet.

After the 1952 election, however, the Senate's select committee, of which McCarthy was the most famous, or infamous, member, was looking for a young lawyer to serve as special counsel. One name, above others, came forward: while still in law school at Virginia, this attorney had written a paper denouncing Roosevelt's "sell-out" at Yalta; had worked in the Justice Department's Internal Security and Criminal Divisions; and more than any of his brothers or sisters, he resembled his father. "He hates the same way I do," said Joe Kennedy of this son. The son, of course, was Robert F. Kennedy. Step-by-step and through his children, Joseph Kennedy was establishing control in Washington.

5   At just about the same time, the United States was establishing, or reestablishing, control in the island of Cuba. Ever since the Spanish-American War of 1898, Cuba had lain within America's sphere of influence, although in the island's elections of the mid and late 1940s, America's favored Cuban politician, Fulgencio Batista, had been voted out of the presidency. He had gone off to exile in Florida. There he had set himself up in Daytona Beach, tending to his Miami real estate holdings to stay rich and rowing a shell on the Halifax River to stay fit. *Time* described him as a "hairy, muscular man's man," ready at any time to take power in Cuba.

In late 1952 he did so, returning to Havana (with the quiet support of the Truman administration) and staging a military coup. Truman recognized the new regime immediately.

So by the time President Eisenhower took office, Fulgencio Batista, America's protégé, already was well settled into Cuba's own executive mansion, a grand palace with a glorious view of the Havana harbor. Sitting there behind his antique desk, he was positively heroic, bull of neck, cleavaged of jaw, white of teeth, and broad of grin. Thus, at least, he appeared on a cover of *Time*, his mug silhouetted against a Cuban flag—an emblem plainly modeled on the Stars and Stripes.

The symbolism was telling. For as its last will and testament, the Truman administration left with its successors in Washington a document classified as NSC-141. It applied the earlier NSC-68 to Latin America:

> In Latin America we seek first and foremost an orderly political and economic development which will make the Latin American nations resistant to the internal growth of communism and to Soviet political warfare. . . . Secondly we seek hemisphere solidarity in support of our world policy and the cooperation of the Latin American nations in safeguarding the hemisphere through individual and collective defense measures against external aggression and internal subversion.

As 1952 gave way to 1953, Josef Stalin was approaching his personal end. Although a window in his Kremlin office remained lit throughout the winter nights, he was spending almost all his time at his dacha in Kuntsevo, outside the capital. When he did go to Moscow, it was in a procession of fast black limousines; the drivers overtook each other frequently, changing places so no one on the streets could tell which automobile, behind its lace curtains, contained Stalin. He saw nearly everybody save his drivers and special guards as potential assassins. Only among the silver birch trees and dense pine forests around his estate did he feel at home. Always a small man, he had shrunken noticeably; he had become a tiny, gray-haired old man, failing in strength.

Late in February 1953, he gathered around him at Kuntsevo his top aides, Georgi Malenkov, Lavrenti Beria, Nikolai Bulganin, and Nikita Khrushchev. On the last night of the month, they dined together, downing enormous quantities of vodka, and Stalin was jovial. But on the next day, a Sunday, he did not set forth from his villa.

A guard that evening passed along word that Stalin had failed to telephone for his dinner. Rushing from their own dachas, the four aides entered their master's room and found him, fully dressed, lying on a rug. He had collapsed from a cerebral hemorrhage.

CHAPTER 2

Peace, Prosperity, and Progress

1   Early in the summer of 1952, before the presidential campaign had heated up, President Truman would call reporters into the Oval Office and discuss the possibility that Dwight D. Eisenhower would become the next President. How well, reporters would ask, did Truman think Ike would do in the office? "He'll sit here," Truman would remark (tapping the desk for emphasis), "and he'll say, 'Do this! Do that! And *nothing will happen.* Poor Ike—it won't be a bit like the Army. He'll find it very frustrating."

Truman may have been doing his last bit for the Democratic party: remembering Truman's comments, the Washington press corps watched President Eisenhower with care, propagating the legend that he had no idea how to grasp the levers of power. But the legend hardly could have been farther from reality.

Like most Presidents, Eisenhower early on established a White House routine. Awakened by his valet, a black sergeant named John Moaney, he would arise, shave, and comb his thinned-out white hair, then for a few moments practice golf swings as he stood before one of the upstairs bedroom windows. Before putting his club in its bag again, he often paused to enjoy the view: the South Lawn with its magnolias planted by President Jackson, the Washington Monument, the Jefferson Memorial, and the flat gray-brown of the Potomac. Then he ate breakfast from a tray, skimmed the major newspapers of the morning, and dressed, in wintertime donning a then-fashionable gray flannel suit. Once in the Oval Office, he sat down behind the huge rosewood desk, sometimes glancing outside at *Marine One*, the presidential helicopter always available at his beck and call.

Contrary to Truman's prediction, however, Eisenhower did not just give orders. Many were fooled by his grandfatherly mien and his bumbling syntax. Virtually from day one in the White House, Eisenhower was grasping real political power.

His first step, undertaken while he still was just President-Elect, was the fulfillment of his most important 1952 campaign pledge, his flight to Korea; in that flight he proved himself a master of public relations. Even before dawn on November 29, 1952, he slipped secretly from the back door of his Manhattan town house, hunched down in a limousine as it whisked him to his airplane, and took off without the press knowing anything of his whereabouts. As he was in the air, a line of prominent visitors streamed in and out of his front door, creating the impression that they had been doing business with the President-Elect inside. Only after his plane landed in Seoul was word of his presence leaked to the press—given no chance to question the merits of his trip, reporters in Korea were reduced to racing after him with notepads and cameras as he reviewed troops, crunched over the battlefield ice, visited a mobile hospital, talked briefly with President Syngman Rhee, and then flew back to the States. He accomplished little (the Korean armistice came into being only after Ike had become President, and then in part because he had threatened to use atomic bombs against the Chinese), but his trip was undeniably dramatic. As he moved into the White House he controlled the nation's attention.

Then he moved to seize control of the political repression already widespread in the land. On the evening of February 2, 1953, wearing a somber double-breasted suit, President Eisenhower delivered his first State of the Union address. After some preliminaries, he repeated a statement he had made during the campaign in Green Bay, Wisconsin: the major responsibility for eliminating subversives from the U.S. government, he stated, lay squarely with the White House.

Ike's first power move, domestically, was toward the State Department; given the widespread distrust of diplomats in general and Dean Acheson in particular, State was a popular—and easy—target. But who was going to carry out the attack? During his time as President-Elect, Eisenhower's first choice for Secretary of State was John J. McCloy. A balding, beefy, easygoing man, Mccloy had risen from the wrong side of the tracks in Philadelphia to the Harvard Law School, a big-time legal post on Wall Street, then Assistant Secretary of War under Roosevelt, head of the World Bank, High Commissioner in West Germany, and then back to New York. McCloy eventually would be chairman of Chase Manhattan Bank, really a financial secretary of state. And as a golf-playing success, he was Ike's kind of man.

But he also was a friend of Dean Acheson, and so Eisenhower had to look elsewhere. For Secretary of State he settled on another Wall Street lawyer, John Foster Dulles.

On a personal level, Eisenhower could barely tolerate Dulles. Where Eisenhower rarely bothered to attend church, Dulles, the son of a Presbyterian minister (and grandson of Robert Lansing, Woodrow Wilson's second secretary of state), was all pontifical; he "gave the impression," quipped one Democrat, "that he had a direct line to the Almighty." Where Eisenhower often fumbled for words, Dulles was a walking thesaurus. Where Eisenhower was trim and neat, Dulles wore green suits, drooping socks, ugly neckties, and usually had foul breath. But they agreed more than they disagreed, and Dulles, ever ruthless, was useful. Dulles could serve as Ike's lightning rod, and uproot without qualms the "subversives" in State.

So Dulles it was, as secretary of state, and when in early 1953 the Eisenhower administration took office, Dulles from his office on the seventh floor of the new State Department building proceeded to institute a reign of terror. Hardly had he taken office than he began to demand "positive loyalty" (apparently including slavish devotion to Dulles) of the Foreign Service; and to make sure everyone was positively loyal, he appointed Scott McLeod, an ex-FBI agent and associate of Senator McCarthy, as the State Department's chief security officer. In McLeod's—and Dulles's—witch-hunting mentality, criticism equaled treason.

Soon therefore, up and down the halls of the State Department, the McLeod-Dulles purge "burned its deadly way . . . , immolating along the way the careers of several hundred officers and employees." From the overseas libraries of the U.S. Information Agency, Dulles even ordered the removal of books authored by "Communists, fellow travelers, et cetera." Who was an "et cetera"? Whoever Dulles said.

Yet cowing the State Department was one thing and controlling the Congress was another; Joe McCarthy was riding higher than ever and, although a Republican, was hardly going to submit to guidance from the White House. Yet in his desire to harness McCarthy, President Eisenhower had a most important ally—McCarthy himself. By early 1953, McCarthy's most recent biographer has written, "Americans were realizing that Joe was not just an Irish, two-fisted, anti-Communist. He was a rather frightening right-wing extremist who was capable of attacking anyone who stood in his path. Journalists, clergymen, professors, engineers, librarians, senators, generals, Cabinet members, the President—no one was safe." McCarthy was also an alcoholic, spinning out of self-control. Eisenhower's strategy was to give McCarthy the rope with which he could hang himself; the rope was named Charles E. Bohlen, appointed by Eisenhower in March 1953 as ambassador to the Soviet Union.

Charming and strikingly handsome, Bohlen had gone to Harvard, where he had majored largely in liquor and women. Captivated by the early romance of the Russian Revolution, he had read Russian novels, learned Russian songs, even screwed a Russian girl: "This," he had quipped to Paul Nitze, his friend, "is the way to learn Russian." He had entered the Foreign Service, become one of the State Department's foremost Soviet experts, loathed Moscow, and with a record that was spotlessly clean, been Ike's ideal choice for ambassador. McCarthy tried to smear him as a leftist—to "the extreme right-wingers," Bohlen commented, "the gauntlet had been flung down [by Eisenhower]"—but Bohlen's credentials were impeccable, and the Senate gave him its eager confirmation.

Suddenly McCarthy had peaked. He did thunder away a while longer, but he made the mistake of attacking the integrity of the U.S. Army; by the end of 1953, the Senate had subjected McCarthy to a vote of censure. The only Democratic senator who failed to vote against McCarthy was John F. Kennedy.

2   Even as President Eisenhower was taking over the reins of the United States government, the Soviet government was undergoing a profound change. At 7:40 A.M., March 4, 1953, Eisenhower strode into the Oval Office to receive his first visitor of the day, CIA Director Allen Dulles. Smoking a pipe and wearing a bow tie, Allen Dulles, brother of the secretary of state, looked like an elderly professor of English, and he could be as obscurantist as any academic. This morning, however, he got straight to the point: according to overnight intelligence reports, Josef Stalin had died. For all his brutality, Stalin during the war had developed a great respect for Eisenhower. But now the key question was—who would succeed Stalin?

Commenting several years later on Nikita Khrushchev's eventual rise to power, Britain's Prime Minister Harold Macmillan expressed bewilderment. "Khrushchev is a mystery," Macmillan penned in his diary. "How can this fat, vulgar man with his pig eyes and ceaseless flow of talk, really be the head—the aspirant Tsar—of all those millions of people of this vast country?" Khrushchev did lack Macmillan's elegance. But he was shrewd, and while others high in the Soviet system had hovered almost exclusively around Stalin, Khrushchev had made many trips to the countryside, whence he came, working for agricultural improvements and forging a network of allies. Well-positioned politically, Khrushchev soon was able to oust Stalin's apparent favorite, Georgi Malenkov; by September 1953, the man whom Stalin had called "Mikita" and forced to squat while he did Russian dances was first secretary of the Central Committee of the Communist Party. Now he could do favors for even more people, and thus consolidate his power as Russia's new boss.

3   John F. Kennedy, too, was moving upward. He took part in a marriage his father had arranged for its maximum political advantage.

As reported on the front page of the Sunday *New York Times*, the wedding of John Kennedy and Jacqueline Bouvier occurred on September 12, 1953, in Newport, Rhode Island's St. Mary's Roman Catholic Church. Most of the U.S. Senate, flown up by Joseph Kennedy for the occasion, was present; so was Joseph Martin of Massachusetts, the Republican Speaker of the House, along with top people of the press, Hollywood, and Wall Street. Richard Cushing, archbishop of Boston, intoned the nuptial mass, and read out a special blessing from the Pope. As the new couple passed down the aisle on their way outside, three thousand people were standing ready to cheer and to ogle. The reception took place nearby at Hammersmith Farm, a twenty-eight-room shingle-style cottage belonging to the Auchincloss family, into which Jacqueline Bouvier Kennedy's mother had married. After John and Jacqueline had left for a first honeymoon night at the Waldorf-Astoria, guests drank champagne on the broad lawns, or wandered down to the dock that later would berth the presidential yacht, *Honey Fitz.*

Being photogenic, the new Mrs. Kennedy was going to be an asset to her husband's career. Joseph Kennedy had seen to that. She also was going to stay married. Joseph Kennedy saw to that, too.

Joseph Kennedy also saw to it that John had at his disposal a top-flight legislative assistant and speechwriter—the twenty-four-year-old Theodore Sorensen. Tall, dark-haired, and bespectacled, Sorensen, a lawyer out of Nebraska, was loyal, and he possessed a skill John Kennedy never could master: he could write English. The speeches and articles of many a Washington politician were written, in fact, by aides. Sorensen wrote the best prose of the lot. He proved to be especially good at writing speeches that attacked the foreign policies of Dwight D. Eisenhower.

4   By the middle of 1953, President Eisenhower had worked out his basic foreign policy plan, called Operation Solarium after the sun room in the White House where he and his advisers had held their secret sessions. In public Eisenhower said, after the Korean armistice had gone into effect on July 27, 1953, "We have won an armistice on a single battleground—

not peace in the world. We may not now relax our guard or cease our quest.'' In private, he wanted to contain communism with a large-scale nuclear threat and small-scale covert wars.

Nuclear weapons, he calculated, would be cheaper than another dragged-out Korean-style war. Covert wars, he believed, would be an improvement if failures could be hidden from view and if successes could be seized upon as successes.

Nuclear weapons and covert wars would be smart politics at home and efficient implements abroad. Both would allow Eisenhower to control any risks. Or so he thought.

One covert war took place in Iran. Back in 1951, an Iranian politician named Mohammed Mosaddegh had risen to the premiership, riding the tide of rising nationalism and challenging the control long exerted by the British-controlled Anglo-Iranian Oil Company over his country's petroleum deposits. The British firm had been exploiting Iran for years, granting the Persians only about 20 percent of the profits from their own oil. Enter the United States, upsetting Great Britain's cozy deal: in 1952, the last year of the Truman administration, Aramco, the U.S.-based oil company, approached the Saudis, offering them 50 percent of the proceeds from Arabian oil. Across the Persian Gulf, Premier Mosaddegh insisted on the same arrangement. Anglo-Iranian, however, treated him with contempt, utterly refusing any new deal.

In Washington, Secretary of State Dean Acheson actually sympathized with Mosaddegh, even offering to mediate. Soon, however, the Democrats were out of the White House.

John Foster Dulles wanted nothing to do with mediation. Nationalism he found an anathema and, besides, the British, knowing just which buttons to push, had been whispering to Washington that Mosaddegh either was a Communist or was becoming a puppet of Tudeh, Iran's Communist party. The rumor was enough for Dulles. Fully supported by Washington, the large oil companies, British *and* American, refused to buy Iranian oil. Mossadegh, who had expropriated the oil wells, had the petroleum but no access to markets, and Iran slid into depression. At that point, in the summer of 1953, Dulles, Eisenhower, British intelligence, and Kermit Roosevelt of the CIA, all of whom had been in consultation, decided to move. Throwing dollars around Tehran and especially toward top officers in the Iranian army, officers already bitterly anti-Mossadegh—all of this being classified for many years to come—the CIA stirred up massive street demonstrations in the Iranian capital, and helped the military put Mossadegh under house arrest.

The premier, whom Dean Acheson had described as a "pixie," so bald that he had a "billiard-ball head," was finished. And fresh back from the ski slopes of Switzerland, to which he had been exiled temporarily, Mohammed Reza Pahlavi assumed his seat upon the Peacock Throne. During his coronation, he offered a toast to the head of the CIA operation, Kermit Roosevelt: "I owe my throne to God, my people, my army, and to you." And the Anglo-Iranian Oil Company was back in business, with terms almost as favorable as before, except that now it had to cut the American majors into the deal.

So covert action could indeed yield results! And confronting another revolutionary movement, the anti-French insurgency in Vietnam, the Eisenhower administration applied the tactic again. Going public, to an extent, President Eisenhower himself supplied the rationale. In his press conference of April 7, 1954, he thought aloud about what might happen if the Indochinese peninsula went Communist:

> First of all, you have the specific value of a locality in its production of materials that the world needs. [Ike did not specify those materials. Perhaps he meant rice for Japan.] Then you have the possibility that many human beings pass under a dictatorship that is inimical to the free world. Finally, you have broader considerations that might follow what you would call the "falling domino" principle.
>
> You have a row of dominoes set up, you knock over the first one, and what will happen to the last one is a certainty that it will go over very quickly. . . .
>
> It takes away, in its economic aspects, that region that Japan must have as a trading area or Japan, in turn, will have only one place to go—that is, toward the Communist areas in order to live.
>
> So the possible consequences of the loss are just incalculable to the free world.

The implication of this, the domino theory, was that somebody—namely the United States—had to stop the first domino from falling. But largely covertly. After the French lost in Vietnam in the spring of 1954, and a seemingly pro-Western government emerged in Saigon, President Eisenhower quietly gave that government aid; and U.S. advisers taught the South Vietnamese to fight a conventional war, as in Korea.

Eisenhower's policy of covert action enjoyed another success, indeed a smashing success—in Guatemala. Later, in fact, the Eisenhower administration looked to what had happened in Guatemala as the key to how to handle Castro in Cuba.

Guatemala, as journalists in the States in the 1940s and 1950s described the place, was about the size of Kentucky, albeit populated by dirt-poor peasants who were descended from the Mayans and who, under the tropical sun and along the mist-filled hillsides, worked almost as chattel on the U.S. corporate-controlled coffee and banana plantations. Insofar as Guatemala existed in the North American imagination, it was hot, snake-ridden, corrupt, and, above all, down there. The idea that such a classic banana republic could have endangered the security of the United States—before the 1950s—was farcical.

Yet suddenly, early in the 1950s, Guatemala loomed up in the magazines and newspapers of America as if it were some prehistoric monster, fiery of eye and slobbering of mouth, about to gobble up the entirety of the American Republic. For the Guatemalan government had had the temerity to institute some land reforms. Headed by Jacobo Arbenz Guzmán, son of a Guatemalan mother and an émigré Swiss druggist, the administration in Guatemala City was challenging the absolute preeminence of the country's real ruler, the United Fruit Company.

Guatemala, like its neighbors around the Caribbean Basin, for decades had held a special niche in the North American imagination. Even before the U.S. Civil War, the region had seemed America's "backyard," the part of the property where you raise a garden, get a suntan, let the dog run loose, and set up a fence to keep intruders out. If you are not safe in your backyard, you are not safe anywhere.

This suburban homeowners' mentality led directly to the Spanish-American War of 1898. Americans today remember the

Spanish-American War, if they remember it at all, as a series of faded and ancient photographs: here, the battleship *Maine* lying on its side in the Havana harbor; there, Colonel Theodore Roosevelt, his teeth bared and his glasses glinting as he bullies his way up San Juan Hill, or whichever hill it was, actually; and over there, Admiral George Dewey and his flotilla in the heart of Manilla Bay, shooting up Spanish ships so ancient they might have been galleons. Yet we hardly bother to dust off the pictures, for the war seems so quaint.

Anything but romantic, actually, the Spanish-American War offered a clear view of how Americans, at the turn of the twentieth century, had come to view the world. One young man, Smedley T. Butler (who later became a general in the Marine Corps), enlisted because he had heard that the Spanish, from down in Cuba, were going to come up and encamp themselves on his family's Pennsylvania farmland. Americans as a whole saw Spain as the villain of a melodrama—bigoted, venal, and abusive—lording it over an island only ninety miles from the U.S. border. So, in going to war against Spain, Americans convinced themselves that they were doing so for humanitarian reasons. Some people were so moved. Out in the Philippines, however, America quickly transformed itself from the liberator of an oppressed people into their new oppressor, fighting a war of conquest that dragged on for four years of ambushes, garrotings, executions, and street fighting. In Cuba, too, the indigenous fight for freedom flared on, leading the U.S. to impose a military government—a euphemism for jails, torture, and hangings.

Few atrocities—committed by Americans—reached the pages of the U.S. press. Cuba, in the popular conception, was not after all truly a colony. It was rather a maiden, white of course, in the words of historian George Black, "passively awaiting salvation or seduction."

The Caribbean maiden of the American imagination, though, quickly transformed herself into a child, a rather hyperactive black child. A 1904 political cartoon depicted Uncle Sam leaning out an open window and looking in dismay at a little black boy, who was jumping up and down in the dust. The child's straw hat bore the label "San Domingo," and in his right hand he held an open straight razor, the blade of which was entitled "Revolution." The caption: "Maybe I'll have to bring the boy into the house to keep him quiet." President Theodore Roosevelt's version of that caption, expressed at the same time and by which he meant to keep the "dagos" in order, was his corollary to the Monroe Doctrine: "Chronic wrongdoing, or an impotence which results in a general loosening of the ties of civilized society," he told Congress, "may in America, as elsewhere, ultimately require intervention by some civilized nation, and in the Western Hemisphere the adherence of the United States to the Monroe Doctrine may force the United States, however reluctantly, in flagrant cases of such wrongdoing or impotence, to the exercise of an international police power." T.R.'s successors, William Howard Taft, Woodrow Wilson, and Calvin Coolidge, accepted this role of the U.S. as hemispheric policeman, sending the Marines repeatedly into the countries around the Caribbean.

But then, in 1933, President Franklin D. Roosevelt implied that such intervention was a thing of the past.

Sunday, March 4, 1933, in Washington was a cloudy, cheerless day, the air as chill as the mood of the thousands who had thronged to the Capitol. This was Inauguration Day, a time of national consecration; most of the country's banks had closed, and the crowd gathered beneath the inauguration stand feared for the future. As noon came they waited in silence. Then, coatless and hatless, Franklin D. Roosevelt appeared, moving out slowly on to the high white platform. His face grave, he took the oath of office and, turning to the sea of faces below him, started to speak.

This was to be FDR's most famous inaugural address, and its language still rings in the memory: "This is preeminently the time to speak the truth." "The only thing we have to fear is fear itself." And "the good neighbor."

In proclaiming this, the Good Neighbor Policy, FDR described the "neighbor who respects his obligations and respects the sanctity of agreements in and with a world of neighbors. We now realize as we have never realized before our interdependence on each other; that we cannot merely take, but must also give."

Roosevelt hardly had invented the term "Good Neighbor"— it was used in the Treaty of 1848, by which the U.S. seized one third of the territory of Mexico—but he did give it currency. During the early years of his administration, a historian has commented, a veritable cottage industry of Good Neighborism flourished in America: "There were state-based Good Neighbor Committees and Good Neighbor Leagues and Good Neighbor Commissions, all working to improve cultural ties [with Latin America] and publishing guides for newly arrived refugees and émigrés." The phrase found its way into Broadway, with a 1941 play called *The Good Neighbor*, and into the nation's school books. Before 1933, the texts had gloried in American imperialism; after 1933, imperialism was something only the Europeans and the Japanese practiced. The underlying U.S. contempt for Latin America, to be sure, scarcely had changed at all: in a 1940 public opinion poll, Americans overwhelmingly identified the "Latinos" as "lazy," "ignorant," "emotional," and "darkskinned." Still, to nearly a generation of historians, the Good Neighbor Policy was a grand success—after all, Roosevelt had stopped intervening in Latin American affairs.

The policy may have been a success. That we stopped intervening, however, is a myth.

FDR's treatment of the Latin republics differed from that of his predecessors largely in that he had no *need* to send the Marines in. For the Marines had done their work well already. When they withdrew from the region, they had left behind the *gendarmerie* (in Haiti), the National Guard (in Nicaragua and the Dominican Republic)—the local forces of repression. In El Salvador, the murderous Maximiliano Hernández Martíncz; in the Dominican Republic, the megalomaniac Rafaél Leonidas Trujillo; in Nicaragua, the shrewd and corrupt Anastasio Somoza García—all flourished as dictators because, for monies under the table, they welcomed the presence of American investment. And in Cuba, wielding power behind the scenes, the U.S. government in mid-1933 engineered the rise to power of the stocky young Cuban Army sergeant, Fulgencio Batista y Zaldívar. "He may be a bastard," FDR was to say of Batista, "but he's our bastard."

Roosevelt might have said "racketeer." With the coming of Prohibition in the 1920s, mob money flooded Havana—with Batista and his henchmen always on the take—turning the waterfront into one long row of hotels, brothels, and bars. "Don't try to consume all [the alcohol] in the first few days," the English-language *Times of Cuba* cautioned tourists. "Remember that Cuban distilleries work night and day." The tourists paid little heed; and when in 1927 Juan Trippe, a Yale graduate and World War I flying ace, opened an air link of his Pan-American Airways between Miami and Cuba, the tourists arrived in even greater droves than before. So even more mob money flooded the island.

As it did so, some of it went respectable, undergirding establishments such as the Women's Club, the Mother's Club, the Little Theater and Choral Societies, the Country Club, and the Yacht Club—all good Yankee institutions. And working out of such institutions, good Yankee businessmen paid off Batista and his cronies with good big bribes.

The Cuban upper classes in turn thought of themselves as almost American. All "rich Cubans had money in North America," writes a historian; "most had been educated there, many looked on North America as their social guarantor; some were really more North American than Caribbean." The Cuban-American bond seemed unbreakable.

But the Good Neighbors became Bad Neighbors. In May 1945, as World War II was ending in Europe, Henry L. Stimson, Wall Street lawyer and venerable secretary of war, said to John J. McCloy, Wall Street lawyer and assistant secretary of war, that America's domination of the Caribbean Basin was different from Russia's domination of Eastern Europe. Said Stimson to McCloy: "I think that it's not asking too much to have our little region over here which has never bothered anybody."

Stimson was speaking for the new Truman administration. In the eyes of Truman and his advisers, the sin of the Soviets was that they wanted to run their neighbors' internal affairs—whereas the saintliness of the Americans was that, as long as their own neighbors followed Washington's lead in international affairs, we let them run their own internal affairs. In practice, to be sure, letting the countries around the Caribbean run their own affairs meant allowing right-wing dictatorships, winked at by Washington; in effect the Good Neighbor Policy now meant the U.S. financing of tyranny.

Precisely because it did finance tyranny, however, the U.S.

early in the Eisenhower era found itself in a remarkably Soviet-like position, running a neighbor's internal affairs.

Jorge Ubico, the dictator of Guatemala in the 1930s and early 1940s, had practically inherited the place, as his godfather, a great land baron, had developed much of the country's coffee industry. Ubico himself seemed a bit of a clown: after a riding accident left him impotent, he surrounded himself with busts of Napoleon and, at parade-ground reviews, tried to jut his jaw out like Mussolini's. But he knew where his bread was buttered. In return for bribes and support, he let the United Fruit Company—Boston-based, and with investments all around the Caribbean—hold title to 112 railroad miles, tracks that linked United Fruit–run plantations in the interior to United Fruit–run docks and warehouses by the sea. By both seas, in fact, for—his palm well-greased—Ubico gave United Fruit exclusive rights to a Pacific as well as a Caribbean port. After a few more bribes, he even granted United Fruit a ninety-nine-year lease on more than half of Guatemala's land.

But did Ubico, and the land-owning oligarchy he represented, have special ties with the U.S. government? By the time the Eisenhower administration came into office in early 1953, Ubico was long gone from Guatemala, having been overthrown and flown to exile in New Orleans. Still: in its negotiations with Ubico, United Fruit had used the legal services of the New York firm Sullivan and Cromwell—the executive partner of which was John Foster Dulles, President Eisenhower's first secretary of state.

Yet more: as the Eisenhower administration was organizing its roster, early in 1953, a certain pattern emerged.

Allen Dulles, John Foster's brother and new CIA director, also had been a Sullivan and Cromwell partner. Before World War II, he had helped arrange German financial penetration of Guatemala.

John M. Cabot, Assistant Secretary of State for Inter-American Affairs, was from Boston, the site of United Fruit's headquarters. He had been the company's major stockholder.

Sinclair Weeks, Secretary of Commerce, had been the director of United Fruit's registrar bank.

Robert Cutler, Special Assistant to the President for National Security Affairs, had been board chairman of Old Colony Trust, the company's transfer bank, as well as board chairman of United Fruit itself.

John J. McCloy, lawyer, World Bank president, and friend of Eisenhower, had sat on the United Fruit board of directors.

Robert Hill, U.S. ambassador to Costa Rica, had been a board member of United Fruit.

Whitney H. Shephardson, an official of the Council on Foreign Relations, had been a director of International Railways of Central America, a subsidiary of United Fruit.

Some of these officials had forsworn their interests in United Fruit. The import of the Ubico–United Fruit–Washington network, nevertheless, was that the Eisenhower administration looked askance at the idea of any change at all in the Guatemalan status quo.

And the Guatemalan status quo had changed. During the time of the Truman administration, a cluster of reformists from Guatemala's military had seized power, then held elections. The eventual victor was Jacobo Arbenz (son of an émigré Swiss druggist) who, by the early 1950s, was instituting a modest program of land reform. And land reform meant expropriation of some of the holdings of the United Fruit Company.

La Frutera, as the Guatemalans called the firm, reacted with vigor. Edward L. Bernays, a United Fruit public relations wizard, launched a press campaign intended to pressure Washington into toppling Arbenz. Washington did not need much pressuring, but, still, Bernays had no intention of letting events take care of themselves. He struck up a relationship with Arthur Hayes Sulzberger, publisher of The New York Times; Sulzberger sent a reporter to Guatemala; La Frutera and the State Department showed the reporter just what they wanted him to see; the reporter did his job. In a series of articles about Guatemala, The New York Times reported that the Arbenz government was fully in the grip of international communism. Bernays, in 1953, also persuaded Henry Luce to run a photo spread in Life on Guatemala's "Red" land reform: Life even carried a picture of barefooted peasants drinking champagne. The Russians, obviously, were coming.

As "I anticipated," Bernays said later, U.S. "public interest in the Caribbean skyrocketed." With Senator Joe McCarthy already stirring up Americans with his anti-Red rantings, people were looking southward, into America's "backyard," and they were lusting for action.

In 1954, a reporter visited the seventh-floor State Department office of John Foster Dulles. He found the secretary "purring like a giant cat" at the thought of what was to come.

Plenty was to come. In March 1954, the National Security Council authorized the Eisenhower administration to:

a. Create and exploit troublesome problems for international communism . . . and retard the growth of the military and economic potential of the Soviet bloc.
b. Discredit the prestige and ideology of international communism, and reduce the strength of its parties and other elements.
c. Counter any threat of a party or individual *directly or indirectly responsive to Communist control* [emphasis added] to achieve dominant power in a free-world country.
d. Reduce international communist control over any areas of the world.
e. Strengthen the orientation toward the United States of the peoples and nations of the free world. . . .
f. . . . develop underground resistance and facilitate covert and guerrilla operations and ensure availability of those forces in the event of war. . . .

U.S. government responsibility for such operations was not to be "evident," and "if uncovered the United States government can plausibly disclaim any responsibility for them. Specifically, such operations shall include . . . propaganda, political action; economic warfare; preventive direct action, including sabotage, anti-sabotage demolition; escape and evasion and evacuation measures; subversion against hostile states or groups including assistance to underground resistance movements, guerrilla and refugee liberation groups; support of indigenous and anti-communist elements . . . ; deception plans and operations. . . ."

Worldwide, costly, and above all secret, this plan, coded as NSC-5412, sanctioned threats, bribes, murders, indeed just about all measures short of nuclear war; and it ended, in the words of one historian, "all pretensions about the territorial integrity, national sovereignty, and international law." It provided the rationale for action against the Arbenz government in Guatemala.

Operation PBSUCCESS, code name for the plan to overthrow Arbenz, was proceeding in secrecy. Secrecy was Eisenhower's way. Despite his bumbling, grandfatherly mien, he was a sharp politician, wanting always to be able to proclaim successes and to disown failures. Hence his taste for covert action: if Arbenz fell, Ike could take credit; if Arbenz remained, someone other than Ike would be at fault. But Ike did not intend to have Arbenz remain in power. For at some point in the summer or early autumn of 1953, Eisenhower's clandestine chain of command—Ike to the Dulles brothers; Allen Dulles down through the CIA bureaucracy; CIA headquarters to the station chief in Mexico, E. Howard Hunt, later of Watergate infamy—received marching orders.

The first step was to find a new ambassador for Guatemala, someone who could coordinate the impending intervention from within the embassy. This someone should be loyal, ruthless, and, in case the coup miscarried, a Democrat. A name surfaced: a good old boy from South Carolina and ambassador to Greece, John E. Peurifoy.

Peurifoy was anything but a standard ambassador. He had attended West Point (1926–1928), but had dropped out. He had studied business at American University in Washington and taken the foreign service examination, but had flunked. After the war, he had gone to law school at George Washington University, working daytime as an elevator boy in the Capitol, but had ended up taking a job as a clerk in the State Department. There, however, he had found his niche, serving in effect as a spy for Secretary of State Dean Acheson and ferreting out incriminating gossip about accused spy Alger Hiss; Acheson had promoted Peurifoy to the position of assistant secretary in charge of administration. Able now to do favors for people, Peurifoy had developed a network of right-wing allies, and on the basis of such contacts had wangled an appointment as ambassador to Greece. In that capacity his major distinction had been his flamboyant attire and his love of racing about Athens in a British sports car.

In October 1953, Eisenhower made him our man in Guatemala City. Operation PBSUCCESS was now underway.

PBSUCCESS was an ambitious scheme, using implements of economic warfare to "destabilize" (a term later applied to Castro's Cuba and Allende's Chile) Arbenz's Guatemala. Washington cut off foreign aid to the country, blocked loans from the Export-Import and World Banks, and, in 1954, started searching and seizing merchant ships bound for Guatemalan ports. With the White House hoping to plunge Guatemala into financial chaos, CIA agents in Guatemala City approached high-ranking officers of the army, proffering bribes if they would betray Arbenz.

In the United States most of this was kept quiet. In Guatemala, however, it was an open secret. So certain was President Arbenz that the U.S. was arranging a coup that in the spring of 1954 he panicked, sending an appeal for help to the Kremlin. Moscow was delighted to assist.

Moving fast, the Soviet government ordered the shipment of two thousand tons of matériel, rifles, bullets, and small cannon, from the Skoda factory near Prague to the Polish port of Stettin on the Baltic. Loaded aboard the *Alfhem*, a Swedish freighter supposedly heading for Africa, the crates bearing the weapons were listed in the ship's manifest as optical supplies. The CIA, however, learned otherwise. Slipping aboard the ship while it was still in Stettin, an agent spotted the arms, and sent to Washington a microdot containing the words, "My God, my God, why hast thou forsaken me?" Decoded, the message meant that the *Alfhem* was transporting military supplies. When the ship reached Guatemala, Ambassador Peurifoy was waiting for it on the pier.

Alfhem arrived at Guatemala on May 17, 1954. Now having a pretext, the Eisenhower administration launched the coup.

"There's no school this afternoon because there is going to be a revolution at five o'clock!"

The date was June 17, 1954, and Danny Peurifoy, son of the ambassador, had rushed to the residence to tell his mother,

Betty Jane, the news. She was surprised, for the ambassador had told her no details, but she was delighted, for her husband now had reached the peak of his career. The only thing was, what took place was not much of a revolution.

Sponsored by the CIA, Carlos Enrique Castillo Armas, a fugitive Guatemalan colonel of Mayan descent, led a ragtag band of about 150 men to the Church of the Black Christ, six miles inside Honduras; there he waited. That was it. That was the Guatemalan part of the revolution.

But, then, Castillo Armas was only a puppet, the puppet master being the CIA. Working with Ambassador Peurifoy, their handpicked diplomat, CIA agents had rounded up a crew of Guatemalan exiles, provided them with Spanish-language radio scripts, sequestered them in stations in the Honduran jungle, paid them to claim that they were broadcasting on the Voice of Liberation, somewhere near Guatemala City, then had them report the "invasion" of the country by a huge counterrevolutionary army.

The report was a lie, but no matter; the propaganda had its desired effect, especially since it was accompanied by a couple of small-scale bombing raids. Then, with Castillo Armas and his barefoot band virtually tiptoeing in across the border, Ambassador Peurifoy, to magnify the "danger," ordered U.S. citizens in Guatemala City to leave. Peurifoy himself was acting under orders; Secretary of State Dulles had told him "to crack some heads together," meaning that Peurifoy was to activate the coup against Arbenz.

Arbenz got the point. On June 27, 1954, he fled his capital, escaping to exile in Mexico.

For the Fourth of July, 1954, the Peurifoys invited several hundred Guatemalans—right-wing Guatemalans—to the embassy to celebrate. They all sang "The Star-Spangled Banner," and Betty Jane Peurifoy penned a bit of doggerel that Henry Luce published in *Time.* It concluded:

> *Pistol-packing Peurifoy looks might optimistic*
> *For the land of Guatemala is no longer communistic!*

Although saying nothing of the CIA's involvement, the Eisenhower administration milked the Guatemalan episode for all it was worth. Central America, proclaimed John Foster Dulles,

was now free of "Communist imperialism," and Generalissimo
Castillo Armas had added a "new and glorious chapter to the
already great tradition of the American States." Castillo Armas
himself, beribboned and braided, and wearing a military hat
with leather visor over his wisp of a dark mustache, went to
Washington. There he received a twenty-one-gun salute,
gawked at the sights, and then flew to Denver, where President
Eisenhower was recuperating from a heart attack.

Also visiting Ike in Denver, Vice President Richard M. Nixon
then set off on an official tour of the Caribbean Basin, climaxing
the trip with an appearance in Guatemala. In Guatemala City,
a photographer snapped him as he read, or purported to read, in
Spanish, a glossy magazine entitled *Union Sovietica.* He also
had a look at some of the weapons from the *Alfhem.* Most were
obsolete—the Soviets had cheated Arbenz, perhaps because the
Communist element in his government had been puny. "This
is the first instance in history," Nixon asserted nonetheless at
the airport, "where a Communist government has been replaced by a free one."

Nixon saw Arbenz's fall as a victory; another foreigner in
Guatemala, an Argentinian medical student named Che
Guevara, saw that fall as a lesson. Subsequent revolutions,
Guevara concluded, would have to be on their guard against the
CIA's black propaganda. In the CIA itself, number-two man
Richard Bissell, a tall, storklike man with an engineer's brain,
saw in the Guatemalan affair a model to be applied elsewhere
in Latin America, as in Cuba.

And in March 1960, Bissell received President Eisenhower's
go-ahead to organize a "Program of Covert Action." The target
this time was not Arbenz but Castro. A new objective, but the
old tactics—President Eisenhower's Guatemala tactics were
prelude to President Eisenhower's and President Kennedy's,
Cuba tactics. And those tactics led straight to the crisis of
October 1962.

But a question remains. Was Arbenz's government Communist?
Or at least was it ripe for a Communist takeover? No. According
to a 1953 study by the State Department itself, Guatemala
possessed no more than "two or three dozen" Communist leaders and "almost without exception they are indigenous to the

area and are Mexico-trained rather than Moscow-trained, although some have visited the Soviet orbit and may have received brief instruction there." On May 11, 1954, furthermore, John Foster Dulles told the Brazilian ambassador that "it will be impossible to produce evidence clearly tying the Guatemalan government to Moscow." And a year later, Dulles learned that his analysts had found "nothing conclusive" linking Arbenz, or even Guatemala's almost invisible Communist minority, to the Soviet Union.

Arbenz, without question, had bought bloc-made weapons. But he also had tried to purchase Western-made weapons—and Washington not only had refused his offer but also had pressured European arms-makers into refusing to sell.

So, in the end, Colonel Jacobo Arbenz was up a creek without a paddle. Which was precisely what Eisenhower and the brothers Dulles had intended.

A few months after the Guatemalan affair had ended, General James Doolittle—Jimmy Doolittle of the 1942 firebombing raid on Tokyo—authored a secret report that sought to justify the Arbenz overthrow and that looked ahead to more such overthrows. In fighting the Cold War, claimed the Doolittle Report,

> hitherto acceptable norms of human conduct do not apply. If the United States is to survive, long-standing American concepts of fair play must be reconsidered. We must . . . learn to subvert, sabotage, and destroy our enemies by more clever, more sophisticated, and more effective methods than those used against us. It may become necessary that the American people be made acquainted with, understand, and support this fundamentally repugnant philosophy.

"More clever, more sophisticated, and more effective methods": late in 1954, the CIA came up with just such a method, the development of a lightweight, high-flying airplane that, equipped with special cameras, could take advantage of photographic advances so great that the newest lenses from fifty thousand feet in the air could record the numbers on auto license plates. The airplane, eventually designated the U-2, was the brainchild of Richard Bissell. A tall, bespectacled man, Bissell had been a brilliant undergraduate at Yale, leader of a coterie that had devoted itself, above all, to attacking all orthodoxy. He had gone on to become a Yale professor of economics, outraging colleagues by his openness and creativity. After 1947, he had entered the CIA. While far from being a right-wing fanatic, Bissell had applied his unsurpassed brainpower to leaflet drops and strafing missions over Guatemala. Then he had turned his energies to the U-2.

In doing so, he set up shop on the Mall, in a rickety building that was almost a shack and that, in World War I, supposedly, had been a whorehouse. In such digs, nonetheless, he oversaw the growth of the U-2. The plane had its first test runs in Nevada, early in 1955. By the middle of the year the plane was a proven success.

While U-2 prototypes were soaring over the wastes of the West, another U.S. intelligence mission was getting underway, this one underground—in Germany. With President Eisenhower's approval, CIA agents burrowed a tunnel from West Berlin to East Berlin, and in a narrow passageway far below where the Old Reichstag had stood, they tapped into Communist telephone lines. In charge of this operation was Richard Bissell.

As brilliant as he was, however, he forgot a detail: heat melts snow. During the winter of 1955–56, one particular potato field just east of Berlin, unlike all the other nearby fields, was not white but brown—a fact soon brought to the attention of the Soviet authorities. And on the evening of April 15, 1956, Soviet and East German troops poured into the tunnel as the Americans fled in haste to the West.

Pravda called the tunnel an example of the "perfidy of the American and British aggressors." The *New York Herald Tribune* termed it "a venture of extraordinary audacity . . . a striking example of their [American intelligence forces] capacity for daring undertakings."

5   Shortly before the Soviets cleared the tunnel, Nikita Khrushchev, wearing one of his floppy-armed, shiny suits that barely covered his paunch, entered a secret session of the Twentieth Party Congress, turned a picture of Stalin's face to the wall, waddled up to the lectern, and stunned his listeners. In what was to become known, once it was smuggled to the West, as his "secret speech," he declared:

> It is impossible and foreign to the spirit of Marxism-Leninism to elevate one person and transform him into a superman with supernatural characteristics akin to those of a God.

Denouncing the cult of Stalin, Khrushchev went on to propose "de-Stalinization" (meaning the decentralization of power and the release of political prisoners), to suggest that the Kremlin could recognize different brands of communism, and to endorse, in Russia's relations with the West, the principle of "peaceful coexistence."

The "secret speech" was typically Khrushchevian, at once shrewd and reckless. While it enabled him to tar his domestic rivals as Stalinists, its acknowledgment of many roads to socialism was direct incitement to an anti-Communist rebellion in Poland. To save his own skin politically, Khrushchev in the summer of 1956 had to fly to Warsaw to oversee a crackdown. Still, in words that he must have known would be leaked, he had spoken of "peaceful coexistence"—having consolidated power at home, he was signaling the world abroad that he was ready for an end to the Cold War.

6   While Khrushchev was in Warsaw, the Democrats were in Chicago, holding their presidential convention. That Adlai Stevenson, the former governor of Illinois and 1952 Democratic presidential nominee, would be the nominee again was a foregone conclusion. The only question was: who would be the vice presidential nominee?

Joseph Kennedy had spent the four previous years running John for the vice presidential nomination, and the effort bore all the hallmarks of the later presidential campaign: national publicity (the June 12, 1956, issue of *Look* carried a piece entitled "Can a Catholic Become Vice President?"); a show of strength in the New England states outside Massachusetts (two Democratic governors, Dennis J. Roberts of Rhode Island and Abraham A. Ribicoff of Connecticut, endorsed Kennedy for Vice

President); alliances with Democratic bosses throughout the country (such as Chicago's mayor, Richard Daley); and the burnishing of John F. Kennedy's reputation as a hero. The device chosen for enhancing the image was a book that bore John F. Kennedy's name, *Profiles in Courage.*

The book became a best-seller (Joseph Kennedy having purchased enough copies to place the work on *The New York Times'* list) and it won the Pulitzer Prize (Joseph Kennedy probably having manipulated the selection committee). But John F. Kennedy was not the author.

Profiles in Courage spelled out the stories of U.S. senators who, down through the ages, had risked their careers by casting unpopular votes. The theme was appealing and Jack Kennedy had come up with the idea; he had sketched out an outline, made notes, and dictated a few facts to secretaries. Then he had turned the writing over to others—professors Arthur Schlesinger, Jr., James MacGregor Burns, and Allan Nevins, then to his senatorial aide, Theodore Sorensen, who had coordinated a unifying draft. Returning to the enterprise, Kennedy had made a few changes and additions.

Profiles in Courage implied that Senator John F. Kennedy, like his senatorial subjects, was courageous. He was certainly determined to win: autographed copies of the book were distributed to every member of the 1956 Democratic national convention.

The vice presidential nomination in the end went to Tennessee's Democratic Senator Estes Kefauver. But John Kennedy had shown considerable strength on the convention floor—and the moment the November election was over, he launched his bid for the presidency.

The Republicans, of course, renominated President Dwight D. Eisenhower. One campaign banner read: "IF YOU DON'T LIKE PEACE, PROSPERITY, AND PROGRESS, VOTE STEVENSON!"

7   As if to commemorate the holiday, a U-2 spy plane on July 4, 1956, flew over Moscow. The pictures it took are still state secrets. Had the aircraft passed over Spaso House, the residence of the American ambassador, however, it could have recorded on film the mansion, the garden, a cluster of Americans eating hot dogs from a grill, the ambassador, Charles Bohlen, and the ambassador's special guest, the bald, wide-bellied figure of Nikita Khrushchev. By his portly presence, Khrushchev sought to embody the spirit of "peaceful coexistence." He praised Mrs. Bohlen on the corn she was raising, bantered with some journalists, exchanged quips with an American professor, then drank a toast to the health of President Eisenhower.

Bohlen knew, at the time, of the U-2 project. Khrushchev soon found out.

The U-2s were spying on more places than just the Soviet Union. In his diary entry for October 15, 1956, President Eisenhower noted: "Our high-flying reconnaissance planes have shown that Israel has obtained some 60 of the French Mystère pursuit planes, where there had been reported the transfer of only 24."

Through the U-2 photographs, the Eisenhower administration realized that, in October 1956, something was afoot in the Middle East. And indeed it was: in retaliation against Egypt's seizure of the Suez Canal—and apparent mobilization against Israel—Britain, France, and Israel secretly planned an armed attack up the Nile. Hardly had the attack begun, however, than through the ineptitude of Britain's Prime Minister Anthony Eden, who quailed before the thought of bloodshed, it faltered. Then it collapsed altogether: Khrushchev threatened that if the British and French failed to leave Egypt, he would "bust" their countries with Soviet missiles; U.S. officials similarly vowed to ruin the pound and shut off oil to Great Britain; and President Eisenhower, in a furious phone call to London, reduced Eden to tears. The Suez fiasco soon came to an end.

November 6, 1956, was election day. The Eisenhowers helicoptered to their Gettysburg farm to vote, then returned to the White House in the late morning. At noontime Ike saw the latest U-2 reports: he had feared a Soviet move into the Middle East, but the photos showed that Syrian airfields were devoid of Russian planes. So he relaxed, sure of peace and sure of victory over Stevenson.

That evening, Eisenhower visited his campaign headquarters in the Sheraton Park Hotel, eager to hear Adlai Stevenson concede. "What in the name of God is that monkey waiting for?" Eisenhower exclaimed. "Polishing his prose?"

Eisenhower had reason for arrogance, for he had just manhandled Stevenson at home and Eden abroad. His contempt for Eden ran especially deep. The Suez invasion, he exploded at one point, was "the damnedest business I ever saw supposedly intelligent governments getting themselves into." But Eisenhower's greatest cause for pique was that the Israelis, the French, and the British had failed to seek his approval, indeed had tried until the last possible moments to keep the Suez mission a secret.

And one did not get away with trying to keep secrets from the U.S. government. In case the Western powers had any doubt, the United States now made the rules—and had its U-2s up there on the lookout for any violations.

8   Or so it seemed. But late in 1956, two episodes showed that America's power had limits.

As the Suez invasion was getting under way, a revolt, encouraged by the Voice of America and Radio Free Europe (paid for by the CIA) erupted in Hungary—only to be crushed by Soviet tanks. Short of all-out war, the United States had no way to extend aid. "Poor fellows, poor fellows," President Eisenhower lamented to a journalist who had mentioned the Hungarians. "I think about them all the time. I wish there were some way of helping them." There wasn't.

Then, on the night of November 24–25, 1956, eighty-some Cuban revolutionaries boarded a little ship called the *Granma* and, from the Mexican port of Tuxpan, set out in the darkness for Cuba. Their leaders were a young Argentinian medic named Che Guevara and a flamboyant Cuban Fidel Castro, son of one Angel Castro.

Angel Castro, a native of Galicia, had signed up for a hitch in the Spanish Army, and had ended up fighting against the Americans in the war of 1898. After Spain's defeat, he had stayed on in Cuba, and since he was a strong, well-built young man, he had taken a job as a laborer with the United Fruit Company. He hated the gringos, apparently, but he kept his mouth shut and saved enough money to buy land near Santiago on the southern coast. Near his farm the United Fruit Company had maintained one of its compounds, with a private police force and, for the benefit of American employees alone, a polo club. The Yankee presence may have been a goad: Castro had prospered so much that, by the early 1950s, his sugar fields had employed more than five hundred men, and he had been able to send his son to law school.

Fidel Castro headed off for the law faculty at the University of Havana, careening along the highway in an automobile presented to him by his father. According to Juana, his sister, he was an unfocused young man, but ambitious nonetheless, determined at all costs to make a name for himself: soon after enrollment he garnered attention by riding a bicycle headlong into one of the university's brick walls. He was not much of a student. By his own admission, he "never went to lectures, never opened a book except just before examinations." No matter: as a student orator he was brilliant; and as a hoodlum—for he was part of the big car and submachine gun *gangsterismo* that was the bane of respectable Cubans—he had a pronounced talent for revolutionary speechifying. Rising fast in Havana's underworld, he was dedicating himself to the overthrow of Batista.

By 1953, the year Dwight Eisenhower became President, Fidel Castro had emerged as leader of a group of about 150 young Cubans, diverse in their background, a few students but mostly farmers, clerks, laborers, waiters, yet united in their love of revolutionary danger. At first they called themselves, simply, the Movement, but on July 26, 1956, they staged an insurrection. Ever after, they termed themselves July 26.

Conspiring in their rooms in Havana, the group planned to travel eastward, some by train and some by car, to Oriente Province; there, on July 26, which was Carnival, a day when defending troops were likely to be drunk, they would seize the Moncada barracks at Santiago. A few of the group, frightened, deserted. But the rest forged ahead. At 5:30 A.M., July 26, 1953, a column of cars, Chevrolets and Fords, with one Chrysler, pulled up to the barracks gate. The occupants of the lead car, disguised as sergeants, demanded admission. Fidel Castro was driving the second car.

Just what happened next has never been clear, although some of the cars at least did penetrate the base. But whatever the details, the attackers soon found themselves trapped by their cars, facing hostile fire from several directions; and then they were captured. Put on trial, Fidel Castro, the ringleader, received a prison sentence of fifteen years.

During the trial, however, on October 16, 1953, the Batista government allowed Castro to speak in his own defense. The speech made him a martyr.

"Once upon a time, there was a [Cuban] Republic," Castro may have said. (We have no trial transcript, but he claimed that a pamphlet he wrote later, "History Will Absolve Me," was based on the speech.) "It had its constitution, its laws, its civil rights, a President, a Congress, and law courts. Everyone could assemble, associate, speak, and write with complete freedom."

Cuba never had been such a republic. By romanticizing the past nonetheless Castro created a contrast between that past and what he what he called the present *"monstrum horrendum . . . a man named Batista."* Batista, in Castro's portrayal, "has not even human entrails . . . has, furthermore, never been sincere, loyal, honest, or chivalrous for a single moment of his public life. Only one man in all these centuries has stained with blood two separate periods of our historic existence and has dug his claws into the flesh of two generations of Cubans. . . . That grip, those claws [are] familiar: those jaws, those death-dealing scythes, those boots."

Turning from Batista-the-monster, Castro flailed away at the system over which Batista presided: he spoke of "700,000 Cubans without work," an exaggeration, of "30 percent of our farm people [who] cannot write their names and . . . 99 percent [of whom] know nothing of Cuba's history," a curious bracketing, and of "the capitalists [who] insist that the [Cuban] workers remain under a . . . yoke." Then he swept into his conclusion:

I know that imprisonment will be as hard for me as it has ever been for anyone—filled with cowardly threats and wicked torture. But I do not

fear prison, just as I do not fear the fury of the miserable tyrant. . . .
Sentence me, I do not mind. History will absolve me.

Castro's prison term, carried out in a jail in the Isle of Pines,
was hardly as horrible as he had forecast. He faced no torture,
and he was allowed to read, voluminously—Kant, Shakespeare,
Hugo, Lenin, and biographies of Franklin D. Roosevelt. And he
communicated with his fellow conspirators, locked up in nearby
cells. Then, on May 15, 1955, Batista let him go. To this day
we are unsure why—perhaps Batista had figured he had better
show the Americans that he wasn't such a bad guy, after all. In
any case, Castro left with a group of his comrades for Mexico.
From there he determined to have another go at Batista.

There, holed up in a farm near Mexico City, he also made the
acquaintance of Che Guevara, himself now an exile from Guatemala. They hit it off: Guevara saw in Castro a great leader and
a romantic adventurer; Castro saw in Guevara a seasoned revolutionary and a clever strategist. So on the night of November
24–25, about a year after they had met, Castro and Guevara,
along with eighty-two other exiles, boarded a sailing ship called
the *Granma* and, from the Mexican port of Tuxpan, set out in
the darkness for Cuba.

They barely made it. On the morning of December 2, 1956,
they saw the green of the Sierra Maestra rising up from the blue
of the sea; but the wind stopped, leaving the *Granma* becalmed.
A Batista reconnaissance plane spotted them and turned back
toward land, obviously to report their location. Then a frigate
appeared on the horizon. Paddling frantically, the Castro-
Guevara group—the July 26ers—reached land, only to discov-
erer that it was not land but a swamp, swarming with crabs and
thick with undergrowth. Only three hours later did the column
get onto ground, pushing through cane fields in the direction of
the Sierra.

Thus young Fidel Castro flung himself into his destiny. He was
hardly known in Washington at this time, but already the major
lineaments of his character had become apparent. He was, in
the words of Hugh Thomas, a British historian and author of the

most definitive study of Cuba in English, "nationalistic, unconventional, ambitious, and audacious." Thomas spotted in Castro an "addiction to revolution," a "Garibaldian romanticism as expressed . . . in the revolutionary slogans . . . *Patria o Muerte!* . . . *Venceremos!* (Fatherland or Death! We Shall Conquer!). . . . It is almost as if Castro and his colleagues were in love with the concept of revolution, or with the word."

Thomas made another and telling comment:

If Castro coveted power, and if, once obtained, he like most other politicians would not give it up without a struggle, and if he was certain to use that power in a revolutionary style, the U.S. would inevitably be implicated. . . . Castro's own temperament required tension, probably demanded an enemy. . . . To choose to be free meant for many Cubans, and above for Castro, to act in a way most calculated to anger the U.S.

CHAPTER 3

Fidel

1   To American tourists in the 1950s, Cuba seemed just the right combination of the exotic and the familiar. Beyond the broad sweep of the Havana harbor, commanded on both sides by tall, modern buildings, the city was a rabbit warren of twisting alleys, two-story houses with wrought-iron railings, Spanish doors that opened into courtyards with benches, flowers, and grandiose fountains. Cuba may have had a high standard of living, on paper, but that standard was an average: for each of the landowners and professional people who lived in mansions overlooking Havana's harbor, dozens more lived in the sewerless slums that spread outward from the capital, or in the overgrown, snake-infested hamlets of the countryside. Batista's Cuba pitted rich against poor, owner against tenant, white against black. And all the while Batista holed up in his palace, where he had surrounded himself with busts of Lincoln. He had no idea how to handle one of the threats to his rule, a law student named Fidel Castro.

But Castro sensed how to handle Batista. He had to make Batista reveal himself for what he was, an American puppet.

"Why, these people are no more fit for self-government than gunpowder is for hell!"

The speaker, asked if he thought that the Cubans should be free, was General William Rufus Shafter, one of the heroes of the Spanish-American War; the people to whom he was referring, the Cubans, he regarded with loathing. During the war, barefooted Cuban guerrillas had fought alongside U.S. troops, in many cases valiantly, but most of those rebels were of African descent and, in the eyes of the white Americans, little better than thieves. So what was America to do with this now-liberated "rabble"?

Up in Washington, Orville Platt, a senator from Connecticut, had an idea. Cuba could have a constitution, and thus be free, nominally, but that constitution would contain the following provisions: 1) Cuba would build sewers and eliminate mosquitoes, making the island safe for U.S. private investors; 2) Cuba would grant the U.S. a ninety-nine-year lease of the harbor at Guantánamo, making the island safe for the U.S. Navy; and 3) Cuba would acknowledge America's right, when the U.S. saw fit to do so, to intervene in the island militarily, making the Caribbean safe for U.S. interests. In 1901, after intense U.S. pressure, delegates to the U.S.-convened Cuban constitutional convention wrote these provisions—the Platt Amendment—into their document. Wrote General Leonard Wood, another hero of the Spanish-American War, to Theodore Roosevelt, "There is, of course, little or no independence left Cuba under the Platt Amendment."

But Cuba had become bound to America by more than words. With lobbyists from the American Sugar Refining Trust spreading dollars around Capitol Hill—the company was itching to import cheap sugar from Cuba and thus undersell American domestic producers—the Senate in 1903 ratified a trade treaty with Cuba, and Yankee dollars poured into the island's sugar fields. To safeguard the investment in the face of repeated rebellions, the U.S. Marines went into Cuba in 1906, in 1912, and 1917—on the last occasion, ostensibly, to guarantee the flow of sugar to the American troops in France.

The military interventions came to an end (until after Fidel Castro had risen to power). But another sort of intervention took place, the influx of dollars and Yankees, especially after World War II. With new telegraph and telephone connections between the U.S. and Cuba, new ferry service between Havana and West Palm Beach, new air routes into Cuba from New Orleans,

Tampa, and Charleston, and with as many as twenty-eight Pan Am flights a day between the island and Florida, the tourist industry stood on the brink of explosive takeoff.

With U.S. dollars pouring into the hotels and casinos, furthermore, Cuba was starting to look American. American cars crowded the streets, Havana newspapers advertised tires, sewing machines, refrigerators, all American-made. Movie houses played American films; nightclubs featured American jazz, and served American bourbon; theaters staged American musicals. And with highways, railways, and a Havana harbor that at night glowed with the lights of the cruise ships, Cuba seemed almost like America; according to a U.S. Commerce Department report, the island enjoyed "one of the highest standards of living in Latin America."

It certainly had a slob of a dictator. Eating and drinking hugely, Batista was growing fat. For hours at a time, his press secretary later revealed, he would "play canasta with his military friends or watch horror films." He would spend more hours showering, changing clothes, combing his hair, knotting his neckties, and listening to private telephone conversations his secret police had taped. He had mistresses galore. He was increasingly out of touch with his people.

The people over whom he presided, or lorded, furthermore, were having to endure rampant unemployment, spreading corruption, and financial control by the chieftains of the American Mafia. Cuba under Batista was wealthy by Latin-American standards, but the distribution of its wealth was skewed, the many poor being very poor and the few rich being very rich—a state of affairs that, in Washington, seemed to bode no trouble.

Time cast Batista in the role of America's helpmate. And he certainly helped—himself and his buddies to the loot, more even than before. Their hands out and their palms greased, the members of the Batista machine flaunted their wealth with abandon. Robert Alden, a *New York Times* correspondent, paid a Christmas visit to one of the favored casinos: "The women," he wrote, "wore chinchilla capes and sported diamonds as big as robins' eggs. Thousands of dollars changed hands at each throw of the dice." Then the elite would drive off in their Cadillacs and Lincoln convertibles, racing through the streets as if to run down the less fortunate.

Some of the Yankees saw this, some did not, but on the whole to the tourists it made no difference. Havana was fun, fun, fun. Las Vegas south!

For nearly half a century, U.S.-made maps of Florida had included Cuba, as if the island were nothing more than a tropical extension of territorial America. And, in the American thinking of the early 1950s, why not? Cuba—after all—was nothing more than one of those wayward Latin societies, symbolized in movies and on television by the native dancer Carmen Miranda, feather-brained, over-sexed, and given to gyrating her pelvis while, on her head, balancing a bowl of bananas. Great! Cuba, obviously, was America's distant cousin, with baseball, Coke bottles, and one-armed bandits. Cuba was coming along: one of her athletes, Minnie Minoso, starred for the Cleveland Indians and then the Chicago White Sox!

The trouble with the American vision was that, during World War II, another Cuban was named school athlete of the year, but instead of professional baseball he chose professional revolution. He was Fidel Castro.

February 16, 1957: setting out by car from Havana, a middle-aged American couple started off toward the wilds of southeastern Cuba, at various military checkpoints passing themselves off as tourists. The husband actually was Herbert Matthews, a *New York Times* reporter and an old Cuba hand (Ernest Hemingway had called him "brave as a badger"); he had told the U.S. embassy nothing of his trip, and indeed had taken his wife along as camouflage. Then, when he reached the foothills of the Sierra Maestra, he left his wife with friends, and embarked on the mountain climb by foot.

He was off in search of the scoop of his lifetime. Rumor in Havana had had Fidel Castro dead, killed by Batista's forces somewhere in the jungles. Through a secret emissary, however, Matthews had learned that Castro was alive, well, and ready to grant an interview. Matthews met Castro at dawn on February 17, 1957, and learned of Castro's return to Cuba.

The *Granma* had managed to land, with Castro and his band hiding out in cane fields. Then they were betrayed by a guide. As they came out from among the stalks, on the afternoon of

December 5, 1956, they walked into machine-gun fire. Many died, some became prisoners; a few, including Guevara, Fidel, and Raúl Castro, escaped, somehow slipping up to the mountains. The band now numbered sixteen men. Desperate, they ate herbs and raw corn, and Fidel sucked cane stalks. Occasionally peasants gave them meals. On Christmas Eve they arrived at the base of the Sierra Maestra, Cuba's traditional last refuge for fugitives and criminals.

A mountain range about a hundred miles long, running along Cuba's southeastern coast, the Sierra Maestra was the wildest part of the island, its slopes rising precipitously from cactus plants and near-desert conditions at its base to tree ferns and rain forests around its peaks. There, close to the highest point, the Pico Turquino or the Blue Mountain, the remnants of the July 26ers set up camp.

The Guatemalan revolution had failed, in part, because the U.S. public heard only one side of the story—that of the United Fruit Company. Guevara had learned that lesson well: the survival of a revolution, he had concluded, depended on winning the early sympathies of the American public; that public, later on, might become disenchanted, but by then the revolution could be in place.

Hence, through underground channels, the invitation to Herbert Matthews to come to the Sierra. He and Castro talked throughout the day and on into the night.

A week later, the first of Matthews's three-part series on Castro hit the front page of *The New York Times*. "The personality of the man is overpowering," Matthews wrote. "It was easy to see that his men adored him. . . . Here was an educated, dedicated fanatic, a man of ideals, of courage, and of remarkable qualities of leadership. . . . [O]ne got a feeling that he is now invincible." Castro, in Matthews's account, was a "powerful six-footer, olive-skinned, full-faced, with a shapely beard. He was dressed in an olive gray fatigue uniform and carried a rifle with a telescopic sight of which he was very proud." Castro, Matthews believed, was Jeffersonian, "radical, democratic, and therefore anti-Communist," with "no animosity toward the United States and the American people."

Matthews's series ignited a firestorm, for he predicted that

"General Batista cannot possibly hope to suppress the Castro revolt." Infuriated, the Batista government accused Matthews of having invented the whole story. But, in rebuttal, *The New York Times* printed a photograph taken during the Sierra Maestra interview: right there, under a wooden lean-to, with trees and sunshine in the background, Castro in his fatigues was lighting a cigar and Matthews, wearing a beret and chomping on his own cigar, was scribbling away on a notepad.

Yet Castro's eventual victory was hardly certain. In countries such as China, Guatemala, and Colombia, guerrilla forces had survived for years, but without short-term success. Cuba, however, was different. In the words of Hugh Thomas, the island's most prominent English-language historian:

> The reasons for Batista's fall did not lie in the Sierra. The field of struggle was in Havana, and in Santiago, and in Washington as well.

Batista, to be sure, still had friends in Washington. But he was demonstrably losing friends in Cuba; and so, to the U.S. administration, he was ever more a liability. The way to avoid a real revolution in Cuba, American officials were starting to think, might be to let Batista go and to replace him with someone right-wing *and* popular.

2   1957 began well for John F. Kennedy. Thanks to the Democratic national convention, he had had national exposure. Now, thanks to Majority Leader Lyndon B. Johnson (and to Joseph Kennedy, who pressured Johnson), he had the prestige of a seat on the Senate's Committee on Foreign Relations. And soon, thanks to Henry Luce (his father's pal), he had his picture on the cover of *Time*.

To be President in 1961, he needed more: he needed to win reelection to the Senate by so stunning a victory in 1958 that he automatically would be far ahead of any rivals. And his father was going to arrange it all. Over a dinner in Palm Beach, one of John's buddies started to tease him about some woman or other he had had. Slapping the table, Joseph Kennedy glared down and ordered:

You're not to speak like that any more. There are things that you just can't bring up any more, private things. You've got to forget them. Forget the "Jack" you once knew. From now on you've got to watch everything you say. The day is coming, and it's coming soon, when he won't be "Jack" any more at all—not to you and not to the rest of us either. He'll be "Mr. President." And you can't say or do anything that will jeopardize that.

So commanding, Joseph Kennedy had created what his biographer termed "a publicity buildup unprecedented in U.S. political history." But whether son John would jeopardize the campaign—and indeed the presidency—was another matter.

3   Mid-1957 brought a whisper of East-West reconciliation: fearing that the U.S. would supply the West Germans with nuclear weapons, Chairman Khrushchev floated the Rapacki Plan (Adam Rapacki was the Polish foreign minister), a scheme that would have left Central Europe (including East Germany and Poland) nuclear-free. And in the early autumn of 1957, George Kennan, original author of the containment policy and by this point a visiting professor at Oxford, gave a series of lectures on the BBC, urging a "disengagement" for Central Europe. But back in his P Street home in Georgetown, Dean Acheson was furious with Kennan—Kennan, Acheson stated in a press release, had "never grasped the realities of power relationships." And the White House simply ignored the Rapacki Plan.

Then the American people found a new worry. It was called *Sputnik.*

"It was Us versus Them," a journalist remembered. "It was the American way of life, not to mention tailfins, Wrigley's Spearmint gum, Wednesday night bowling, and attending the church of your choice, going against the godless horde."

The reporter was referring to the mania in America that followed the launching, in October 1957, of the Soviet space satellite, *Sputnik.*

"Listen now for the sound which forevermore separates the

old from the new": so whispered an NBC television announcer; and peering into their oval-screened sets, millions of Americans heard, from beyond the earth, *Sputnik*'s beep-beep-beep. The sound was eerie. And scary. Egged on by his constituents, Senator Henry Jackson demanded a "National Week of Shame and Danger."

The American public was jumpy. So was H. Rowan Gaither, Jr., an official of the Ford Foundation—unless the country pumped up its defense spending to nearly $50 billion a year, warned a commission that Gaither had chaired, the U.S. might lose the Cold War. America, Gaither concluded, had to goose up the arms race, and do so fast. Congress complied, raising America's annual defense budget to nearly $45 billion.

The Gaither Report was classified. Administration officials nonetheless leaked enough of it to justify an arms buildup.

Far behind in the arms race now, Khrushchev countered with a scheme for an atom-free zone in the center of Europe. Eisenhower, advised by former Secretary of State Dean Acheson, turned the idea down flat.

By late 1957, hopes for a thaw in the Cold War had all but vanished. Indeed, the newspapers were full of the darkest stories. The Soviets were leading in the arms race! America was facing a missile gap! America might be conquered! From his U-2 reports, President Eisenhower knew that the rumors were false. But the reports were good news for the Democrats, and with a recession looming, the White House moved to boost defense spending.

So contracts went out and the missile program took off. Convair and Martin got the go-ahead for the Atlas and the Titan, intercontinental ballistic missiles; Ramo-Woodridge got responsibility for systems engineering in the missiles; North American got to build engines for the Jupiter, the Army's counterpart of the Navy's Thor; Chrysler got the right to assemble the Jupiters; and, as primary contractor and design coordinator for all the above rockets, Douglas Aircraft got the contract to construct the airframes. The Pentagon was spreading the wealth around.

It also was spreading the missiles around. Florida's Cape Canaveral soon was ablaze with missile firings, most of them unsuccessful. But toward the end of the year a rocket lifted a nose cone 300 miles above the earth and 1,300 miles down the Atlantic channel.

Then, in November, the Soviets launched a space satellite that contained a puppy—when the animal died in orbit, American reporters wrote of Communist "beastliness"—and President Eisenhower urged the missile-makers to make their missiles even faster.

On Christmas Day, 1957, a certain American was in Havana. He stayed in the embassy, attended early mass, then spent the rest of the day with his chum, Fulgencio Batista. The American, whose father had extensive investments in Cuba and benefited from Batista's protection was Senator John F. Kennedy.

Soon after the turn of the year, John Kennedy had a series of encounters with another gentleman, although these were not so convivial as his time with Batista: on several occasions, after Democratic party meetings, he shared rides back to Georgetown with Dean Acheson. Their relationship was uneasy. "I would not say that we were in any way friends," Acheson later remembered. "We were acquaintances." Acheson distrusted Kennedy, or, more exactly, Kennedy's father, whom the former secretary of state dismissed as a social-climbing bootlegger. The younger Kennedy, in Acheson's judgment, was little more than a spoiled brat for whom the father had purchased a seat in Congress. Kennedy in turn was stiff with Acheson, deferential, as if Acheson made him feel like a kid again.

4   Although neither had declared for the presidency formally, the contest between John F. Kennedy and Richard M. Nixon was heating up already. Trying to prove his foreign policy credentials, Nixon in the spring of 1958 embarked on a goodwill tour to Latin America. The goodwill turned to ill will. Riding in a big, black, tail-finned Cadillac limousine in Caracas, Nixon found himself surrounded by a phalanx of hostile youths. Shortly before, a military junta had overthrown the dictator Marcos Perez Jimenez (known to his pals in the Eisenhower administration as "P.J."). Secretary of State John Foster Dulles had praised him for providing "in Venezuela a climate which is attractive to foreign capital to come in"; and when P.J., along with his hated chief of police, had to skip the country, the Eisenhower administration quickly granted them asylum. So the United States, in the eyes of many young Venezuelans, was a sponsor of torture and murder.

As his procession crawled along a tree-lined avenue in Caracas, Nixon could see a horde of youths, wearing short-sleeved shirts and holding anti-U.S. banners, approaching from across a park. As they reached the street, they shouted, stoned the cars, smashed some of the windows, crunched fenders. Surrounding Nixon's own limousine, they rocked it, shook their fists at him, and some even tried to open the rear doors. Seated beside Nixon, a Secret Service agent drew his gun and said, "Let's get some of these sons of bitches." Nixon, however, restrained him, and the limousine somehow pulled free. Acknowledged one rueful journalist: "A national defeat has been parlayed into a personal political triumph"—Nixon's proving to the world that he was indeed tough.

When Nixon returned to Washington, he recommended that the U.S. "must do a more effective job of reaching the opinion-makers of Latin America. . . . We must develop an economic program for Latin America which is distinctively its own." Nixon reprinted the advice in his memoirs; apparently he did not see the contradiction.

By the time of Nixon's tour, Fidel Castro had been in Cuba's Sierra for about a year. His guerrilla band had grown into a guerrilla army, possessing its own hospital, butcher shop, and cigar factory, and able to roam at will over about two thousand square miles of southeastern Cuban countryside. The force could strike in the cities, too, where incidents of sabotage were multiplying—just as Castro intended. Occasional incidents of sabotage lured Batista's police to commit counterrevolutionary atrocities, which did nothing to prevent further sabotage and only made the romance of guerrilla war ever more attractive to young men and women.

Like an expert in judo, Castro was using Batista against himself; for while some thought of Batista as a thug, actually he was just poor at being a dictator. Batista simply had no way of countering Castro's interview with Herbert Matthews.

The immediate effect of Matthews's reportage was that, in the United States of 1957 and 1958, Fidel Castro, in certain circles at least, became a folk hero, "larger than life," one historian has written, "Robin Hood to Batista's grotesque Sheriff of Nottingham." With the public momentarily enthralled, CBS sent a television crew into the Sierra to film a documentary, eventually entitled "Cuba's Jungle Fighters." Staring straight into a camera lens, Castro declared—undoubtedly for the benefit of American viewers—that he was not a Communist. He seemed to be telling the truth; and in March 1958, the Eisenhower administration slapped an arms embargo on Cuba. Since, through raids on police stations and military outposts, the July 26ers had been helping themselves to all the arms they could use, the embargo for all intents and purposes was aimed at Batista. And when, in mid-1958, Batista launched a major offensive against the July 26ers in their mountain redoubts, failed to dislodge them, and lost face, Washington seemed ready to see Batista depart.

Or almost ready. On December 8, 1958, Arthur Gardner, U.S. ambassador to Cuba (1953–57) and an ardent Batista supporter, sent a message to Vice President Nixon, urging that the "Miami matter . . . be opened at once. . . ." Gardner wanted Nixon to explore ways to keep Castro out of power.

Gardner may not have been speaking for Eisenhower, directly. But American business leaders in Havana, officials from Esso and United Fruit, passed word to Earl T. Smith, an investment broker and the newest U.S. ambassador, that Castro's movement was dominated by Communists; Smith passed the word along to Washington; CIA officials closeted themselves with Miami-based William Pawley, a onetime airplane salesman who had helped the CIA set up its private airline and who was a buddy of Batista; and Pawley on December 9, 1958, flew to Havana, and offered Batista a new setup in Daytona Beach. Batista, Pawley and his Agency allies thought, was finished anyway: so if Batista would leave Cuba before it was too late, the U.S. could replace him with one Rivero Agüero, a moderate lawyer, who might be able to patch together a government on national unity. Castro's movement would die a-borning—if Batista took the next plane out.

But he only diddled, and with each passing day, Castro's popularity grew. Finally, at the very end of 1958, when all hope for an Agüero ministry had faded, Batista collected his money, liquor, and mistresses, said good-bye to the Mafia and to Havana, and flew to Madrid. Ambassador Smith left, too.

5   As Smith left, Fidel Castro was launching his final push toward Havana, starting off from Santiago by the eastern end of the island. His forces met some slight resistance, for a few of the Batista soldiery had not yet had word that all was over. Many of them, however, joined with Castro's column. Castro himself, sometimes walking, sometimes riding a jeep, waved his hands and worked the crowds as if he were an American politician running for election. While he had not exactly won a military victory, people had grown sick of the old Batista crowd, and responded to Castro and his July 26ers as if they were conquering heroes. And all along the towns and villages on the way to the capital, the people became aware that the *barbudos*, the bearded ones, despite their khakis and omnipresent guns, "did not drink, did not loot, conducted themselves as if they were saints. No army had ever behaved like this in Havana."

Once in Havana, on January 8, 1959, Castro's triumph seemed complete. As his cars, jeeps, tanks, and trucks drove in from the east, television cameras covered his route of entry; and along every street and corner, from the outlying slums to the old quarter and finally to the presidential palace, huge crowds sang and embraced, and held up placards inscribed: "GRACIAS, FIDEL!" With his rifle with its telescopic lense slung over his shoulder, he mounted the palace steps, then stood at a microphone to address his people.

"As I watched Castro I realized the magic of his personality," wrote an American woman who was in the crowd below. ". . . He seemed to weave a hypnotic net over his listeners, making them believe in his own concept of the functions of government and the destiny of Cuba." After he had finished, he moved on to the Campamento Colombia, the fortress nearly, and as he did so crowds parted for him as the Red Sea had parted for Moses.

.   .   .

"When Mrs. Bonsal and I landed at the Havana airport on the rainy evening of February 19, 1959, we were cordially greeted by old and new friends." Thus began the memoir of Philip W. Bonsal, Earl Smith's replacement as U.S. ambassador to Cuba. Unlike the buffoonish Smith, Bonsal, a slender six-footer, was a professional diplomat, fluent in Spanish, and deeply versed in Latin American affairs. In Cuba he was an immediate hit, for after he had walked down the ramp from his airplane, he strode up to one of Castro's bearded revolutionaries, a man with a submachine gun slung over his shoulder, shook the man's hand, and expressed admiration for the Fidelistas' courage. Widely "reported in the Cuban press," *The Christian Science Monitor* reported, his gesture "endeared him immediately to Cubans."

For a time, the sentiment was mutual. In April 1959, at the invitation of the American Society of Newspaper Editors, Castro flew to the States. Although President Eisenhower refused to meet him, the press heaped him with praise, the CIA briefed him (on the menace of communism), Vice President Nixon conversed with him (Nixon thought him "sincere [but] incredibly naive about communism), and Castro posed for photographs at the Lincoln Memorial. To be sure, Castro made a few Americans nervous: Oregon's Democratic Senator Wayne Morse regarded Castro's springtime war-crimes trials of Batista's old supporters as nothing more than kangaroo courts (in one case, Castro indeed had overruled an acquittal, himself giving a group of Batista pilots thirty years' confinement); and Nixon thought Castro had paid him little attention. Yet Castro "could probably be handled," Ambassador Bonsal said to a caller, "and he, Bonsal, could handle him if he were left alone. . . . Castro was a terrific person, physically and mentally, he was far from crazy, he was not living on pills [as some of the U.S. newspapers had alleged], and he was not a Communist."

So when Castro returned to Cuba in May 1959 (he had visited Canada and Brazil as well as the United States), he had received America's right hand, if not of fellowship, then at least of sufferance. As far as the Eisenhower administration was concerned, Castro and Cuba were free to go their own way. Free, that is, as long as their way did not involve communism.

.   .   .

If Bonsal really had thought he could "handle" Castro, then he was soon disillusioned. U.S.-Cuba relations were spiraling downward, fast.

A few days after he had come back to Havana, Castro presented his cabinet with a draft version of an agrarian reform law. Written by Guevara, or by a Guevara aide, and inspired by the Guatemalan reform law, the Cuban measure would authorize the government to take much of the island's land back from its owners—many of them companies based in America—and hand it out to the peasants. The cabinet approved, and in a ceremony up in the Sierra Maestra, promulgated the law. The date was May 17, 1959.

The reaction in the United States was sharp. On Wall Street the value of Cuban stocks, especially in sugar and the utilities, plummeted; and a spate of articles in the American press portrayed Castro's Cuba as turning to communism. Before May 17, 1959, *Time* and *Newsweek*, between them, had run only one piece on communism in Cuba; after May 17, 1959, their issues were chock-full of such stories. Through the embassy in Havana, the American companies whose fields had been expropriated pressed Castro for compensation.

Castro offered to pay them back, in the Cuban currency and at a rate far below that which they demanded.

Late in May, a Spanish-speaking hit squad tried to kill Castro; Cuban intelligence believed the group had come from the soil of an American ally, Trujillo's Dominican Republic. Castro sent a hit squad of his own to Santo Domingo, but all his men were killed or imprisoned. Castro tried to buy weapons in Britain and Belgium; the U.S. government, citing the raid on the Dominican Republic, pressured those two countries into withholding sales.

In June, President Eisenhower made a prophetic comment. CIA Director Allen Dulles already had been lobbying Eisenhower to take Guatemala-type action against Castro and, in March, even had handed the President a document entitled "A Program of Covert Action Against the Castro Regime." As in the case of Guatemala, the proposal combined intelligence-gathering, a government-in-exile, covert action, a paramilitary force, and propaganda. Fearing perhaps that so far he lacked a good pretext, Eisenhower gave Dulles no commitment. In June, however, he told his Cabinet that if the Russians took over Cuba, he "would have to go to Congress to start war" against Castro.

6   Late in July 1959, Vice President Richard Nixon, positioning himself as an expert on foreign policy, flew to Moscow. Shortly before Nixon's flight, Nikita Khrushchev had indicated that he could be flexible on Berlin and had agreed to a conference of foreign ministers. The conference idea went nowhere, for Secretary of State Dulles was ill with cancer and could not attend. Through a Nixon visit, nonetheless, President Eisenhower wanted to see if a Cold War thaw truly was in the offing. Nixon, running for President, turned the visit into a political circus. Reporters accompanying Nixon sang:

> *Moscow Kremlin, here I come,*
> *What a place to campaign from!*

The place in question was the American Exhibition at Sokolniki Park, where in a glass pavilion the U.S. government was staging a display of the latest American goodies—a Pepsi-Cola machine, Polaroid cameras, a color television studio, and a mock U.S. kitchen, replete with sink, stove, toaster, and refrigerator. Leading Khrushchev into the kitchen and standing with him by the washing machine, Nixon expounded America's various advantages over Russia. Khrushchev seemed unimpressed, but *Time* thought Nixon "the personification of a kind of disciplined vigor that belied tales of the decadent and limp-wristed West."

Having thus put Khrushchev in his "place," the administration in Washington braced itself for the chairman's impending visit to the States. Khrushchev's visit actually involved a bit of a puzzle. At about the time of his "Kitchen Debate" with Nixon, he received, through diplomatic channels, an invitation to go to America. Since Eisenhower, for nearly a year, had been trying to avoid a summit meeting, the invitation to Khrushchev was surprising. Yet it was also surprising to Eisenhower: the invitation had been issued in his name, but he had given no such authorization. Someone in the State Department, on his or her own initiative, or through a misunderstanding, had asked for the Khrushchev visit. On learning all this, President Eisenhower blew up in a rage, but he had lost control of the situation—Khrushchev had accepted publicly.

Putting the best face on it all, Eisenhower on September 15, 1959, rode out to Andrews Air Force Base in Maryland to greet Khrushchev's airplane, a huge Ilyushin. A coterie of little girls was on hand to offer the chairman flowers, and college students, specially recruited for the occasion, held up banners that read "WELCOME KHRUSHCHEV." Once Khrushchev was on the tarmac, Eisenhower greeted him coolly, for the President had no wish to appear chummy with Khrushchev. After both men had read off greetings, they entered the presidential limousine; and as the car rolled along the parkway back to Washington, military helicopters roared overhead, securing the route. Placards along the sidewalk before the White House called the Russian a "tyrant."

Khrushchev's American visit turned into a spectacle. Setting off on a tour of the nation, the chairman and his party gawked at an IBM plant, fell in love with San Francisco, lunched with Frank Sinatra and Shirley MacLaine in Hollywood; and Khrushchev lost no chance to plug his theme of "peaceful coexistence." He even disavowed his earlier statement "We will bury you," that he claimed had been misreported. "I say it again," Khrushchev declared, "—I've almost worn my tongue thin repeating it—you may live under capitalism and we will live under socialism and build communism. The one whose system proves better will win. We will not bury you, nor will you bury us."

In Iowa, Khrushchev celebrated the corn harvest. In Camp David with Eisenhower, he agreed to cut the Red Army by one million men. And in the White House, just before his return to Moscow, he shamed the still reluctant Eisenhower into agreeing to hold a summit meeting in Paris, in 1960. A summit, both leaders conceded, might defuse the Berlin tension.

7   Speaking to about three hundred supporters under the chandeliers in the Senate caucus room, John F. Kennedy announced his candidacy for the presidency. He had just won reelection to the Senate, a mega-landslide victory in Massachusetts of 73 percent of the votes cast; and, dutifully, the Kennedy minions in the press, all of them directed by Joseph Kennedy, were doing their duty. *The Ladies' Home Journal, Reader's Digest*, Luce's *Life*, and others all ran features on one of the Kennedys or another; *The Saturday Evening Post* carried an article entitled "The Amazing Kennedys"; Theodore Sorensen–written and John F. Kennedy–signed pieces appeared in *Foreign Affairs* and *The New York Times Magazine;* another book appeared, *A Nation of Immigrants*, Sorensen-written and Kennedy-signed.

So all, by the turn of the year, was prepared. Kennedy's announcement was timed to hit the next morning's papers, the first Sunday of the New Year. The issues on which he would run, he said, were:

> How to end or alter the burdensome arms race, where Soviet gains already threaten our very existence. How to maintain freedom and order in the newly emerging nations. . . . And how to give direction to our traditional moral purpose, awakening every American to the dangers and opportunities that confront us.

Kennedy already had identified the warring words of his campaign, and indeed of his presidency: ". . . threaten our very existence. . . . freedom and order. . . . dangers and opportunities. . . ."

8   In its edition of February 22, 1960, in the month after John F. Kennedy had announced for President, *Time* carried a striking photo of a missile. Taken from under the archway of a rolled-back gantry gate (the scaffolding used while a missile was still under construction), the picture showed, in the foreground, a sentry and his guard dog and, in the background, the converging tracks on which the gate had been rolled. And right in the middle, visible under the arch and silhouetted against the sky, stood a missile—fueled, erect, and, as *Time* boasted, seventeen minutes from Red Square.

The rocket, situated at Feltwell Air Base near England's North Sea coast, was an intermediate-range ballistic missile, an IRBM, with a 1,700-mile range and a thermonuclear warhead. It was called a Thor.

Encouraged by the Gaither Report and subsidized by Congress with billions of dollars, the defense industry was on the move. By the early spring of 1960, government-paid-for earth-moving equipment was at work all across America's western states, digging out launching sites for hundreds of intercontinental ballistic missiles. When finished, these sites, clustered around twenty major bases from Montana to Texas, were to be "hardened," built of concrete far under the ground and covered with steel doors that, supposedly, could withstand the heat and pressure of even a direct nuclear attack. After such an attack, then, at least according to U.S. government estimates, the doors would open, the ICBMs, about one hundred feet long, would emerge from their silos, streak up toward the sky, and reach Moscow in thirty minutes.

Moscow must have got the message. These pieces of information, or threats, appeared in the public domain, compliments of the U.S. Defense Department, in *U.S. News & World Report's* edition of July 18, 1960.

Time, the weekly news magazine, also underlined the threat to Moscow: "ALARMING AMERICAN REVELATIONS OF AGREEMENT FOR MISSILES IN ITALY," *Time* trumpeted, quoting from Rome's Communist daily, *L'Unità*. The "Red worry," *Time* added, "was well founded. Italy, after long debate, had decided to install two squadrons of intermediate-range (1,500 miles) ballistic missiles. . . . While Italians leaked their decision to a semi-official news agency, the missile they will get, the American-designed Jupiter, was again proving its bright new reputation for reliability. In summery twilight test-firing [at Canaveral] it blasted aloft on its tenth successful flight (out of 15 tries, only one blowup . . . since Chrysler Corp. started supplying the birds off its assembly line)." *Time* also carried a map of Europe, a diagram of how far the IRBMs could reach into Russia: those in Britain had a range as far as Moscow; those to be based in Italy, near Venice and on Sardinia, could reach Moscow, Kiev, and the Crimea; and those in Turkey could drop their payloads all the way to Tashkent and the Urals.

Turkey?

Turkey. In 1959, the Eisenhower administration arranged a deal for the construction of an IRBM base in eastern Turkey, right up against the Soviet border. These Jupiters, pointed toward the Black Sea, the Caspian, and beyond, were provocative.

They were inaccurate; they required hours to fire up; and they were so thin-skinned that a sniper, sequestered in the ravines of easternmost Turkey, could have shot them down with a bullet. The Jupiters could have served one purpose, and one purpose alone. They signified an offensive, first-strike capability on the part of the United States against the Soviet Union.

9   If the Jupiters were provocative, so was the Kennedy campaign. In a brazen display of power over reporters—or at least of the power of his father's money over them—John Kennedy dared the press to print the truth. And it feared to do so.

What the public got during the Wisconsin campaign, Kennedy's first major primary after his announcement, were statements like:

> A bareheaded, coatless man, lithe as an athlete, his face still unlined, his eyes unpuffed with fatigue, wandering solitary as a stick through the empty streets and villages of Wisconsin's far-northern Congressional District.

This description of Kennedy in Wisconsin in the winter of 1960 was by journalist Theodore H. White, who later, in his best-seller, *The Making of the President, 1960,* treated Kennedy almost worshipfully. Backed by his father's money, Kennedy did work hard in the Badger State, and so did all the members of his family, as was duly noted in the papers.

What the public did not get during the Wisconsin campaign, however, was news about the Judith Campbell affair. Taking time off to hobnob with Frank Sinatra during a Las Vegas stop-over, John Kennedy met a gorgeous young woman named Judith Campbell, and could not resist. How much of her story, as Campbell herself has told it, we are to believe is anyone's guess: she claimed that she had been ignorant of the fact that she had been consorting with mobsters. Perhaps so. But what rings true in her memoirs was the attitude of John Kennedy. As she documents, he practically advertised their liaisons—as if proving his own invincibility.

Shortly after their introduction, she wrote, Kennedy called

"to ask if I would have lunch with him. . . . He was having a press conference in the covered section between the [Sands'] casino and the pool area, and he suggested that I meet him there around twelve-thirty [on February 8, 1960]. . . . When I arrived he was addressing a group of newspapermen. I tried to be as quiet as a little mouse as I moved over to a bench across the way. Jack immediately saw me and called out: 'Judy, I'll be right with you, we're just finishing up.' I could have fallen off the bench in a dead faint. 'Fine, take your time,' I managed to vocalize to my complete surprise, my face turning every shade of red. All the newspapermen had turned around to look at me. Jack didn't seem to mind at all. He didn't even flinch."

And so it continued. After a three-hour lunch on Sinatra's patio, they went to a reception in Kennedy's honor in one of the banquet rooms of the Sands. "There was no avoiding Jack at the reception . . . ," Campbell wrote. "Every time he made his way over to me in the crowd . . . [and] came over and touched my hand, all eyes were focused on us."

But nobody printed a word. It was as if the Kennedys had the press in their thrall.

10   The Eisenhower administration was drawing the sword. From deep within the government, officials were filling the Washington air with the cry of betrayal. Who had lost Cuba? Former Assistant Secretary of State for Latin American Affairs Roy Rubottom was one scapegoat (Rubottom "favored Castro," declared former Ambassador to Cuba Arthur Gardner), and William Wieland, who had been in charge of the Caribbean desk of the State Department, was another. Both indeed had helped clamp the arms embargo upon Batista. But the archvillain, in the eyes of the archconservatives, was Herbert Matthews, who, after the initial enthusings prompted by his articles from the Sierra, found himself branded at best as a fool and at worst as a traitor. In a parody of *The New York Times'* own want-ad advertisement, the May 1960 issue of William F. Buckley's *National Review* ran a cartoon: sitting astride a map of Cuba labeled "Police State of Cuba" was a revolutionary, wearing fatigues, holding a rifle, and sporting a black beard. The caption: "I got my job through *The New York Times.*"

The major enemy, of course, was really not Matthews but Castro. The U.S.-Cuban relationship was degenerating so badly that, by late 1959 and early 1960, it resembled the 1941 prelude to war between the U.S. and Japan.

On October 11, 1959, an airplane dropped three bombs on a sugar mill in Piñar del Río; without producing evidence, Castro claimed the plane had flown down from Florida. Cuba sent Washington a formal protest.

Ten days later, a former pilot with Batista flew over Havana and dropped a stack of anti-Castro leaflets. This airplane clearly had come from Florida. Castroite antiaircraft guns fired after the plane; the projectiles fell into the city streets and killed three people. Castro claimed the aircraft had dropped bombs.

Early in November 1959, *Revolución* carried a piece about the presence in Mexico City of Soviet Vice Premier Anastas Mikoyan. The Cuban paper hinted that Castro, too, would welcome a visit.

In early January, Castro took over more U.S. property, six sisal plantations, this time offering to pay 50 percent of the stated value; Washington rejected the offer as too low.

On January 12, 1960, an unmarked airplane out of Florida dropped incendiary bombs on seven sugarcane fields northeast of Havana.

At this moment, the American government might have called back the dogs of war. But, wrote Hugh Thomas, an historian of Cuba,

> Eisenhower did nothing about the plans for backing the counterrevolutionaries. Instead, he went on a short journey "to see South America for himself." But the incendiary raids by exiles from Florida continued. . . . [I]ncendiary bombs fell on Puerto Padre and upon several canefields in the north. There were other raids, one by a U.S.-built aircraft of Moroccan registration.

Then, early in February 1960, Anastas Mikoyan, the mustachioed deputy premier of the Soviet Union, arrived in Havana. He also had been in the United States (he had dined with Allen

Dulles and told him that Moscow hoped to set up a trade mission in Cuba) and Mexico. He had worked out a trade agreement with the latter country. Washington so far had raised no objections, although it was watchful. In Cuba, then, he proposed a trade of industrial goods and oil for sugar. That proposal seemed to catalyze the trouble to come.

Castro took Mikoyan up on the offer—and then demanded that Esso, which had plants in Cuba, refine the Soviet oil. At the behest of the State Department, the company refused to do so. Castro seized its plants, without tendering payment.

On March 4, 1960, *La Coubre,* a French cargo vessel loaded with munitions for Cuba, blew up in the Havana harbor, killing many people. Carelessness on the part of stevedores may have caused the explosion. Castro nonetheless blamed the CIA, and he asked the Soviets for arms.

On March 17, 1960, President Eisenhower authorized a "program" for the overthrow of Castro. The document he signed was entitled "A Program of Covert Action Against the Castro Regime," and it listed four points of attack: (1) "creation of a responsible and unified Cuban opposition to the Castro regime located outside of Cuba"; (2) a "powerful propaganda offensive" against Castro; (3) creation of a "covert action and intelligence organization within Cuba"; and (4) "the development of a paramilitary force outside of Cuba for future guerrilla action." All this, Eisenhower said later, was a "program," not a "plan."

CHAPTER 4

Ninety Miles Off Our Shore

1   While such endeavors were proceeding, the 1960 presidential campaign was starting to heat up. The press was focusing its attention on West Virginia.

The familiar picture of the Kennedy campaign in West Virginia, as sketched by the court historian Theodore H. White, was that of the Kennedy, aided by Franklin D. Roosevelt, Jr., campaigning up and down the hills and dales of West Virginia, smiling, shaking hands, and showing voters in the Mountain State that Catholics could be as human as Protestants. This description was valid, as far as it went.

It just did not go very far. While anti-Catholicism did exist in West Virginia, the Kennedy camp exaggerated the degree of prejudice by flooding the coal towns with leaflets that denounced Papism—so that John Kennedy, on television, could make a display of the kind of bigotry he had to combat. Television, of course, cost money, and here, as Theodore White detailed, Kennedy simply swamped his rival, Democratic Senator Hubert H. Humphrey, forcing the Minnesotan into using personal money simply to stay on the air. But the money had another use, one unmentioned in White's account. It was "widely reported," a recent historian has recounted, that during the West Virginia primary large amounts of Kennedy money wound up in the pockets of potential Kennedy voters. Charles D. Hylton, Jr., editor of the *Logan Banner*, reported that, in Logan County, payoffs "ranged anywhere from $2 and a drink of whiskey to $6 and two pints of whiskey for a single vote." Later, in December 1961, FBI listening devices picked up evidence of large Mafia donations to the West Virginia campaign that had apparently been disbursed through Frank Sinatra. It was this under-the-table money, used to make payoffs to key election officials, that was to be perhaps the deciding factor in the contest.

None of this made the news at the time, or the quasi-official histories published soon thereafter. Nor did John Kennedy's continuing affair with Judith Campbell—especially not since, in April 1960, according to her own story, she was introduced by Frank Sinatra to Sam Giancana, the gangland boss of Chicago.

All this the Kennedys were able to keep out of the public purview. President Eisenhower was not so fortunate. He got caught, in effect, with his pants down.

Tall and gaunt, smiling always through the hideous pain of advanced arthritis, Christian Herter, former governor of Massachusetts, had succeeded John Foster Dulles as secretary of state. He was the most Brahmin of Brahmins from Boston, but even he seemed rattled when, on May 3, 1960, he learned from a cable out of Athens that the unthinkable had happened. A U-2 spy plane, flown by pilot Francis Gary Powers, had flown out of a secret base in Pakistan, set its course for another secret base in Norway, but, about a thousand miles inside the border of the Soviet Union, been shot down. Secretary Herter notified President Eisenhower, who was playing golf in Pennsylvania, and allowed that the pilot probably was dead.

Speaking to the press, President Eisenhower indicated that an American weather plane had gone astray, and that its whereabouts, and the fate of its pilot, were uncertain. The Soviets, however, produced the pilot, Powers, put him on television, and he himself indicated that he had been on a spy mission. So Eisenhower, whom the world had trusted as it had trusted few leaders, was shown to be a liar.

For the newspaper editions of Sunday, May 8, 1960, headline writers and front-page reporters had the story almost of a lifetime. *The New York Times:* "U.S. CONCEDES FLIGHT OVER SOVIET, DEFENDS SEARCH FOR INTELLIGENCE." The *Washington Star:* "KHRUSHCHEV'S STORY PARTLY CONCEDED." The *San Francisco Chronicle:* "MORAL LEADERSHIP OF U.S. HARMED." Said *The Washington Post*, "This country was caught with jam on its hands." "Do our intelligence operatives," asked the *St. Louis Post-Dispatch*, "enjoy so much freewheeling authority that they can touch off an incident of grave international import by low-level decisions unchecked by responsible policy-making power? There must be an investigation of the circles which placed our country before the world in the light of a barefaced liar."

Later in May 1960, President Eisenhower went off to the long-negotiated-for summit meeting, held in Paris; present also were the host, France's President Charles de Gaulle, as well as Britain's Prime Minister Harold Macmillan and the Soviet Union's Premier and Chairman, Nikita Khrushchev. But the meeting broke apart—on arriving in Paris, Eisenhower had paid respects to de Gaulle and Macmillan, while virtually ignoring Khrushchev; and Khrushchev, under pressure from Kremlin hardliners who saw in the U-2 episode a perfect example of American perfidy, stomped out.

Fearing the expense and dangers of the nuclear arms race, Eisenhower and Khrushchev had been groping toward accommodation. Someone in the U.S. government nonetheless had allowed pilot Powers and his U-2 spy plane to violate Soviet air space. Who was responsible? We still do not know.

The U.S. was closing a vise on Cuba. In the midst of reports from refugees that Castro had cracked down on his opponents in the University of Havana and brought freedom of the press to an end, President Eisenhower, on July 6, reduced Cuba's sugar quota practically to zero. Ike had begun an embargo against the island. And at about the same time, the CIA, from a radio station on Swan Island—a lizard-infested pile of guano off the coast of Guatemala—started launching propaganda broadcasts toward Havana. To knowledgeable Cubans and Soviets, these steps seemed a replay of the commencement of the Guatemalan intervention.

In an address in Moscow, Nikita Khrushchev rang the alarm. "Figuratively speaking," he said,

> if need be, Soviet artillerymen can support the Cuban people with their rocket fire if aggressive forces in the Pentagon choose to start intervention against Cuba.

In the Pentagon itself, reported Hanson W. Baldwin, military specialist for *The New York Times*, some of the brass had visions of Cuba as a base for Soviet missiles, but they dismissed the worry on the ground that Khrushchev would see such bases as easy to destroy.

Four days after Baldwin raised the issue of missiles in Cuba, the Democrats poured into Los Angeles to open their national convention. With the Kennedy machine after West Virginia purring from victory to victory in the state primaries, few had any doubt that in the convention itself, JFK would score a win on the first ballot; and with ample precedent of a northern Democratic candidate's balancing the ticket with a southerner (Adlai Stevenson and Franklin Roosevelt alike had looked away to Dixie for their vice presidential choices), few were surprised that Kennedy picked Lyndon B. Johnson, the Senate majority leader from Texas. But, then, the convention was not supposed to be a surprise. As Joseph Kennedy conceived it, it was supposed to package his son for the White House.

An incident almost tore the package apart. Just before the convention got under way, John Kennedy and his friend Red Fay were in Monterey, talking with Hugh Sidey of *Time*. During the conversation, Sidey asked Fay: "Red, how much influence do you feel that the senator's father has had on his career? Do you feel that he is the motivating force behind the amazing drive and ambition of the entire family?" Fay answered, "I think that Mr. Kennedy has been the most vital force in the careers of the Kennedy men and women." Sidey was looking at Fay, not at Kennedy, as Kennedy slashed a finger across his throat. Fay said no more. "God, if I hadn't cut you off," Kennedy said to Fay later,

> Sidey could have headed his article "A vote for Jack is a vote for Father Joe." That's just the material *Time* magazine would like to have—that

I'm a pawn in Dad's hands. That it's not really Jack Kennedy who is seeking the presidency, but his father. That Joe Kennedy now has the vehicle to capture the only segment of power that has eluded him. That once in the White House it will be Dad directing the policy with Nice Jack agreeing, "Right again, Dad."

But *Time* printed none of this, possibly because *Time*'s owner, Henry Luce, was a political ally of the Kennedys. And with Joseph Kennedy in France, precisely to give the impression that he had stayed out of the campaign, John Kennedy picked up all the Democratic marbles.

"It has been a long road . . . to this crowded convention city," he declared. Looking out toward the setting sun, on July 15, 1960, and addressing a crowd of thousands packed into the Los Angeles Coliseum, John F. Kennedy was accepting his party's nomination for President.

"Now begins another long journey," he continued, as an estimated 35 million Americans watched him on their television sets, "taking me into your cities and homes all over America. Give me your help,

> [the huge crowd cheered]
> give me your hand,
> [it cheered again]
> your voice,
> [rising to its feet now,
> the immense crowd roared]
> and your vote!

The Republicans early in August 1960 nominated Richard M. Nixon for President. Shortly after they did so, President Eisenhower secretly authorized $13 million for the CIA-run guerrilla war against Castro. And in his secret quarters down on the Mall, Richard Bissell, the CIA chieftain who had fathered the U-2, took charge of the Cuba operation. The problem was, the secret was soon no secret.

2   The contest between Kennedy and Nixon kicked off in earnest after Labor Day, 1960, with Kennedy himself giving a speech in Detroit. His manner, one historian has noted, was taut, tense, and rushed. And with his Harvard accent and habit of jabbing the air with his fist, he appeared unnatural to many. [I]n Detroit many thought his fast-paced delivery sailed right over most people's heads.

He was, furthermore, several points behind Nixon in the polls; to catch up, the Kennedy campaign made elaborate use of now-famous advance men, agents who would proceed Kennedy to an airport and there, for the benefit of television cameras, organize crowds of young women who would go wild when the candidate landed.

The candidate also sought to outflank Richard Nixon—on the Right. In general terms, Kennedy charged that the Eisenhower administration had allowed the United States to slip behind the Soviet Union, behind in influence, behind in economic growth, behind in missiles; and the last of these charges gave rise to Kennedy's allegation, albeit false, of a missile gap. In specific terms, Kennedy, starting with an October 6, 1960, speech at the Cincinnati Garden, accused Eisenhower of creating in Cuba "Communism's first Caribbean base": "We did nothing," Kennedy claimed, "to persuade the people of Cuba and of Latin America that we wanted to be on the side of freedom."

In making these attacks, in practically accusing Eisenhower of appeasement, Kennedy had reckoned without the President's well-honed sense of timing. On October 13, 1960, about three weeks before the election, President Eisenhower banned all U.S. exports, save medicines and food, to Castro's Cuba. In a quick sidestep, the Eisenhower administration now had outflanked *Kennedy* on the right.

During the famous television debates, Kennedy and Nixon outdid each other in their expressions of loathing for Castro. Then, late in October, Richard Goodwin, a Kennedy aide and a former clerk to Supreme Court Justice Felix Frankfurter, took matters into his own hands. During Kennedy rallies around the country, Goodwin had circulated questionnaires, intended to identify what the voters wanted to hear. What he had learned was that, to Americans, Castro was more of an ogre than Khrushchev. Nixon seemed to have made the same discovery, for on October 17, 1960, speaking to the American Legion Convention in Miami, he had proposed ringing Cuba with an all-out "quarantine" (a term that, almost exactly a year hence, Kennedy himself adopted). All this Goodwin had confided to Kennedy. And flying into New York, Kennedy had told him to "get ready a real blast for Nixon."

Goodwin did so. While Kennedy was asleep in the Carlyle Hotel, Goodwin typed out a statement (and issued it to the press without clearing it with the exhausted Kennedy). The United States had an obligation, the statement went, to help those Cubans "who offer eventual hope of overthrowing Castro. Thus far these fighters for freedom have had virtually no support from our government."

As the Kennedy camp knew full well, for CIA Director Dulles had briefed candidate Kennedy on the plans for an assault on Cuba, Goodwin's statement was untrue. Issuing these words, however, was a shrewd move. Vice President Nixon, a major mover behind the invasion plot, was pledged to secrecy, and so could say nothing in rebuttal.

But the press, or at least a small part of the press, could say something. On October 30, 1960, *La Hora*, a Guatemalan newspaper, revealed that an invasion of Cuba was "well under way, prepared not by our country, which is so poor and so disorganized, but implicitly by the U.S.A." Few in the States, of course, read *La Hora.* One who did, however, was Ronald Hilton, an academic at Stanford and editor of a monthly newsletter, the *Hispanic American Report;* in his November issue, he stated that Castro knew all about the invasion plans. Picking up Hilton's report, *The Nation* ran a description of the Guatemalan base wherein the CIA was training Cuban exiles for a hit at their homeland.

But *The Nation* was small and left-leaning. American voters went to the polls in almost total ignorance of what loomed over Cuba.

3   Election night, November 8, 1960, found the whole of the Kennedy family at Hyannis Port, milling in and out of Robert Kennedy's house, wired up as a vote analysis and telephone communications center. At first, at about 10:30 P.M., as the vote tallies began to trickle in from the industrial—and heavily Catholic—states of the Northeast, the results looked good; the IBM computer was predicting a Kennedy victory in the popular vote of 56 percent. But then disappointing telephone calls came in from Ohio: the northeast corner of the state was safely Democratic, but Cincinnati, although heavily Catholic itself, was Republican in its leaning, and going for Nixon; elsewhere in that populous state Nixon was enjoying a landslide. From farther out and down—Wisconsin, the old border states, and the prairies beyond the Mississippi—Nixon looked unbeatable. With Lyndon Johnson on the ticket, the South was still solid for the Democrats; and Texas, as Johnson phoned Hyannis Port, "was close, but safe."

But from Illinois, with its potentially controlling number of electoral votes, the Kennedys were hearing nothing. Unnerved almost, the candidate himself telephoned Chicago's Mayor Richard Daley. Daley, according to John Kennedy's friend Ben Bradlee of *The Washington Post*, was reassuring: "Mr. President," Daley stated, "with a little bit of luck, and the help of a few close friends, you're going to carry Illinois."

Kennedy in the end carried Illinois by 8,858 votes, about one voter for each polling place. The "close friends" of whom Mayor Daley had spoken included Chicago mobster Sam Giancana, who, like Kennedy, was carrying on an affair with Judith Campbell.

Kennedy won the election but he paid the price. His two principal political debts now were to Lyndon Johnson and Sam Giancana, both of whom, Johnson because of Texas's intense conservatism and Giancana because of the losses the Mafia had entailed in Cuba, were out for Castro's head.

Such debt, however, when in the morning Kennedy learned of his narrow victory and Secret Service details closed in on the Kennedy compound, probably were the last thing on the family's mind. They were, instead, simply elated. For they had

once again proved that they were supreme masters at building up and projecting idealized images of themselves through massive publicity blitzes and saturation advertising. Their victory, for it was very much a family victory, was the culmination of a long, sustained drive for power that had been in motion for decades, and they were fully justified in being immensely proud of their accomplishment.

4   Soon after the election, John Kennedy was in Washington, paying a visit to the P Street, Georgetown, residence of former Secretary of State Dean Acheson. The older statesman found the visit irritating, partly because Kennedy turned down a proffered martini and partly because of the photographers who tromped through the parlor to preserve the President-Elect's every twitch.

Kennedy had come, he explained, to solicit Acheson's advice on three impending Cabinet appointments: Treasury, Defense, and State. Nervously, Kennedy promised Acheson that, at State, he would tolerate no "soft" liberal; that ruled out Connecticut Governor Chester Bowles and the Democratic two-time nominee Adlai Stevenson. But then who? Acheson himself? Although lusting again for government involvement, Acheson thought himself—much to Kennedy's relief—too old. J. William Fulbright, chairman of the Senate's Committee on Foreign Relations? Acheson dismissed the idea: Fulbright, from Arkansas, was against civil rights and, besides, was lazy. Acheson had a thought: Jack McCloy? John J. McCloy, from behind the scenes, was unrivaled as a foreign-policy mover and shaker. But, as Kennedy pointed out, he was a Republican. JFK could go with some Republicans: C. Douglas Dillon (an old chum) at Treasury and Robert S. McNamara at Defense. At State, however, he wanted a Democrat.

Acheson came up with a third name: Dean Rusk. Kennedy had never heard of him. Rusk, Acheson explained, had been a Rhodes Scholar out of Georgia, a crackerjack wartime officer in Asia, a fine assistant secretary of state for the Far East under Truman, and throughout the Eisenhower years, president of the Rockefeller Foundation. Acheson thought Rusk would be perfect. Kennedy said he would see.

The scene then shifted to Palm Beach, where Kennedy had a long-sought rest at his father's estate, swam in the sea, played golf, watched movies (*The Sundowners* and *Fanny*), talked with reporters, read reports, and planned his administration. The appointments that interested him most were in the area of national security.

For Secretary of State he accepted Acheson's recommendation of Dean Rusk. Rusk—tall, balding, self-effacing, a good company man—was perfect. Kennedy wanted to be President—and his own secretary of state.

For Secretary of Defense, McNamara. Once a business professor at Harvard, McNamara had become president of Ford Motor Company, known there for his mathematical giftedness, efficiency, and eagerness to further the company fortunes.

For National Security Adviser, he got McGeorge Bundy, the dean of Kennedy's alma mater, Harvard College. Undeniably brilliant, Bundy had been a Harvard junior fellow, as well as collaborator in the memoirs of former Secretary of War Henry L. Stimson. Bundy had had no direct experience in national security affairs. But he did know how to move paper, and to shape the flow of memoranda to suit the boss.

For slightly lower positions, the State Department got Chester Bowles, liberal governor of Connecticut, and the Defense Department got Roswell Gilpatric, a Wall Street lawyer. Both held the rank of undersecretary.

The White House role of "special adviser," with tasks undefined, went to the Harvard historian Arthur M. Schlesinger, Jr. Formerly a speechwriter for Adlai Stevenson, Schlesinger was under pressure to prove his loyalty to Kennedy. He also was under pressure to show himself as tough as the rest of the Kennedy team.

With the exception of Rusk, members of the team were relatively young, in their forties, and they were to hit Washington in a mood that was almost swashbuckling. "Euphoria reigned," Schlesinger himself wrote; "we thought for a moment that the world was plastic and the future unlimited." The Kennedy group, commented David Halberstam, author and at the time reporter with *The New York Times*, saw the "Eisenhower people as having shrunk from the challenge set before them. . . . It was not surprising, for the Eisenhower people were men of the past who had never been too strong on ideas. . . . But this new administration understood ideas and understood the historic link-up between our traditions and those in the underdeveloped world; we too were heirs to a great tradition, we too had fought a colonial power. . . . [Such an attitude inspired] the Kennedy administration to dizzying heights of . . . discussion; instead of looking behind them, the Kennedy people were looking ahead, ready for a new and more subtle kind of conflict [than Eisenhower ever envisioned]." Third World countries could—and should—have their revolutions, all right. But they were supposed to let America, with all its technological know-how, run their revolutions for them. And it followed that, if the unwashed masses around the world persisted in trying to run their revolutions by themselves, and for themselves, then we had the right to crush them.

In Cuba and Indochina alike, the Kennedy administration was determined to crush revolution. Save for their revolutionary movements, those two countries had little in common. To the White House, however, that fact was irrelevant. If only America could apply the right kind of force, President Kennedy would be able to chalk up victories on both sides of the world.

President-Elect Kennedy did converse at length with two officials from the Eisenhower administration, both of them from the CIA. Late in November 1960, Allen Dulles and Richard Bissell, Dulles's deputy for operations and the man in charge of the Cuba project, flew to Palm Springs. Bissell outlined crisply what he was trying to pull together for Cuba—an anti-Castro force based primarily in Guatemala (to avoid using U.S. soil for launching an attack), privately funded air units, a small navy to be leased in New York and with logistical support from certain of the U.S. Navy's own ships.

After Bissell had finished, Dulles and Kennedy went for a walk in the Palm Springs garden, alone. Allen Dulles was primarily a lobbyist, and had steered the Guatemala and U-2 projects past Eisenhower. Now he was trying to steer the Cuba project past Kennedy.

"Lem, I want to tell you a story!"

The time was just before Christmas, 1960; "Lem" was General Lyman L. Lemnitzer, Chairman of the Joint Chiefs of Staff, and the caller, using a scrambler phone, was Admiral Robert Dennison, Commander in Chief Atlantic. Dennison's office was in Norfolk, overlooking the mouth of the James River. He was a big man, with a bulbous nose and a craggy face, and with a temper to match. On this December day, he was furious, and he had telephoned Washington to let Lemnitzer know exactly what he thought.

Two gentlemen from the CIA, it seemed, had just paid a visit to Vieques Island, a naval base off Puerto Rico. Calling on the vice admiral in charge, they said they had come to requisition the USS *San Marco*, a World War II vintage LSD (landing ship dock) for use on the coastline of Cuba. The vice admiral had called Dennison, indicating that he had better relinquish the LSD.

"The hell I will!" Dennison had exploded; on the scrambler then to Washington, he wanted to know if Lemnitzer knew what was going on. Although military intelligence had reported "strange" goings-on in Washington, Lemnitzer had little specific knowledge. He did promise to find out what he could. Shortly thereafter, Richard Bissell was striding into Dennison's Norfolk office, providing a sketchy outline of the Cuba project. Dennison was aghast—the project seemed amateurish, cutting out the regular military. He tried to learn more details about the operation, but got nowhere. On February 10, 1961, three weeks after Kennedy had taken office, the Joint Chiefs ordered Dennison to hand over the LSD.

With the turn of the year, the U.S.-Cuba relationship, such as it was, hit an all-time low. Castro already had announced his country's diplomatic alignment with the Soviets. Then, at a January 2, 1961, cocktail party in the Cuban embassy in Moscow, Khrushchev exclaimed: "Alarming news is coming from Cuba at present, news that the most aggressive American monopolists are preparing a direct attack on Cuba!" Castro at the same time cut down the size of the U.S. embassy staff in Havana. Eisenhower, on January 3, 1961, severed diplomatic relations with Cuba.

And at some point in January 1961, between New Year's Day and the Kennedy inauguration, Richard Bissell of the CIA let out a contract to Sam Giancana and Johnny Rosselli of the Chicago Mafia to murder Castro. The deal was supposed to be secret, but if Castro did know about it, he scarcely could have been surprised. Journeying around Cuba to factories, cane fields, and public meetings, he knew he was vulnerable: he felt, he said, "like a dove." He apparently consoled himself with the knowledge that Soviet aid was on the way—and that *The New York Times* was providing clues as to the nature of the impending invasion. On January 10, 1961, the *Times* reported the location and purpose of the exiles' base in Guatemala.

Just before the 1961 presidential inauguration, John F. Kennedy joined Dwight D. Eisenhower for a discussion in the Oval Office, and received quite a start. For somebody supposedly vapid, Ike's voice was strong and his gaze direct, and he proceeded to give Kennedy, the much younger man, what almost amounted to a tongue-lashing. The Communists, Eisenhower insisted, were on the march, especially in Indochina: if they got Laos, they could get Southeast Asia; if they got Southeast Asia, they could get the western Pacific.

So went Eisenhower's domino theory. And the first domino—the one Eisenhower wanted Kennedy to prop up to stop the others from falling—was Laos.

Eisenhower then mentioned another domino, Cuba. The incoming President's responsibility, the outgoing President stated, was at all costs to overthrow Fidel Castro.

The date of this conversation was January 19, 1961. Snow fell on the capital that night, and in the morning, riding past the glare of white on the Mall, Eisenhower and Kennedy went together by limousine toward Capitol Hill.

5   "Let the word go forth from this time and place, to friend and foe alike. . . ." At 12:51 P.M., January 20, 1961, John F. Kennedy raised his right hand to take the oath of office of President of the United States. Then he turned to the vast and freezing crowd below the inaugural platform, and delivered his most famous address, declaring

> that the torch has been passed to a new generation of Americans born in this century, tempered by war, disciplined by a hard and bitter peace, proud of our ancient heritage, and unwilling to witness or permit the slow undoing of those human rights to which this nation has always

been committed, and to which we are committed today at home and around the world. . . . And so, my fellow Americans, ask not what your country can do for you; ask what you can do for your country.

Now, as at that time, these words glow. Adlai Stevenson called the speech (written by Sorensen) "inspiring"; Hubert Humphrey considered it "America's message to the world."

It was a message all right—a message of anticommunism, a message of military buildup, a message that might have warmed the heart of John Foster Dulles, moldering in his grave.

A message that Castro and Khrushchev must have read with considerable concern. For soon after Kennedy's inauguration, Castro, in an effort to appease the new administration, demobilized his militia. Khrushchev took similar steps: he cut back on the jamming of Voice of America and he released two U.S. flyers who, in an ostensibly weather-researching plane, had gone down over Siberia.

Kennedy reciprocated almost immediately, stopping U.S. Post Office censorship of Soviet magazines, inviting the Kremlin to engage in civil aviation talks, and ordering Chief of Naval Operations Admiral Arleigh Burke, well known on the lecture circuit, to temper his anti-Soviet rhetoric. Burke obeyed, then went around the back of his commander in chief by leaking word of the order to *The New York Times*. The conservatives loved it. Giving a joint press conference in the Capitol, Senators Barry Goldwater, the department store heir from Arizona, and Strom Thurmond, the former football coach (known on Capitol Hill as "Stud Thurmond") from South Carolina, denounced Kennedy's instruction to Burke as "gag-rule diplomacy."

And poof! The short-lived détente, such as it was, was dead, especially with a January speech Khrushchev gave in Moscow to assembled Communist dignitaries. In a declaration as ringing as Kennedy's inaugural address, the chairman proclaimed that in the countries of Asia, Africa, and Latin America revolution was the wave of the future and that the Soviets, not the Americans, would be able to ride that wave. He went further still: in Castro's victory in Cuba, he saw proof positive that the "onslaught of the imperialists" was being crushed by a triumphant "war of national liberation."

President Kennedy was not amused. On the evening of Janu-

ary 30, 1961, he delivered to Congress his first State of the
Union message, speaking in the House of Representatives. The
"great chamber," wrote Tom Wicker of *The New York Times*,

> harshly bathed in television lights, was filled to capacity, the beautiful
> Kennedy women dazzled the populace from its galleries, the floor was
> crowded with senators and diplomats, justices and the new cabinet, as
> the President—lion of the hour—delivered his speech.

After a Sorensen-written lead-in, Kennedy declared: "I speak
today in an hour of national peril and national opportunity."
The audience was hushed, listening attentively, especially to
the next two sentences: "Before my term has ended, we shall
have to test anew whether a nation organized and governed
such as ours can endure. The outcome is by no means certain."
Skimming over the nation's economic problems (the country
still was feeling the effects of the 1958 recession), he honed in
on matters of national security. In parts of the speech, his tone
was soft: he called for the creation of the Peace Corps and for a
massive Latin-American aid program to be termed, in English,
the Alliance for Progress. But most of his words were harsh. He
wanted a massive military buildup, and he implied that the
United States was bent on eliminating Castro and the Cuban
revolution:

> Communist domination in this hemisphere can never be negotiated.
> We are pledged to work with our sister republics to free the Americas
> of all such foreign domination and all tyranny.

And lest Khrushchev should miss any of the above, he underlined America's dedication to "the ultimate freedom and welfare of the Eastern European peoples"—a passage certain to
elicit cheers in the bars of Milwaukee and Chicago.

He finished the speech with an expression of grimness. "Our
problems," he insisted,

> are critical. The tide is unfavorable. The news will be worse before it
> is better. And while hoping and working for the best, we should prepare
> ourselves now for the worst.

Even more than the inaugural address, the speech to Congress
in late January 1961 was the kickoff of the Kennedy foreign

policy drive—a drive intended to show the world, America, and perhaps Kennedy himself that he was tough. Determined to show everyone concerned that America could meet all military eventualities, Kennedy and his new Defense Secretary, Robert McNamara, crafted the "flexible response," meaning the production of "tactical" nuclear weapons (so America could fight "small" nuclear wars) and the development of the Special Forces, or Green Berets (so Americans could smash the guerrillas); and Kennedy's 1961 budget increased defense spending by 15 percent.

The push for an invasion of Cuba, meanwhile, continued unabated. The CIA's Allen Dulles, with his professorial manner, ever-puffing on his reassuring pipe, seduced Kennedy into the belief that the proposed invasion of Cuba could not fail. The attacking forces would land at the south central port town of Trinidad (close to the Sierra, so that if anything went wrong, the refugee force, like Castro himself, could head for the hills), and at least 25 percent of the Cuban population, once learning of the strike, would rise in revolt against Castro.

Dulles was about a year past customary retirement age, and had indicated that, soon, he would step down. But he staked the rest of his career on the truth of his predictions.

The morning after Kennedy's state of the union address, a stubby, bald, and erect old man emerged from his office on the principal floor of the Capitol and with a stately tread walked through the Speaker's lobby. Other old men, fixed forever in gloomy oil portraits, looked down on him from their frames on the walls. He was a Democrat and a Texan, Speaker of the House Sam Rayburn, and he was off to do battle on behalf of the new President, installed just eleven days before. Rayburn's opponent in that battle was going to be Judge Howard Smith, also a Democrat, nominally, a Virginian, and chairman of the House Rules Committee.

The issue between Rayburn and Smith seemed purely procedural: would the House accept or reject Rayburn's resolution to add to the Rules Committee one Republican and two Democrats? But what really was at stake was whether Rayburn, and through Rayburn President John F. Kennedy, could control the House of Representatives.

Congress, and particularly the House, consisted of an array of almost feudal duchies, the standing committees, and among those committees none was more powerful than the Rules Committee. So mundane seemed its activities: it set the House calendars; it determined whether a member could amend a bill; *it decided whether the House as a whole could consider a bill.* Thus it set the agenda; and as those two foxes, Rayburn and Smith, knew perfectly well, whoever controls the agenda wields the real power.

Down on Pennsylvania Avenue, John Kennedy could fly around in helicopters and charm the nation on television, and his wife could redecorate the White House. But as long as Howard W. Smith, a stoop-shouldered dairy farmer from northern Virginia, controlled, as he did control, through the innumerable deals he had cut during his long tenure on the Hill, the Rules Committee, President Kennedy would have no true power over Congress. Kennedy's only hope lay in packing the Rules Committee, adding to it two fresh Democrats, committed to JFK's prolabor legislative proposals and unbeholden to Judge Smith.

After much debate that wintry day, Rayburn in the rostrum presided over the vote. The voting was done by voice, the names of the House members sounding like a cross section of America: Abitt . . . Abernathy . . . Adair . . . Addabo . . . Addonizio . . . Albert . . . So far the vote was tied. Soon came more names, from all over the country. Blatnik . . . Blitch . . . Farbstein . . . Feighan . . . Inouye . . . The galleries were still, the clerk's voice droned, members shouted their votes; on both sides of the aisle, the Democratic and Republican leaders were huddled over tables, keeping score on tally sheets.

In the end, the Rayburn resolution won, but barely, only by 217 to 212. And to achieve even that slender a victory, Rayburn, and the Kennedy White House behind him, had had to make so many political promises that, before the administration was a month old, it already had expended its political capital. Rayburn died within a year; Kennedy had to water most of his proposals to Congress to such an extent that they were virtually meaningless; and he never did get around to major civil rights legislation.

The old Republican charge against President Truman was the question "Who lost China?" The question was unfair; China was never Truman's to lose. Reporters much later charged that, in early 1961, Kennedy lost Congress. The charge also was unfair; Congress was never Kennedy's to lose.

In fact, he could barely control his own administration. The Kennedy campaign against Nixon had been based above all on the claim that President Eisenhower had allowed the U.S. to fall behind the U.S.S.R. in the nuclear arms race. On the evening of February 6, 1961, however, Defense Secretary McNamara gave his first Pentagon backgrounder to the press. There, in response to a question about the missile gap, he said he had been going through classified material. Then he blurted out, ''There is no missile gap.''

As soon as the words were out of his mouth, he knew he had made a mistake: he was acknowledging that Kennedy had lied.

Two days later, in his own press conference, Kennedy fudged. ''It would be premature,'' he said quickly, ''to reach a judgment as to whether there is a gap or not a gap.''

As if to add to Kennedy's sudden troubles, Fidel Castro went on Havana television, proclaiming that Cuba had obtained, or soon would obtain, 55 tanks, 100,000 rifles and submachine guns, 80 antiaircraft guns, and eight Soviet-made MIG fighters. He ended the broadcast by daring anyone to invade.

6   To rescue his nearly stillborn Presidency, Kennedy had to move, and move fast. But in what direction? An arms buildup would win support but it would take time. And few cared about Laos, or even knew where it was. Berlin? The Soviets had substantial forces in Eastern Europe. That left Cuba. Perhaps because of Castro's dare, however, Cuba made Kennedy nervous: he could risk no failure.

Mounting a massive lobbying campaign, the CIA assured the President that failure was out of the question. As Richard Bissell presented the invasion plan (approved reluctantly by the Joint Chiefs) on March 11, 1961, everything indeed looked good. The invasion force could land in about a month at Trinidad, a town on the middle of Cuba's southern shore line. The people there would be friendly; B-26s, disguised and flown out of Nicaragua, could keep Castro's forces back from the beachhead; and if anything did go wrong, the invaders, in the manner of Castro himself, could take refuge in the Escambray Mountains nearby. As Bissell argued seductively, Kennedy would have no need to land American troops.

Smoothly and equally seductively, Allen Dulles described the downpour of rain about to descend on the Caribbean. It would come by the end of April, and then an invasion would be impossible for weeks. And by then, Castro would have received even more Soviet weaponry.

Kennedy understood the implication. He had to move now, or maybe never, at least not with a small force. He did not approve the project, but he did not disapprove it, either.

But he did change the plan. A landing at Trinidad, a well-known resort, could be headline grabbing—in JFK's judgment, too much so. For if it failed, and therefore Kennedy failed, all the world would know.

So the CIA redesigned, selecting a landing site almost directly below Havana, at an obscure place called the Bay of Pigs. The site was far from ideal: it was ringed by swamps, its water was underlain by coral, and at its beachhead stood a complex of apartments set up as public housing. But Kennedy wanted obscurity in the landing, and so obscurity he got. What no one in Washington seemed to realize was that Castro's agents were reporting all the preparations—and that standing high over the apartment complex were floodlights, lights that when turned on illuminated the beach.

Some doubts were surfacing. Flying with the President to Palm Beach late in March 1961, Arkansas's courtly J. William Fulbright, chairman of the Senate Foreign Relations Committee, raised a problem of foreign relations. The Bay of Pigs project, Fulbright contended, was anything but secret; even if the mission succeeded it "would be denounced from the Rio Grande to Patagonia as an example of imperialism." One can imagine Kennedy's response—how many votes were down there?

On into early April, Professor Arthur Schlesinger put his misgivings on paper, even though Kennedy scarcely had invited him to do so. Schlesinger saw an invasion of Cuba as a series of unending complications, even disasters. "If we could achieve [a victory] by a swift, surgical stroke, I would be for it," he wrote to Kennedy. Yet "a) no matter how 'Cuban' the equipment and personnel, the U.S. will be held accountable for the operation, and our prestige will be committed to its success," and "b) since the Castro regime is presumably too strong to be toppled by a single landing, the operation will turn into a protracted civil conflict." And if a rebellion against Castro (an uprising confidently predicted by Dulles) flopped? "Pressures will build up," Schlesinger went on, "which will make it politically hard to resist the demand to send in the Marines." And then? Castro and his legions would head for the hills, and the Soviets would seek "to convert the conflict into another Spanish Civil War."

In typing these thoughts, Schlesinger had no illusions. A memorandum from a professor was hardly going to slow the momentum of government policy, once in train. The professor nonetheless did his duty: he tried.

Former Secretary of State Dean Acheson also tried—he made fun of Kennedy to his face. "I was very much alarmed about the thing," Acheson recalled in a 1964 oral interview,

> and said I hoped he [JFK] wasn't serious about it. He said, "I don't know if I'm serious or not, but this is the proposal, and I've been thinking about it and it is serious—in the sense . . . I'm giving it very serious thought." I remember saying that I did not think it was necessary to call in Price Waterhouse [the public accounting firm] to discover that 1,500 Cubans weren't as good as 25,000 Cubans. It seemed to me that this was a disastrous idea. We talked about it for a little bit and then I went off. I really dismissed it from my mind because it seemed like such a wild idea. While I was in Europe the Bay of Pigs came off and this really shattered the Europeans. They had tremendously high expectations of the new administration, and when this thing happened they just fell miles down with a crash.

Kennedy may have scoffed at Fulbright and Schlesinger, regarding them as liberal, and possibly even soft on communism. In Acheson, however, he had more than met his equal; Acheson had been the very father of the containment policy. Acheson's own doubts must have stung Kennedy to the quick. For shortly after his talk with Acheson, he retreated in haste to his father's estate in Florida.

Of that visit we know certain facts. On Good Friday, the President and Mrs. Kennedy lunched at the home of one of Joseph Kennedy's Palm Beach neighbors, Earl Smith, the former ambassador to Cuba. President Kennedy played golf at the Palm Beach Country Club; while he was on the links, Secret Service agents told him of a rumor that Castroites were hatching a plot to kidnap his daughter, Caroline. When on Easter morning, the First Family attended services at St. Edward's Church, police protection was exceptionally heavy. President Kennedy played golf again, with his father and Ambassador Smith, swam in the ocean, watched movies in the evenings, and talked with his father. On Tuesday, April 4, 1961, he flew back to Washington.

Before flying to Palm Beach, as McGeorge Bundy noted, Kennedy himself had seemed dubious about the invasion of Cuba. After his return to Washington, however, as Bundy again noted, he "really wanted to do this. . . . [W]hen he came to the moment of truth—the decision to go or not go—he had made up his mind and *told* us. He didn't *ask* us."

On April 7, 1961, *The New York Times*, in a short, underplayed article, revealed the impending assault. "INVASION REPORTED NEAR," stated the headline; picking up the story, CBS that night claimed that the invasion plans were in "their final stages."

Kennedy was outraged. "Castro doesn't need agents over here," he screamed at Pierre Salinger, his press secretary. "All he has to do is read our papers. It's all laid out for him." Kennedy was forgetting that, a few weeks before, Osvaldo Dorticos, Cuba's President, had laid the same plans out to the United Nations.

7   Riding in a motorcade to the District's Griffith Stadium, President John F. Kennedy tossed out the first ball of the baseball season. The date was April 12, and he had been in office for nearly three months. He watched the game for a few innings—the Washington Senators lost as usual, going down to the Chicago White Sox 4 to 3—and then he left. He had to prepare for a critical press conference.

For several days Washington had been a-buzz with a wondrous rumor—that the United States was going to invade Cuba and overthrow Fidel Castro. Kennedy desperately wanted to quash the rumor, but hardly had he entered the State Department's amphitheater that evening than he realized that the rumor was at the top of the reporters' agenda. From the press conference:

> *Reporter:* Mr. President, has a decision been reached on how far this country will go in helping an anti-Castro uprising or invasion of Cuba?
>
> *The President:* First, I want to say that *there will not be, under any circumstances, an intervention in Cuba by the United States armed forces* [emphasis added]. The government will do everything it possibly can, I think it can meet its responsibilities, to make sure that there are no Americans involved in any actions inside Cuba. . . .
>
> The basic issue in Cuba is not one between the United States and Cuba. It is between the Cubans themselves. I intend to see that we adhere to that principle and as I understand it this administration's attitude is so understood by the anti-Castro exiles from Cuba in this country.

Kennedy was shading the truth. Even as he spoke, Cuban exile forces at bases in Florida, Nicaragua, and Guatemala were poising for an armed strike at Cuba, and Americans themselves were not going to be involved in that invasion—directly. But they certainly were going to be involved indirectly. Later, in fact, the Kennedy administration would lay plans for an intervention in Cuba that would be direct, and carried out, in Kennedy's press conference words, "by the United States armed forces."

Feeling trapped, apparently, Kennedy at his press conference of April 12, 1961, promised to keep Americans out of the action in Cuba. And to make good on that promise, he decided to withhold American air support as the invaders landed at the Bay of Pigs.

In mid-April 1961, the attack began anyway. Scrambling off old landing craft, the Cuban exile brigade, numbering about 2,500 men, waded ashore. Some got stuck in the coral, others ran into gunfire, and heard the chop-chopping of helicopters; all were stunned when they hit the beach. It was nighttime. But they were bathed in light anyway.

CHAPTER 5

Bay of Pigs

1   Early in the morning of April 18, 1961, a radio message reached Fidel Castro, wide awake in the presidential palace. He lost no time. Placing his air force on alert and mobilizing a battalion by the rail line that led down to the Bay of Pigs, he himself boarded an airplane, flying south to take overall command.

He had prepared well for this night—having accepted the tutelage of Che Guevara. Guevara, having been present in Guatemala during the overthrow of Arbenz, had realized that America, like other imperial powers before it, had succeeded in Guatemala by using the classic tactic of divide and conquer: the CIA had separated Arbenz from his army, and indeed from his people. Guevara had advised Castro therefore to let the old Batista officers go to Florida, establish a popular militia, and jail any remaining opponents. Castro, always a quick study, had complied and so, when the invaders came, his forces were ready.

Ill-trained, waterlogged, some stuck on the coral reefs, and almost all of them under close observation from the time they hit the Bay of Pigs, the invaders had no chance. By the afternoon of the first full day of the attack, a Castro helicopter was clattering up and down the beach at will, swooping to treetop level to fire on the remnants of the invading force. Sweeping onto the beach, the people's militia captured about 1,400 prisoners of war and transported them to Havana in sealed trucks. Many did not survive the trip.

Appearing on Havana television the next day, Castro was beside himself with glee. He pointed at maps with a stick, he held up captured documents, he made fun of the CIA: "Imperialism examines geography, analyzes the number of cannons, of planes, of tanks, of positions. . . . The imperialists don't give a damn about how the population there thinks or feels!" That population all over Cuba, as it watched Fidel on old round-screened television sets, laughed, cheered, and hurrahed. Any illusion that the Cuban people had been about to rise up against Castro now lay shattered.

Up in Miami, in a heavily guarded hangar the CIA was using to house Cuban exile leaders, the mood was bitter. The anger was directed at President Kennedy: in the eyes of the émigrés, he was at best an incompetent, at worst a traitor. Arthur Schlesinger, Jr., the historian and White House aide who had been assigned to the Cuba project, was present; he called the White House from a wall phone in the hangar. After some time he reached Kennedy.

"This is a Pearl Harbor," he told the President. "They're [the Cuban émigré leaders] really upset!"

Later that day, Schlesinger was back in Washington, talking with Kennedy in the Oval Office.

"We can't win them all," Schlesinger later remembered JFK as saying, "and I have been close enough to disaster to realize that these things which seem world-shaking at one moment you can barely remember the next. We got a big kick in the leg—and we deserved it. But maybe we'll learn something from it."

Then Kennedy added: "How can I have been so stupid, to let them [the CIA] go ahead?"

Kennedy must have felt as if he were in a pressure cooker. He was reaching out for help.

First from his just-defeated rival for the White House, Richard M. Nixon. Residing still in northwest Washington, Nixon was nearby; Kennedy phoned, asking him to come by the White House. Arriving at the Oval Office on April 19, 1961, Nixon inwardly must have gloated; a year before he himself had been in overall charge of the Cuba project, and now his nemesis, John Kennedy, was presiding over an abject failure. From the record of their conversation, however, Nixon must have kept his sense of triumph to himself. Kennedy, rising from his rocking chair, pacing and swearing, asked Nixon what *he* would do now.

"I would find a proper legal cover and go in," said Nixon, now in the role of counselor. "There are several justifications that could be used, like protection of American citizens living in Cuba and defending our base at Guantánamo."

Nixon's words were mild, judicious. What he left unspoken, however, was that if Kennedy failed to dislodge Castro, the next Republican candidate for the White House—Nixon hoped to be the one—would have at his disposal a campaign charge that JFK could never confute. All the next Republican candidate had to do to win was to ask: "Who lost Cuba?"

Second, in his search for advice, Kennedy met at Camp David with former President Eisenhower. Eisenhower was less circumspect than Nixon, dressing Kennedy down like he was a naughty urchin.

"Why on earth," Ike demanded, had Kennedy in the end withheld the needed air support?

"Well," Kennedy stammered, "my advice was that we must try to keep our hands from showing in the affair."

Eisenhower was blunt. As the two men looked out onto the Maryland mountains beyond Camp David, the old general asked: "How could you expect the world to believe we had nothing to do with it? Where did these people get the ships to go from Central America to Cuba? Where did they get the weapons? . . . I believe there is only one thing to do when you go into this kind of thing: it must be a success."

And third, Kennedy heard from his old man, down in Palm Springs. Joseph P. Kennedy was brutal. He said to his son, the President of the United States: "You blew it!"

Having thus heard the word of the Lord, or at least of his father, which in John Kennedy's estimation was about the same thing, JFK resolved to push forward, to overcome his humiliation at the hands of Fidel Castro. As he did so, his brother, Robert F. Kennedy, whom he had made attorney general, shifted his own attentions from law to diplomacy. Of the two Kennedy brothers, Robert was the meaner, the one more like their father. With Robert pressing him on, President Kennedy now wanted to get really tough with Castro.

Giving a press conference in the State Department auditorium on April 20, 1961, President Kennedy took responsibility for the Bay of Pigs failure. But then he stated, defiantly:

> The complacent, the self-indulgent, the soft societies are about to be swept away with the debris of history. Only the strong, only the industrious, only the determined, only the courageous, only the visionary, who determine the real nature of our struggle, can possibly survive.

Uttering the sweeping language of Theodore Sorensen, Kennedy seemed to be saying that, at last, he had become truly tough. At last he was going to destroy Castro.

Why had the first effort to destroy Castro—the Bay of Pigs attack—gone wrong? Confronted with such a failure, John Kennedy did what most good American politicians do in similar circumstances: he appointed a committee to study the matter. This particular committee was chaired by General Maxwell Taylor, whom Kennedy was whisking ahead of numerous Army rivals to become the Chairman of the Joint Chiefs of Staff. Taylor, the very model of a politician's general, performed admirably. Heading the "Cuba Study Group," he determined that the problem at the Bay of Pigs lay not so much in President Kennedy's ineptitude as in the CIA's rosy reports of the imminence of anti-Castro revolts.

General Taylor did his work well. The roots of the Bay of Pigs fiasco had lain, he concluded, not with the Democrats but rather with the Republicans! Taylor's report bespoke nothing of the wisdom, let alone the legality, of the attempt to overthrow Castro.

Indeed, stipulated the Taylor board,

> There can be no long-term living with Castro as a neighbor. . . . While inclining personally to a positive course of action against Castro without delay, we recognize the danger of dealing with the Cuban problem outside the context of the world situation.

Added Robert F. Kennedy, taking charge of the new program against Castro:

The Cuban matter is being allowed to slide. Mostly because nobody really has the answer to Castro. Not many are really prepared to send American troops in there at the present time, but maybe that is the answer. Only time will tell.

Were the Kennedy brothers considering an invasion of Cuba? Just days after the Bay of Pigs disaster, President Kennedy authorized Operation Mongoose, an effort that, in his words, would "use *our available assets* [emphasis added] . . . to help Cuba overthrow the Communist regime."

2   Mid-April 1961 brought a flowering of the cherry blossoms around the Tidal Basin—and within the Kennedy administration, a flurry of action. The White House wanted to show the world that it was, after all, tough.

Having criticized the Eisenhower administration for allowing the nation somehow to fall behind the forces of international communism, the Kennedy people were eager to show that they alone could roll back the tide, and just about anywhere would do. They chose Laos. Landlocked and abutting North Vietnam, Laos was an easy target for Communist influence; indeed, the CIA-backed forces of the Laotian monarchy were losing control of their own country. And U.S. Ambassador Winthrop Brown was urging Washington to bomb the Communist redoubts. President Kennedy, however, held back: he feared a nuclear confrontation with the Soviets, or at least a Russian show of force around Berlin. So he tried to "save" Laos through diplomacy. Early in May 1961 he dispatched Averell Harriman, the railroad heir and wartime ambassador to Moscow, to a fourteen-nation conference in Geneva. Harriman regarded the Kennedys as mere parvenus, but he did do the President a favor; he secured an agreement that, for the time being at least, made Laos neutral. So Kennedy had not won in Laos, but he also had not lost.

Laos, of course, was a Southeast Asian sideshow. The major issue was Vietnam where, according to intelligence reports, Communist guerrillas were controlling more and more of the countryside. To Kennedy and the leading figures in his administration, the pattern was familiar. During World War II and soon thereafter, Communist guerrillas in China had controlled more and more of the countryside. JFK had no wish to be accused of having lost Vietnam.

"We're in this one [the fight against the Communists in Vietnam] all the way," President Kennedy declared, as in 1961 he increased the U.S. troop level in Vietnam by more than tenfold. Robert F. Kennedy echoed the thought. "We are going to win in Vietnam," the attorney general stated during a February 1962 visit to Saigon. "We will remain here until we do win."

President Kennedy sought to score another win close to home, in Canada. In March 1961 John Diefenbaker, the Canadian Prime Minister, had visited Kennedy in the Oval Office. Kennedy had shown the older man around the room, pointing out the desk, made from the timbers of a British frigate wrecked in the Artic in the nineteenth century, a collection of whale teeth lined up along the shelves, and on one of the curved walls, an oil painting of the American Lake Erie victory over the British in the War of 1812. Then they had talked, Diefenbaker sitting on the sofa by the fireplace and Kennedy easing his back into his white-padded rocking chair. Diefenbaker had bored Kennedy with complaints about Canada's trade imbalance with the U.S., then infuriated him by urging accommodation with Cuba. Kennedy had agreed to pay a state visit to Ottawa, however, and on May 16, 1961, made the trip.

Born in 1895 (and thus a quarter-century older than John F. Kennedy), John G. Diefenbaker's most vivid memory from childhood was that of riding a train with his family as they migrated from Ontario to the Saskatchewan prairie: all along the route above the U.S. border, railroad stations were crowded with Ukrainians, Poles, Hungarians, and French; and aboard the train itself his family seemed to be the only one that spoke English. Off the train and on to the homestead, Diefenbaker and his brother helped their father build their farmhouse, a two-room shack. John Diefenbaker reached adulthood in the flat plains, isolated farms, and fearsome winters of the Canadian West, well versed in poverty and hardship.

Yet by dint of hard work, young Diefenbaker pulled himself

upward, soon after service in the First World War becoming a lawyer. He specialized in defending the poor; and in court he grew famous for "an unerring sense of timing, a well-developed gift of pantomime, and [an] ability to seize upon dramatic situations," traits that launched his career in politics. Midway through 1957, he won election as Canada's Prime Minister, sweeping into power at the head of a large Conservative majority.

Three months later, Queen Elizabeth II arrived in Ottawa to open the new session of the Canadian Parliament. Accompanied by the Royal Canadian Mounted Police, decked out in their ceremonial coats of scarlet and with their sabers flashing in the morning sun, she set out from the Governor-General's residence in an open landau, rode down Sussex Drive as it curved along the river to the Rideau Canal, and then, as great crowds cheered, mounted the foot of Parliament Hill. Her carriage pulled to a stop beneath the neo-Gothic clock tower that loomed over the Parliament Buildings, and she processed inside. With her speech, she officially launched the Diefenbaker era.

Of all the foreign embassies in Ottawa, the one closest to the Parliament Buildings was that of the United States—so close that its front door on Wellington Street looked straight up toward the clock tower, straight up to the very center of the Canadian government, as if through its embassy the American government were keeping permanent watch on the Canadian.

Or at least so suspected Diefenbaker. While not exactly anti-American, the Prime Minister did view a certain caste of Americans—the well-educated, the well-financed, and the well-connected—with the slit eyes of suspicion. For he still thought of himself as a poor boy from the prairies, the very antithesis of an American named John F. Kennedy. Indeed, the Diefenbaker-Kennedy relationship was troubled almost from the start.

Late in the afternoon of May 16, 1961, President and Mrs. Kennedy flew on an official trip to the Royal Canadian Air Force Station, just south of Ottawa. Showers and a cold wind swept the runway, and after handshakes out by the airplane, the Kennedys and their hosts scurried to the hangar. Speaking there from a podium, Governor-General Georges Vanier welcomed the President, in French.

Diefenbaker also spoke. *"Monsieur le Président,"* he said, *". . . soyez les bienvenues au Canada."* So mangled was the Canadian leader's French that Mrs. Kennedy, standing nearby, looked stricken. With obvious relief, Diefenbaker switched to English, saying, "I welcome you as a great American. . . ."

Then Kennedy went to the microphone. Having just listened to the Prime Minister, he stated, he himself felt "encouraged to say a few words in French." His own French being execrable, everyone laughed. Everyone, that is, but Diefenbaker.

Then Kennedy mispronounced Diefenbaker's name. The "baker" was as in a baker of bread; Kennedy referred to Prime Minister "Diefenbawker." The Prime Minister, again, was unamused.

Leaving the airport, the Kennedys, the Diefenbakers, and Governor-General and Mm. Vanier took the nine-mile drive into town, riding past the thousands of tulips and daffodils that filled the banks of the Rideau Canal. Hundreds of flags, Stars-and-Stripes and Red Ensigns, snapped in the breeze; and along the principal intersections, from the Lord Elgin Hotel around to Parliament Square, huge crowds cheered the presidential arrival. JFK had drawn more onlookers than had the Queen. Confessed Diefenbaker to reporters: "I hope he doesn't come across the border and run against me."

Under a clear blue spring sky, Kennedy and Diefenbaker laid a wreath at the War Memorial, just off Parliament Hill, then walked up toward the East Block, where the Prime Minister had his offices. Noticing photographers nearby, Kennedy "bounded up the stairs to the second floor . . . and was greeted by grinning secretaries standing in the hallway," a journalist noted. "[He] eyed them appreciatively as he strode along, flirting with them in his boyish magnetism. He was so unlike John Diefenbaker." Said Ellen Fairclough, a Canadian cabinet colleague: "If Diefenbaker ever found a woman in his bedroom, he'd scream for help."

Once inside Diefenbaker's office, the two men talked in a businesslike way. Kennedy, wrote a Canadian official who was present, was "well briefed and sensitive to the Canadian outlook. . . . Alert and intelligent, he talked quietly and persuasively, and often with a light touch. . . . The Prime Minister gave every appearance of enjoying the exchanges." The discussion ranged far, touching on foreign aid, European integration,

Laos and Vietnam, and Cuba. Canada was trading with Cuba (by this time the U.S. had slapped an embargo on the island); but he would refrain, JFK promised, from invoking the economic penalties of the Trading with the Enemy Act. Unless, he added, we "receive provocation."

Diefenbaker did have a question—were there nuclear weapons in Cuba? Kennedy thought not. But if so, and before he did anything, he assured the Prime Minister, he "would talk with Canada." He pronounced it "Canader."

Moving on, Kennedy said he certainly hoped that Canada would join the Organization of American States; once in the regional organization, the President opined, Canada could help stabilize Latin America, "more dangerous than any other place in the world." But, Diefenbaker objected, if Canada joined the OAS and then followed the American line, the Latin Americans would see Ottawa as Washington's puppet. Kennedy, however, dismissed Diefenbaker's concern as trivial, pressing hard for Canadian membership. Diefenbaker said no. This "was the first of a number of occasions," the Prime Minister commented later, "in which I had to explain to President Kennedy that Canada was not Massachusetts or even Boston."

Then Kennedy came to the issue he wanted most to raise, the point on which he wanted most to impose his will on Canada. And all goodwill evaporated.

America had placed nuclear weapons in several NATO countries. But many Canadians, Diefenbaker stated, wanted no part of nuclear weapons on their soil: the Prime Minister ticked off the opposition he had heard from academics, the clergy, and a Canadian organization known as the Voice of Women. Yet such views were neutralist, Kennedy shot back, and Canada was allied by treaty with America. The President's implication was plain: Diefenbaker had to accept nuclear weapons or violate his country's legal obligations. Diefenbaker and Kennedy then went off to lunch.

After they had done so, a Canadian staffer, tidying up the Prime Minister's office, noticed a document wedged behind a cushion of a couch. A single piece of paper, the document bore the title "Memorandum for the President" from "WWR" (W. W. Rostow of the U.S. State Department) and the subtitle "What We Want from the Ottawa Trip."

Someone in the American party had left the document behind. And the paper found its way, even before the day was over, to Diefenbaker (who refused to return it to the Americans). The conference over, Diefenbaker closed his office doors and read the document over and over. Later he would charge "arrogant pressure" by that "young son of a bitch." Kennedy would return the honor by terming Diefenbaker a "prick."

President Kennedy, the memo urged, should *"push* the Canadians toward an increased commitment" to the Alliance for Progress (the U.S. aid program in Latin America), *"push* them toward a decision to join the OAS" (which the Canadians, fearful of compromising their independence, had been reluctant to join), and *"push* them toward a larger contribution for . . . foreign aid generally." Diefenbaker himself had penciled in the lines under the word "push."

Diefenbaker then found insult added to injury. Throughout the evening's white-tie dinner at the American embassy, Kennedy virtually ignored Diefenbaker, spending most of his time with the bland-faced Lester Pearson, leader of the Liberal opposition. Kennedy and Pearson "chatted, gossiped, and laughed, sharing a sardonic humor that Diefenbaker never really understood," a Canadian recalled:

> There were only twenty guests at the dinner table, with the President sitting across from Pearson and beside Diefenbaker. Kennedy made it abundantly clear which man he preferred talking to, as they sliced into their filet mignon; his preference was especially obvious after the ladies withdrew, following the strawberry tart dessert, and the men stayed sipping their brandy and smoking cigars. Half a dozen joined them at this point, but Kennedy still concentrated on Pearson.

"We all saw it," said one of the Canadians present. "It was absolutely discourteous. But Kennedy was insensitive to Diefenbaker's feelings."

President and Mrs. Kennedy left Ottawa the following morning and, at the airport, a Royal Canadian Mounted Police band played, "Will Ye No Come Back Again." John Kennedy did not come back again. Helicoptering from Andrews Air Force Base to the White House, and talking with aides, he erupted with expletives: "boring," "insincere," "shallow," "bastard," and he applied them all to Diefenbaker. Kennedy, Sorensen later acknowledged, was "pissed off with [Diefenbaker]. He was aggravated. Diefenbaker got under his skin."

And no wonder. Kennedy had come to persuade Diefenbaker to take American nuclear weapons—and Kennedy had failed.

Kennedy was running great risks. During a springtime visit to Chicago, he saw Judith Campbell quite openly. She was staying at the Ambassador East and, according to her memoirs, telephoned him.

" 'I'll be over for sure,' he said. 'Don't worry. . . . Everybody knows I'm in town and there's nothing unusual about my dropping over to see someone.' He made it sound so normal, but as I sat there waiting for his knock on the door, I tried to envision what his visit entailed—the limousines, the motorcycle cops, the secret service, the mapping of the route, the control of traffic lights, the blocking off of streets, and Jack in his limousine discussing affairs of state, or politics, with men who would be left waiting while we kissed and talked of love." In Washington, too: early in May 1961 a presidential limousine picked Campbell up right in front of the Mayflower Hotel. Upstairs in the Executive Mansion, then, JFK took her to the main bedroom. The furniture, she noticed, was from Kennedy's Georgetown house, a locale she had known quite well. The "twin beds were on the right and we turned left," she wrote, "into a small alcove leading to another bedroom with a large double bed. There was a stereo in the alcove and Jack put on the music from *Camelot*." On this occasion she stayed so late that she was about to miss her flight back to Chicago. But no difference! A car from the White House whisked her across the river and an order from the White House called back her commercial airplane, already partway down the runway of the National Airport and full of grumbling passengers. People stared at her as she walked down the aisle to her seat.

Was Judith Campbell exaggerating Kennedy's recklessness? Perhaps so. Three points, however, are clear. First, between January 22, 1961, and March 22, 1962, telephone logs indicated seventy telephone calls between Judith Campbell's number and the White House. Second, by her own confession, Judith Campbell had been consorting not only with Kennedy and Sinatra but also with Sam Giancana, boss of the Chicago underworld. And third, on March 22, 1962, President John F. Kennedy lunched in the White House with FBI Director J. Edgar Hoover. We have no record of their conversation. But that day marked the last telephone contact between Judith Campbell and 1600 Pennsylvania Avenue.

Like his father, John F. Kennedy was an adventurer, political and sexual, and in his fling with Judith Campbell he seemed to have thought himself invulnerable. J. Edgar Hoover, we can only assume, had showed him his limits.

But a Kennedy pattern had been established—win, flaunt, dare others to get in his way. With regard to Judith Campbell, his nemesis was J. Edgar Hoover. With regard to the island of Cuba, his nemesis was Nikita Khrushchev.

Khrushchev was also the nemesis of Secretary of State Dean Rusk. In May 1961, in a closed session with William Fulbright's Senate Foreign Relations Committee, Rusk sounded an ominous warning. Khrushchev's long-range bomber force, Rusk admitted, was limited. But, Rusk posed, what if Khrushchev decided to put missiles in Cuba?

Missiles in Cuba, Rusk testified,

> could reach parts of this country which may be more difficult to reach otherwise. [This would] impose a degree of blackmail upon the United States in dealing with our problems in all parts of the world.

Rusk must have been speaking for Kennedy. For on May 25, 1961, President Kennedy appeared before a joint session of the Congress, only twelve weeks after his State of the Union message (one Washington columnist dubbed Kennedy's new talk the "*Re*-State of the Union"), and his tone was almost frantic. Citing great global dangers and "urgent national needs," he asked Congress for a vastly expanded military force—more howitzers, more helicopters, more personnel carriers, more Army reserve divisions, fifteen thousand more Marines. He wanted Congress to triple its commitment to nuclear fallout shelters.

Faced with diplomatic frustration abroad and political weakness at home, President Kennedy in the late spring of 1961 was resorting to a classic political ploy. He was asking the Congress to remilitarize America.

3   Hoping to dramatize his demand, he set off, at the end of May 1961, for Europe and a summit meeting with Khrushchev. Fearing that such a meeting would enhance Khrushchev's worldwide appeal, Kennedy had been reluctant to go. But he had overcome his reluctance: coming so soon after the Bay of Pigs fiasco, a summit meeting, with its attendant publicity, could bolster Kennedy's domestic image. Besides, Khrushchev had challenged Kennedy directly. "It is not yet too late to prevent what may be irreparable," Khrushchev had written to JFK right after the Bay of Pigs:

> The U.S. government can still prevent the flames of war that have been lit by the interventionists . . . from growing into a conflagration that will be impossible to extinguish. I earnestly appeal to you, Mr. President, to call a halt to the aggression against the Republic of Cuba. Military technology and the world political situation are such today that any so-called little war can give rise to a chain reaction in all parts of the globe.
>
> As for the Soviet Union, let there be no misunderstanding of our position: we will give the Cuban people and their government every assistance necessary to repulse . . . armed attack on Cuba.

Challenged, JFK began to bone up for a summit meeting with Khrushchev. And on the night of May 30, 1961, President and Mrs. Kennedy boarded *Air Force One* at New York's Idlewild Airport, and flew up and over the Atlantic toward France.

The visit to Paris started off badly, with Pierre Salinger nearly losing his job as press secretary. The Kennedy administration, of which Salinger was the official spokesman, was determined to avoid another Bay of Pigs—and it sought therefore to eliminate the conditions that could give rise to another Castro. One such condition lay in the Dominican Republic, a Caribbean country whose thirty-one-year dictatorship under Rafael Trujillo was an ideal target for revolutionaries. As President Kennedy was flying to Europe, in fact, a conspiracy was hatching in Ciudad Trujillo (now Santo Domingo), and the plotters had received machine guns and grenades from the CIA. (To the Kennedy administration, Trujillo was even more dictatorial, and thus even more likely to trigger revolution, than Batista.) And on the night of May 30, 1961, as Trujillo was being chauffeured down a seaside highway for a tryst with his mistress, ambushers stopped the car, forced him out, and shot him to death. Hearing of the assassination, the U.S. ambassador dashed off a cable to the State Department, which relayed the news to the White House staff, then in Paris. The next morning, Pierre Salinger gave a press conference, and let slip that Trujillo was dead.

Yet reports of the assassination had not yet reached the papers. The world's press was agog: did the Kennedy administration have prior knowledge of Trujillo's murder? Had Kennedy ordered the murder?

Secretary of State Dean Rusk was worried. "If people think we did anything to Trujillo," he said, "they might look at this as a license to go after Kennedy." Salinger himself said later that he had never seen Kennedy so angry.

As Kennedy's airplane pulled to a stop on the runway outside Paris, on the morning of May 31, 1961, the President stepped out the forward door and onto the top of the ramp. Waiting for him at the foot of the steps was the towering figure of France's President Charles de Gaulle. They greeted each other, in English, and after Kennedy had accepted a salute from the color guard, they rode in state, in a caravan of Citroëns, from the Orly Airport to the center of Paris.

After luncheon in the Elysée Palace, Kennedy and de Gaulle closeted themselves, discussing the issues of the day. If Kennedy held Diefenbaker in contempt, then he regarded de Gaulle with awe. Hero of France's wartime resistance—in June 1940 Brigadier General Charles de Gaulle had made the dangerous flight over German-occupied France to Britain, and then, four years later, having led a military contingent called Free France, had marched in triumph down the liberated Champs-Elysée—de Gaulle had become France's President in 1958, and was known worldwide for his intransigent defense of his country's independence. De Gaulle was one of the few persons to whom Kennedy listened. And de Gaulle had some advice for Kennedy.

As their discussion turned to Indochina, the old general insisted that Kennedy proceed with caution. "The more you become involved out there against communism," he warned,

the more the Communists will appear as the champions of national independence, and the more support they will receive, if only from despair. . . . You will sink step by step into a bottomless military and political quagmire, however much you spend in men and money.

De Gaulle refrained from stating the obvious. His advice applied not only to Asia but also to Cuba.

Kennedy in response asked, "You've studied being head of a country for fifty years. Have you found out anything I should know?"

Yes, de Gaulle stated, the head of a country should follow his own judgment. Not, de Gaulle implied, that of his father.

On the morning of June 3, 1961, the President flew to Vienna to meet with Khrushchev. The summit began the following morning.

Pulling up to the door of the U.S. embassy residence, a massive stone-and-stucco Viennese edifice, a black Chaika, a solid Russian-built limousine with lace curtains around its back windows, screeched up to a halt. As it did so, President Kennedy, bursting forth like a bronco buster sprung from his chute, bounded from the residence and dashed down the steps.

"How are you?" JFK said with his most charming smile to his fat, bald guest. "I'm glad to see you."

Khrushchev lumbered out of the Chaika. Keeping his face immobile, he shook the President's hand.

Under a cold wet Austrian sky, a new summit meeting had got under way—and for John F. Kennedy, it was a disaster. Khrushchev stunned him. "The conclusion of a peace treaty with Germany cannot be postponed any longer," the Russian said bluntly. "A peaceful settlement in Europe must be attained this year." Khrushchev was renewing his ultimatum on Berlin.

"Berlin is the testicles of the West," Khrushchev said. "Every time I give them a yank, they holler."

Fumbling for a response, Kennedy talked about access routes to Berlin. If necessary to keep the city open, Kennedy said, the U.S. would go to war.

Khrushchev spat contempt—he had heard the same threat before, from Eisenhower. Over Berlin, Kennedy would not dare go to war, Khrushchev taunted.

Had Khrushchev ever admitted to a mistake, Kennedy stammered?

"Certainly," Khrushchev snapped.

In 1956, he said, "I admitted all of Stalin's mistakes."

Aboard *Air Force One* on the return flight to Washington, Kennedy paced up and down the aisle, swearing, practically ranting about that man Khrushchev. Kennedy had been desperate to wring some admission, some confession, from the old Russian leader. But now, en route to the States, he knew he had won precisely nothing.

High over the Atlantic, he seemed to reach a resolution. Now he was going to be really tough with the Communists.

Back in the White House, President Kennedy received encouraging news: as new spy satellites revealed, the Soviets possessed not four hundred ICBMs, as JFK had feared, but only four. So the famous missile gap did exist—in America's favor. More confident now than in Vienna, Kennedy went on national television, assuring his country that he would stand fast on Berlin. He also called up the reserves, and asked Congress for $3 billion more to be spent immediately on the military.

But Kennedy's language itself was especially resolute. "We must be patient," he said on television.

We must be determined. We must be courageous. We must accept both risks and burdens, but with the will and work freedom will prevail.

Khrushchev's response was crude but effective. With thousands of East Germans fleeing to the West, he had his forces in

August 1961 erect the cement-block wall, topped with guard houses, barbed wire, and guns.

Now it was Kennedy's turn. Early in 1962, President Kennedy and top Pentagon officials began discussing the idea of a U.S. nuclear first strike against the Soviet Union.

"Why," Khrushchev demanded of his advisers in 1962, "[do] Americans have so many bases around the Soviet Union, and we have no bases near the United States?"

4   But Khrushchev soon would have such bases. For the Kennedy administration was gearing up for a direct assault on Castro. Giving up his day-to-day chores at the Justice Department, Robert F. Kennedy was emerging as the man in charge of the proposed assault. Mean, determined, and forceful, he certainly was the right one for the job. The plan was code-named Mongoose, after the little animal that kills the cobra.

Was Castro on a Kennedy hit list? Assassination certainly was on John Kennedy's mind, as we know from a statement by Kennedy's buddy, Florida's conservative Democratic Senator George Smathers. Smathers's oral history is on deposit in the John F. Kennedy presidential library. "I don't know whether he brought it [Castro's murder] up or I brought it up," Smathers stated:

> We had . . . conversation of assassination of Fidel Castro [after the Bay of Pigs], what would be the reaction, how the people would react, would the people be gratified. I'm sure he had his own ideas about it, but he was picking my brain on this particular question as I had heard many times he picked the brains of others. And on those occasions he would very rarely express his own view because he wanted to know what the other man's view was before he made up his mind. . . . But the question [of the assassination of Castro] was whether or not it would accomplish that which he wanted it to. . . . And I talked with him about it and, frankly, . . . I wasn't so much for the idea of assassination, particularly when it could be pinned on the United States.

We cannot pin the idea of assassination on President Kennedy, at least not directly. But indirectly? On October 5, 1961, McGeorge Bundy issued National Security Action Memorandum #100, entitled "Contingency Planning for Cuba." Addressed to Secretary of State Dean Rusk, it mentioned the desirability of "a plan . . . for the indicated contingency." The meaning of such jargon? The next day, a study group of the National Security Council learned that, in preparation, was a "contingency plan in connection with the possible removal of Castro from the Cuban scene."

The CIA weighed in with a cautionary note—perhaps Allen Dulles was trying to ingratiate himself with the Kennedy White House. Castro's loss now, concluded the CIA's Board of National Estimates, "by assassination or by natural causes, would have an unsettling effect, but would almost certainly not prove fatal to the [Cuban] regime." Assassination alone, that is, would not solve the Cuban problem: indeed, the Kennedy administration was making sure that Operation Mongoose would not involve assassination alone. In an article in *Look*, Fletcher Knebel, a journalist and later an author of best-selling thrillers, explained what Kennedy intended:

> In October 1961, President Kennedy, still bearing his scars from the [Bay of Pigs] disaster, secretly ordered the Joint Chiefs of Staff to prepare an invasion plan for Cuba—to be used if and when needed. This top-secret plan took months to prepare, but when the strategists and computers had finished, with every plane, warship, and assault unit tagged, it was calculated that the first troops could hit the Cuban beaches eight days after a "go" signal.

Fletcher Knebel, a skilled reporter, had written his *Look* piece on the basis of inside sources, persons who may have wanted to fudge the truth. Documents now declassified, however, reveal that those sources were essentially correct. On November 30, 1961, the National Security Council, in a study entitled "The Cuba Project," outlined its goal with regard to Castro:

> The United States will help the people of Cuba overthrow the Communist regime from within Cuba and institute a new government with which the United States can live in peace.

Two days before the issuance of this directive, a bulletproof Buick passed out through the gate of the CIA's fortified complex on the southern bank of the Potomac and streaked across the

Key Bridge to Georgetown. There it parked before an elegant brick house. The occupant of the car got out and climbed the front steps. He would not ride in that Buick again. He was Allen Dulles, and now, seven months after the failure—his failure— at the Bay of Pigs, he suddenly was out as CIA Director.

The White House already had his replacement in mind: John McCone, an immensely successful California industrialist (he was a founder of the San Francisco–based Bechtel engineering company), a right-wing Republican, and a viciously effective administrator.

McCone's nomination for CIA director sailed through the Senate. And with McCone in place, the Kennedy administration could move against Castro, this time with real menace.

5   Early in December 1961, Fidel Castro made it official. For months his regime had been accepting more and more aid from Russia, aligning itself more and more closely with the Soviet bloc. Now, on December 2, he appeared on Havana television, giving a speech that shocked the world. For many years, he stated, even at university, he had been a Marxist-Leninist, and had hidden his views for the sake of gaining power. Among those he had deceived was *The New York Times* reporter Herbert Matthews. But now, Castro insisted, the truth could be told—Cuba's government henceforth would be by "collective leadership."

Was Castro indeed speaking the truth? Perhaps so. Possibly he had been a closet Communist all along. But, just as possibly, he was positioning himself for entry into the Moscow-led Warsaw Pact, an alliance that promised for its members security and mutual defense. For Castro was certain that the Americans would come again, this time with far greater force than at the Bay of Pigs. The target date for such an assault, his intelligence estimated, would be October 1962.

6   Six days before Christmas, 1961, Joseph Kennedy was in Palm Beach, playing golf with his niece Ann Gargan, when he collapsed. Unaware of what was wrong, Gargan notified Rose

Kennedy, who thought her husband merely tired. So by the time the senior Kennedy was placed in a hospital, he was on the verge of death. He did survive, after a tracheotomy, but he had suffered a severe stroke that for the rest of his life left him paralyzed and unable to speak.

The effect on his children, and especially on President Kennedy, was profound. Joseph Kennedy "had been so independent, so in control, always able to do just what he wanted to do," said his chauffeur. "Seeing him in that wheelchair tore them apart."

Since the father could no longer pressure the sons, they might at last have become more conciliatory, less insistent on toughness. For whatever their reasons, personal or political, though, they turned on Castro with a vengeance.

7   For Robert Kennedy was on the move. At a secret meeting in his office at the Justice Department, on January 19, 1962, he demanded that "no time, money, effort, or manpower be spared" in bringing about "the overthrow of Castro's regime."

President Kennedy's own hostility to Castro had hardened substantially. "I think," said Ray Cline, a CIA official, in an oral interview,

> the very bitter personal feeling that both Jack and Bobby had—I called it an obsession once in writing and Arthur Schlesinger jumped down my throat, and Mac [McGeorge] Bundy, for saying that the President was obsessed. But whatever, he was certainly very determined to try to get even with Castro for what he thought of as a humiliation at the Bay of Pigs.

"President Kennedy indicated," noted another CIA official present at the January 19, 1962, meeting, "that the final chapter [on Castro] had not been written—it's got to be done and will be done."

The next day, Major General Edward Lansdale, plain-looking man with a habitual smile, but a gritty veteran of the 1950s anti-insurgent wars in the Philippines, took command of Operation Mongoose. His model was the American Revolution.

"Americans once ran a successful revolution," he wrote to his news staff:

> It was run from within, and succeeded because there was timely and strong political, economic, and military help by nations outside who supported our cause. Using this same concept of revolution from within, we must help the Cuban people to stamp out tyranny and gain their liberty.

As France had intervened militarily against Britain, so must America intervene militarily against Castro.

CHAPTER 6

Mongoose

1 *February 1962*

STATEMENT OF THE SOVIET GOVERNMENT!

So trumpeted the headline of *Pravda*, on the cold Moscow morning of February 19, 1962. As Muscovites read on, accustomed as they were to studying the papers for any changes in the party line, they must have sensed that the Kremlin was laying out a justification for something. "By what right and by what law," the front-page article demanded,

> does the U.S. government organize and direct aggression against another country accusing it of having established a social system and a state different from what the United States wanted? If the U.S. government arrogates this right to itself, it is standing on very shaky ground, because it does not . . . possess the military might that would permit it to dictate conditions to other countries. The U.S. political leaders should take into account that there are other countries possessing no less terrible weapons, standing guard over peace, and prepared to prevent the unloosing of a new war.

U.S. intelligence analysts would have read this article, although what import they saw in it, no available record shows. Speaking on behalf of Khrushchev, nonetheless, *Pravda* was sending Kennedy a blunt warning: don't invade Cuba! Or else!

. . .

Despite the threat, General Edward Lansdale was busily at work in a Pentagon office, organizing Operation Mongoose. Lansdale, wrote a *New York Times* reporter, was

> one of the most unusual members of the United States government. It was as if [he] had been invented with the Kennedy administration in mind. He was a former advertising man, a former Air Force officer, a CIA agent now, a man deeply interested in doing things . . . the right way. . . . He had risen to fame within the government as an anti-bureaucratic figure of no small dimension, and State, Defense, and the CIA were well stocked with his enemies. . . . He was the Good American because in part his own experience had convinced him that Americans were, in fact, good, and that the American experience and American ideals were valid elsewhere. . . . [He had served in Asia where he had concluded that] Asians could have nationalism, but nationalism on *our* terms: nationalism without revolution, or revolution which we would run for them—revolution, it turned out, without revolution.

Applying the same attitude to Cuba, Lansdale detailed a six-phase schedule for Operation Mongoose. Including political, psychological, sabotage, and intelligence actions—as well as attacks "on the cadre of the regime, including key leaders"— the plan was to culminate with "an open revolt and overthrow of the Communist regime." Its phases were:

   I. *Action.* March 1962. Start moving in.
  II. *Build-up.* April–July 1962. Activating the necessary operations inside Cuba for revolution and concurrently applying the vital political, economic, and military-type support from outside Cuba.
 III. *Readiness.* 1 August 1962. Check for final policy decision.
  IV. *Resistance.* August–September 1962. Move into guerrilla operations.
   V. *Revolt.* First two weeks of October 1962. Open revolt and overthrow of the Communist regime.
  VI. *Final.* During month of October 1962. Establishment of new government.

But was the U.S. military going to support this plan directly? That "vital decision," Lansdale noted—the date was February 20, 1962—had not yet been made.

.   .   .

On the subject of a direct and armed assault on Cuba, the Kennedy administration seemed to be wavering. Back in January 1962, Lansdale had talked at length with Robert Kennedy, and had come away believing that "we are in a combat situation—where we have been given full command." But on February 26, 1962, the White House reduced Lansdale's "Cuba Project" simply to a program for gathering of intelligence.

Why the Kennedys changed their minds is unclear. Perhaps they were afraid of premature leaks.

This much we know. On February 27, 1962, FBI Director J. Edgar Hoover informed Robert Kennedy, his nominal boss, that Judith Campbell, President Kennedy's favored paramour of the moment, had talked at least six times on the telephone with Johnny Rosselli of the Chicago mob. If the Kennedy brothers had any thought of replacing Hoover, the director implied, they had better forget it: at any time he could expose the Judith Campbell liaison.

All this is established fact. What is unclear is just what happened next. Did Robert Kennedy know of Judith Campbell? In her memoirs, she indicated that, during the same time period that she and John Kennedy were having an affair, the new senator from Massachusetts, Edward M. Kennedy, made a pass at her. Did Robert know that? During the winter of 1962, we know, Judith Campbell was carrying messages back and forth between President Kennedy in Washington and mobster Sam Giancana in Chicago. Did Robert Kennedy know that? It seems likely that he did. In an interview with the London *Sunday Times*, Campbell has stated that she carried "intelligence data"—as well as money—between JFK and Giancana "on at least twenty occasions." The money was used to finance Kennedy's primary victories in West Virginia and Chicago; the data had to do with plots to assassinate Castro. "Fairly early on," Campbell stated,

> Jack told me outright. He said the envelopes contained "intelligence material" and that it involved the elimination of Castro.

On March 22, 1962, then—and this too is established fact—Hoover lunched with President Kennedy in the White House, and laid out what the FBI had learned about Judith Campbell's ties with the mob. Soon thereafter the White House logged no more telephone calls between President Kennedy and Camp-bell. The JFK-Campbell affair, we assume, was over.

At about this time, midway through March 1962, the Kennedy White House revived Operation Mongoose. The opera-tion was to be a deep secret.

March 1962
After a cool Christmas and New Year season, the weather in Cuba was turning sultry—and the news correspondingly was becoming ominous. The Havana newspapers almost every day were reporting an impending invasion. On what were the re-ports based? We have no access to Cuban documents. We do, however, have declassified American papers: according to Gen-eral Lansdale's schedule, the U.S. government intended by the end of July 1962 at least to "penetrate the [Cuban] regime."

For by the middle of March 1962, Operation Mongoose was breathing the breath of wholly new life. President Kennedy may have seemed to have recoiled from any direct action against Castro. On March 14, 1962, nevertheless, the official guidelines for Operation Mongoose indicated clearly that

(a) In undertaking to cause the overthrow of the Castro government, the U.S. will make maximum use of Cuban resources, internal and external, but recognizes that final success will require *decisive U.S. military intervention* [emphasis added].
(b) Such Cuban resources as are developed will be used to prepare for and justify this intervention, and thereafter to facilitate and support it.

Two days after General Lansdale drafted these words, he showed them to President Kennedy. One thing is for sure: JFK did not disavow the document.

Going into Cuba, however, as the President must have real-ized, was scarcely going to be easy. For it was "evident," in the words of an intelligence report, "that Fidel Castro and the revo-lution retain the positive support of a substantial proportion of the Cuban people." And a State Department report, sent over to the White House on March 27, 1962, estimated that the Soviet Union already had sent Cuba $100 million worth of equipment such as torpedo boats, mortars, and antiaircraft guns; several hundred Cuban soldiers had gone to Communist countries for training.

President Kennedy nevertheless was feeling belligerent. In an end-of-the-month interview with *The Saturday Evening Post*, he proclaimed that

> In some circumstances we might have to take the initiative. . . . Khrushchev must not be certain that, where its vital interests are threatened, the United States will never strike first.

April 1962

Giving credence to Kennedy's threat, the U.S. government early in April 1962 made the Jupiter missiles in Turkey fully operational. The Jupiters, as the White House leaked to the press, were "ready and manned."

At the same time, the administration renewed contact with Johnny Rosselli and the mob. The CIA made the contact, and in a Miami parking lot passed along to Rosselli poison pills that the Mafia, through its networks, was to smuggle into Cuba and, somehow, slip into Castro's food. Within a month Rosselli reported that the "medicine" was safe in Cuba.

But the White House had no intention of relying just on the Mafia. As *The Wall Street Journal* revealed—in a leak that caused General Lansdale to suspect a security violation—

> U.S. policymakers debate whether to aggravate Cuba's economic troubles by sabotage. Foes of the idea get the upper hand. They prefer to save secret agents for eventual direct efforts to overthrow the Red regime.

Just as that issue of *The Wall Street Journal* was going to print, the U.S. Navy went to sea, staging a vast military maneuver described in the press as "Operation Quick Kick." From the huge naval base at Norfolk and out past the promontory called Old Point Comfort, from the Marine station at Cherry Point, just south of Cape Hatteras in North Carolina, from over the sand dunes and sea oats that lay just to the east of the air base in Myrtle Beach, South Carolina, from the Cooper River docks at Charleston, South Carolina, and out around Fort Sumter on its mid-harbor island, 79 ships, 300 aircraft, and more than 40,000 troops took part in the operation.

The exercise lasted until May 11, 1962. It blanketed the Caribbean, with ships making runs toward Cuba and landing

Marines in mock raids on Vieques Island, just east of Puerto Rico.

On April 28, 1962, in the Kremlin, Premier Khrushchev met with Osmani Cienfuegos, Cuba's minister of public works. What they talked about was secret. U.S. intelligence in Moscow nonetheless knew that Khrushchev was up to something.

Late April 1962 found Nikita Khrushchev vacationing at his dacha in the Crimea. As he walked along the beach one morning with Marshal Rodion Malinovsky, the Soviet defense minister, Malinovsky pointed a finger out across the Black Sea. Even as they spoke, the general declared, U.S. nuclear missiles were across the water in Turkey, capable of destroying all Russia's southern cities.

"Why do the Americans have such a possibility?" Malinovsky asked. "They have surrounded us with bases on all sides, and we have no possibility or right to do the same!"

Malinovsky's complaint must have had a sharp impact on Khrushchev—from this moment onward he began to rush forward the idea of putting missiles in Cuba. He may have been toying with the thought earlier; Castro later claimed that he had requested Soviet missiles as early as February 1962. But Khrushchev now, with the Jupiters operational and the U.S. military apparently practicing for a strike at Cuba, had to feel a sense of alarm. According to later Soviet sources, the chairman kept coming back to three imperatives: 1) he had to end the double standard whereby America could place missiles on Russia's perimeter but not Russia on America's; 2) he had somehow to magnify the U.S.S.R.'s nuclear striking power which, as Defense Secretary McNamara had boasted, lagged far behind America's; and 3) he had to deter an American invasion of Cuba.

Upon his return to Moscow at the very end of April 1962, we know, Khrushchev bounced the Cuban missile idea off the prim and intelligent First Deputy Prime Minister Anastas Mikoyan; Mikoyan looked on the proposal with horror. The Americans, Mikoyan believed, were certain to react with rage.

Thinking the gamble might be worthwhile, however, Khrushchev asked a group of his closest advisers, including General Malinovsky and Foreign Minister Andrei Gromyko, also to evaluate the idea. Did they think the Soviets could put missiles in

Cuba without being spotted by U.S. intelligence? What they answered, we do not know. But would Castro indeed accept the missiles? The committee of advisers agreed to send a mission to Havana to find out.

2   *May 1962*

General Lansdale was nervous. Mongoose preparations were moving along more slowly than he had hoped, and he was feeling the heat from Robert Kennedy. "I am concerned," he wrote on May 7, 1962, to his immediate subordinates,

> that we are losing sight of our sound original concept, in Operation Mongoose, of careful integration of the independent elements of government in planning and operations. . . . It is clear that each operational representative must keep his own top boss informed. . . . If this is not clear, then we invite the danger of matters falling between the chairs.

What was bothering Lansdale was that, pushed ahead by the Kennedys and fueled by a fortune from the CIA, Operation Mongoose was producing just one more inept and cumbersome bureaucracy, out of anybody's control. By midspring, 1962, the operation indeed had become huge, having transformed Miami virtually into CIA-City South. Each noontime's Eastern Airlines flight from Washington was known as the Miami Milk Run; the majority of passengers frequently were with the CIA. A World War II air base at Richmond, in the scrublands just south of Miami—where a hurricane had destroyed the hangars—had come to house a CIA radio station, code-named JM/WAVE. Up in Coral Gables, the University of Miami served as a depot for arms; CIA personnel kept in shape using its athletic fields, and young Cuban exiles masqueraded as students. Close by the campus, the University Inn was in effect the largest CIA station outside headquarters in Langley, Virginia. Senior agents actually lived farther uptown, in the DuPont Plaza Hotel, an establishment that overlooked the mouth of the Miami River and from which they could see the causeways that led to Miami Beach. They had drinks together in the lounge of the Holiday Inn, nearby, and during working hours spread out all over the city to run some fifty-five dummy companies, real estate agencies, gun shops, fishing stores, even, on Okeechobee Road, the thoroughfare that angled into the city from Hialeah, a marketing firm.

With all these fronts, the operation was becoming chaotic; hence Lansdale's insistence on organizational tightness. But perhaps his worry was exaggerated. On May 8, 1962, even while the "Quick Kick" maneuvers were still taking place, Lansdale presided over *another* joint military test run. Code-named "Whiplash," this new set of sea games was designed explicitly to test procedures that would be used in an invasion of Cuba.

Like "Quick Kick," "Operation Whiplash" received widespread coverage in the U.S. press, and the Soviet embassies in Washington and Havana could hardly have missed the significance. In a 1977 magazine article, indeed, General Igor D. Statsenko stated that the springtime 1962 maneuvers strengthened Khrushchev's hand in his wish to send missiles to Cuba.

Another item in the news had to have alarmed the Kremlin still further. On May 12, 1962, a heavily armed ship attacked a Cuban Coast Guard vessel, just above Santa Cruz del Norte, and killed two of Castro's sailors. Alpha 66, a Cuban exile group that received funding from Henry Luce's *Life*, claimed responsibility for the attack. Their ship had put out of Miami.

Early May 1962 found Secretary of Defense Robert McNamara in Athens, addressing a meeting of NATO foreign and defense ministers. The symbolism of Athens was obvious: Greece and neighboring Turkey alike were bristling with Jupiter missiles.

Speaking from a lectern, McNamara, bristling himself with statistics and jargon, announced the doctrine that since early winter had been bubbling up through the Pentagon bureaucracy: the strategy called "counterforce." Meaning? "We may be able to use our retaliatory forces to limit damage done to ourselves and our allies," McNamara explained, "by knocking out the enemy's bases before he has had time to launch his second salvos."

By targeting Soviet bases rather than cities, McNamara claimed, the U.S. would induce the Soviets to do the same. That way a nuclear war would end fast, and millions of lives would be saved.

. . .

As if to rebut McNamara directly, Khrushchev flew to Varna, a resort on Bulgaria's Black Sea coast, and gave his own speech. "Would it not be better," the chairman asked, "if the shores on which are located NATO's military bases and the launching sites for their armed rockets are converted into areas of peaceful labor and prosperity?"

Khrushchev obviously was worried. The U.S., he complained, was pulling Turkey "deeper and deeper into the coils of the NATO military alliance."

In President Kennedy's view, of course, the U.S. *had* to strengthen its allies. For the Russians were coming, the Russians were coming, especially in Laos and Vietnam.

Wedged up against the southern border of China, flanked by Thailand, Burma, and Cambodia, and landlocked, Laos had the appearance of sleepiness, peacefulness, and, according to the 1962 Geneva Convention, neutrality. Laotian neutrality was a farce. North Vietnam used Laos as a highway for military goods to the south; America ignored the Geneva agreement, setting up the pro-Western regime of Laotian General Phoumi Nosovan; and the Pathet Lao, the country's Communist party, joined by neutralists, had put itself in charge of an ever-growing number of villages and towns. By the late spring of 1962, Laos, at least as viewed from halfway around the world in the Oval Office, seemed a domino on the verge of collapse.

Desperate to avoid a failure, Kennedy sent the Seventh Fleet into the Gulf of Siam. Thailand had said nothing, publicly at least, about a danger to their security. The White House nonetheless claimed that the U.S. naval force moved into Thailand's waters "at the decision of the Thai government."

Kennedy also sent U.S. Marines to the border of Laos. And in the country itself, Air America, the CIA's air wing, flew supplies to pro-Western elements—triggering a resurgence of the Pathet Lao and subverting Laotian neutrality.

Why these U.S. actions? As Roger Hilsman, President Kennedy's Assistant Secretary of State for Far Eastern Affairs, later told Congress, "If we had . . . used the [Geneva] negotiations as an excuse to withdraw from Laos . . . we in effect would have been turning it over to the Communists."

But even America's allies were dubious about the worth of Laos. During a Potomac River cruise aboard the presidential yacht, Britain's Prime Minister Harold Macmillan, present with Kennedy on a summertime state visit, spied a racing scull gliding along the water.

"What have we here?" the elegant Macmillan wisecracked. "The Laotian navy?"

In the end, Kennedy's interest in Laos gave way to interest in Vietnam. Laos was only a highway to Vietnam, to the Mekong Delta; and the great prize was the Mekong Delta.

In the late spring of 1962, the Mekong Delta, fingering around Saigon toward the South China Sea, had the "appearance of a land of milk and honey. The onset of the monsoon . . . had quickened the rice seeds into shoots that were pushing green, and would soon be ready for . . . transplanting into . . . the paddy fields that stretched out in an expanse from both sides of the road[s]. The landscape looked flat, but it kept the eye busy. Narrow dikes to trap the water for the rice plants checkered the paddy fields. The checkerboard of the paddy fields and the dikes was in turn crisscrossed by the straight lines and sharp angles of canals for irrigation and transport. The lines and angles of the canals were occasionally interrupted by the wide bend of one of the rivers that fed the Mekong."

In the late spring of 1962, however, those rivers, for Americans and South Vietnamese government forces, had become about the only safe means of movement. Roads, particularly secondary roads and particularly at night, were guerrilla-infested; and guerrillas were pressing ever more closely in toward Saigon.

And, in the late spring of 1962, President Kennedy stepped up America's troop commitment to South Vietnam. He did so with little enthusiasm. "The troops will march in," he said in a conversation, "the bands will play; the crowds will cheer; and in four days everyone will have forgotten. Then we will be told we have to send in more troops. It's like taking a drink. The effect wears off and you have to take another."

Why did Kennedy jack up the pressure in Vietnam? A gain for communism, he believed, was a loss for America; and with the Republican party ready to pounce on him, he had no wish to "lose" Indochina. Yet more still was involved—what we were doing seemed good for Vietnam. Like most Americans of his generation, President Kennedy was convinced that America was a force for good in the world. America's leadership, in the words of Pulitzer Prize–winner Neil Sheehan, seemed a "benevolent form of international guidance. It was thought to be neither exploitative, like the nineteenth-century colonialism of the European empires, nor destructive of personal freedom and other worthy human values, like the totalitarianism of the Soviet Union and China and their Communist allies. Instead of formal colonies, the United States sought local governments amenable to American wishes and, where possible, subject to indirect control from behind the scenes. Washington wanted native regimes that would act as surrogates for American power."

The problem was, the Vietnamese Communists had no intention of serving as surrogates for American power. Nor, for that matter, did Castro's Cuba. In both countries, therefore, the White House detected evidence of the global march of communism. Laos, Vietnam, Cuba, it didn't matter which—the Kennedy administration was determined to stop communism dead in its tracks.

Khrushchev detested jazz, claiming to find it "decadent," but at the end of May 1962, he went to the Red Army sports palace to hear Benny Goodman; he had gone at the prodding of Jane Thompson, wife of U.S. Ambassador Llewellyn Thompson. But he ended up enjoying himself, and when singer Joya Sherrill came out in a low-cut white dress, he stood and cheered. After the concert he attended a bash at Spaso House, the U.S. embassy.

Khrushchev liked the Thompsons. He could talk with Jane about her efforts to grow corn in the embassy garden, and he regarded Llewellyn, a long-faced midwesterner who had worked his way through college, as solid and honest. But the Thompsons were leaving Moscow: their daughter, Sherry, was in early adolescence, and they thought Moscow no fit place for an American teenaged girl. So Khrushchev had come to the embassy party to pay his respects.

Khrushchev, however, was not wholly straight with Thompson. He said nothing of the fact that, even as they downed their toasts, a Soviet delegation was in the air, flying in the night toward Cuba, ostensibly to study irrigation problems but actually to broach with Castro the idea of shipping missiles to his island.

June 1962

With the coming of the summer's heat to Washington, President Kennedy, allowing his brother Robert to handle Cuba, was turning his attention to politics at home. To hold on to Democratic seats in Congress in the upcoming November election, and thus to salvage the programs that could help with his own reelection two years later, he needed some kind of political victory. Yet securing such a win was going to be tough. His relations with Congress were virtually nonexistent: former Speaker of the House Sam Rayburn was gone now and former Senate Majority Leader Lyndon Johnson, as Vice President, was sitting back and letting JFK solve his own political problems. And those problems were sticky. Conservative Democrats in the South considered Kennedy a radical on race; liberal Democrats in the North were appalled by what they thought was his lack of commitment to justice. Facing gusts from right and left, he tacked toward the right, remaining largely aloof from racial issues. Southerners in Congress patted him on the head, becoming more accommodating on administration proposals for an increased minimum wage.

Yet Kennedy himself once had asked aides, "Who gives a shit about the minimum wage?" He craved a *big* win. And he would get it, thanks to the machinations of Robert McNamara and Roswell Gilpatric over in the Pentagon.

What happened left Washington agog. It was called the TFX scandal.

.   .   .

Early in June 1962, Deputy Defense Secretary Roswell Gilpatric received a prominent visitor, Henry M. ("Scoop") Jackson. Jackson physically was on the short side, and ungainly (detractors said he walked like a penguin), but he was a powerhouse in the capital and, as a Democratic senator from Washington State, he was an effective advocate for the Boeing Corporation. Some called him the "senator from Boeing," a label he never bothered to deny. It was in his capacity as Boeing's representative, in fact, that he had come to see Gilpatric. And he was disturbed. Rumor had it, Jackson reportedly told "Roz" Gilpatric, that Boeing did "not have a snowball's chance in hell of securing the TFX contract." Gilpatric, silken and smooth, dismissed the reports.

Back in their offices over Puget Sound, however, Boeing's top officials—Senator Jackson's major backers—remained suspicious. They had been compiling intelligence reports, and they had no liking at all for what they were learning: Vice President Johnson had been pulling strings on behalf of General Dynamics; Navy Secretary Korth had been beating the drums for General Dynamics; and Deputy Secretary Gilpatric, a lawyer, had been a partner in Cravath, Swaine & Moore, special counsel to General Dynamics. The TFX bidding, Boeing suspected, was rigged.

The TFX story had started "as a gleam in the eye of General F. F. Everest, in 1959 the incoming commander of the Air Force's Tactical Air Command. "At that time," *Fortune* reported, "[the] industry was working on advanced fighter planes, a result of having nosed around the Air Force to see what was wanted and needed. The new commander, however, was about to put the companies on a radically different track. On Hank Everest's mind was a fighter-bomber that would meet the new and tougher conditions that he envisioned for the mid-1960s. . . . [T]he best Air Force fighter, the Republic F-105, was in a vulnerable position with only 44 suitable take-off and landing fields and these long since pinpointed on Soviet military maps. So Everest's initial requirement for a new fighter was that it should . . . be able to fly from the U.S. to [Europe] nonstop, and to the Far East with a single refueling. Such long legs . . . demanded a large wing area, but Everest also wanted his fighter to be able to dash in at tree-top levels doing 1,000 miles per hour [hazardous for a big-winged plane]. On top of all this, he expected his plane to have the virtuosity of a hummingbird, able to 'loiter'—at subsonic speeds for reconnaissance and ground support missions—or do aerial combat at 1,700 m.p.h." How was one airplane to do all these things? Everest's answer, on paper, was that the craft could have fold-back wings, giving it both range and stability. "Everybody thought Everest was nuts," one plane builder told *Fortune*. "He was asking for too much of a state-of-the-art advance."

Indeed, Thomas Gates, Jr., President Eisenhower's last Secretary of Defense, gave the dream plane, the TFX, little support. General Everest's idea seemed like one big white elephant; and President Eisenhower may well have had the TFX in mind when, in his Farewell Address, he warned the nation against the excesses of the "military-industrial complex."

For Defense Secretary Robert S. McNamara, however, the TFX seemed just what the doctor, or more exactly President Kennedy, had ordered.

But the TFX scandal had its origin in the huge Pentagon office of Defense Secretary Robert S. McNamara. McNamara had hit Washington, after his Senate confirmation early in 1961, with the force of a missile. Encouraged by President Kennedy, he was determined to revamp the military services, making them mean and lean, or at least lean. He embodied the meanness. With his thin, grim mouth and his dark suit jackets buttoned primly around his thin waistline, he made the Pentagon brass think of an athletic accountant. And he did strike terror in the hearts of the brass. More precisely: he intended to eliminate waste in defense spending by forcing interservice cooperation. So— hardly had he taken possession of his Pentagon office than he announced plans for a new jet fighter, one to be used by the Army, Navy, and Air Force alike. The Navy and the Air Force both had been screeching for a new fighter. (The Army, with its special needs, backed out of the picture.) Contract bidding for the airplane, to be called the Tactical Fighter Experimental, or TFX, was to start on October 1, 1961. The contract, in the area of $7 billion, was the largest the government ever had dangled before the munitions lobby.

The TFX, furthermore, coincided with the new administration's belief in a "controlled response" (the theory that the U.S. should have military options other than all-out nuclear war). As McNamara saw it, the TFX would be able to zip into the Soviet Union, drop little A-bombs, and zip out again, crossing the tundra to safety; and, as the most versatile fighter available, the TFX could be shared by the Air Force and Navy, allowing the administration to claim that it had cut costs.

Or so calculated Secretary McNamara; actually, he had managed to alarm both Air Force and Navy. In the Air Force, General Everest "feared the Navy might seize the occasion to delay the TFX 'The Navy's problem,' said Everest, '[was that] carriers can do the ferrying. The Navy didn't need the plane and we thought they would see the TFX as a threat. If someone else can operate without relying on this 40-knot barge called a carrier, it demolishes the carrier. Carriers did do a great job in the Pacific, but the TFX could make them less important: four hours to Europe vs. four days, from base to the Mediterranean." The Navy, furthermore, *was* unhappy with the proposed TFX, although for reasons beyond those ascribed by General Everest. As conceived in McNamara's office, the TFX was too heavy and too long to fit on the carrier decks.

So McNamara compromised, agreeing to a TFX that lay somewhere between Air Force and Navy requirements. As a Pentagon wag put it, the T in TFX "stood not so much for 'Tactical' as 'Togetherness.' "

But the big question was whether McNamara's compromise really could fly or whether he was simply squandering $7 billion. No one knew.

What observers *did* know was that, even while still on the drawing boards, the TFX was inseparable from politics. Boeing had its paid lobbyists in Washington, but so did General Dynamics, and General Dynamics furthermore had the support of big state congressional delegations, those out of Connecticut, New York, California, and Texas.

In its geographical spread, General Dynamics had become an empire, nearly as large as the ancient Roman and Chinese empires, certainly larger than the nineteenth- and early-twentieth-century Austro-Hungarian one; a glance at a map of the United States would have made the point. Center and southward, in the heart of the vast Texas plain, was Dallas–Fort Worth; here, adjacent to the airstrip it shared with the Carswell Air Force Base, was General Dynamic's mile-long, aluminum-sided Texas plant, soon to be the home of the TFX jet fighter plane. Out in California, in Pomona and San Diego, twin General Dynamics factories manufactured intermediate-range ballistic missiles. Back toward the east and north, in Warren, Michigan, a sprawling industrial suburb of Detroit, a General Dynamics subsidiary called Land Systems made tanks for the Army. Farther to the east still, where the Thames River flowed through the Connecticut landscape, widened between New London and Groton, and spilled into the Long Island Sound, the Electric Boat Company, also a General Dynamics division, cranked out nuclear submarines, each able to carry multiple warheads, each priced at more than $100 million, and each nearly as long as the Washington Monument. Over in Long Island, the Grumman Company was General Dynamics' largest subunit. Across the East River bridges and down in lower Manhattan, the law firm of Cravath, Swaine, & Moore served as General Dynamics' general counsel. General Dynamics was headquartered in New York.

It was in the New York office that the top General Dynamics officials mapped out their strategy in the matter of the TFX. For the TFX affair boiled down to political warfare between General Dynamics and its archrival out in Seattle, Boeing Aircraft.

The Texans especially had lined up in force behind the General Dynamics TFX bid: the list included Vice President Lyndon B. Johnson, Fort Worth's young and hardworking U.S. Representative James Wright, Navy Secretary Fred Korth, and Korth's immediate predecessor in the Navy job, a Texan who had resigned to run for governor, John Connally. And a young man from a state into which General Dynamics was trying to expand, Massachusetts, was doing his bit for the aid of the company. His name was Edward Moore Kennedy.

Hence the visit of Senator Henry Jackson early in June 1962, to the Pentagon office of Deputy Secretary Roswell Gilpatric: Jackson was as sure as were his backers out in Seattle that the TFX bidding was rigged. And so it was—through the device of the defense contract, the Kennedy administration was consolidating its hold on two regions of the country that would be critical in the 1964 presidential election: Texas, and the corridor that ran along what now is Interstate 95, from Rhode Island down through Connecticut, and then the heavily industrialized reaches of western Long Island.

Such was the Kennedys' political game.

Cuba, in the rainy month of June 1962, was an island of discontent. The U.S. had engineered Cuba's ouster from the Organization of American States, persuaded most of the Western hemisphere to cut diplomatic ties with Cuba (Mexico and Canada refused to do so), and clamped Cuba in the vise of an economic embargo; Cubans definitely were feeling the pinch. On June 16, 1962, wrote Hugh Thomas,

> demonstrations occurred in the city of Cárdenas. Housewives marched into the streets beating pots and pans. Tanks were dispatched by the heavy-handed Major Jorge Serguera, the provincial military commander, to overawe them. . . . Afterwards, demonstrations occurred at Santa Clara and at El Cano near Havana, where one young militiaman was killed and another wounded by the police in a confused incident. The government reacted as if terrified by what further crises they might encounter: the shops at El Cano were confiscated, the inhabitants lost all their cars, telephones, and lorries, and were forced into unemployment and submission. The local militia, which had proved notably inadequate in this trial, was purged and reorganized.

Such evidence of discontent was duly noted in Washington and in Havana alike. Havana itself was awash with rumors of impending invasion—several politicians in Congress were shouting for invasion and White House officials were speaking frankly about getting rid of Castro—and midway through the month of June 1962, Che Guevara and Fidel's brother, Raúl, flew secretly to Moscow; they had gone off in response to the visit by the Soviet delegation. "The only thing we asked the Russians to do," Fidel Castro later said to a French journalist,

> was to make clear to the U.S. that an attack on us was an attack on the Soviet Union. We had extensive discussion before arriving at the proposal of installing guided missiles, a proposal which *surprised us at first and gave us great pause* [Castro's emphasis]. We finally went along with the Soviet proposal because, on the one hand, the Russians convinced

us that the U.S. would not let itself be intimidated by conventional weapons and secondly because it was impossible for us not to share the risks which the Soviet Union was taking to save us.

This account by Castro sounded a bit like "After you, Alphonse." Yet in another interview, this again with the *New York Times* reporter Herbert Matthews, Castro said emphatically:

[W]e felt ourselves in danger from the U.S. We consulted with the Russians, when they suggested the missiles, we immediately said, "Yes, by all means."

Whatever the details, one major point remains. On June 10, 1962, Khrushchev, with the support of his closest aides in the Kremlin, handed down a secret order. The Soviet military immediately was to beef up its combat forces in Cuba—and as stealthily as possible to send missiles to the island.

By the end of June 1962, according to a memorandum prepared for General Lansdale's "special group," a "maritime operation to emplace a cache of arms and demolitions was accomplished without incident." The CIA, in plain English, had smuggled in some weapons.

Early to mid-July 1962
By the Fourth of July holiday, the CIA had increased its U-2 flights over Cuba, supplementing spy reports of many Soviet ships in the Havana harbor. (Simultaneously, Raúl Castro, Fidel's brother, flew to Moscow to work out details of the missile deal.) But right after Independence Day, General Lansdale, who had been to Florida, went to Robert Kennedy with happy news. "My visit to the Miami area," Lansdale wrote in a July 5, 1962, memorandum,

included discussions with the operations staff of the CIA station, which carries the brunt of current work on Operation Mongoose. I was pleased to note that CIA has built a team which has a number of people experienced in operations into Communist-controlled areas (Europe and Asia), whose know-how strengthens the operations of people with Latin American experience. . . . Overall, this is a splendid effort by CIA.

Mounting the podium before a "peace conference" in Moscow, Khrushchev was virtually ranting. Referring to McNamara's "monstrous proposal" for a joint counterforce strategy, Khrushchev bellowed, "Are there no armed forces in and near big cities? Wouldn't atom bombs exploded according to McNamara's rules in, say, the suburbs of New York bring fiery death to that great city?"

Khrushchev then denounced Kennedy, for all the world to hear. "Some statesmen in positions of responsibility," Khrushchev claimed,

> even declare openly their willingness to "take the initiative" in a nuclear conflict with the Soviet Union. . . . Their reasoning is: hurry up and start the war now, or the situation may change.

The situation was indeed changing. On July 15, 1962, a fleet of Soviet cargo ships steamed down the Black Sea, heading for the Mediterranean and then Cuba. By the time the ships had reached the Aegean, they were under U.S. aerial observation. According to a report sent back to Washington, they were "riding high in the water"—meaning that their cargo was light, probably military equipment.

Mid- to Late July 1962
Always busy with his memos, General Lansdale on July 23, 1962, summarized, for the eyes of Secretary McNamara, what Mongoose so far had accomplished: a Defense Department working group; an interrogation center at Opa-locka, Florida; the acquisition of PT boats; radio broadcasts into Cuba; the use of Avon Park, Florida, as a training base for Cuban refugees; overflights of Cuba; contingency plans for air strikes against Cuba and an air-sea blockade of the island; and a "cover and deception plan." Lansdale's description of this last plan remains declassified.

But what was the U.S. to do next? Lansdale spelled out the options, complete with advantages and disadvantages:

Option #1: "Cancel operational plans; treat Cuba as a bloc nation; protect hemisphere from it." In short, scrub Mongoose. Doing so, Lansdale contended, would save money and show the world that the U.S. now espoused "the principle of non-intervention." But then he listed ten objections.

Option #2: "Exert all possible diplomatic, economic, psychological, and other pressures to overthrow the Castro Communist regime without overt U.S. military commitment." Again, Lansdale acknowledged, the U.S. would display its "devotion to the principle of non-intervention." But, he pointed out, "except in degree, this has essentially been the U.S. policy since . . . 3 January 1962, and it has not been successful."

Option #3: "Commit the United States to help the Cubans to overthrow the Castro Communist regime, with a step-by-step phasing to ensure success, including the use of U.S. military force if necessary." Lansdale was happier about this option—it "would permit the United States to control the timing of operations against Cuba"—but he believed also that the longer the U.S. postponed an invasion of Cuba, "the higher the cost will be in American lives."

Option #4: "Use a provocation and overthrow the Castro Communist regime by U.S. military forces." Lansdale listed eight advantages. The only real disadvantage was that it "could inspire Soviet counter-action in other areas"—but, then, the Soviets might act in those other areas anyway.

So here was the CIA's strategy: threaten Castro, feint toward him with large and menacing forces, have complaisant magazines like *Reader's Digest* tell him how his days were numbered, provoke him into a rash action, such as an attack on Guantánamo, then finish him off. But would President Kennedy sign off on the plan?

As MIG jet fighters, newly supplied by the Soviet Union, roared overhead, Fidel Castro addressed a mass really in downtown Santiago; the date was July 26, 1962, and he was commemorating the anniversary of the revolution. He was all defiance. "And therefore we must prepare," he proclaimed,

> not only because we know that imperialism threatens us, not only because Mr. Kennedy, who is a stubborn gentleman, has the fixed idea of attacking our country, which we know, but also because the world lives under the danger of imperialist aggression, because the progressive nations live under the danger that the imperialists threaten.

The End of July 1962
Dean Acheson had developed doubts about Kennedy's ability

now to handle the Cuban problem. "I have a curious and apprehensive feeling," he wrote to his old boss, Harry S Truman,

> as I watch JFK that he is a sort of Indian snake charmer. He toots away on his pipe and our problems sway back and forth around him in a trancelike manner, never approaching but never withdrawing; all are in a state of suspended life, including the pipe player, who lives only in his dream. Someday one of the snakes will wake up, and no one will be able even to run.

And what was the snake charmer, JFK, proposing to do about Cuba? Was he going to seek a pretext, and then invade?

Perhaps even he, as July turned into August, did not know. But two more documents give us a clue as to his thinking. On July 31, 1962, General Lansdale produced a new study, one "not releasable to foreign nationals." Cuba soon would undergo a revolt, Lansdale forecast, "supported by the United States through propaganda, covert operations, and other actions as necessary." And then? Lansdale's policy proposal contained a heading entitled "U.S. Military Reaction." The proposal, declassified, exists in the John F. Kennedy presidential library. The three pages that follow "U.S. Military Reaction," however, are deleted.

Why should the CIA have blacked out three pages of a document that discussed plans for an American invasion of Cuba—unless those plans were for real?

And then, also at the very end of July 1962, as we learn from the U.S. Senate's 1975 investigation of CIA activities, the "Kennedy administration pressed the Mongoose operation with vigorous language." Given the foul mouths of the Kennedy men, we can imagine readily the meaning of "vigorous language."

But language to what end? If we can tolerate government prose, what we encounter is fascinating: "Although the collection of intelligence information was the central objective of Mongoose until August 1962," asserted the Senate's report, "sabotage and paramilitary actions were also conducted, including a major sabotage operation aimed at a large Cuban copper mine. Lansdale described the sabotage acts as involving 'blowing up bridges to stop communications and blowing up certain production plants'."

The administration had taken great pains to avoid implicating President Kennedy in any Pearl Harbor–type attack on Havana. But here it was. The blowing up of bridges and production plants could have meant only one thing: provoking Castro into doing something rash, such as trying to overrun Guantánamo.

Much to the annoyance of the powers-that-were in Washington, however, Castro did nothing. He fortified his bastions around the island, but he refrained from any move whatsoever toward Guantánamo.

He was refusing to be type-cast, certainly not as Hollywood loved to type-cast its villains, dark-complexioned and conspiratorial. He was just sitting there.

John F. Kennedy and his father.

Fidel Castro in Havana.

1

2

ABOVE. Fulgencio Batista and Richard M. Nixon.

LEFT. Allan Dulles.

President-elect John F. Kennedy and Vice President-elect Lyndon B. Johnson talking with reporters in the lobby of New York's Carlyle Hotel, January 1961.

6

8

ABOVE. Kennedy and Prime Minister John Diefenbaker, Ottawa, 1961.

LEFT. JFK and McGeorge Bundy.

JFK and Prime Minister Harold Macmillan, the White House, 1961.

ABOVE. Senator Kenneth Keating.

LEFT. William D. Pawley, former U.S. ambassador to Cuba, in Miami, 1961 with two survivors of the Bay of Pigs fiasco.

In the Kennedy Palm Beach estate. Left to right: Lyndon Johnson, JFK, Robert McNamara, Maxwell Taylor, and Roswell Gilpatric.

12

The Oval Office, October, 1962. Left to right: Anatoly Dobrynin, Andrei
Gromyko, and JFK. Back of the head: Llewellyn Thompson.

MISSILE TRANSPORTERS

SUPPORT AREA

UNCOVERED LAUNCHER

CANVAS COVERED LAUNCHER

GUIDANCE AREA

PERSONNEL TRENCHES

13

Soviet Cruise missile site, Isle of Palms.

Soviet truck in the area of the Havana harbor.

15

Construction of Soviet I.R.B.M. at Remedios.

The U.S. naval base at Guantanamo Bay.

Adlai Stevenson speaking in the United
Nations.

John Scali.

CHAPTER 7

Provocation

1 *Early August 1962*

At some point early in August 1962, an elegant gentleman entered a plush Citroën and swung onto Kalorama Road, away from the mansion that housed the French embassy. Somewhere in the Washington area he met with John McCone, Allen Dulles's successor as head of the CIA The elegant gentleman was Philippe L. Thiraud de Vosjoli, Washington chief for French intelligence, and McCone was worried. A hard-driving and extremely right-wing industrialist, he had received several reports of Soviet missiles in Cuba, as well as of an unusually large number of Soviet ships in Cuban ports. And from his experience in engineering, he was certain that in Cuba something big was going on. White-haired and steely-eyed, he put his suspicions to de Vosjoli—and he asked the Frenchman to go to Cuba to have a look around. De Vosjoli accepted the assignment.

In his memoirs, he described his spy efforts thus:

[M]y reports started mentioning the arrival of Soviet ships in Havana and, strangely, in Mariel, a small harbor seldom appearing on the maps of Cuba. Other ships were landing people and cargoes in harbors where the Soviet flag had, until now, been a rarity. . . .

Soldiers were reported to be guarding a cavern where work was being conducted secretly. Photographs taken by [an] agent showed that a large hole was being drilled through the ceiling of the cavern to the pasture 50 feet above. This hole had the appearance of a large tube, big enough to hold a missile and oriented in the direction of the United States. The Cuban informed insisted that its function was to launch missiles . . .

Upon de Vosjoli's return to Washington, CIA Director McCone became agitated, demanding then and there that President Kennedy take the missiles out of Cuba.

McCone was a Republican, a powerful figure in whom the Kennedy brothers placed little trust. Soon he may have leaked to Republicans in Congress word of the missiles, so the GOP could accuse JFK of appeasement.

It was hardly true that Kennedy was appeasing Castro. Under the blazing early August sunshine, U.S. military units in the Carolinas carried out a joint exercise called "Swift Strike II." Four Army divisions, out of Fort Jackson in South Carolina, and eight air squadrons out of the Shaw, Myrtle Beach, and Cherry Point Air Stations—seventy thousand persons in all—carried out the war exercise, and for the first time practiced unconventional warfare.

Early to Late August 1962

On August 7, 1962, an unusually large number of U.S. naval vessels put out to sea from Jacksonville, Key West, and Guantánamo. According to a recent intelligence report, "one and possibly two Cuban exile groups have acquired B-26–type aircraft and have planned raids on Cuban targets." The aircraft, the report went on, "will head for southern Florida upon completion of raids." So the U.S. ships were in position to lend help if Castro's forces came after the raiders. How the Cuban raiders had obtained the B-26s, the report did not say.

Back in late July, General Lansdale had presented President Kennedy with four possible courses for dealing with Cuba, and JFK had approved "Course B": to "exert all possible diplomatic, economic, psychological, and other pressures to overthrow the Castro regime, without *overt* employment of U.S. military" [emphasis added]. But now, on August 8, 1962, Lansdale after consultation with Robert Kennedy drew up yet another memo. Its subject: "Stepped Up Course B." Meaning? Another document, typed up the same day, discussed the "possibility of a . . . sustained occupation" of Cuba.

But stepping up "Course B" meant something more. During an August 10 meeting in Dean Rusk's office on the seventh floor of the State Department, McCone laid out his reasons for believing that Cuba was getting missiles; and Defense Secretary McNamara raised the thought of murdering Castro.

In a memo he wrote the next day, General Lansdale used the expression "including liquidation of leaders." His immediate assistant, William K. Harvey, in a follow-up memo, persuaded him to delete those four words. Putting such language in writing, Harvey contended, not so tactfully, was inadmissible and stupid.

Over the next week, then, as the U.S. press gleefully pointed out, fifteen new Soviet ships, five of them passenger vessels, reached the ports of Cuba. Some of the ships were being unloaded at night—and they were being unloaded with forty-foot cranes. Trucks pulling away from the piers were covered with tarpaulins.

How the press had learned these facts is unclear. The source, perhaps, was McCone. We do know that, on August 20, 1962, Director McCone told President Kennedy flatly that the Soviets in Cuba were building offensive missile installations.

JFK may have distrusted McCone, but the director was precisely the kind of immensely successful older man to whom Kennedy had always looked up; certainly Kennedy now took McCone's concern seriously. In National Security Action Memorandum #181 of August 23, 1961, Kennedy ordered Joint Chief Chairman Maxwell Taylor to increase "with all possible speed" the actions "projected for Operation Mongoose Plan B plus." Kennedy still was refraining from attacking Cuba overtly. His directive nonetheless allowed the U.S., in the words of one academic historian, to deliberately "seek to provoke a full-scale revolt against Castro that might require U.S. intervention to succeed."

The End of August 1962

Just before midnight on August 24, 1962, two motorboats out of Florida slipped under Cuba's radar screen, edged past a flotilla of Czech-built patrol boats, and, entering Havana Bay, approached the Hotel Icar in suburban Miramar, right by the water's edge. The occupants of the motorboats, exile students trained and equipped by the CIA, pulled up so close that they could see, framed in the light from the hotel's windows, men in uniforms pacing back and forth. Castro, the students knew, often had drinks and dinner in this hotel. So they opened fire, and then fled into the night. The hotel was pockmarked by the shells from the boat.

Castro indeed was present—but unhurt. The next day he sent a formal protest to the United Nations.

And the night after that, August 26, 1962, more boats out of Florida pulled up to the Havana shoreline, attacking the Sierra Maestra Hotel. These attackers, too, escaped.

"There is evidence," the CIA concluded a few weeks later,

> that the Cuban leaders were very fearful of a U.S. attack during the summer months [of 1962]. There were numerous "invasion scares" which reached a peak toward the end of August and then began to level off. As early as . . . June, Cuban officers were reported [word deleted] to be fearful of an attack by the U.S. and pessimistic as to the outcome *unless the invasion took place after September when "the danger will be over"* [emphasis added].

August 29, 1962

At a morning press conference in the State Department auditorium, President Kennedy was visibly shaken: a reporter had asked him about Soviet forces and missiles in Cuba, and about reports of an impending U.S. invasion.

Flustered, he could only stammer a response:

> I'm not for invading Cuba at this time. No, I don't—the words do not have some secondary meaning. I think it would be a mistake to invade Cuba, because I think it would lead to—that it should be very—an action like that, which could be very casually suggested, could lead to very serious consequences for many people.

August 31, 1962

Amid reports that the Soviets had just landed twelve thousand troops in Cuba, Senator Kenneth Keating, the handsome, white-haired U.S. Senator from New York (Rochester), and a Republican, rose from his desk in the Senate. He had in his possession, he told his colleagues, in a speech that immediately flashed out across the wire services, evidence of Soviet "rocket installations in Cuba." He urged Kennedy to take action.

2   *September 1962, the first Week*

The American press smelled blood, Kennedy blood. In its first issue for September, *U.S. News & World Report* stated that Cuba was receiving "Soviet rockets with a range of up to 400 miles." *Time* weighed in with a cover of President James Monroe, and implied that President Kennedy was abandoning the Monroe Doctrine. Writing in *Life*, Clare Boothe Luce, wife of publisher Henry Luce, demanded immediate action:

> Time is running out in Latin America and the cold war is being lost there. . . . What is now at stake in the decision for intervention or non-intervention in Cuba is the question not only of American prestige but of American survival.

Perhaps in response to his critics, President Kennedy on September 4, 1962, admitted in a press conference that the Soviets had many troops in Cuba, as well as surface-to-air missiles. Then he declared:

> There is no evidence of any organized combat force in Cuba from any Soviet bloc country; of military bases provided to Russia; of a violation of the 1934 treaty relating to Guantánamo; of the presence of offensive ground-to-ground missiles; or of other significant offensive capability. . . . Were it otherwise the gravest issues would arise.

The day after this announcement, a U-2 photographed a Soviet MIG jet fighter on a Cuban airstrip. More photographs showed MIGs being unloaded at the ports.

To receive Chairman Khrushchev's response to President Kennedy's September 4, 1962, statement, Theodore Sorensen, JFK's tall and bespectacled speechwriter, rode up Sixteenth Street to the Soviet embassy. There Ambassador Anatoly Dobrynin conveyed the message from Moscow. Assuring Sorensen that all military activity in Cuba was defensive, Dobrynin read, from Khrushchev:

> Nothing will be undertaken that could complicate the international situation or aggravate tension between our two countries . . . *provided*

there are no actions by the other side which could alter the situation
[emphasis added].

Reinforcing this not-so-veiled threat, Khrushchev, who was
vacationing at his dacha at Petsamo, in the Georgian Republic,
entertained a visit from Robert Frost, the poet, and Stuart Udall,
Kennedy's Secretary of the Interior. Making sure that the old
poet was comfortable, Khrushchev drew Udall aside. "Now as
to Cuba," the Soviet leader said,

> —here is an area that could really lead to some unexpected conse-
> quences. . . . [Castro] hasn't much modern military equipment, so he
> asked us to supply some. But only for defense. However, if you attack
> Cuba, that would create an entirely different situation. And it is un-
> thinkable, of course, that a tiny nation like Cuba would ever attack the
> United States.

At the end of the week, the Kennedy administration took two
new steps, one public and the other private. The public step:
President Kennedy asked Congress to allow him to call up 150,-
000 reserves; the reason, said the White House, was the continuing tension over Berlin. The private step: the Air Force's Tactical Air Command "established a planning group charged with
the task of developing a complete air plan; its objective was to
achieve the complete destruction of the Cuban air order of
battle."

September 1962, the Second Week
Politics was going on as usual. Publicly, President Kennedy had
sent in federal troops to ensure the entry of James Meredith, a
young black man, into the University of Mississippi; privately,
he was assuring, or trying to assure, southern white leaders that
his support for civil rights was lukewarm, at best. And the
Defense Department still was calibrating where would lie the
administration's advantage in the matter of the TFX award.

By Labor Day, 1962, Boeing and General Dynamics resembled, in the words of one journalist, "a pair of exhausted run-
ners who had put out all they had into a sprint for the finish line
only to find the tape had been moved a mile farther down the
track. They had been racing at top speed ever since the previous

October. Both had invested a great chunk of their technical resources in the contest—Boeing had a thousand people assigned to the TFX, General Dynamics had made it the sole concern of virtually an entire division (Fort Worth)—and they had committed capital in equal measure. Money was pouring out of their treasuries at the rate of over $1 million a month. Now each had to shore up sagging morale and get on with another lap, one that would be just as long, just as tough . . . as the first." For, having received a pro-Boeing recommendation from his own Source Selection Board—a recommendation based on both price and quality—Secretary McNamara had postponed the contract decision.

Then, on September 11, 1962, Boeing and General Dynamics submitted to the Pentagon their fourth, and last, set of technical proposals. And on October 15 (the same day the U-2s started picking up pictures of the missile sites in Cuba), the Bureau of Naval Weapons announced its preference for the Boeing design.

In fact, Boeing at last seemed to be on the brink of victory: on the "basis of lower quoted costs, greater weapon selectivity and carriage capability, less chance of engine damage from foreign objects, a better deceleration mechanism . . . and superiority in all major operating characteristics," the Source Selection Board now gave its final recommendation to Boeing. So did the Pentagon's Air Council, stating flatly that Boeing's proposal was clearly preferable. And lined up behind Boeing, a reporter commented, was "undoubtedly the most glittering array of top brass since the Japanese surrender ceremonies aboard the battleship *Missouri:* General Curtis LeMay, Chief of Staff of the Air Force; ten assorted generals and admirals of the Air Council; General Walter C. Sweeney [of the Tactical Air Command]; General Mark E. Bradley of Logistics Command; Lt. General Bernard Schriever of Systems Command; Admiral George Anderson, Chief of Naval Operations; Admiral William E. Ellis, Assistant Chief of Naval Operations for Air; Rear Admiral Kleber S. Masterson, Bureau of Weapons; plus the five general and flag officers of the Source Selection Board itself.

Rarely if ever had Washington witnessed such interservice consensus: the brass had favored Boeing *unanimously.* All that remained was the announcement of the award.

Correctly handled, the TFX contract was going to be of major importance in Kennedy's reelection bid. But so was Cuba: Cuba had to be handled correctly. And the Cuban problem was getting out of control.

The *Omsk*, a Russian freighter and the first of the Soviet "large-hatch" vessels, on September 8, 1962, had steamed into the Cuban port of Casilda; it was just the kind of ship that could haul missile equipment. Then, on September 11, 1962, Castro, in a three-hour radio speech picked up in Miami, declared that the United States was "playing with fire and with war." And, simultaneously, TASS, the Soviet news agency, warned that any attack by the United States on Cuba or upon Soviet ships bound for Cuba would mean war. The Soviet paper implied that the war would be nuclear.

In the face of such threats, Robert Kennedy recorded what had to be his brother's worry: "Cuba obtaining [nuclear] missiles from the Soviet Union would create a major political problem here." RFK went on:

> We would have to anticipate there would be surface-to-surface missiles established in Cuba. What was going to be our reaction then?

Time for figuring out that reaction was running short. On September 12, 1962, the biggest headline on the front page of the Cuban newspaper *Revolución* proclaimed: "ROCKETS WILL BLAST THE UNITED STATES IF IT INVADES CUBA!"; on September 12, 1962, Fidel Castro's brother, Raúl, said in a broadcast he himself had given that "the Cuban people will be the last target of imperialist aggression. The first shot will end imperialism." Both boasts reached the U.S. press.

At his own news conference the next day, September 13, 1962, President Kennedy tried to reassert his own toughness. Reading from a prepared statement, but emphasizing its main points with his customary choppy hand gestures, he said that Fidel Castro, "in a frantic effort to bolster his regime," had tried to "arouse the Cuban people by charges of an imminent American invasion." In an effort to reassure the American public, he went on to say that Soviet activities in Cuba presented the U.S. with no serious threat; he denied again that he was hatching a scheme for an invasion of Cuba. He did warn, however, that if Cuba "should ever attempt to export its aggressive purposes by force . . . or become an offensive military base of significant capacity for the Soviet Union, then this country will do whatever must be done to protect its own security and that of its allies."

So by mid-September 1962, all the principals, Kennedy, Khrushchev, and Castro, were rattling their sabers. And none of them, so far, was willing to stop rattling.

September 1962, the Third Week
Midway through the month, U.S. intelligence sources reported, the *Poltava*, another Soviet large-hatch ship, put in at the port of Mariel, just west of Havana. As those sources also reported, from September 15 to 17 longshoremen unloaded the ship's cargo of medium-range ballistic missiles—at least eight missiles—hoisting them aboard convoys bound for San Cristóbal, out toward the island's western tip. On September 17, 1962, U.S., or U.S.-connected intelligence sources, spotted yet another convoy, containing long-trailer trucks, moving out of the port areas and into the western provinces.

Out in the heat and dust of Bakersfield, California, the next day, former Vice President Richard M. Nixon, running for the governorship of the Golden State, thundered against Kennedy: the U.S. *had* to stop the flow of Soviet arms into Cuba, Nixon declared, and to do so, America had to "quarantine" the island. Several Republican senators soon joined in the chorus: Jacob Javits and Kenneth Keating of New York, Barry Goldwater of Arizona, Hugh Scott of Pennsylvania, John Tower of Texas, and Strom Thurmond of South Carolina.

The U.S. Air Force, meanwhile, was getting ready—with a vengeance. Flying out of various air bases in the South, Tactical Air Command aircraft trained for bombing raids on Cuba, even making runs over the water toward the island. The Air Force's target date for the completion of the exercises was October 20, 1962.

A month before then, on September 20, 1962, the *Los Angeles Times* blasted its readers with the headline "MYSTERY CARGO UNLOADED IN CUBA!" "A mysterious Soviet arms shipment to Cuba has U.S. intelligence and defense officials puzzled and concerned," claimed the following article, written by Washington-based correspondents Robert A. Allen and Paul Scott:

A large lead casket, the weight of which left deep tracks in an unpaved road, was unloaded from the Soviet freighter *Hortensia* when it docked at the Cuban port of Casilda on August 9. Accompanied by 800 Soviet military "pallbearers," the heavily guarded cargo was rushed to Banes [in eastern Cuba], which is now ringed by heavy Soviet military and ground-to-air missiles.

The town of Banes and the port of Casilda have been closed for weeks to all Cubans, even Castro's military personnel. More than 500 Cuban families were evacuated from these areas more than three months ago.

The heavy lead casket looked very much like the storage crates used by the U.S. military to ship nuclear warheads from one part of the country to the other, according to a Defense Intelligence Agency's analysis of information from eyewitness Cuban refugees.

According to another U.S. intelligence report, one that reached the Oval Office on September 19, 1962, Fidel Castro's private pilot, after a night of drinking in Havana, had boasted: "We will fight to the death and perhaps we can win because we have everything, including atomic weapons."

The next day, a Defense Intelligence Agency bulletin reported twelve about-to-be-operational surface-to-air missiles sites in Cuba (the New York *Daily News*, to whom the classified bulletin may have been leaked, put the figure at thirteen); and *Krasnaya Zvezda (Red Star)*, the official Soviet military newspaper, stated that, for the defense of Cuba, Russian nuclear submarines were ready to put out to sea.

Then, on September 21, 1962, in the face of more warnings still—in a broadcast on Radio Havana, and relayed by the Baltimore *Sun*—Cuban official Blas Roca declared that the moment the U.S. stepped into Cuba, the "missiles will start functioning"—President Kennedy asked Secretary McNamara for "assurance as to the currency of contingency planning for Cuba"; he also wanted to know how many Americans would die in an assault on the surface-to-air missile sites.

September 1962, the Fourth Week
Kennedy's request to McNamara gave the contingency planning new urgency, especially since, on September 22, 1962,

U.S. planes spotted a Soviet convoy of one tanker, four freighters, and two submarines only two hundred miles northeast of Cuba. Throughout the last week of September 1962, indeed, lights in many Pentagon offices burned all night. And on September 24, 1962, young Marines in Guantánamo started working around the clock to ring the base with new fortifications.

Only two days later Castro announced on television that at Banes, on Cuba's north coast and just above Guantánamo, the Soviets were going to build a fishing port. Because a U-2 almost simultaneously spotted Komar-class (PT-like) Soviet vessels in the waters near Banes, U.S. officials feared that the port would house something more deadly than trawlers.

On September 26, 1962, the U.S. House of Representatives overwhelmingly sanctioned the use of force, if necessary, to restrain Cuban "aggression." On the same day, a U.S. military attaché in Mexico reported that, in the view of senior Mexican officers, the United States was preparing to launch an armed attack against Cuba.

The Mexicans had a point. On September 27, 1962, Air Force Chief of Staff General Curtis LeMay received, and approved, the plan for an air attack on Cuba, a hit to be carried out just before an airborne assault and an amphibious landing.

By the end of the month, Kennedy administration officials must have been feeling unprecedented pressure. On September 28, Navy airplanes spotted on the deck of the Cuba-bound Soviet vessel *Kasimov* crates that clearly contained Soviet IL-28 light bombers, aircraft that could carry nuclear payloads. On September 29, 1962, a U-2 flight over the western end of Cuba, and over the Isle of Pines, just to the south of the main island, photographed a surface-to-air missile site and, on the coast, a cruise missile installation. And on September 30, 1962, *U.S. News & World Report* bespoke the presence of five thousand to ten thousand Soviet troops in Cuba; and, said the magazine, "more are arriving constantly."

On September 30, 1962, Secretary of State Dean Rusk granted a television interview to Howard K. Smith. In his courtly southern voice, Smith asked if the U.S. might close overseas bases in return for a Soviet withdrawal from Cuba. "This is not a negotiable point," Rusk snapped. "You cannot support freedom in one place by surrendering freedom in another."

3   *October 1 to October 4, 1962*

Kicking off the month, Secretary McNamara directed Admiral Robert Dennison, Commander in Chief of the U.S. Atlantic Command, "to be prepared to institute a blockade against Cuba"; Navy and Air Force brass received orders to position equipment and planes for an air strike. "To mask widespread preparations for the actions proposed," McNamara's instructions concluded, ". . . we [should] announce that our forces [are] preparing for an exercise. PHIBRIGLEX 62, a large-scale amphibious assault exercise, [will provide] a cover for our Caribbean preparations."

Meeting the next morning, October 2, 1962, with the Joint Chiefs, McNamara outlined six conditions that would justify a U.S. attack on Cuba:

1. Soviet action against Western rights in Berlin. . . .
2. Evidence that the Castro regime has permitted the positioning of [Soviet] bloc offensive weapons on Cuban soil or in Cuban harbors.
3. An attack against the Guantánamo naval base or against U.S. planes or vessels outside Cuban territorial space or waters [this was the Mongoose scenario].
4. A substantial popular uprising in Cuba, the leaders of which request assistance [also the Mongoose scenario].
5. Cuban armed assistance to subversion in other parts of the Western Hemisphere.
6. A decision by the President that the affairs in Cuba have reached a point inconsistent with continuing U.S. national security.

The last point being a loophole wide enough to fly a Jupiter missile through, McNamara was virtually urging overt action against Cuba. But was he speaking for himself alone? We have no hard evidence that President Kennedy had seen McNamara's directive. We do know, however, that on October 3, 1962, JFK urged McNamara and the Joint Chiefs to intensify plans for an air strike against Cuba and to "wargame" its "effectiveness."

McNamara responded the next day, October 4, 1962, assuring JFK that an air attack could work. The Navy and the Air Force alike, McNamara had written out for Kennedy, have made detailed target studies; target folders are in the hands of crews; and crews are familiar with their assigned targets. As new missile sites are located, they are picked up in the target and attack plans within a few hours of receipt of photographs.

Probably the two men conversed at length on the subject. Certainly Kennedy read McNamara's words with "interest," offering no discouragement.

Another October 4, 1962, meeting indeed found Robert Kennedy on the warpath. Sitting with McCone, Lansdale, and others of the Mongoose group, the attorney general lashed out at McCone's failure so far to topple Castro. This may have been one of the occasions when "Bobby" jabbed his finger in McCone's chest; McCone's own notes refer to his encounter with Robert Kennedy as a "sharp exchange." With or without physical violence, however, Robert Kennedy obtained his, and the President's, wished-for agreement on the need for "more dynamic action," such as capturing Castroite soldiers and mining Cuba's harbors. The group in fact endorsed "all efforts . . . to develop new and imaginative approaches," enabling the U.S. to get "rid of the Castro regime."

October 5 to October 9, 1962
October 5 and 6 were Friday and Saturday, and weekend drivers on four-lane highways out of northern and midwestern states would have noticed the military convoys—olive-drab trucks rumbling along with their headlights on, even in daytime. The U.S. military was starting to move, as Army and Marine troops headed for embarkation centers, airplanes flew south, and trucks built up the supplies of gasoline and oil in Florida bases. One by one great Navy ships were slipping out of Norfolk, steaming south.

After some covert exchanges, the British on October 8, 1962, agreed to let the U.S. store supplies at Mayaguana, in the then-British Bahamas. The British government had insisted on two conditions: that nothing "be put in writing," and that the U.S. not put the Bahamian facilities "to active use," at least not without Great Britain's approval. On the same day, a squadron of Cuban exile commandos hit Cuba's eastern port of Isabela de Sagua, killing twenty persons, including some Russian soldiers.

Sensing the rush to war, Walter Lippmann, the famed columnist, on October 9, 1962, raised a flag of caution. "It is obvious," he had written, "that Castro is being armed against a re-run of the raid on the Bay of Pigs in April, 1961." Then, quoting Winston S. Churchill, he proffered a piece of advice for President Kennedy:

> Those who are prone by temperament and character to seek sharp and clear-cut solutions of difficult and obscure problems, who are ready to fight whenever some challenge comes from a foreign power, have not always been in the right. On the other hand, those whose inclination is to bow their heads, to seek patiently and faithfully for peaceful compromise, are not always wrong. . . . How many wars have been averted by patience and persisting good will. . . . How many wars have been precipitated by firebrands?

October 10 to October 12, 1962

With the congressional elections about three weeks away, President Kennedy came out of the White House on October 10, 1962, lending his own magnetism to the cause of the Democratic candidates. He did not venture far from the capital, only to Baltimore, but he took that city by storm. In the largest political demonstration ever held in Baltimore, more than two hundred thousand people lined the route from Patterson Park, where the presidential helicopter landed, to the Fifth Regiment Armory, where he launched an appeal for the Democrats. Eight thousand onlookers were inside the armory; nearly every time he finished a sentence they cheered and clapped.

The Republicans fired back. While Kennedy was in Baltimore, Senator Keating spoke again in the Capitol; his latest information, he claimed, indicated that the Soviet rockets in Cuba could reach the Panama Canal, or the heart of the United States.

"When are the American people," he demanded, "going to be given all the facts about the military buildup in Cuba?"

While Keating himself spoke, Key West became the target of "high gear" military airlift operations. And to support the invasion plan for Cuba, the Joint Chiefs ordered the transfer of a Marine brigade from the West Coast to the East.

Thursday afternoon, October 11, 1962, found President Kennedy landing at New York's La Guardia Airport; when he appeared at the door of the presidential airplane, the cheering

from the crowd below was tumultuous. At the base of the ramp
was a handsome forty-three-year-old man who fingered his hat
nervously and seemed somewhat lost in the crowd. He was
Robert Morgenthau, the man whom Kennedy had come to help.
Help he would need: faithful ever to the Democratic party (his
father was Henry Morgenthau, Jr., President Roosevelt's Secretary of the Treasury, and his grandfather was Henry Morgenthau, President Wilson's ambassador to the Ottoman Empire),
Robert Morgenthau had taken on the thankless task of trying to
unseat Governor Nelson Rockefeller. He had little chance, but
that fact made no difference: the throng at the airport had come
to see President Kennedy.

Perhaps presidential popularity rises in times of crisis. Cuba
was on many people's minds. But so was Berlin: news reports
were indicating the imminence of a new Berlin crisis.

Meanwhile, the *Independence* moved out of Norfolk, heading for southern waters. McCoy, MacDill, and Homestead Air
Force Bases, all in Florida, were stockpiling war matériel and
stepping up training exercises.

In a special benefit for the Committee for a Democratic Congress, Washington's Ontario Theater in the evening staged the
premiere performance of *The Longest Day*, the film about the
Allied invasion of Normandy; the event had all the fanfare of a
Hollywood Academy Awards night. When actor and songwriter
Paul Anka appeared, women screamed; they shrieked again
when up the red carpet walked Henry Fonda. An ROTC honor
guard from Georgetown University—present because of the pa-
triotism of the event—fired three volleys into the air, and with
bayonets affixed to the ends of their rifles, they started in with
their drill. At that moment, Attorney General and Mrs.
Kennedy appeared; just as he reached the red carpet, Robert
Kennedy managed to get himself nicked by the tip of a flying
bayonet.

Friday morning, October 12, 1962, President Kennedy hit the
campaign trail again, swinging from New York, where he had
spent the night, to New Jersey and Pennsylvania. It was Columbus Day, so speaking in front of the Newark City Hall, he said:
"My grandfather, John F. Fitzgerald, who used to be a mayor of
Boston and was a congressman, used to claim that the Fitz-
geralds actually were Italian and were descended from the Ger-
aldinis, who came from Venice. I have never had the courage to

make that statement, but I make it here on Columbus Day."
The crowd went wild.

Over in Pennsylvania, after several motorcades, Kennedy
spoke for a few moments in Aliquippa. "I come to this community not as a candidate for office," he said, "but I come here to
ask the people to vote Democratic on November 6, 1962."

Even though out of Washington, President Kennedy instructed CIA Director McCone (who also was out of Washington) to distribute further intelligence about the Soviet missiles
in Cuba strictly on a "need to know" basis; JFK was trying to
guard all secrets. At the requests of the Joint Chiefs, meantime,
a Pentagon conference of "operations and logistics planners"
began to work out, for the prospective invasion, "specific actions to be taken to increase readiness and reduce reaction
time."

Off Cárdenas during the night, a Cuban exile boat caught up
with a Castro vessel, attacked it with gunfire, and let it sink.
According to the next morning's Washington Post, the U.S.
government claimed it had no way of guaranteeing the safety of
Cuban shipping against Cuban exile attacks, even if those attacks were launched from American territory.

4   *October 13, 1962*

Using Saturday morning and afternoon to campaign in the Midwest, President Kennedy on October 13, 1962, landed in Louis-
ville, where he spoke at Churchill Downs, the racetrack, and
denounced Homer Capehart, the Republican senator from
across the Ohio River in Indiana. Capehart had called for American armed intervention in Cuba. Looking down at the crowd
that filled the great grass oval, Kennedy claimed that talk such
as Capehart's only "strengthens the claims of our adversaries."
Up in Indianapolis, then, JFK lauded the virtues of Democrat
Birch Bayh, who was trying to unseat Capehart. Vice President
Lyndon B. Johnson, meantime, was off on a seven-state political
tour starting in Florida and ending in Oregon.

Down in Puerto Rico, where muggy weather presaged a hurricane, a spokesman for Alpha 66, the Cuban émigré hit squad,
bragged to reporters that his group was plotting two more raids

soon, including one against British shipping to Cuba. London sent a formal protest to Washington.

5 *October 14, 1962*

After early morning mass in Indianapolis, Kennedy spoke again in support of Birch Bayh, delivering his message at the Indianapolis airport. Gushed *The Washington Post:* "Like his predecessors, Franklin D. Roosevelt and Dwight D. Eisenhower, John F. Kennedy has a magic that can never be fully explained. Like them he irritates and infuriates the opposition and excites the faithful." Late in the morning, he flew back to Washington.

Shortly before the President returned, Secretary of State Dean Rusk was in attendance at the Washington National Airport, waiting to greet Algeria's acting chief of state, Ahmed Ben Bella. Having spoken at the United Nations, Ben Bella had come to Washington to pay his respects to President Kennedy. He stayed at Blair House, just across Pennsylvania Avenue from the White House. The only bothersome point of the Ben Bella visit was that he was scheduled next to visit Cuba.

The Rusk–Ben Bella motorcade whisked past Washington's old Griffith Stadium, where the Washington Redskins were in the process of reaching a 17–17 tie with the St. Louis Cardinals. In a downtown Washington television studio, National Security Adviser McGeorge Bundy was meeting questions on "Issues and Answers." As always he was masterful. "I know there is no present evidence, and I think there is no present likelihood," that Cuba would have a "major offensive capability." He let slip the presence in Cuba of IL-28 aircraft, but he downplayed the significance. "So far," Bundy avowed, "everything that has been delivered to Cuba falls within the categories of aid which the Soviet Union has provided, for example, to neutral countries like Egypt or Indonesia."

That evening, in a scatter-gun battle on the Caribbean, an Alpha 66 crew sank a Cuban patrol boat and brought two wounded prisoners to Miami.

6   *October 15, 1962, the morning and afternoon*
The sky over Cuba for several days had been cloudy, and the
U-2s had stayed at their bases. The morning of Monday, October 15, 1962, however, brought clear weather, and a U-2 camera
soon was recording the missile sites in the western reaches of
Cuba. Developed in Florida, the photos were in Washington by
midafternoon.

Late in the afternoon, Ray Cline, a high-ranking CIA official
whose specialty had been Taiwan but whose acuteness was
known throughout the agency, saw the pictures. He was adamant. The pictures had to go all the way to the top.

Part II
Deception

CHAPTER 8

The Autumn Campaign

1 *October 16, 1962, Tuesday*

After several days of rain, the morning dawned clear in Washington. The sun rose gentle and bright, soon gleaming down on tree leaves that were just starting to yellow. People had no need yet for overcoats and, since the first frost had not yet come, car engines still turned on with ease. From all around the District of Columbia, from the then-rural foothills of Virginia and the Potomac shoreline along the border of Maryland, from the elegant suburbs out past the Washington Cathedral, from the old brick houses of Alexandria, from the tract homes around Arlington, from the vast black slums of the District's two eastern quadrants, the morning rush began, members of Congress and doormen, high civil servants and operators of elevators, military brass and secretaries, lawyers and bureaucrats, lobbyists and reporters, all converged on the city. Traffic was thick. Many turned on their car radios: announcers told of the Yankees' final victory in the World Series the night before, 1 to 0 over the Giants out in Candlestick Park; Connie Francis was singing "Don't Break the Heart That Loves You," and Elvis Presley crooned "Return to Sender"; a voice that spoke in pearly tones described a one-day-only sale on mink hats at Hecht's at Metro Center, Twelfth and G streets; another voice pitched Buick's pride and joy, the new, 1963 Le Sabre ("full-size room for six adults to ride in real easy-chair comfort''), available at area dealerships. The nation's capital was settling in for the second workday of the third week of October 1962.

In their Fifteenth Street offices, two blocks down from McPherson Square, *The Washington Post's* editorial staff, chaired by Ben Bradlee, natty in a striped, English-cut shirt, started the daily ritual, scanning the incoming cables for the placement of the next morning's articles. Two items were of obvious front-page import.

The Soviets had accused the Kennedy administration of fomenting a "war psychology"—this was the year after the building of the Berlin Wall. With that charge looming, furthermore, General Secretary Nikita Khrushchev, the short, stocky, bald-headed mineworker who had clawed his way to the top of the Soviet system, had summoned new U.S. Ambassador Foy Kohler for a three-hour dressing down. According to Radio Moscow, the session had taken place in an "atmosphere of sincerity and mutual understanding." Khrushchev, actually, had used the conference to storm against the buildup of U.S. bases in Italy and Turkey; he then had insisted that Soviet activities in Cuba were strictly defensive. This article would go front page, top left.

Another piece soon flashed into the *Post's* offices, this one datelined Havana. After a visit to the White House, Ahmed Ben Bella, the Algerian premier, had flown to Cuba. Mounting a podium beside Fidel Castro, he had declared that "Algeria is and will be with Cuba."

From New Jersey, in the course of the day, came the results of the latest Gallup Poll. Rumor had it that the United States was about to invade Cuba but the American public, Gallup's pollsters had discovered, was nervous: Gallup's interviewees did *not* think that the Cubans themselves would topple Castro, but they *did* fear (by a 51 percent majority) that an invasion of Cuba would bring war between America and Russia.

Another item, which would end up on the second page, top, sent *Post* photographers, along with television network crews, scurrying to the Oval Office. For at midmorning, Walter Schirra, his wife, and his two blond-haired children, a girl and a boy, were scheduled to meet with the President.

Only days before, Schirra, an astronaut, had made a much-heralded Pacific splashdown. His six orbits around the earth had proceeded smoothly enough: given his weightless condition, he had radioed down at one point, "I suppose the song 'Drifting and Dreaming' would be apropos"; and over Ecuador, he had broadcast a cheery "*Buenos días,* y'all!" Still, his space suit had overheated dangerously. The White House had said by telephone after the landing, "You did a wonderful job, and we are very, very pleased." So now, on the morning of October 16, Commander Schirra, tanned, short-haired, and attired in a dark civilian suit, was chatting with the President.

As the cameramen squinted and clicked, John Kennedy, resting his back in his white-cushioned rocking chair, smiled at the family seated on the sofa just to his right, and ended up giving them a full eighteen minutes. Rising then, he led them out on to the White House lawn; there the children petted Macaroni, the pony of his own daughter, Caroline. JFK gave no hint of the presence of missiles in Cuba.

At least he did not do so that morning, in public.

"On Tuesday morning, October 16, 1962, shortly after 9:00, President Kennedy called and asked me to come to the White House. He said only that we were facing great trouble."

Thus began the missile-crisis memoir of Robert F. Kennedy. Responding immediately to his brother's request, the attorney general raced by limousine from his Justice Department office down Pennsylvania Avenue to a back entrance of the White House. The President told him the news. "I had no doubt," Robert Kennedy later recalled, "we were moving into a serious crisis."

That same morning, President Kennedy also telephoned John J. McCloy, a Republican, a New York attorney, with a home in Stamford, Connecticut, and a member-in-good-standing of America's foreign-policy establishment. McCloy sometimes bridled at being called "establishment." Beefy and athletic as a lad, he had been born on Philadelphia's North Nineteenth Street, a working-class neighborhood; and he had had to fight his way for an education, first at Amherst College and then at Harvard Law School. But establishment he did become—as personal attorney for the Rockefeller family; as Assistant Secretary of War under

War Secretary Henry L. Stimson, just before and then during World War II; as the U.S. High Commissioner to Germany after the war; and, on behalf of the Kennedy administration, as chief lobbyist on Capitol Hill for the creation of the Arms Control and Disarmament Agency.

Like his old mentor, Henry L. Stimson, McCloy was, in foreign policy, a hard-liner. Although he was about to fly off on legal business to Europe, he told the President, he would be back within the week. In the meantime, since JFK had asked, McCloy had one piece of advice about the missiles in Cuba: act, act fast, and act with force.

Just before the general meeting he had called convened, President Kennedy also conferred, in the White House, with Charles Bohlen, formerly the ambassador to Russia and presently the just-confirmed ambassador to France. Tall, elegant, and charming, with an impeccable educational background and an unsurpassed knowledge of Kremlin politics, Bohlen, like his friend McCloy, was a pillar of the foreign policy establishment. JFK made it a point to tell him of the missiles.

As sunlight streamed across the President's desk, Bohlen had a clear impression of Kennedy's thoughts. "[T]here seemed to be no doubt in [JFK's] mind, and certainly none in mine, that the United States would have to get these [missile] bases eliminated. . . . [T]he only question was how it was to be done."

Few, if any, of the men assembling in the Cabinet Room late in the morning of October 16, 1962, were likely to disagree. These men, the core of what would be called the Executive Committee of the National Security Council, or Excomm, were all, in one degree or another, controllable:

Ambassador Charles ("Chip") Bohlen was present just for the day.

U. Alexis Johnson, Deputy Undersecretary of the State for Political Affairs, was a bit down the pyramid of Executive Branch power.

Lyndon B. Johnson, oversized of height, girth, ego, and ambition, was, at the moment, only the Vice President. Like Victorian-era children, American Vice Presidents were best seen and not heard.

McGeorge Bundy, the National Security Adviser, with cold

eye and slashing mind, had his very roots in the tradition of interventionism: his father, Harvey Bundy, had been an aide to Henry L. Stimson in the Roosevelt War Department; and "Mac" himself, once a Junior Fellow at Harvard, had collaborated with Stimson on the old statesman's memoirs, *On Active Service in Peace and War.* McGeorge Bundy, to be sure, was toady to no one, not even to the President of the United States: "Goddammit, Mac," someone had heard Kennedy exclaim, "I've been arguing with you about this all week long." Consonant with his upbringing, nonetheless, Bundy was devoted to duty, and as National Security Adviser, his duty was to serve the interests of the President.

Roswell Gilpatric, the Deputy Secretary of Defense, and George Ball, his counterpart in the State Department, were both distinguished and wealthy New York lawyers. At the moment, however, they played secondary roles, expected to support their principals, the Secretaries of Defense and State.

Edward M. Martin, a State Department specialist in Latin America, was subordinate to George Ball.

General Marshall S. Carter had come over from the Central Intelligence Agency, but there he was only second in command. (John A. McCone, appointed CIA director by Kennedy, was not present; a widower, he had flown to the West Coast for a new marriage.)

General Maxwell Taylor, the trim, crisp, and handsome Chairman of the Joint Chiefs of Staff, had struck some people as a rebel—back in the Eisenhower era he had got into trouble advocating a "flexible response" for the military in place of the then-prevailing doctrine of "massive retaliation." Yet to President Kennedy, Taylor's principle, stressing speed and surprise, had seemed a blazing call to action. Taylor, whom Kennedy had picked as Chairman over dozens of higher ranking brass, was loyal to the Chief.

Theodore Sorensen, clean-cut, dark-haired, was the presidential speechwriter and scribe.

Bostonian Kenneth O'Donnell, lean, slight, dark, and buddy of Robert Kennedy from Harvard football days, was a political operative, not a framer of policy.

C. Douglas Dillon, who had met John Kennedy at Harvard, was a Republican, a Wall Street banker, and Secretary of the Treasury; his military knowledge was slight.

Besides two officers from the CIA, Robert Kennedy, and Eve-lyn Woods, JFK's private secretary, that left only two more original Excomm members, Secretary of State Dean Rusk and Secretary of Defense Robert McNamara.

Rusk. Tall, balding, inclining toward the rotund, Rusk was middle of age, balanced of view, and placid of manner. He seemed so dull, in fact, that McGeorge Bundy had opposed him for the Secretaryship, convinced that Rusk's was a second-rate mind. Rusk, actually, was keenly intelligent, for he had been a Rhodes Scholar; and he was ambitious enough to have become, with the support of President Eisenhower's Secretary of State, John Foster Dulles, head of the Rockefeller Foundation. Rusk was quiet, controlled, anything but a maverick.

And McNamara. A driven man, he had risen like a meteor from a business professorship at Harvard to the presidency of the Ford Motor Company. He did have an independent streak. Rather than live among other automotive executives in the Grosse Pointes, he and his wife, Marg, had bought a mansion off Washtenaw Avenue in Ann Arbor; the environs of the University of Michigan had held out more promise of culture than had the gilded ghetto on riverfront Detroit. Once in Washington, as Kennedy's Secretary of Defense, he had shown this same independence. With his lean frame, rimless glasses, slicked-back black hair, and keen mathematical mind, he had become the scourge of the services, imposing unity, tightening budgets, eliminating waste, and always—always—clicking out statistics. The military of course had howled, and the howling had echoed all the way down to the two-week summer camps of the Army and Navy Reserves. McNamara had remained undeterred. As a representative of the White House, his job was to render the American forces—with their cooperation if possible but against their wishes if necessary—lean, mean, ready to move, all on behalf of the President.

A few others would join Excomm, but this list constituted its core, and Kennedy had picked it with care. The full National Security Council, established by Congress in 1947, made him uncomfortable. It was large, hard to manage, and leaky. But Excomm, especially with Robert Kennedy hovering in the background, gave JFK just what he needed, a small, cohesive, and controllable group that represented political support for the action he craved.

As the President had ordered, Excomm held its first meeting in the Cabinet Room at 11:45 A.M. A tape recorder was running.

After the President had entered and sat, his daughter, Caroline, came in; he spoke a few words with her, and the men around the table chuckled. She left. Then Arthur Lundahl one of the CIA officers, spoke up, confirming the existence of a medium-range ballistic missile site in west central Cuba. The missiles, housed in canvas-covered trailers, were identifiable by their length. The U-2 photographs revealed no nuclear warheads.

When the intelligence briefing was finished and the CIA officers departed, Dean Rusk spoke up. President Kennedy was seated at the middle of the table, just across from Rusk, his back to the sun from the windows. "Mr. President," Rusk said, "this is, of course, a . . . serious development. . . . I . . . think we have to set in motion a chain of events that will eliminate [the launch site]. I don't think we can sit still. The questioning becomes whether we do it by [a] sudden, unannounced strike of some sort, or we build up the crisis to the point where the other side has to consider very seriously about giving in."

General Maxwell Taylor chimed in; he was seated in a brass-studded, black leather armchair near the end of the table. "[W]e're impressed, Mr. President," he said, "with the great importance of getting a . . . strike with all the benefit of surprise. . . . Hit 'em without any warning whatsoever."

Perhaps worried, President Kennedy here raised, briefly, the question of Soviet motives. The transcript catches his manner of speech: "What is the, uh, advant—. . . . Must be that they're not satisfied with their ICBMs [Inter-Continental Ballistic Missiles]. What'd be the reason that they would, uh . . . ?"

General Taylor was quick with an answer: "What it'd give them is . . . [a] launching base for short-range missiles against the United States to supplement their . . . ICBM system." In General Taylor's expressed judgment, the balance of terror might well tilt in favor of Russia.

A few moments later, Secretary Rusk lent support to Taylor's contention. If the Russians "could provoke us into taking the first overt action," Rusk said in his soft Georgia accent, "then . . . they would . . . what they would consider justification for making a move somewhere else."

In a chair close to Rusk's, "Mac" Bundy added his bit: "It's important, I think, to recognize that they did make this decision [to put the missiles in Cuba], as far as our estimates now go, in early summer, and this has been happening since August."

Soon after Bundy's statement, we encounter another voice, coming through on the transcript: "Uh, eh, well, this, which . . . ;" President Kennedy was speaking. He was starting to tick off options: "One is the strike just in these three bases . . . ," he was saying. "[T]he second is the broader one . . . on the airfields and on . . . anything else connected with, uh, missiles. Third, is doing both of those things and also . . . launching a blockade. . . ."

Leaning forward over the table, close by Bundy and Rusk, the President's brother now spoke. "We have [another choice], really," Robert Kennedy said, "which is the invasion." He had not said "an" invasion; he had said "the" invasion.

RFK also passed a note to his brother: "I now know," the message stated, "how Tojo felt when he was planning Pearl Harbor."

Bundy then requested that subsequent Excomm meetings be secret, described to anyone who did learn of them as "intensive budget review sessions." The group disbanded, for the moment, at 12:57 P.M.

But Robert Kennedy's note was curious. Did he mean that America was plotting its own day of infamy? Did he mean that America, like Japan in 1941, had embarked on a mission ultimately self-defeating? Did he mean that he and his brother were accepting great political risks?

2   After the morning Excomm meeting disbanded, John and Robert Kennedy walked back together toward the Executive Mansion. The President was due to host a luncheon for Hasan al-Rida al-Sanusi, the thirty-four-year old Crown Prince of Libya. Libya was a U.S. ally; and Crown Prince Hasan, expected to succeed his uncle, King Idris, was his country's first official visitor to the United States. So the luncheon, attended by several high U.S. officials and half a dozen Libyans, was an important affair.

In a toast at the luncheon, wrote Marie Smith, society reporter for *The Washington Post*, "President Kennedy told the royal visitor the hospitality his country has shown Americans who served in military and civilian capacities in Libya is 'well known here' and 'warmly appreciated.' Most of us," the President added, "have not been to your country," but it has "played a part in our history" and the " 'Shores of Tripoli' are well known to all of us." In his reply, Prince Hasan expressed hope that, together, the United States and Libya would "play a great and important" role in establishing throughout the world the principles of justice and peace. Just over five feet tall, the Prince wore a black braid-trimmed robe and a red fez with a black tassel. President Kennedy did not get back to the Oval Office until 3:57 P.M.

Almost immediately, then, he rode by limousine to the State Department to address a conference of editors. His speech was full of platitudes; only once, at the end, did he allude to anything exceptional going on. He quoted a passage from Robert Graves, the English poet:

> Bullfight critics row on row
> Crowd the enormous plaza de toros;
> But only one is there who knows,
> And he is the one who fights the bull.

Then, amid the sounds of puzzled laughter, he returned to 1600 Pennsylvania Avenue for late afternoon chit-chat, again with the Libyan Crown Prince. To editors and Libyans alike, he conveyed the impression of calm.

Over in Foggy Bottom, however, where the blocky State Department building rises high among the rows of narrow, nineteenth-century townhouses, Secretary Rusk, Undersecretary Ball, Assistant Secretary Edwin Martin, Deputy Undersecretary Johnson, Soviet specialist (and until recently Ambassador to Russia) Thompson, and United Nations Ambassador Adlai Stevenson all met in intense midafternoon conversation. Exchanging ideas, they prepared for the President a memorandum entitled "What Course of Action Should We Follow If Construction on Missile Sites Continues?" Rusk also consulted with an afternoon visitor, the tall, elegant, mustached former Secretary of State and current Democratic elder statesman, Dean G. Acheson, who had been driven down from his Maryland farm. Henceforth a full participant in the Excomm sessions, Acheson was cautious. Until more information was available about the nature of the missiles, he refused to recommend any specific action. Still, he felt a sense of urgency—the administration, in his judgment, hardly could sit back and wait for the missiles to be armed with nuclear tips.

At dusk, as the lamps came on along the Ellipse and down around the Jefferson Memorial, the members of Excomm again filed into the Cabinet Room. They had gained two new colleagues: Paul Nitze, physically fit, tanned, with thick, wavy white hair, a former Wall Street banker, then Dean Acheson's brilliant protégé at State and now one of Robert McNamara's assistant secretaries; and Adlai Stevenson, who had flown down from New York for the White House luncheon. Kennedy had invited Stevenson to take part in Excomm.

Why Stevenson? He had, after all, little in common with Kennedy. After his abortive bids for the presidency, Stevenson had become bloated, putting on so much weight around his hips and his butt that he waddled. In the Kennedys' judgment, he was mentally soft as well: when JFK told him, early in the afternoon of October 16, of the missiles in Cuba, Stevenson reportedly responded, "Let's not go to an air strike until we have explored the possibilities for a peaceful solution." Stevenson nonetheless had his uses. Still the darling of the Democratic liberals, he was JFK's insurance against too much sniping from the left. So here he was, Illinois's former governor, Adlai Stevenson, once the giant of the Democratic party, squeezing himself into a chair alongside a dozen or so other Democrats (and some Republicans), all of whom were far more powerful than he and who barely managed to acknowledge his presence.

Then the President entered, taking his own seat at the middle of the long, gleaming Cabinet table. Under the gaze of Gilbert Stuart's oil portrait of George Washington, Excomm's second meeting began. The time was 6:30 P.M.

3   The first words of the session, President Kennedy's, were: "Uh, anything in 'em?" The President was referring to the newest U-2 photographs from over Cuba, taken at his directive that afternoon.

"Nothing in the additional film, sir," responded Marshall Carter of the CIA. "[But we] have a much better reading on what we had. . . . There's good evidence of . . . a capability of from sixteen or possibly twenty-four missiles."

Obviously looking over a display of photographs and maps, JFK said: "Uh, General, how long would you say we had, uh, before these—at least to the best of your ability for the ones we now know—will be ready to fire?"

"Well," General Carter stated, "our people estimate that these could be operational within two weeks." A single missile, he added, might achieve operational capability "much sooner."

Half a dozen more pages of the transcript are devoted to discussions of the photographs. And only then did Secretary McNamara take the floor. Even just reading the transcript, you can hear his precise, mathematical drone.

"Mr. President," he was asking, "could I outline three courses—"

"Yes," Kennedy said.

"—of action we have considered," the Defense Secretary continued, "and speak very briefly on each one? The first is what I would call the political course of action"—diplomatic communications with Castro and Khrushchev. Having raised this choice, however, McNamara dismissed it. "This [option]," he stated, "seem[s] to me likely to lead to no satisfactory result, *and it almost stops subsequent military action* [emphasis added]. . . ."

A second course, he then said, "would involve declaration of open surveillance [and] a blockade against *offensive* weapons entering Cuba in the future."

At this point, McGeorge Bundy and Robert McNamara engaged in a brief conversation. What they said, however, we do not know. The words are blacked out; in the lingo of the CIA, the transcript has been "sanitized."

The third course was military, meaning a massive aerial assault. "The Chiefs," McNamara declared, "are strongly opposed to [a] limited air attack. [They are thinking not of] twenty or fifty sorties or a hundred sorties, but probably several hundred sorties." "Such an assault on Cuba," the Defense Secretary acknowledged, almost certainly "will lead to a Soviet military response of some type someplace in the world. It may well be worth the price.''

What was that price? Alongside the massive air strike, McNamara urged, the United States should stage a ''large-scale mobilization, a *very* large-scale mobilization [emphasis in the transcript], *certainly exceeding the limits of the authority we have from Congress* [emphasis added].'' The Kennedy administration, McNamara was proposing, should violate the will of Congress.

From across the Cabinet table, Robert Kennedy added a point. ''Of course, the other problem is . . . in South America a year from now,'' he said. ''And the fact that you've got . . . *these* things [the missiles] in the hands of the Cubans . . . some problem arises in Venezuela, . . . you've got Castro saying, 'You move troops down into that part of Venezuela, we're going to fire those missiles.' '' The missiles, actually, were in Russian hands. RFK feared nonetheless that, armed with missiles, Cuba might deter America's ability to wage banana wars. Of McNamara's suggestion that the administration start what in effect was war, and do so without a congressional declaration, Robert Kennedy offered no dissent.

The U.S. Constitution was one thing and tactics were another; and Excomm's deliberations soon narrowed to tactical questions. Should the U.S. launch an air strike, specifically against the missiles? The missiles were mobile and could be pulled ''in under trees and forest,'' General Taylor warned, and so the results might be disappointing. Should the strike be more general, including an attack by land, air, and sea against Havana? No one turned the idea down, but President Kennedy did wonder about the existence of Cuban antiaircraft units. Should Cuba be blockaded? ''Then,'' Robert Kennedy commented, ''we're gonna have to sink Russian ships.''

Any steps, therefore, involved risks. Determined, however, to do *something*, President Kennedy raised the issue of readiness. General Taylor was reassuring, speaking of ''air defense measures'' previously taken. We have ''moved fighters into the southeastern United States,'' he reminded the President, and we are ''gradually improving . . . our patrol procedures . . . *under the guise* [emphasis added] of . . . preparations for that part of the country." McNamara added: "I believe that military planning has been carried on for a considerable period of time . . . [it is] is well underway."

Toward the end of the meeting, Bundy asked Secretary McNamara about the missiles' probable effect on American-Soviet relations, and McNamara replied that, in the opinion of the Joint Chiefs, the impact would be substantial. Yet he then conceded: "I don't think there is a military problem here. . . . [T]his is a domestic, political problem." McNamara's expertise had not lain in politics. So he may have been suggesting that the missiles in Cuba were, after all, defensive.

The meeting adjourned at 7:55 P.M. As the members rode off on their separate ways in the darkness, one point was clear: scorning Adlai Stevenson's hope for a "peaceful solution," the Kennedy government was opting for the use of force; and by using force, the administration was hoping to improve Democratic chances in the November election.

Seated under the portrait of Benjamin Franklin in the Green Room that evening, Secretary and Mrs. Rusk hosted a state dinner for Libya's Prince Hasan; the Prince and his aides had been staying across Pennsylvania Avenue in Blair House. The Prince was in good spirits, doing something, commented *The Washington Post*, "that is not the accepted practice in his own country in northern Africa. He shook the hands of all the ladies who came down the receiving line and spoke a few words to each in French. No curtsies were in order, not even from the beautifully dressed wife of Libyan Ambassador Mohieddine Fekini. Mme. Fekini, dressed in an exquisite pale blue Western evening gown, ornamented with a bead fringe, shook hands, like everyone else, with the man who will be her country's next King. . . . Among the 106 men and women seated at the beautifully decorated horse-show table . . . included the Chief Justice and Mrs. Earl Warren, the Secretary of Health, Education and Welfare and Mrs. Anthony Celebrezze, and the Secretary of the Air Force and Mrs. Eugene M. Zuckert. . . . Before the toasts of good will by Secretary Rusk and the Prince, guests dined on consommé, filet of sole, roast duck with orange sauce, braised celery and potatoes, Bibb lettuce salad, and fresh fruit Roman-off. At the end of the dinner, Prince Hasan said he had sensed deep affection for his country in his talks with President Kennedy earlier in the day."

President and Mrs. Kennedy were apart from the group, dining privately with Mr. and Mrs. Joseph W. Alsop. One of America's preeminent journalists, Alsop, a distant cousin of President Franklin D. Roosevelt, had been a participant, even before Pearl Harbor, in General Claire Chennault's American Volunteer Group of aviators out in the China theater. Now he wrote a nationally syndicated column. He was steady of gaze, natty of dress, and hawkish of view.

Did JFK discuss the missiles with Alsop? The dinner conversation, according to the presidential appointment book, now available, was "off the record." In his column, nonetheless, Alsop soon emerged as one of Kennedy's staunchest supporters.

After the dinner in the Green Room was over, and the Libyans escorted back to Blair House, Secretary Rusk went straight to the State Department; his seventh-floor office windows were lighted until well after 11:00. In conference with his closest aides, Rusk made one determination. For the moment, at least, the presence of the missiles in Cuba was supposed to be secret.

So most of Washington that night, October 16, 1962, seemed perfectly normal. The Bayou, a striptease joint at 3135 K Street, featured a string of young women described on the marquee as the "Foggy Bottom Six." *West Side Story* was showing at the Warner Theater on Eleventh Street; at the Apex on Massachusetts Avenue, Peter Sellers and Margaret Leighton were starring in the *Waltz of the Toreadors.* For the higher-minded, Vladimir Ashkenazy, who had just won the Tchaikovsky Prize in piano, was performing in Constitution Hall, a bit down Seventeenth Street from the Old Executive Office Building; the featured soloist for the National Symphony's season's opening, he played Prokofiev, then the Soviet favorite, Shostakovich, and, finally, Beethoven's *Emperor* Concerto. The evening was a black-tie affair with two representatives from the administration, Labor Secretary W. Willard Wirtz and his wife, and Presidential Assistant-Professor Arthur M. Schlesinger, Jr., and his wife. For the less exalted, television offered some classic choices: Jack Benny or "The Untouchables" at 9:30; "The Garry Moore Show" at 10:00; Sid Caesar at 10:30. From 11:00 to 11:30, area news junkies picked up Ray Scherere and Martin Agronsky on NBC's "Commentary"; their news round-up said nothing of missiles in Cuba. Nor, of course, did Johnny Carson, at 11:30. But, by then, most people in the Washington area had gone to bed.

Most, that is, except for the Secret Service, preparing throughout the night for the President's trip of the morrow. October 17 was going to be a busy day for President Kennedy. Scheduled to make campaign speeches in Connecticut and New York, he would have to postpone until evening any further meetings with Excomm.

He was determined to maintain appearances. He wanted to keep the secret.

4   *October 17, 1962*

Pulling out of the CIA's fortresslike complex in northern Virginia and streaking down the George Washington Parkway, an automobile was fast approaching the District. The morning sky was cloudy, and as the vehicle crossed the Theodore Roosevelt Bridge, the river below was gray. Moments after it had passed the State Department, the car was wheeling up alongside the Ellipse toward the White House. People relaxing in Lafayette Park might have noticed the auto's arrival as it turned in through the right front gate of the White House, but they scarcely could have known its importance: it was a Buick of nondescript color and, with its Dynaflow holes by the side of the engine, it looked like hundreds of other Buicks that regularly plied the streets of downtown Washington. This Buick, however, was special. It was extra-heavy, for its chassis and doors were armored, and its windows were made of bulletproof glass. And the occupant of its rear seat was the Director of the CIA, John McCone. Under the North Portico of the White House, McCone got out of the car.

Back in early October 1962, while vacationing at the Hammersmith mansion in Newport, Rhode Island, Kennedy had introduced McCone, fifty-nine, to the press as the new CIA chief. From the President's viewpoint, McCone was an ideal choice. Canny and tough, he was widely respected in Washington: a founder of the Bechtel-McCone engineering firm, McCone during World War II had made $44 million. Later he chaired the Atomic Energy Commission. If Allen Dulles was known as a kindly-looking pipe smoker, then McCone was feared as one who, provoked, could turn the air blue. He was a prodigious worker with a steel-trap mind. He was, furthermore, a Republican. Like his exemplar in politics, Franklin D. Roosevelt, Kennedy knew the value of bringing the other party into government, especially in a time of tension.

The tension scarcely could have been more acute than it was on the morning of Wednesday, October 17, 1962, when McCone reached the White House. Having flown back in the night from the West Coast, he had received a briefing at the agency's Langley headquarters, and now, at 9:35 A.M. at the White House, he was about to be a full participant in Excomm. He talked with Bundy, then rode straight to the State Department.

At about the time of McCone's departure from the White House, another car pulled up under the Portico. This automobile was a black limousine, a Mercedes-Benz, and it had driven down from the German embassy, housed then in a stone mansion on the tree-shaded corner of R Street and New Hampshire Avenue. As a White House attendant opened the car's rear door, Dr. Gerhard Schröder, West Germany's foreign minister, stepped out.

Schröder had become a political star. Son of a minor railroad official in Germany, he had been the perennial head of his class, still possessing, said his enemies back home, a top pupil's condescending manner. But to one person at least he must have been ingratiating—West Germany's Chancellor Konrad Adenauer. Adenauer had been Schröder's champion; in the West German capital, Schröder was called, behind his back, "Bonn's oldest young man." With his trim form and smooth dark hair, he resembled a male model. He was also tough, and he had flown to Washington to represent Adenauer on a most urgent mission, one having to do with Berlin.

Berlin had been a perennial trouble spot: the Wall had gone

up the year before Schröder's visit and, in the autumn of 1962, the city seemed on the brink of a crisis again. American and Soviet commanders had been squabbling anew over whether U.S. bombers had violated East German airspace and whether Soviet border guards had restricted access unlawfully. Would the two sides start shooting? In Washington, administration officials were giving out that, come winter, the U.S. might find itself at war. Commented *The Washington Post* in an article about Schröder's visit: "The most intriguing foreign policy question in Washington today is why the Kennedy administration has raised a public cry about a coming Berlin crisis. . . . Some American experts say that the bits and pieces of evidence thus far do point to a new round of Soviet pressure. Other experts and many of America's allies disagree. JFK, Rusk, McNamara, and an assortment of top aides all share the crisis hunch. There is another aspect, too, and that concerns the U.S. election. The Republicans have made Cuba a major issue and the administration is being beleaguered across the land. New crisis talk from Washington about Berlin in these final three weeks of the campaign would take some of the edge off Cuba as an issue. Of course no one admits out loud that the Berlin crisis talk has a domestic political reason but Washington cynics see it that way."

Over in Bonn, however, Chancellor Adenauer, the wizened old fox, had his own reason for alarm. His nominal ally, President Charles de Gaulle, the intransigent wartime hero of the French nation, was cutting loose his moorings in the North Atlantic Treaty Organization. NATO was American-run, but America, de Gaulle was intimating with ever-growing plainness, no longer should be master of Europe. The Kennedy administration, in turn, was manifesting an ever-growing hostility toward de Gaulle. (A secret CIA report, signed by Director McCone on September 7, 1962, was entitled "Consequences of the Death or Assassination of de Gaulle." The memorandum shied away from any recommendation of murder. It did state nonetheless that any "successor to de Gaulle would, of course, be unable to command the unique authority enjoyed by his predecessor. . . .") Feeling caught in the middle, therefore, Adenauer wanted to know—was NATO unraveling? Would Kennedy be steady on Berlin?

Followed into the White House by an entourage of German

officials, Gerhard Schröder had come to find out. He need not have worried.

Again, we have no transcript. Yet we do possess President Kennedy's notes and doodles, scrawled over a piece of White House stationery. Some of the markings reveal nothing, just squares overlapping squares and rectangles enveloping words. But the words, where we can decipher them, are "military defeat," "access," "psychological . . . pressures"; and then "action, action, action." Schröder left the White House at 10:30 A.M.

In the midst of the racket and hubbub in the World War II–vintage terminal of the Washington National Airport, a loudspeaker squawked: "Will Mr. Charles Bohlen please report. . . ." About to depart for Paris, Ambassador Bohlen made his way to a telephone. On the line was the tense, combative, Boston-Irish accented voice of Kenneth O'Donnell, the wiry little Kennedy operative. "The President," O'Donnell snapped from his own telephone in the White House, "wants you to sit in the [Excomm] meetings."

Handsome and gracious, Bohlen handled O'Donnell with ease. It was actually in the President's best interest, the ambassador explained, that the U.S. have Bohlen in Paris as scheduled; anything else would alert the press, suggesting that something unusual was going on; Kennedy thus would lose any advantage of surprise. Before O'Donnell could raise a protest, Bohlen pointed out that he had left his recommendations with Secretary Rusk. We have Bohlen's notes: ". . . it seems to me essential," he had written, that this channel [diplomacy] should be tested out before military action is used." He had emphasized, however, that the missiles simply *had* to come out of Cuba. So informing O'Donnell, Bohlen hung up, and soon his airplane was banking through the clouds above the Potomac River toward New York. From there he would proceed to Europe.

Adlai Stevenson's departure from Washington caused little distress in the White House. Due back at the United Nations,

Stevenson had taken time, in his Mayflower Hotel suite, to write a letter to President Kennedy:

Dear Mr. President,

I have reviewed the planning thus far and have the following comments for you:

. . . Because an attack [on Cuba] would very likely result in Soviet reprisals somewhere—Turkey, Berlin, etc.—it is most important that we have as much of the world with us as possible. . . . We must be prepared for the widespread reaction that if we have a missile base in Turkey and other places around the Soviet Union surely they have a right to one in Cuba. If we attack Cuba, an ally of the U.S.S.R., isn't an attack on NATO bases equally justified? One could go on and on. . . . I know your dilemma is to strike before the Cuban sites are operational or to risk waiting until a proper groundwork of justification can be prepared. The national security must come first. *But the means adopted have such incalculable consequences that I feel you should have made it clear that the existence of nuclear missile bases anywhere is negotiable before we start anything* [Stevenson's emphasis].

JFK read this letter as being the height of presumption. Adlai Stevenson, even more than before, was on the outs.

At some point late in the morning, a coded message from Moscow flashed into the Soviet embassy. Situated on Sixteenth Street, a half-dozen blocks straight north from the White House, and protected by a heavy, black wrought-iron fence, the building had a foreboding air: window shades across its four-story gray-stone façade were kept drawn, and its gray-green mansard roof bristled with the branches of antennae. This morning's particular communication had come from no one less than Soviet Premier Nikita Khrushchev, and it was intended for Georgi Bolshakov, a diplomat who enjoyed behind-the-scenes access to Robert F. Kennedy. Bolshakov's job was to slip out, passing a Khrushchev memorandum to the President's brother.

Wily peasant that he was, Khrushchev had intended his wording at once to warn and to lull. The Soviet Union, Bolshakov was to convey to the attorney general, was sending weaponry to

Cuba, but for defensive purposes alone. Khrushchev had made no mention of missiles.

The State Department Building, a few wags had noted, was almost Soviet in style. Newly built, it stood out in stark contrast to the brick apartments and seedy townhouses of old Foggy Bottom. Seen from the front, on C Street, the structure seemed mammoth, a huge sandstone rectangle punctuated with smaller rectangles that were windows. A stainless-steel overhang shadowed the glass front doors, as in Soviet hotels; and on the morning of October 17, 1962, a long row of black limousines filled the driveway in front of the doors. For Excomm had resumed its deliberations, this time in Undersecretary of State George Ball's conference room upstairs on the seventh floor. Directly across the hall from Ball's office, the room was windowless, with "leather arm chairs marching in straight rows on either side of a long table." The style suggested the "lowest common denominator agreed upon in a committee of warring decorators." Yet the chamber did have one advantage: George Ball, a big, rumpled-looking man, and Dean Rusk, whose office also was on the seventh floor, could pop in whenever their duties allowed.

The committee—minus President Kennedy, Vice President Johnson, and Ambassador Stevenson, and plus CIA Director John McCone and former Secretary of State Dean Acheson—assembled in what one document called a "blur of meetings." People came and went, the journalist Elie Abel recounted, "some talking, some scribbling notes. Dean Acheson . . . found it all rather formless and confused. When someone was hungry, sandwiches and coffee were sent for. It may have been by tactful design, but, more likely, was a product of the random comings and goings, that Acheson and Adlai Stevenson—who despised each other—never found themselves in the room at the same time. . . . Acheson, long before the missile crisis, had marked Stevenson down as woolly-minded and soft. Stevenson, for his part, tended to put Acheson in the 'warhawk' party. . . . Dean Rusk—the senior Cabinet officer and, in a sense, the host—refused to exercise the chairman's function."

Yet out of this chaos, a pattern did emerge; Robert Kennedy took over as discussion leader, or just whip. Necktie loosened, shirtsleeves rolled up, his fingers ever ready to jab somebody in the middle of the chest, the youthful-looking RFK challenged one older speaker after another, asking questions that were pointed, even rude, and, everyone suspected, keeping a mental list of where everyone stood.

Under RFK's goading, where everyone stood was becoming clearer than it had been the day before. McNamara wanted a blockade of Cuba.

Having consulted with the Joint Chiefs, he stated in his crisp monotone, he had learned that, in their judgment, the previous day's talk of a "surgical" air strike against the missiles was impractical. Cuba was armed already and, if attacked, it could strike back effectively: any U.S. action, therefore, would have to destroy many installations on the island, and *that* would necessitate an all-out invasion. And with an unknown number of missiles in Cuba, aimed directly at America, was an invasion feasible? McNamara feared not. Instead of an air strike he urged a blockade.

Dean Acheson was outraged. Although the elder statesman, at sixty-nine years old, he still bore the dapper style of a British Guardsman; and he still, in foreign policy, favored vigorous, even provocative, action. Twenty-one years before, as President Roosevelt's Assistant Secretary of State for Economic Affairs, Acheson had made certain that Japan could purchase no oil in America, practically guaranteeing that the Japanese, starved for fuel in their Asiatic war, would lash out at America. Acheson now was little changed: "[The] decision has to be made now, or not at all," declare his handwritten notes," . . . This is time of minimum risk—I would act!" For a blockade, he pointed out to McNamara across the table, would have no effect on whatever Soviet missiles were in Cuba already. A blockade might stop shipment of new missiles, Acheson contended, but it would do nothing to remove the old ones.

Acheson wanted more than a blockade. He wanted, if necessary, an invasion.

Air strike proponents, such as Treasury Secretary Douglas Dillon, the President's chum from Harvard, fell in line behind Acheson. A blockade, they contended, would have one effect only, that of shifting the confrontation from Cuba to the Soviet Union. In response to a blockade of Cuba, Khrushchev might blockade Berlin again.

So whose view would triumph? McNamara's or Acheson's? No one knew. At some point in the course of the day, however, Robert Kennedy joined forces with McNamara. "My brother," he lashed out at Acheson, reiterating his note to the President the day before, "is not going to be the Tojo of the 1960s."

So the real duel of the day turned out to be one between former Secretary of State Dean Acheson and a man young enough, at thirty-seven, to be his son, present Attorney General Robert F. Kennedy. Acheson wanted action, but Kennedy, to the apparent astonishment of those assembled in the seventh-floor conference room, wanted caution. Kennedy's position was puzzling to Acheson, for the elder statesman thought the Tojo analogy to be spurious: the Japanese attack at Pearl Harbor, he insisted, had been unprovoked. RFK, however, stuck by his own position.

By noontime, the clouds over the capital had scattered, leaving the sky over Washington a clear and sparkling blue. Glinting in the sunshine, a train of black Cadillac limousines, parked in a row under the North Portico of the White House, slid into motion, speeding out onto Pennsylvania Avenue, rounding Blair House and the Renwick Gallery on the corner of Seventeenth Street, then racing up Connecticut Avenue to the steps in front of the dusky brick St. Matthew's Cathedral, just off Connecticut on Rhode Island. The time was 12:45 P.M.; President Kennedy was showing himself in public, first for National Prayer Day services at the cathedral, then for a stag luncheon with the Libyans, at their embassy tucked away by a park behind Massachusetts Avenue.

He returned to the White House at about 2:30 P.M. Soon thereafter he rejoined the motorcade which now streaked down toward the Navy Yard, over the Anacostia River, down the tree-lined Suitland Parkway, and, finally, through the main gate of Andrews Air Force Base.

Boarding *Air Force One*, Kennedy took off for Connecticut, flying up to campaign for the Democrats. All he had on his mind was politics as usual, or at least he sought to create that impression.

5   The autumn campaign was close to its climax. Out in Kansas City, Vice President Lyndon B. Johnson, sporting a big smile and waving a ten-gallon hat, strode into the ballroom of the old Muehlebach Hotel, the establishment from which Boss Tom Pendergast had ruled the western half of Missouri. Count Basie was entertaining the audience, who had paid a hundred dollars a plate for this Democratic party fund-raiser; up behind the dais sat St. Louis Cardinal outfielder Stan Musial, Missouri Senators Stuart Symington and Edward V. Long, former President Harry S Truman, hollow-cheeked now and gaunt, and Congressman Richard Bolling, the Missouri Democrat for whom LBJ had come to campaign. Baseball announcer Joe Garagiola introduced Johnson; Johnson, at the lectern, praised Bolling, praised the Democratic administration, praised himself, praised the memory of Franklin D. Roosevelt, and said hardly a word about John F. Kennedy.

Farther out, in Southern California's Santa Ana, incumbent Republican Congressman James B. Utt called President Kennedy a "compulsive liar, at least a pathological liar." Utt was referring to a Cleveland speech in which JFK had promised that the Cuban economy was collapsing.

And up in San Francisco, high over the bay in the ballroom of the Mark Hopkins Hotel, another Republican, former Vice President Richard M. Nixon, described himself as an "unemployed Californian who expected to have a job in January on Inauguration Day at Sacramento." Having lost the presidency to Kennedy, Nixon now was running for the governorship. He thought he might well win—after his remarks in the Mark Hopkins, more "than 600 insurance underwriters put down their coffee cups to laugh, cheer, and applaud." Nixon refrained from making derogatory remarks about Kennedy.

The Mark Hopkins audience well knew the significance of the Nixon campaign. If Kennedy faltered . . .

At about 4:25 P.M., *Air Force One* crossed western Long Island and nestled down toward the small airport at the edge of Bridgeport, Connecticut. A big, sprawling industrial town with lots of brick smokestacks, and Italian and Irish workers who lived in neat little houses, Bridgeport was natural Kennedy country. And Kennedy had come to repay a political debt. John M. Bailey, Connecticut's political boss and now national Democratic chairman, had supported Kennedy early for the presidency; and so had Abraham Ribicoff, Bailey's protégé, who recently had resigned as Kennedy's Secretary of Health, Education, and Welfare to run for the Senate from Connecticut. Ever mindful of his ethnic New England support, Kennedy had flown in to campaign for Ribicoff.

Besides, Connecticut, for the Kennedy administration, was critical. A state just loved by political analysts, it seemed to have everything: wealthy suburbs like Westport; dreary industrial cities like Bridgeport and, apart from Yale University, New Haven; war production in Groton and New London; a commercial center in Hartford; towns, villages, even apple and turkey farming. And the state was almost evenly divided between Democrats and Republicans. So Connecticut was representative of the nation at large, and given the narrowness of Kennedy's victory in 1960, the Connecticut races were crucial in 1962.

On hand to greet the President as *Air Force One* touched down at Bridgeport were Sam Tenesco, the mayor, John M. Golden, the state's Democratic national committeeman, Abraham Ribicoff, and Governor John Dempsey, stocky, dark-haired, Irish-American, and Democratic. The Democratic machine had turned out as a welcoming committee; and the AVCO Manufacturing Company had let its employees out of work to hear the President. After a drum and bugle corps had performed near the terminal, JFK gave a short speech. At 4:40 he left by motorcade for Waterbury.

Three press buses followed the limousines; and all along the route northward, through Stratford on the Housatonic River, Shelton, Derby with its eighteenth-century houses, Ansonia with its factories, and finally Waterbury, heavily Italian in its makeup, great crowds gathered. *The New York Times* estimated more than 200,000 persons. In Waterbury, Kennedy spoke on the Green, surrounded by seedy office buildings and drugstores, but in full view of the original settlers' houses and the newer, Renaissance-style Church of the Immaculate Conception. At 6:45 he left for New Haven.

Darkness had fallen, and along the highway hundreds of people waved torches and flashlights as the motorcade pulled by. In one village, Kennedy stopped the procession, got out of his car, waited for the photographers to race up, then purchased a basket of fresh Connecticut apples.

As with all Kennedy campaign appearances, this one was carefully stage-managed, designed to reach its climax in New Haven. Local Democratic Congressman Robert N. Giaimo (pronounced "Jyemo") rode down from Waterbury in the limousine with the President; Abraham Ribicoff, slender and dark-complexioned, greeted the President as JFK mounted the steps to New Haven's City Hall; Governor Dempsey introduced Kennedy to the crowd that had gathered in the green below. Kennedy then spoke, making predictable remarks—reminding his audience that Connecticut Democrats had given him his first push into national political prominence, and urging his listeners to give the Democrats a straight party vote.

Only one episode marred the scenario. A group of students, collegiate with their short haircuts, tweed jackets, and crew-necked sweaters, had walked over from Yale. As Kennedy spoke they booed. They booed long, lustily—and loudest when he mentioned medical care for the aged. Amused, Kennedy intimated to his mostly working-class audience below: "They [the Yalies] will learn, as the country has learned, that the Democratic party is best for them." This brought forth, from the perimeter of the crowd, prolonged cries of "No! No! No!"

All but breaking off his speech, Kennedy soon had himself driven to the New Haven airport. At about 9:30 P.M., his airplane began its descent again toward Andrews Air Force Base. Off in the blackness of the night, lights were shining from the dome of the U.S. Capitol.

As the presidential airplane landed, Robert Kennedy and Theodore Sorensen were waiting, huddled in a limousine to avoid attention. Wrote Sorensen of the moment:

I have the most vivid memory of the smiling campaigner alighting from his plane, waving casually to onlookers at the airport, and then instantly casting off that pose and taking up the burdens of crisis as he entered his car and said almost immediately to the driver, "Let's go,

Bill." I had prepared a four-page memorandum outlining the areas of agreement and disagreement [among the Excomm members], the full list of possibilities and (longest of all) the unanswered questions. With this to ponder . . . the President decided not to attend our [Excomm] session that night. Dropping him at the White House, the attorney general and I returned to the State Department.

6   Like President Kennedy, Secretary of State Dean Rusk was keeping up appearances by attending parties, first at the German embassy, in honor of Foreign Minister Schröder, and then in the grand ballroom of the Mayflower Hotel, where Libya's ambassador Fekini was throwing a bash for Haasan Al-Ride, his Crown Prince. In the center of the ballroom, wrote a society reporter for *The Washington Post*, "dolphins spouted water into a little pool surrounded by cherubs, and lobster shells dressed up like chefs twirled in a continuous waltz."

But rising up and over the swamps around South Carolina's Shaw Air Force Base that same night, a wing of RF-101 reconnaissance airdraft, Voodoos, were streaking southward, reaching the ocean at about Savannah, crossing land again over what now is Walt Disney World in Florida, and passing Key West en route to Cuba. As a fighter jet, the Voodoo was not much: it handled, said one of the Shaw pilots, "like a cow." It did, however, have one advantage. At low altitudes, even at treetop level, it could dash about at great speed, confusing antiaircraft gunners and, once over target areas, snapping close-up infrared photographs. The Voodoos returned to Shaw without incident; their negatives, developed and hastened to Washington, revealed the existence of an SS-5 IRBM site in Cuba. No SS-5 was yet on the island. This particular Soviet missile, nonetheless, possessed a range of 2,200 nautical miles, enough to reach the frozen wastes of Canada.

In the course of the evening, also, an order flashed forth from the Pentagon: the Joint Chiefs of Staff were accelerating a military buildup in the southeastern states. From as far west as Fort Bliss, in the desert beside El Paso, and as far north as Fort Myer, just outside Washington, convoys of olive-drab vehicles, their headlights blazing, started rumbling along the highway toward Florida. Air Force planes, too, moved southeast, landing lights showing in the night as they eased into Tampa's MacDill Air Base. Journalists, scenting a story, wondered if these movements had anything to do with Cuba. An Air Force information officer at MacDill said no.

7   But from a secret location at Tyuratam, out on the steppes of the Kazakh Soviet Socialist Republic, the U.S.S.R. launched its first reconnaissance satellite, *Cosmos X.* Flying in a low orbit, only 122 miles from earth, the vehicle headed onto a course that took it straight over the Jacksonville Naval Air Station and MacDill, as well as U.S. bases in Puerto Rico, Louisiana, and Texas. Four days later, *Cosmos X* came down again. With its own cameras, it had been tracking the American buildup.

As the first snowfall of the autumn covered the roofs of the Kremlin, the reporter Seymour Topping relayed a special report to *The New York Times.* The item would appear in the next morning's edition. *Izvestia*, the official Soviet newspaper, had published a warning to America and to President Kennedy. A U.S. attack on Cuba, *Izvestia* had stated, would mean war.

CHAPTER 9

Politics as Usual

1   *October 18, 1962*

The morning's news was unsettling. Launched in the night from Canaveral, the spacecraft *Ranger V* had failed; and a front-page photograph in *The Washington Post* revealed the vehicle as nothing more than a shower of burning parts as they cascaded through the darkened sky. Was the U.S. space program, which President Kennedy virtually had made his own, likewise going down in flames?

The press also had got wind of certain military movements. *The Christian Science Monitor:* "[T]he United States Caribbean Command, with headquarters in the Canal Zone . . . has for the first time participated in a two-day air-drop and air-landing exercise in Honduras." *The New York Times:* the by-now undeniable buildup of airpower in the southeastern American states was, in the words of a Pentagon spokesman, "an ordinary thing to do in the light of Cuban possession of jet fighters"; actually, stated the *Times*, "a considerable military deployment [is] underway. . . . The Navy [has] long scheduled a Navy-Marine amphibious exercise called PHILBRIGLEX-62. . . . [There are] 5,000 Marines at sea and 40 ships converging on the Caribbean. The purpose of the exercise [is] to liberate the mythical 'Republic of Vieques' an island just off Puerto Rico] from the rule of a tyrant named Ortsao—Castro spelled backward." The *Times* also reported the shift of a U.S. Navy jet squadron to Key West. And the *San Francisco Examiner:* "The U.S. has moved some of its fastest and most heavily armed Navy jet fighters to within four minutes flying time of Cuba"; the fighters in question were twelve in number, F-4B Phantom 2s, and amongst the palm trees and bougainvillea of Key West, their pilots were ready to take off again on a moment's notice.

Behind the red brick façade of the British embassy in Washington, up near the Naval Observatory on Massachusetts Avenue, Sir David Ormsby-Gore, the ambassador, was hearing a peculiar tale. He did not, of course, allow himself to look perturbed. A descendant of the ancient English aristocracy—his mother had been a Cecil, which family had supplied Westminster with ministers and officials since the sixteenth century, and his father was the fourth Baron Harlech—Ormsby-Gore, slender and well-dressed, carried himself with an air of inner assurance. He had become ambassador to the United States in 1961 and, two decades before in London, he had been a friend of the young John F. Kennedy. Now, on Thursday morning, he realized that his old chum Kennedy might be up to something, something big.

Outside his office window, the embassy's garden was ablaze with yellow chrysanthemums, and the leaves on the dogwood trees had just turned to scarlet. Ormsby-Gore's attention, however, must have been focused altogether on two compatriots sitting in the leather chairs in front of his desk. They both were British officials, Major General Sir Kenneth Strong and Sir Hugh Stephenson, Deputy Under Secretary of State in the Foreign Office, and what they had observed during a sojourn in Washington was highly intriguing. Down at the Pentagon, where General Strong had been on a consulting assignment, some of his counterparts, American, had set up cost in their offices. Out on the diplomatic cocktail circuit, furthermore, as Stephenson had become aware, high-ranking State Department officials such as Llewellyn Thompson, U. Alexis Johnson, George Ball, even Dean Rusk, all had kept disappearing. Was all this just coincidental? No, one of Ormsby-Gore's visitors thought, "something funny" was going on. But what? Some kind of crisis had to be in train, a major international crisis; probably, the

Britishers guessed, it had to do with Cuba. As Strong and Stephenson departed the embassy, they agreed that, whatever else they could dig up, they would pass along forthwith to Ambassador Ormsby-Gore.

Under a cool and cloudless sky, a morning ceremony took place in the Rose Garden. As President Kennedy, slim and agile in a dark blue suit, strode forth from the Oval Office just after 9:30 A.M., the small crowd that had collected along the lawn broke out in applause. JFK took his place at a lectern, reading from a prepared script as he presented Harmon International Aviation Trophies. These awards were for excellence in flying, and the winners were: U.S. Air Force Lieutenant Colonel William R. Payne, who had flown a B-58 bomber to two supersonic records; U.S. Navy Commanders Ross and Prather, the latter posthumously, for having ascended, over the Gulf of Mexico, higher than anyone before in the open gondola of a manned balloon, and at more than 100,000 feet, conducted scientific experiments (Prather had drowned in the descent); and Jacqueline Cochran, the aviatrix, who in 1960 in a T-38 jet fighter had established four records for speed, two for distance; and in a F-104 jet she had flown twice the speed of sound. Then, the awards distributed and the handshakes given, the President went back to the Oval Office to prepare for a Cabinet meeting.

To a casual onlooker, the Rose Garden ceremony might have seemed merely perfunctory. Washington insiders, however, would have known differently: JFK was a master of using ceremony to further his own agenda, his political agenda. For the very cast of characters in the Rose Garden that morning suggested politics. The group (many of whom were the military brass, braided and beribboned) included:

James E. Webb, the stocky, jut-jawed Kennedy-appointed administrator of the National Aeronautics and Space Administration (NASA). Once a poor boy in North Carolina, Webb had scrapped and scraped his way upward, becoming a lawyer, a World War II Marine flyer (eventually heading the Marine Corps air station at Cherry Point, North Carolina), and a postwar official in President Truman's Department of State. During the Eisenhower era, Webb had held directorships in the McConnell Aircraft Corporation of St. Louis, the Kerr-McGhee Oil Company of Oklahoma City, and the Oak Ridge Institute of Nuclear Studies near Knoxville, Tennessee. Webb therefore was a key player in what President Eisenhower in his Farewell Address had dubbed the "military-industrial complex"; under James Webb, who knew his way around, NASA was constructing its space control center in the Texas of Vice President Lyndon B. Johnson.

Igor I. Sikorsky, head of Sikorsky Aircraft of Stratford, Connecticut. Born into the Russian intelligentsia (his father had been a professor and his mother a physician), Sikorsky had emigrated to America, taught mathematics to other Russians in New York, and then made a fortune in aviation—he had designed both the Pan Am Clipper ships and the helicopter. He was a "scientific genius and a man of deep spiritual qualities," or so at least declared a politicians to whose campaigns he had contributed lavishly, Connecticut's Republican Senator Prescott Bush. Bush's son was named George. And Sikorsky was a subcontractor for General Dynamics.

Fred Korth, Secretary of the Navy, and formerly president of a Fort Worth bank, Continental National. Although now in Washington, Korth was using his official position to drum up new accounts for the bank: in letters that bore the seal of the Navy Department, he was inviting prospective clients for cruises aboard *Sequoia*, the presidential yacht, and over drinks on the deck he was soliciting their deposits. His bank's biggest customer had been General Dynamics.

And Jacqueline Cochran. After a poverty-stricken childhood in the Florida panhandle, where she had had to endure alcoholic foster-parents, she had migrated to Manhattan, working there as a hairdresser. Blond, pretty, and bright, she had had an affair with Floyd B. Odlum, a big financier. He had encouraged her to take flying lessons. Although she barely had gone through grade school, she had mastered the navigation textbooks and, in only three or four lessons out on Long Island, had become an accomplished pilot. She had been a wartime pilot, a news reporter in the Far East, and then, finally marrying Odlum, the manager of his six-hundred-acre ranch at Indio, California.

Her accomplishments had been spectacular. Yet in the Rose Garden ceremony, she was almost a stand-in for her husband; for *he* had become one of the most powerful figures in America. Brazen and portly, Odlum, a preacher's son from Michigan, had been a 1920s Wall Street wizard. Noting his addiction to wide-brimmed hats, checked suits, and gaudy suspenders, New York reporters nicknamed him "Farmer Floyd." They should have called him "Horse Trader": smelling the advent of trouble, he sold his stock market shares in early 1929, and survived the great crash with a pile of $14 million. In 1935, *Fortune* put him high on a list of "the 30 men who run America." Accordingly, in 1940, he took a post in President Franklin D. Roosevelt's wartime administration—the directorship of the contract division in the Office of Production Management. In that capacity he steered defense contracts to favored firms, that is, firms in which Floyd B. Odlum was a major investor, blue-chip firms such as General Motors, Ford, Standard Oil, U.S. Steel, and a Fort Worth airplane construction company, Convair. Back in the private sector he staged a postwar corporate reorganization, merging Convair with the Electric Boat Company of Groton, Connecticut. Electric Boat was the nation's major manufacturer of submarines. Odlum's new conglomerate took on the name of—General Dynamics.

Floyd B. Odlum also paid his political dues. In 1949, reported *Life*, he "helped raise anywhere from $1.5 to $6.5 million for the Democratic party."

So the ceremony in the Rose Garden of the White House on October 18, 1962, was almost a General Dynamics family reunion, perhaps even a recognition of the good deeds done for the Democratic party by Floyd B. Odlum and by General Dynamics. And the ceremony was a classic Kennedy ploy: putting on a good show and hiding scandal. In this case the scandal would be called "TFX".

Kennedy was hiding yet another scandal. The administration had denied consistently any knowledge of missiles in Cuba. As Excomm convened on October 18, 1962, however, a CIA officer passed out copies of a memorandum about Cuba. The memo is worth quoting:

"In March 1962, two amphibious tracked carriers were observed at the military garrison of Jovellanos, Matanzas Province. Uncovered rockets were visible on the carriers where canvas covers had been rolled up and secured with straps at the side of the rockets. . . .

"At 1100 hours, 9 August 62 [a] source observed numerous Soviet vehicles between Placelas and La Esperanza, Las Villas Province, proceeding northwest on the Central Highway. The vehicles in the convoy consisted of 20–25 large Soviet trucks and Low-Boy-type trailers, about 15 of which were transporting JS model tanks, one 'tank-like vehicle of tracked mobility with long canvas-covered rectangular object mounted on top of tank frame, . . . identifiable as a JS tank chassis modified for transport of ROCKETS or SURFACE-SURFACE MISSILES. . . .'

" ——— reported driving in an easterly direction on Avenida 23, Marianno, Havana, on 12 September 62, when he encountered a convoy of 20 Soviet-driven trucks pulling canvas-covered 65–70 feet long trailers, proceeding west towards Ciudad Libertad. Upon arrival at Ciudad Libertad, the militia jeep escort leading the convoy was waved off and the convoy entered the installation. The trailers were loaded with what source believed to be large missiles which extended over the end of the trailer. Canvas, over what appeared to be wood framers, presented the silhouette of what source believed were four fins on the trailing edge of the missile. The source drew sketches of the load silhouette, which resembled a SURFACE-TO-SURFACE SS-4 'SHYSTER.' The SS-4 'SHYSTER' is a single stage, vertically launched, liquid propellant, medium range ballistic missile with a range of 500 to 700 nautical miles."

So here, in documents spread out along the long table in the seventh-floor conference room of the U.S. State Department, was hard evidence that, from as far back as March 1962, the CIA had known that Soviet missiles were going into Cuba. In no way could the administration have been ignorant of the facts.

In October 1962, two publications challenged the administration directly to fess up: on October 1, *U.S. News & World Report* stated that "competent authorities at [the Guantánamo] Navy base believe Washington is underplaying the Soviet buildup in Cuba—and are puzzled why"; and on October 12, the *Los Angeles Times*, describing a report that Representative A. Paul Kitchin, a Pennsylvania Republican, had turned over to a special House subcommittee (Kitchin had been to Guantánamo, and had learned there that between September 23 and September 29, 1962, 213 Soviet ships had unloaded cargoes in Cuba), declared flatly that Kitchin's information "contradicts government figures on arms buildup in Cuba."

So why the cover-up? The answer may be inferential but it also seems inescapable, for the political interest of the Kennedy administration clearly lay in feigning unawareness of any missiles in Cuba. For if the Soviets had been *sneaking* missiles into Cuba, their doing so, once revealed with hard U-2–gathered photographic evidence, would appear an act of infamy—another Pearl Harbor. With the Soviets caught out in an act of clear-cut villainy, the American public would applaud the building of the TFX.

For the administration suddenly was confronting a most acute problem. On September 3, 1962, the *Washington News* carried a damaging story. According to "reliable sources" in the State Department—that meant a leak—the Soviet arms buildup in Cuba was for "apparently defensive reasons." The leak's implication must have been crystal-clear: if anyone was on the offensive with regard to Cuba, it was not the Soviet Union but rather the United States.

One thing was for sure. The Kennedy administration could afford no more such leaks. To the American people, the villainy of the *Soviets* had to be made clear. It had to be, in the words of former Secretary of State Dean Acheson, "clearer than truth."

2   Late in the morning of October 18, 1962, Dean Acheson was in the Oval Office, having come to consult with the President. Democrats held him in the highest regard—and he held himself in the same regard. *Present at the Creation* was the title he would give to his memoirs, and for two decades he had seen himself as the progenitor of America's rollback policy. Rollback meant the destruction of the Soviet bloc, an objective that made for good politics but, from the perspective of Presidents, scary policy.

Acheson, however, had the luxury of not being President. Rising from his rocking chair, the actual President, John F. Kennedy, walked to the French windows. Gazing down on the Jackson magnolia, he stood in silence for many long moments.

Then, turning back to Acheson, he said, "This is the week when I had better earn my salary."

Several writers have quoted this comment. They have failed, however, to dwell on the obvious: Kennedy had refused to disagree, or agree, with Acheson. Acheson may have been trying to pin the President down. Any limits placed on JFK by international law, the much-older man said, were "a crock." Kennedy nevertheless remained noncommittal. And in the end, the President got what he wanted. Acheson promised to fly to Paris, there to inform President de Gaulle of Kennedy's decision, whatever that decision might be.

Glancing out a window of the State Department's seventh floor, an official looked at the curvilinear driveway below. It was packed with limousines, their polished bodies glinting in the rays of the morning sun. The official passed the word: if Rusk and Ball really wanted the press to start sniffing around, all they had to do was let those cars stay parked down there, right in full view of the street. The cars disappeared forthwith, moved to the garage under the east side of the building.

Excomm was worried about something other than moving cars. According to a CIA report being passed around the table, the Soviets in the night had moved four Komar missile boats from the Havana area to the port of Banes, about seventy-five miles northwest of Guantánamo. The Komars resembled PT boats on which missile tubes had been installed; and their missiles had a range of ten to twelve miles. The Komars thus presented little danger to the U.S. itself—indeed they now were farther from Key West than before. So why had the Soviets changed their location?

Were they intended to deter an American attack on Cuba and out of Guantánamo? Were they poising for a strike at Guantánamo in a preemptive attack?

In either case, their repositioning must have reflected Soviet fears of an American invasion of Cuba, and those fears alone would have caused trouble for the White House politically. News of the Komars did not reach the press.

. . .

But what *was* America going to do? On October 18, 1962, wrote Anatoly Andreivich Gromyko, son of the Soviet Minister, President Kennedy "issued instructions for the formation of two secret subcommittees from among the advisers who had participated in formulating the 'decisive steps.' The groups were to present the President with a detailed plan for the execution of both an air strike against Cuba and also a naval blockade. A regular 'witches' Sabbath' began in the Pentagon, the CIA and the Department of State. The American military clique proposed that Kennedy institute a blockade of oil destined for Cuba from the Soviet Union. This raw material, which is necessary for any economy, was also declared 'offensive' on grounds that it was indispensable to military operations. The extreme right had pushed Kennedy into taking such steps which would leave the other side no alternative but to reply with . . . force."

Was Gromyko-the-younger writing the truth? Did Excomm break down into "secret subcommittees"? Were they working out plans for both air strike and blockade? Was the administration plotting an oil blockade against Cuba? Had the "extreme right" pushed Kennedy into leaving the Soviets "no alternative" but force?

We can turn for answers to the account of Theodore C. Sorensen, in his memoir, *Kennedy.* On "Thursday [October 18, 1962] in the State Department's conference room," he wrote, "subcommittees were set up to plot each of the major courses in detail." Excomm was meeting in secret; therefore the subcommittees were meeting in secret.

"We chose" to recommend, Sorensen continued, for he himself sat on the blockade subcommittee, "a blockade against offensive weapons only. Inasmuch as the President had made clear that defensive weapons were not intolerable, and inasmuch as the exclusion of all food and supplies would affect innocent Cubans most of all, this delineation helped relate the blockade route more closely to the specific problem of missiles and made the punishment more nearly fit the crime." So far, then, Gromyko's interpretation was on target. But was the blockade to include oil?

The "next question," Sorensen commented, "and one that would recur throughout the next ten days, was whether to include 'POL,' as the military called it—petroleum, oil, and lubricants. A POL blockade, automatically turning back all tankers, would lead directly, though not immediately, to a collapse of the Cuban economy. Although these commodities could be justifiably related to the offensive war machine, it seemed too drastic a step for a first move, too likely to require a more belligerent response and too obviously aimed more at Castro's survival than at Khrushchev's missiles. We recommended that this be held back as a means of later tightening the blockade should escalation be required." So Gromyko was partly wrong—and partly right. Sorensen's subcommittee had not labeled oil an "offensive" weapon. The subcommittee, nevertheless, did reserve the right to do so later.

And of Gromyko's claim of right-wing pressure on Kennedy? Out in California, gubernatorial candidate Richard M. Nixon, campaigning from the back of a special train that was chugging through the lettuce fields to Santa Barbara, was denouncing JFK for his "softness" on Cuba. Back in Washington, Barry M. Goldwater, the jut-jawed Republican senator from Arizona, was raising the battle cry for an invasion of Cuba: "I have never met an American," he told reporters at a Capitol Hill press conference, "who prefers slavery to freedom." Up on the seventh floor of the State Department, an official passed to Sorensen the following note:

> Ted—Have you considered the very real possibility that if we allow Cuba to complete installation & operational readiness of missile bases, the next house of Representatives is likely to have a Republican majority. This would completely paralyze our ability to react sensibly & coherently to further Soviet advances.

And down in Cuba, the redeployment of the Komar missile-boats were just the kind of "force" of which Gromyko had written.

So Anatoly Gromyko did have a point. Right-wing pressure on the Kennedy administration was intense—probably no more so than when, on the evening of October 18, 1962, Gromyko the elder went to the White House for a talk with the President.

.   .   .

Foreign Minister Andrei Gromyko was something of a mystery man. Americans knew little about him. One Russian émigré-turned-journalist had written up the bare bones of his life: Gromyko's parents had been semiliterate peasants, and Andrei, born in 1909, had grown up on their farm. After attending school in the village, he had turned up as a student at the Moscow Agricultural Institute, then at the Institute of Economics; thereafter he had become a lecturer at various Moscow Universities—as well as a protégé of Stalin's Foreign Minister, Viacheslav Molotov. During this period, the late 1930s, he had been "an intensely serious young man who did not drink, did not smoke, seldom went out with girls, but worked almost unceasingly." Sent in 1939 as a counselor to the embassy in Washington—at the time he had known no English—he had kept to himself, continuing his "hard-working, austere way of life." Someone among the few who even knew him dubbed him the "oldest young man in Washington." During World War II he had returned to Russia, and American observers lost sight of him almost altogether.

He surfaced again in the postwar years, emerging as the Soviet ambassador to Great Britain and then to the United Nations. In 1957 he became Khrushchev's Foreign Minister. Yet he remained elusive, known to diplomats, in the words of one news magazine, "chiefly for his stony silences." Nothing, added the *New York Herald Tribune*—this was after a 1958 Gromyko visit to the United Nations—"seemed to break the granite solemnity of his face; but sometimes just a brief glimmer of humor showed through. [At] a Soviet party . . . he stared grimly out a window at the heavy rain beating down on the sidewalk. 'Tomorrow,' he muttered, '*The New York Times* will blame it on Gromyko.' "

Now, October 18, 1962, this same Gromyko was back in the States. Actually, he had been there for a week, hidden away in some upstairs room in the Sixteenth Street embassy in Washington, and nobody in the U.S. government seemed to have any idea why. All anyone knew was that he had requested a meeting with President Kennedy, a session scheduled for 5:00 P.M.

Preparations for the conference had been intense. At about 4:30 P.M. Secretary of State Rusk and National Security Adviser Bundy bustled into the Oval Office, both laden with papers. Rusk read aloud from a summation: "You have agreed to receive

Soviet Foreign Minister Gromyko . . . ," he said, addressing himself to Kennedy. "He will be accompanied by Ambassador [Anatoly] Dobrynin and his interpreter, Viktor Sukhodrev. . . . The call was at Gromyko's request but we do not know what subject or subjects he may wish to bring up. Although Berlin will clearly be an important topic of discussion, it seems unlikely that Gromyko will have much new to say substantively on this subject. . . . Other topics which Gromyko might raise include nuclear testing. . . . It is also possible that Gromyko will touch on bilateral issues." The next several lines in the declassified document are "sanitized." Was Rusk referring to Cuba? Perhaps so: Bundy's own memo zinged in on the Cuban issue. "If Gromyko raises this [the Cuban] question—as he may—you will probably want to hear him before you reply. . . . If he does not raise the subject, the consensus last night was that you should remind him of the hazards presented a) by Castro; b) by arms buildup; c) by rumors of offensive weapons."

At 5:00 P.M. sharp, after Ambassador Llewellyn Thompson had joined Rusk, Bundy, and Kennedy, the Soviets tramped in, two embassy officials, the plump, glad-handing Ambassador Dobrynin, Sukhodrev the interpreter (dark-haired and slender, he read American detective novels to keep up with slang, and his pronunciation of English was so good that he could have passed himself off as a native of Cleveland or Detroit), and Gromyko. Plodding through the doorway of the Oval Office, the foreign minister, dark-complexioned, square-shouldered, and heavy, looked uncomfortable, suspicious; and the sleeves of his navy blue suit jacket, tailored in Moscow, looked twice as big as his arms. He sat on the white couch. Theodore Sorensen was present, ready to take notes.

For a few moments, the Oval Office was ablaze with flashbulbs. Then the press was ushered out, and the meeting got under way.

Looking over at Kennedy, seated in the rocking chair, Gromyko brought up the subject of Cuba, referring to attacks on shipping by Cuban exile groups. Charging further that the United States had been "pestering" a small country, Cuba, Gromyko accused Kennedy of having interfered in the island's internal affairs; Cuba was no threat, Gromyko stated, for compared to the United States, a giant, it was only a baby. "As to Soviet assistance to Cuba"—Gromyko was reading from notes—"I have been instructed to make it clear, as the Soviet government already has done, that such assistance [was] pursued solely [for] the purpose of contributing to the defense capabilities of Cuba. . . . If it were otherwise, the Soviet government never would have become involved in rendering such assistance."

In time the President spoke. He said nothing of the missile photographs, so journalist Elie Abel related, restricting himself to reading aloud a statement he had made on September 4—that the U.S. would use "whatever means may be necessary" to prevent aggression by Cuba against any part of the Western Hemisphere—and to saying that the U.S. had had no intention of invading Cuba.

As he left the White House, moments after 7:00 P.M., Gromyko found himself surrounded by reporters. They were clamoring for a statement. All he said of the meeting with Kennedy, however, was "useful, very useful."

So saying, he ducked into a limousine under the North Portico. He had to dress for dinner at the White House.

While Gromyko dined with Secretary Rusk on the State Department's eighth floor—the ceremonial floor—Robert F. Kennedy and several other Excomm members were slipping out of the seventh-floor conference room, riding an elevator to the basement, piling into the attorney general's limousine, parked in the underground garage, and racing up the steep ramp that exited on to the leaf-strewn pavement of Twenty-first Street. The time was about 9:15 P.M. To "avoid the suspicion that would have ensued from the presence of a long line of limousines," wrote Robert Kennedy, "we all went in my car—John McCone, Maxwell Taylor, the driver, and myself all crowded together in the front seat, and six others sitting in back." A few in the rear had to sit on each other's laps; someone wondered aloud what would happen to the Republic if they had an accident. Their destination was the White House.

Once with the President, Robert Kennedy informed him that the group had its recommendation ready: the United States should institute a blockade of Cuba. JFK lost little time—he lost so little time, in fact, that one suspects he had wanted this recommendation all along. Turning to Sorensen, he asked his aide to start writing a speech for delivery on television.

At almost the same time, Robert Kennedy telephoned his own chief aide in the Justice Department, the tall, balding Nicholas deB. Katzenbach, demanding a brief that would give a blockade some legal justification. Katzenbach complied, of course: only two years later, as Undersecretary of State, he would insist that, under the aegis of the Gulf of Tonkin Resolution, President Lyndon B. Johnson could do whatever he wished in Vietnam; Katzenbach would hold, furthermore, that Congress's power to declare war, granted by Article I of the U.S. Constitution, was nothing more than a relic of a bygone age.

And back in the State Department, Leonard C. Meeker, a lawyer and assistant to the assistant of George Ball, started to draft his own analysis. Borrowing a word from President Franklin D. Roosevelt, Meeker urged that President Kennedy call the coming blockade a "quarantine."

For here was the problem, the issue glossed over in most accounts. Earlier in the day, Meeker had advised Excomm that a "blockade of Cuba undertaken unilaterally by the United States in the present circumstances would subject this country to very telling charges of violation of the United Nations Charter and illegal use of force." Under international law, a "blockade" would be illegal—but a "quarantine"? The word "quarantine" was deliciously vague.

3   At some point on Thursday, October 18, 1962, probably late in the evening, for such would have fit his style, Vice President Lyndon B. Johnson placed a telephone call to Jack Krueger, managing editor of the Dallas *Morning News;* Krueger should "prepare for a bombing raid," Johnson told him, "possibly an invasion [of Cuba], maybe as soon as Monday morning." "It's 50–50 we hit Cuba," LBJ went on, "and if you'll get somebody up here [in Washington] and ready, I'll see to it that" he gets the scoop. Johnson had it all worked out. A *Morning News* reporter was to "check in at the Washington Hotel and don't call my office. Just be ready. He'll be told where to go from there."

The *Morning News* sent Hugh Aynesworth, a journalist just back from a nine-day stint in Cuba. Aynesworth was in Washington the next morning.

Even before the reporter had reached the hotel, however, Johnson had been on the phone again to the Dallas paper. "Whoever you send," the Vice President ordered, "tell him he'd better not open his damn mouth about why he's sittin' here. . . . Not if he values his balls."

The 11:00 P.M. Washington-area news programs revealed nothing of such maneuvering. Television screens did show Gromyko, looking lopsided in his ill-fitted suit; a few frames did show jet fighters as they settled down onto their new Florida bases. But the major late evening item was political: in the morning, President Kennedy would be off aboard *Air Force One* for his last swing of the 1962 campaign, off to Ohio, Illinois, Wisconsin, Missouri, New Mexico, and, for reasons left unexplained, Las Vegas.

4   *October 19, 1962*

He was bald, short, and beefy, with fingers that seemed as wide as they were long; his stomach resembled a medicine ball, and when he walked he waddled; yet despite his blockiness the legs and sleeves of his suits were always too big, as if Soviet tailors had just one pattern for everyone. His fingertips were stained a permanent yellow, a consequence of the cheap Russian cigarettes to which he had been addicted since his earliest days in the mines of the Ukraine. He looked working-class, he *was* working-class, and in manner he was appropriately rude, rough, and shrewd. He was also ambitious. He was Nikita Khrushchev, boss of the Soviet Union.

In Khrushchev's Moscow, the first snow of the season had fallen, and down below his office windows, early in the morning of October 19, 1962, the great square of the Kremlin was covered with white. But Khrushchev, surely, was paying little attention to the winter scene outside. For a coded message had just flashed in from Washington, and it demanded Khrushchev's fullest attention. It was Foreign Minister Gromyko's account of his dinner the previous evening with Secretary of State Dean Rusk.

So at least Khrushchev has related. "Gromyko told me," his memoirs state, "that when Rusk invited him to dinner Rusk drank a lot. . . . Rusk told Gromyko, 'We know everything. . . . You are accustomed to living with our missiles encircling you, but this is the first time that *we* face such a threat. That's why we are in such a state of shock and cannot overcome it,' Rusk said. Gromyko answered like a gypsy who was caught stealing a horse: 'It's not me and it's not my horse. I don't know anything.' . . . Gromyko is very moderate in his use of alcohol, and you cannot ply him with liquor. I believe he was sober at the time, and I always trusted his words. . . . After several drinks, Rusk told him, 'We will see this through to the end. Tell Khrushchev we wish we could prevent this from occurring, but anything may happen.' . . ."

Had Secretary Rusk, under the influence of scotch, revealed more than President Kennedy wished? Evidently so, Khrushchev thought.

Gromyko "reported all this to the government and leadership," Chairman Khrushchev went on. "We listened to him but went on with the [Cuban missile] operation. What made the Americans think they had such a unilateral right [to move against Cuba in force]? After all, America had used our neighbors' territory to station its own rockets. Now that we were doing the same, they were threatening us with war. It angered us."

"We received a telegram from our ambassador in Cuba [Alexandr I. Alekseyev], who was on close terms with Castro," state Khrushchev memoirs, referring to the night of October 18–19, 1962. "He said he had just met with Castro. He told us in great detail that Castro informed him he had reliable information that the Americans were preparing within a certain number of hours to strike Cuba. In addition, our own intelligence informed us that such an action was being prepared and that an invasion probably would be unavoidable unless we came to an agreement with the President." Radio Moscow reiterated the Kremlin's fear: in the area of the Caribbean, a Moscow announcer stated, the American Navy was poised for an invasion of Cuba.

The broadcast reached to the far corners of the Soviet bloc, to Poland, Bulgaria, and North Korea, where people, listening to their squawky radio sets, were hearing the Kremlin's warning. Was the warning just propaganda?

Curiously, American newspapers were paralleling the Radio Moscow broadcast; the two principal papers were the Chicago and Tampa *Tribunes*. The *Chicago Tribune:* "Reports smuggled from Havana . . . said today [the dateline was October 19] that Premier Fidel Castro is building a radar line to detect any surprise attack on Cuba. Russian troops and technicians are building an island-encompassing network of radar stations and other electronic installations." The *Tampa Tribune:* "a "Cuban DEW [Distant Early Warning] line, an island-encompassing network of radar stations and other electronic installations similar to that of the U.S. [whose own DEW line stretched across the northern reaches of Canada] to guard against surprise attack from the north. Work on Castro's line has been under way for more than a month. . . . The mass movements of men and material involved are made generally on Sundays, when there are the fewest civilians around. A 25-truck caravan of building materials and equipment was spotted along the Malecon, Havana, seawall, under apparent cavalry escort. It was preceded and followed by horsemen."

Even as the two *Tribunes* were receiving these reports, U.S. armed forces were visibly on the move. Bungalow dwellers near Patrick, Homestead, and McCoy Air Force bases in Florida felt the air jarred repeatedly as more and more jets pulled in overhead for landings. Key West was all a-rumble with the approach of giant Globemaster cargo planes; residents of the island could see the silhouette of the USS *Grant County*, a troop transport ship, as it dropped anchor offshore. Local reporters sensed that whatever was happening was something big.

Up in Washington, Excomm members were still trying to operate in secret. Some were doing their own typing—documents from October 19 are chock-full of misspellings and crossed-out words—and others were pressuring editors into silence. "STAY CLOSE, MCNAMARA TELLS CHIEFS," stated the biggest headline in the next morning's *Washington Post*; and the paper went on to list various reasons why the brass might have to stay in the capital—the "preparation of a new five-year defense program dealing with the future of manned bombers, rival Army–Air Force . . . aviation expansion plans, stepped-up naval shipbuilding proposals"—all the reasons, that is, except the real one. Was Benjamin Bradlee, the thin, nervous, graying editor of *The Washington Post*, and a Kennedy family intimate, responding to White House pleas? We cannot be certain. But what *is* clear is that, at some point during October 19, 1962, President Kennedy himself telephoned Orville Dryfoos, publisher of *The New York Times*, asking that a story about the U.S. force movements be killed. Dryfoos complied.

Yet the effort was hopeless: Washington was so full of leaks that the place seemed flooded. "Yesterday," stated the *Miami News*, carrying a piece by its Washington reporter Hal Hendrix, who had long cultivated sources at the CIA, "the White House said plans are being worked out for a U.S. quarantine on Cuban shipping." Here was Washington at work as usual. Excomm itself did not get around to discussing the word "quarantine" until the evening of October 19; yet the Miami paper printed the word in the *morning.*

The *Miami News* was scarcely the only recipient of inside dope: morning papers carried a syndicated column by Paul Scott and Robert Allen, a reportial team, in which they hinted at the existence of the missiles in Cuba (the State Department was all a-flutter thinking up ways to stop them from printing anything more). In their Queen Anne–style embassy up on Massachusetts Avenue, the British also were glimpsing the truth. Alerted by contacts in the Pentagon, Major General Strong and Deputy Undersecretary Stephenson were closeted with their ambassador again, confiding in Ormsby-Gore that a crisis in Cuba was imminent.

As a presidential limousine pulled under the North Portico of the White House, news photographers clustered round, hoping for shots of President Kennedy. The time was 10:30 A.M. According to press handouts, JFK was due at that moment to start on his final campaign trip.

He did not appear, however, for twelve minutes more, finally entering the limo and giving a wave from the window. The "delay," *The Washington Post* explained the next day, resulted from a "briefing [President Kennedy] received from Secretaries Rusk and McNamara, and General Taylor."

Along with Dean Acheson and all the Joint Chiefs, we know from now-declassified documents, Rusk, McNamara, and Taylor were trying to pressure Kennedy, right then and there, into authorizing an air strike. Moments later, he telephoned his brother, Robert.

"I'll make my own decision . . . ," he said. *Then* he went out to the limousine.

5   As Excomm convened late in the morning in the State Department, Nicholas Katzenbach took the floor. A Princetonian, a Rhodes Scholar, and a former professor of law at the University of Chicago, Katzenbach was the perfect number-two man for Robert F. Kennedy: big, brisk, and aggressive, Katzenbach had made the Justice Department over into a hired gun for the White House. Representing the President even now, his job was to build the best possible case for a blockade. Was a blockade, some around the conference table wanted to know, legal? Katzenbach was firm. Under the laws and the Constitution, he responded, a President could do whatever he had to do to defend the nation. But wasn't a blockade an act of war, one of the Excomm participants queried, and didn't Congress alone have power to declare war? No, Katzenbach snapped, hitting back at both questions: the blockade was justifiable under the "principle of self-defense."

You sense that the Kennedy team was nervous, looking for anything that would bolster its case before the jury of public opinion. Even before lunchtime, a top-secret State Department memorandum, passed around the table by an aide, urged that we eliminate the missiles in Cuba "without use of 'Pearl Harbor' type action." Then said another memo, "Soviets consistently blur U.S. missile programs in other countries by suggesting we are turning missiles over to host country." The author was Roger Hilsman, a lean, bespectacled West Pointer who had fought as a guerrilla in World War II behind Japanese lines and whom JFK had handpicked to head up State Department intelligence. "Just this evening," Hilsman continued, "TASS [the Soviet news agency] put out a story that the U.S. was turning

Jupiters over to Turks, training them in use of missiles." America, Hilsman worried, was in danger of losing the propaganda war. And another State Department memo, destined to be leaked, declared: "Soviet bases are being established in Cuba in secrecy, in accord with secret agreements with the Castro regime, and for purposes that can only be assumed to be aggressive. . . . In contrast, the Jupiter bases in Italy and Turkey were . . . established to strengthen the defense of the West. . . . The contrast with the secretly emplaced Soviet missile bases in Cuba is self-evident."

Putting down at Hopkins Airport, situated in the flat plainland just southwest of Cleveland, *Air Force One*, white with silver-and-gold markings, taxied up to the newly constructed northern Ohio terminal. The airplane whined to a halt. Then a coterie of local Democrats bustled along the tarmac to be first to greet the President: trim little Senator Stephen M. Young, once a farmboy and presently a political hack; tall, solidly built, and wavy-haired Senator (and former long-time Governor) Frank J. Lausche, a Clevelander, a Slovenian-speaker, and an orator, so *Time* had avowed, of the "William Jennings Bryan tradition"; and rotund, five-feet-five-inches tall and almost as round, almost cuddly Michael V. DiSalle, the Governor of Ohio and, by his own estimation, the "champion spaghetti cook of Toledo." Facing a monumental challenge from Auditor James A. Rhodes, a popular Republican from Columbus, DiSalle was up for the political run, or waddle, of his life; DiSalle was desperate for JFK's endorsement. Their greetings to Kennedy, as he trotted down the ramp, were drowned by the roars of the crowd.

With its furnaces flaring red in the night and with its masses of workers with parents or grandparents from the villages of Central and Eastern Europe, Cleveland still was the Ohio power-house, economically and politically, and it was heavily Democratic. Its dominance in the state, however, was peaking: as blacks moved in, whites were moving out; and ensconced in suburbs such as Independence and Parma, the sons of Italy, Bohemia, and Serbia were starting to vote Republican. Farther downstate, moreover, Columbus, the capital, was growing, trying to become the state's banking and insurance hub; and as Columbus grew, so did the fortunes of the Ohio Republican party. So Governor DiSalle's bid for reelection was in peril—and President Kennedy had flown in in the hope that some of his own glamour would rub off on DiSalle.

The President certainly seemed popular. All the way along the route from the airport, up Rocky River Drive, over on Lorain Avenue, up again on West Twenty-fifth Street, then on across the bridge toward the Terminal Tower, the crowds were thick— and ecstatic.

"Strangely," a reporter commented, "placards calling for action in Cuba, so familiar elsewhere, were not to be seen in Cleveland, but there were plenty of others: 'We Love You, John!'; 'Welcome, Giovanni Fitzgerald Kennedy'; 'JFK Is Going Our Way.' " Young, Lausche, and DiSalle accompanied Kennedy into the city.

As the presidential motorcade pulled into Public Square—a New England–type common dominated by the Terminal Tower and overlooking, on this the last day of Indian summer, the blue of Lake Erie beyond the stadium—JFK entered the Sheraton.

Doing so, Kennedy led a trailing band of photographers and reporters along a red plush carpet. Directed by advance men, he turned right, abruptly, the press corps also turning right on his heels. Down the corridor they raced until a wall of Secret Service agents made them stop and wait—while the President of the United States, alone, went into the men's room.

Then he reappeared, retraced his steps, ascended the platform that stood in front of the Terminal Tower complex; cheers from the mob on the pavement below practically shattered the air.

JFK leaned over the lectern. "Ladies and gentlemen, Governor DiSalle, Senator Lausche, Senator Young, and fellow Democrats," he said, "and Republicans who are passing through the Square for lunch. . . ."—and the throng packed into the square roared with laughter. Kennedy's speech itself was routine, containing standard references to housing, jobs, and taxes. Every phrase, however, brought forth huzzahs and cheers, almost as if people were taking cues from local labor leaders.

A young man, stocky and wearing a crew-cut, checked out by the Secret Service, came onto the platform, offering Kennedy a gift—an autographed football from Elyria High School, just southwest of Cleveland.

As the President strode down from the platform, he passed

several women in the crowd. A waitress jumped and squealed (according to the Cleveland *Plain Dealer*): "Isn't he *darling!*"

Said a mink-wearing woman nearby, "He's more handsome than on TV." And a spike-heeled secretary, straining to see, exclaimed when she finally teetered high enough, "Oh, darn it! I left my glasses in the office. Everything is a big blur!"

Everything *was* a big blur. Signs and placards fluttered, hands reached out with gifts of roses, Kennedy waved and pressed the flesh, and then, as the Secret Service closed in around him, he ducked into the waiting limousine.

At 1:05 P.M., JFK motored back to Hopkins Airport. His next destination was Springfield, Illinois.

As *Air Force One* landed at Springfield's Capital Airport— hardly more than a landing strip—Kennedy picked up a new pack of politicos, Illinois's Governor Otto Kerner, Senator Paul Douglas, and Congressman Sidney Yates. Together they rode to Lincoln's Tomb, where Kennedy laid a wreath, then they rode again to the livestock pavilion of the state fairgrounds. After receiving a twenty-one-gun salute there, Kennedy told assembled farmers that "we have achieved the best two-year advance in farm income of any two years since the Depression." Then it was back to the landing strip: Kennedy's stay in Springfield lasted just over an hour and a half. By 3:45 P.M., he was airborne again, heading now for Chicago.

At the approach to Chicago's O'Hare Airport, the sky was turning dark, for a light rain was falling. John Bailey, the Democratic boss, had come out from Connecticut, and along with Governor Kerner and Congressman Yates, he rode toward the city in the presidential limousine. With them in the back of the car was Mayor Richard J. Daley, the short, beefy, Irish-American ruler of the Chicago Democratic machine. Daley had handpicked Yates to run for the Senate against Republican incumbent Everett McKinley Dirksen, and President Kennedy had come to put in a plug for Yates.

Squeezing through a mass of humanity in the Loop, the motorcade at about 5:30 P.M. reached the Sheraton-Blackstone

Hotel, where Kennedy was scheduled to stay for the night. As Secret Service agents moved Kennedy through the hotel's main entrance, lights from inside the hotel illuminated a placard, held high by a picket at the curb. The sign referred to Cuba. It read: "LESS PROFILE—MORE COURAGE!"

After resting and then changing for dinner, Kennedy set out from the hotel again, heading by motorcade for McCormick Place, the great exposition center down on South Lake Shore Drive. The evening was to be an orgy of Democratic politicking.

Despite the darkness and the drizzle, the crowds along Lake Shore Drive were thick, especially around Soldier Field; and over Lake Michigan aerial bombs burst bright, one set of fireworks framing JFK's profile high in the nighttime sky. Accompanied by the sound of cheers and clapping, Kennedy's limousine swung up the incline to the plaza that led to McCormick Place. Surrounded by agents, the President went inside. Met by another round of applause, he entered the huge dining chamber upstairs, taking the seat of honor behind a huge dais, decorated with shamrocks. Down on the floor, five thousand Chicago Democrats, each of whom had paid at least a hundred dollars a plate for the dinner, waited excitedly to hear the President. He did make them wait, but, at last, he rose, walking slowly to the microphone.

The task he faced, building momentum for Sidney Yates's bid for the Senate, was tough and he knew it. Yates, a slender, sharp-faced lawyer from Chicago's North Side, was Jewish, and wealthy enough to be resented throughout downstate Illinois; down there Senator Dirksen was virtually a folk-hero. Daley nonetheless supported Yates, and Yates in the House supported Kennedy, and Kennedy had come to Chicago to support Yates. Such was the name of the game. So Daley introduced Kennedy and, around the tables on the vast floor below the dais, the local politicians, wardheelers, city inspectors, bureau chiefs, committeemen, aldermen, attorneys, city judges, state judges, federal judges, congressmen, and journalists, all of whom played parts in Mayor Daley's organization, put down their coffee cups to cheer and shout and stamp their feet.

The speech was vintage Kennedy or, at least, vintage Sorensen.

"I come here and ask you," Kennedy said to the crowd, "to send Sid Yates to the United States Senate." Shouts and cheers.

"I think you can do it. I think it is time to have a senator . . . who lets you know where he stands, what he is for, what he is against." More shouts and cheers.

"There is only one candidate, Yates," Kennedy continued, "who supported this administration when it sought to expand the coverage of the minimum wage and increase it to $1.25 an hour. There is only one candidate in this race who supported [Senator] Paul Douglas and us in our long fight for legislation to help the chronically depressed areas of Illinois and other states. There is only one candidate in this race who has worked to help build better schools and pay higher teacher salaries—who cared about those who were unemployed or on public assistance—who has been fully concerned about retaining jobless workers. There is only one candidate in this race who has fought throughout his career against feeble substitutes and filibusters in the effort to provide equal rights for Americans of every race.

"There is only candidate in this race who favored protecting American families from harmful and worthless drugs. . . .

"And, finally, there is only one candidate in this race who understands the necessity of helping our older citizens, who have more illnesses and less income than anyone less, pay for their health and hospital insurance through the Social Security system."

Kennedy basked in applause at the end of every sentence. And when he had finished, Mayor Daley waddled up to the lectern, looked down into the audience, spotted a priest, and called for a benediction. Soon thereafter Kennedy went down to the Arie Crown Theater, also in McCormick Place, to extend his greetings to the party workers; they had been listening to him via remote-control speakers. He waved to them all, extended a few handshakes, then left the building. Accompanied by a blare of sirens and a blaze of lights, he returned to his suite in the Blackstone Hotel.

His campaigning for the day was finished. Not once, in public, had he mentioned Cuba.

Across the Chicago River, shimmering in the lights of the Blackstone, the illuminated towers of the Wrigley and *Tribune* buildings jutted high against the nighttime sky. Outside, all seemed still. But inside the presidential suite the telephones were jangling. Kennedy was receiving up-to-the-minute intelligence reports from Washington. He was also receiving a message from Robert Kennedy: the President, according to his brother, should be prepared to return to the capital in the morning.

On the floor just below the President's, Press Secretary Pierre Salinger was also on the phone, speaking with Carleton V. Kent of the *Chicago Sun-Times*. "Pierre, we have it on good authority that the Eighteenth Parachute Corps is standing by for a jump on Cuba," Kent said. "I want a comment from the White House." Breaking off the conversation, Salinger went upstairs to see Kenneth O'Donnell, the longtime Kennedy aide.

"You're going to have to cut me in pretty quick," Salinger said. "I'm flying blind with the press."

"All I can tell you is this," O'Donnell responded. "The President may have to develop a cold somewhere along the line tomorrow. If he does, we'll cancel out the rest of the trip and head back to Washington.

"If I were you," O'Donnell advised Salinger, "I'd stay away from the reporters tonight, even if you have to hide out somewhere."

Back in Washington, that same Friday, Theodore Sorensen had ensconced himself in his White House cubbyhole, scribbling away on a legal pad, trying to draft a proclamation for the President to deliver on television. Sorensen, however, was suffering from writer's block. As he himself put it, all the doubts about a blockade now "stared me in the face: How should we relate [a blockade] to the missiles? How would it help us get them out? What would we do if they became operational? What should we say about our surveillance, about communicating with Khrushchev?" Late in the afternoon, Sorensen rode over to State, where the Excomm members were still in long-run session; he hoped they could supply him with answers.

He got little help. With Kennedy out of town, the participants had set to squabbling, no longer united behind the idea of a blockade. They may have been scared: a blockade of Cuba would "almost certainly," said one of the documents they kept passing back and forth, lead to "strong direct pressures" by the Soviets elsewhere. Sorensen left the State Department, frustrated and floundering.

Back at his desk and fortified "by my first hot meal in days, sent in a covered dish by a Washington matron to whom I appealed for help," Sorensen hit the legal pad again, working on the speech until 3:00 A.M. He stuck with the idea of a blockade. But he inserted another point as well. "In order to persuade the Soviets to pause in their reckless course . . . ," the draft had the President saying, "I am instructing Ambassador Stevenson to propose to the U.N. Security Council . . . steps . . . to guarantee the territorial integrity of Cuba."

Here was a hint of a deal to come. Here also was acknowledgment, tacit but real, of American threats to Cuba's "territorial integrity."

Out in the Midwest the rain had passed through and, in Chicago, lights from the skyscrapers twinkled in the river below. The crowds had long since gone home. In the highest floors of the Sheraton-Blackstone, however, presidential aides were scurrying about, even in the depth of the night; they were in deep communication with officials at O'Hare. For in the morning the President would return to Washington. Sorensen's draft was ready for approval.

As the Washington Symphony opened its season in the evening, comedian Danny Kaye appeared on the podium, and soon had the black-tie audience howling with laughter. Upon entering, he shook hands with the concertmaster, then the first-row violinists, then the second-row violinists, and when he came to Crystal Gothell, the first woman in the section, he gave her a loud juicy kiss. Bounding back to the front of the orchestra, he gave the downbeat and as he did so, somehow, his baton went sailing backward into the audience. A pair of latecomers caught his eye: "Got caught in traffic, eh!" he chortled. To another he said, after he had started the Rossini overture, "No, dear, you're in Row H!" And, "Oh, he's good!" after the French horn player had tossed off a tricky passage. Parodying Leonard Bernstein, he raced through a Strauss polka with his hair flying every which way. The applause was wild—and afterward, at a party in the Sheraton Park Hotel, bejeweled matrons crushed around Kaye for his autograph.

From this gala evening only one thing seemed missing. During the concert, *The Washington Post* noted, "was a conspicuous absence of New Frontier culture-lovers among boxholders."

Where were Rusk, McNamara, Dillon, McCone, and others? Something funny was afoot, and *The Washington Post* sensed it.

CHAPTER 10

Air of Crisis

1 *October 20, 1962*

Reaching the front steps of a two-story red brick house, at East 139th Street in the Mott Haven section of the Bronx, the candidate got out of his car. To the handful of reporters gathered on the sidewalk, he explained that he had been born in that house. Up there had lived, he added, his father, Dr. John J. Donovan, a much-beloved figure in the neighborhood. The candidate, however, did not linger. After shaking hands with a few of the old folks still around who remembered him, he ducked back into his car. He was speeding back to his Manhattan offices.

The candidate was James B. Donovan, forty-six years old, an attorney, and he was running—ostensibly—against New York's redoubtable incumbent Republican senator, Jacob Javits. Yet if ever there was such a thing as a noncampaign, this was it.

For James Donovan, stocky, white-haired, soft-spoken, and well-groomed, was not even a Democrat. Politically, he was an Independent, recruited for the campaign by—President John F. Kennedy. Why? Why, of all people, Donovan? Not "since John Adams defended the British soldiers for the Boston Massacre," a New York judge had commented, had an American lawyer been less popular than James B. Donovan: three years before, Donovan had defended Colonel Rudolf Ivanovich Abel, who eventually was convicted of spying for the U.S.S.R. Donovan's patriotic credentials, to be sure, were unassailable. Wartime counsel for the Office of Strategic Services, he had been a staff officer at the later Nuremberg trials in Germany, and had retired from military service with a Legion of Merit decoration. Dedicated to the American Constitution and its principle of procedural due process, he took up the Abel case, representing the Russian for nothing; and, arguing before the black-robed justices of the U.S. Supreme Court, he contended that Abel, even as a foreigner, had been denied his rights. Abel had been arrested not under a warrant but rather by an alien detention writ. The "constitutional issues have nothing to do with whether Abel really [is] a Soviet spy," Donovan held. "At issue [are] the rights of us all."

Donovan was sound, solid, loyal, and a dreadful politician. In his campaign against Javits he was hardly visible, save for his appearance in front of the house of his birth.

Back in his Manhattan law offices on the morning of October 20, in fact, Donovan gave a press conference—to say he thought he would succeed in persuading Fidel Castro to release the more than one thousand prisoners taken the year before in the Bay of Pigs invasion. Reporters were curious—why, against a politician as formidable as Javits, had Donovan campaigned so little? The answer made the front pages of the New York papers. During most of the senatorial campaign, Donovan had been out of New York, flying back and forth between Miami and Havana, working on behalf of the White House, working for the prisoner release. Donovan was ideal as Kennedy's representative. He was Catholic, he spoke Spanish, and because of his defense of Abel, he had won respect in Havana. Besides, as an old OSS man, he had maintained close ties with the CIA, and with the Kennedys.

The *New York Daily News* considered Donovan to be the "White House's boy." So why the campaign against Javits?

This much we know. President Kennedy saw the return of the prisoners from Cuba as imperative. In the words of secret White House negotiating instructions to Donovan, "It is essential that [Roberto] Geddes [a Cuban who had been captured at the Bay of Pigs] be included in the group of released prisoners. His American wife is emotionally unstable and will undoubtedly go to the U.S. press with stories that could damage the U.S., if her husband is not released."

So the White House feared an involvement of the press. And

Donovan's job, in part, was to help perpetuate a Bay of Pigs cover-up.

Yet the Donovan mission involved another cover-up still. When he flew into Cuba, on August 30, 1962, he rode to the Presidential Palace, and during a four-hour interview, learned of Castro's demand—$2.925 million for prisoners already released and, in the form of food and medicine, $25 million for the rest. But Congress—led by two senators, John J. Williams, a Delaware Republican, and John Stennis, a Mississippi Democrat—had refused to fork out the money. "Not one cent for ransom!" Stennis rasped from the Senate floor. So, in an early version of the Iran-Contra scandal, the Kennedy White House decided to bypass Congress.

Nosing around Washington, Ted Lewis, an investigative reporter for the New York *Daily News*, figured it out. JFK, Lewis revealed in his column of October 11, 1962, had "helped organize" a "private ransom committee, headed . . . by Eleanor Roosevelt, Walter Reuther [head of the United Autoworkers], and Milton Eisenhower [brother of former President Eisenhower]. And he urged citizens to contribute to it. But . . . the idea of the CIA or any other branch of government deliberately and officially putting ransom money on the line was obnoxious."

Hence, probably, the Donovan campaign for the U.S. Senate. As Donovan's papers show, his campaign organization was receiving large contributions from unnamed sources, and where most of the money went was never recorded. A suspicion raised by the press at the time remains: that Donovan's campaign funds came from the CIA, and were earmarked for Castro—to hush up what lay behind the original capture of the prisoners.

Midway through the morning, the lobby of the Blackstone Hotel in Chicago was in a frenzy. Preparing to move the President again, Secret Service agents swarmed everywhere, checking the restrooms, blocking the restaurants, cordoning off the revolving doors and the sidewalk, and, then, when President Kennedy emerged from the elevator, forming a human corridor that led to the limousine outside.

Back in the hotel, Press Secretary Pierre Salinger had announced to reporters that Kennedy had a cold and, rather than campaign further, would return right away to Washington. Buying the story, for the moment, the journalists watched President Kennedy enter the limousine. A chilly rain was falling, and he was carrying a raincoat and a gray hat; normally he went bareheaded. But he looked healthy enough—and then the limousine and its accompanying motorcade raced off to the Chicago airport.

Why the change of presidential plans? Some reporters were growing puzzled, even skeptical. Was Kennedy, some wondered, sick at all?

Pierre Salinger soon had the answer.

"We were airborne at 11 A.M.," he wrote in his memoirs. "At one point in the flight, I found myself along with the President in his private compartment.

" 'Mr. President, you don't have that bad a cold, do you?'

" 'I've had worse.'

" 'Then there's something else?'

"His unprintable answer," Salinger related, "sent a chill through me."

The press bureaus in Washington were frantic with telephone calls. Word had just come in from Honolulu, where Lyndon B. Johnson was on the campaign trail, that the Vice President was returning to Washington via *Air Force Two.* LBJ, too, it appeared, had a cold.

President Kennedy returned from Andrews Air Force Base, this time aboard a helicopter that put down in a circle on the White House lawn. The time was just after 1:30 P.M. Descending from the chopper, JFK dashed past reporters, making straightaway for the Oval Office. There he closeted himself with Theodore Sorensen.

Reaching across the desk, Sorensen handed the President a sheaf of documents, papers on which Excomm members and their advisers had been working throughout the morning. The materials included letters, messages, and contingency papers, and, finally approved by Excomm, Sorensen's draft speech for

Kennedy. JFK glanced at the materials, then headed down to the White House pool.

He took a swim, talking with his brother Robert, seated by the edge of the water. Just before 2:30, the President toweled himself dry, and dressed; together the brothers walked upstairs. The President was about to meet again with Excomm, whose members had been arriving at the White House—and to allay press suspicions, entering by different gates.

For even at this point, midway through the afternoon of October 20, 1962, the White House was trying to mislead the press. Officials were in the Cabinet Room, *The New York Times* would tell its readers the next day, to review "policy, on Berlin . . . The unyielding posture adopted by the Russians . . . this week has spurred the administration to review and refine its planning for all contingencies in and around Berlin."

This diversion of attention from Cuba to Berlin was plausible enough. Berlin had heated up again. But one point the administration did *not* want discussed too loudly was the link between Berlin and Cuba. A certain symmetry did in fact exist. Russia could threaten Berlin and America could threaten Cuba. For political reasons, however, the White House wished to deny that symmetry. What Americans wanted to hear was that Russia could threaten Berlin and that Cuba, a Russian proxy, could threaten America.

2   Braving the chill and drizzle that covered most of America east of the Mississippi, football fans turned out in the afternoon to watch the collegiate games. Northwestern stunned Ohio State, in Columbus, with a last-minute touchdown. Oberlin lost, naturally, humilated 41–0 by Ohio Wesleyan. Texas beat Arkansas. Michigan State thrashed Notre Dame. In New England, the midshipmen from Annapolis downed Boston College, 26–6.

Midway through the afternoon, Admiral Alfred Ward, commander of the Norfolk Navy Base, was relaxing on the grand porch of the Chamberlin Hotel, a multistoried brick edifice that overlooked the mouth of the James River; he was chatting with friends and listening on the radio to the Navy game. He was called to the telephone. Within the hour, Ward, a stocky man with an Alabama accent, had taken off from nearby Langley Air Base, landed in Washington, and gone to the Pentagon. There he received orders.

He was to return right away to Norfolk. From there he was to lead the naval blockade of Cuba.

In the White House itself, President Kennedy was meeting again with Excomm. This was to be the afternoon of decision.

John McCone of the CIA led off, holding up the latest photographs taken from over the territory of Cuba. From around the Cabinet table, Excomm members watched in silence, as if McCone, in the words of one of the participants, was a minister "saying grace."

Then debate opened again. In a "brilliant architectonic presentation," Secretary McNamara argued that a blockade of Cuba would "maintain the options"; National Security Adviser Bundy contended that the most efficient and direct method of removing the missiles from Cuba would be an air strike. Then, as everyone looked at the President, there followed—according to Sorensen—"a brief, awkward silence."

Roswell Gilpatric broke the silence.

"Essentially, Mr. President," he said, "this is a choice between limited action and unlimited action, and most of us think that it's better to start with limited action."

President Kennedy was still. A light rain spattered against the windows of the Cabinet Room.

At last the President spoke. The only course compatible with American principles, he said, softly, was a blockade.

So a blockade it would be, and the discussion turned to details— diplomatic initiatives, public statements, military preparations, the scenario for the blockade (or, as President Kennedy now was calling it, a "quarantine"), final changes in Kennedy's speech. President Kennedy should address the nation, the discussants agreed, two days later, on Monday, October 22, 1962, at 7:00 P.M., on television. Everything now seemed to be in order.

But at this point, probably around 4:30 to 5:00 P.M., Adlai Stevenson waddled in. He had just flown down from New York.

Even though he had missed most of the afternoon's discussion, he expected everyone to listen to his own proposal.

So far the Excomm meeting had been harmonious. Now all hell broke loose.

What the United States ought to do, Stevenson asserted, was to suggest "the demilitarization, neutralization, and guaranteed territorial integrity of Cuba, thus giving up Guantánamo, . . . of little use to us, in exchange for the removal of all Soviet bases on Cuba." And, he added, we should "offer to withdraw our Turkish and Italian Jupiter missile bases if the Russians would withdraw their Cuban missile bases, and send U.N. inspection teams to all the foreign bases maintained by both sides to prevent their use in a surprise attack." This offer "would not sound soft, if properly worded," Stevenson concluded. "It would sound wise, particularly when combined with U.S. military action."

Stevenson was speaking, or at least implying, the unspeakable: that America's nuclear posture was indeed provocative and that America had been indeed threatening Cuba's "territorial integrity."

A few days later, Stevenson was taking the shuttle, flying back to New York. As he settled back in his seat, he opened the newest issue of *The Saturday Evening Post*. On the cover, in garish black and yellow, were pictures of Kennedy and Khrushchev. Stevenson checked the table of contents, then turned to the issue's major article.

He had been tipped off to expect trouble. The article, nonetheless, was stunning.

Written by two Washington journalists, Stewart Alsop and Charles Bartlett, the story was an exposé of what had happened in the Saturday Excomm meeting. According to the article, Stevenson was like Neville Chamberlain, complete with tightly rolled umbrella, mincing into the White House to advocate appeasement. "Adlai wanted a Munich," the piece declared, quoting an official who learned of his proposal to trade the Turkish, Italian, and British bases for the Cuban bases.' "

So somebody inside the Kennedy administration had accused Adlai Stevenson of being a virtual traitor. But who? Stewart Alsop, down in Venezuela when *The Saturday Evening Post* hit the stands, refused to comment. McGeorge Bundy denied everything. Co-author Bartlett, other reporters remembered, had been godfather to the President's son, John F. Kennedy, Jr. So was President Kennedy himself the source?

We probably shall never know. It is clear, however, that the "bitter aftertaste" of the attacks Stevenson faced that Saturday afternoon—attacks permitted by President Kennedy—"stayed with him until his death." And it is equally clear that, in the words of one historian, President Kennedy deliberately "sacrificed" Ambassador Stevenson "to the hawks in order to allow himself to choose the moderate, golden mean."

After the end of the Excomm meeting, the Kennedy brothers, along with Kenneth O'Donnell and Theodore Sorensen, stepped outside the White House. Dusk was falling, and through the mist below the Ellipse, the Washington Monument was almost invisible.

They talked about Stevenson. "He's not strong enough or tough enough to be representing us at the U.N. at a time like this," Robert Kennedy said derisively. Stevenson should be replaced, he went on, supplanted most likely by John J. McCloy.

"Now wait a minute," President Kennedy said. This was in Kenneth O'Donnell's version. "I think Adlai showed plenty of strength and courage. . . . Maybe he went too far when he suggested giving up Guantánamo, but . . . I admire him for saying what he did."

Perhaps.

Perhaps these were indeed the President's words.

By the middle of the next week, nevertheless, JFK had reached McCloy by telephone, asking him to return from Europe and to "help" Stevenson.

3   Late Saturday afternoon was a blur of movements.

From their Glen Ora estate, thirty-five miles out of the capital in Virginia, Mrs. Kennedy at the President's request returned to the White House; he wanted his family close by.

In the Pentagon, the Joint Chiefs of Staff signaled U.S. commanders worldwide that tensions in Cuba might soon call for action.

Out in Southern California's Camp Pendleton, young Marines with shaved skulls and crisp uniforms hopped on to trucks and rode to El Toro, the Corps air station close to Los Angeles. From there they took off in jet transports, heading back east.

All along the East Coast, from Charleston in South Carolina to Halifax in Nova Scotia, American vessels of war were putting out to sea.

Down in Key West, truck convoys, some pulling trailers and all driven by Marines, moved out from the dock area along Roosevelt Boulevard and headed for Boca Chica Naval Air Station, four miles to the north.

Out in the Caribbean, off Puerto Rico, Spanish-speaking Vice Admiral Horacio Rivero was moving a force of more than forty ships and twenty thousand men to stage a mock amphibious assault on the nearby island of Vieques. Then he received orders to reverse course, and he started in the direction of Cuba.

In Puerto Rico itself, Alpha 66, paramilitary Cuban exiles, set off by PT boat for a hit-and-run mission on Cuba. A U.S. newsman learned how this mission, and many like it, started off. "Within the shadow of San Juan's fortress walls," the *New York Herald Tribune* related, "far out among the homes that cluster along the city's hilly fringe, the courier goes his quiet rounds with a few chosen words: '*Es tu turno, Pedro. Dios vaya contigo—y ten cuidado de los MIGs.*' 'It's your turn, Pedro. God go with you—and mind the MIGs.'"

Along the Florida Strait, four American destroyers positioned themselves about halfway between the United States and Cuba.

And in the Guantánamo base, huge troop planes, full of reinforcements, lowered themselves over the harbor, where swampy islets dotted the water, and lumbered down onto the Tres Piedras, or Leward Point airstrip. The lush green hillsides that rimmed the base belonged to Cuba.

"Firm evidence indicates the presence in Cuba of four MRBM and two IRBM launch sites in various stages of construction . . . ," a CIA analyst wrote on Saturday. "We estimate that operational MRBM missiles can be fired in eight hours or less after a decision to launch, depending on the condition of readiness."

The writer made no mention of actual, long-range Soviet

missiles in Cuba. He did, however, spell out an "inventory of other major Soviet missiles now identified in Cuba . . . :

"a. 22 IL-28 jet light bombers, of which one is assembled and three others have been uncrated;

"b. 39 MIG-21 jet fighters, of which 35 are assembled and four are still crated, and 62 other jet fighters of less advanced types;

"c. 24 SA-2 sites, of which 16 are believed to be individually operational with some missiles on launcher;

"d. 3 cruise missile sites for coastal defense, of which 2 are now operational;

"e. 12 Komar cruise missile patrol boats, probably operational or nearly so."

The Soviets, in short, had been anticipating an American invasion of Cuba. And their defenses appeared now to be in place.

Messages were flashing out of Washington.

Douglas Dillon, Secretary of the Treasury, was packing his bags for a trip to Mexico City. He would arrive on Monday, just before President Kennedy announced the quarantine of Cuba; he would proclaim an increase of foreign aid to Latin America— Cuba, of course, excepted.

Walter C. Dowling, the compact, red-haired U.S. ambassador to West Germany, was back home in Atkinson, Georgia, visiting his elderly mother. A telephone call from the State Department summoned him to Washington immediately.

Dean Acheson was relaxing on his farm in Maryland; there he received a telephone call from Dean Rusk. Would Acheson, Rusk asked, drive to the White House in the morning? President Kennedy wished the former Secretary of State to fly to Paris.

Livingston T. Merchant, twice U.S. ambassador to Canada, was a tall, slender, brown-eyed descendant of one of the signers of the Declaration of Independence; now in retirement, he was spending the afternoon watching the football game at Princeton, his alma mater. Afterwards, he dined at the Nassau Inn. Back in his hotel room, then, he had a message: he was to call the State Department without delay. He did so. Secretary Rusk, he learned, wanted him to fly to Ottawa. Merchant would deliver a special message to Canada's Prime Minister, John Diefenbaker.

. . .

These comings and goings still remained secret. But the news-hounds of Washington were baying, smelling a story and tracking the scent.

Hitting the telephone, James Reston—"Scotty"—the premier reporter and columnist of *The New York Times*, reached enough sources to put the pieces together. A Scot by birth and a believer always in clean living and hard work, Reston was the first of the journalists to see the pattern. Figuring that the U.S. was going to throw some kind of ring around Cuba, he rang up George Ball and McGeorge Bundy, challenging them to show he was wrong. They would not do so. They could only beg him, for the moment anyway, to withhold publication. Reston agreed.

But Reston was not alone. Walter Lippmann, the brilliant, hawk-nosed dean of the Washington press corps and devotee of the cocktail circuit, realized on Saturday that he had not seen a high-level administration official at parties in days.

"You know," Lippmann said at a Saturday evening affair to Alfred Friendly, managing editor of *The Washington Post*, "something fishy is going on, and I think it has to do with Cuba."

Rushing to a telephone, Friendly ordered a phalanx of reporters down to the State Department.

At 10:38 P.M.: "A call from Eddie Folliard of *The Washington Post*"—this from Pierre Salinger's memoirs. "He informs me that columnist Walter Lippmann has just told *Post* editor Al Friendly . . . that we're on the brink of war. I call the President. . . . He's angry. 'This town is a sieve.' Then, after a pause, 'Pierre, how much longer do you think this thing can hold?' "

" 'Whatever the story is,' I reply, 'too many good reporters are chasing it for it to hold much longer. I would say through tonight and maybe tomorrow.'

" 'All right, Pierre,' said John F. Kennedy. 'I'll have Bundy fill you in on the whole thing in the morning.' "

4   *October 21, 1962*
Deep inside the bay at Guantánamo, the U.S. carrier ship *Essex*

lay resting at anchor, most of its crew asleep in their bunks. The time was 3:30 A.M. Watchmen on duty in the control tower could barely see the airplanes parked on the deck, for Hurricane Ella had just passed up through the Caribbean, and the night-time air was dense with humidity. About the only noise was that of the water as it lapped up on the sides of the vessel.

Two sounds smashed the stillness: the piping of reveille and the chugging of engines. For a message had just come in from Washington that several thousand Marines were aboard trans-port planes, scheduled to reach Guantánamo before dawn, and the *Essex* was to put out to sea to give the planes protection.

As the Marines landed, they streamed out of their airplanes, and, still in the darkness, the headlights of their vehicles pointed up toward the rim of the base. There they proceeded to dig themselves into bunkers.

Much farther to the north, but still before dawn, a row of destroyers was slipping out from the Navy piers at Norfolk, using the fog to conceal departure. The sun rose soon. But once the flotilla had passed the mouth of the Chesapeake Bay and positioned itself beyond the Outer Banks of North Carolina, it slowed course, awaiting the arrival of a helicopter squadron from the mainland. Aboard the choppers were servicemen who knew Russian—combing through its language-school rosters, the Pentagon had rounded up a dozen or so linguists, now putting them aboard the ships. Thus the destroyers would be ready for encounters with vessels from Russia.

Taking off from the San Juan airport, a group of sixteen Ameri-can reporters flew over to Roosevelt Roads, the U.S. naval reser-vation on the eastern tip of Puerto Rico; from there they had expected to witness the Marine Corps' amphibious mock as-sault on the coral beach of Vieques, just across the Caribbean channel. But the bay at Roosevelt Roads was nearly empty—few ships, fewer Marines, and certainly no invasion.

A Navy officer gave a press conference, purporting to explain what was going on. Hurricane Ella, he stated, had left the fleet scattered. The ships would be reassembled by Monday.

Taking the officer at his word, the reporters relaxed. Some

played cards in the mess, others strolled among the piers and palm trees, watching the sun climb high over the ocean.

One reporter dug up a member of Alpha 66, the Cuban paramilitary unit. The unit, its member swore, would sink any ships headed into Havana—for Britain was defying the American-run embargo of Cuba.

As night turned to day in Washington, the air cleared and churchgoers set off in bright morning sunshine. But Pierre Salinger hardly saw the sun, at least not until much later in the day. Even before dawn he was in the White House basement, meeting with McGeorge Bundy in the Situation Room. There "were guards outside the door," Salinger wrote—"huge maps of Cuba and its sea approaches on the walls—a continuous clatter of teletypes."

"Mac [Bundy] didn't pull punches," Salinger went on. "He told me we were, at that very moment, on the brink of nuclear war. We had absolute evidence of offensive Soviet missiles in Cuba—missiles that could destroy Washington, New York, and all other major cities on the Eastern seaboard and in the South.

" 'They're not yet fully operational,' Bundy told me, 'but they will be in a matter of days. We intend to take whatever action we must—probably a blockade—to force their removal before that time.' "

Salinger learned something else, too, from Bundy: "A highly secret and intricate plan exists for converting our national government from its many and cumbersome peacetime activities to a single-purpose instrument of war. My areas of responsibility were to maintain the President's communications with the people, no matter where he might be, and to halt the flow of all information which might prove useful to the enemy."

Salinger's job, in short, was to make the President's case as palatable as possible. For even as he talked with Bundy, others in the White House were drafting a document called the "U.S. case"—a set of guidelines for briefing America and, indeed, the world.

"It is imperative that we obtain maximum public support . . . for our policies and actions with respect to Cuba." So stated the document. "In developing guidance on the line to be followed . . . ," it went on, "the following main points should be included:

"1. The Soviets stated publicly and privately that only defensive weapons were being sent to Cuba. This is now proven as false as many other Soviet premises. . . .

"2. The Soviets are artificially seeking to create for their own aggressive purposes a connection which would not otherwise exist between Berlin and Cuba. . . .

"3. The great difference between the Soviet base in Cuba and allied bases elsewhere lies in the peaceful purposes of the Free World and the aggressive purposes of the Communist bloc. . . .

"4. This reckless Soviet act has endangered the peace of the world. . . .

"5. The U.S. action is just and self-restrained. . . ."

As if to underline the words "just and self-restrained," President and Mrs. Kennedy, at about 9:30 A.M., went to mass up the street at St. Stephen's Roman Catholic Church. Tucked away off Pennsylvania Avenue, just before the bridge over Rock Creek to Georgetown, the church—called St. Stephen the Martyr—was unpretentious and small, with a brick façade and an abstract glasswork design over the main front door. Photographers were on hand to record the presidential approach. JFK was wearing a dark suit with a narrow necktie and a white handkerchief tucked into the left breast pocket; Mrs. Kennedy was wearing a tweed suit, and her head was covered with a cloth of black lace.

They both looked somber, and they sat through mass with most serious expressions. At 10:46 their motorcade whisked them back to the White House.

Hardly was he back in the Executive Mansion than President Kennedy was occupied with a small meeting in the Oval Office. The sun was high by this point, and its rays, streaming in through the French windows, fell on the carpeting that led to the couch and the stuffed chairs. Ranged around the President, who was in his rocker, were Robert Kennedy, Robert McNamara, Air Force General Walter C. Sweeney, and Chairman of the Joint Chiefs, Maxwell Taylor.

The last three officials were pushing hard on the President, adamant on the need for an air strike. McNamara reported that, on the basis of information obtained the night before, Cuba now had about forty missile launchers; Sweeney urged Kennedy to authorize bombing attacks on the MIG airfields in Cuba; Taylor stated that an initial strike could take out "90 percent of the known missiles," and then a ground invasion could remove any remaining dangers.

At this juncture—probably around noon—a crew of CIA representatives joined the meeting. They had urgent news: eight to twelve Soviet missiles in Cuba, their reports were indicating, now were operational, capable of being fired in three to four hours.

CIA Director John McCone also had come to the White House. He wanted immediate action—bombing action.

President Kennedy, however, stuck with the blockade. Still, as a memorandum of the meeting written by Secretary McNamara shows, he told the generals they should be ready to carry out an air strike at any time after the next twenty-four hours.

Even before the meeting adjourned, a limousine from the British embassy had swung past the West Gate of the White House complex, and come to a halt in the driveway under the North Portico. Out of the car stepped Ambassador David Ormsby-Gore, tall, elegant, wearing a dark suit and a striped shirt with cuff links. He had come, by invitation from the President, for lunch.

As soon as Kennedy was free, he greeted his old friend from London days, and they dined together upstairs in the Kennedy family quarters. After coffee, they sat on the Truman balcony, looking down toward the sailboats on the Tidal Basin and the river beyond. Kennedy let Ormsby-Gore know what was going on.

By early afternoon, Ormsby-Gore was back at the red brick British embassy, wiring a report to Prime Minister Harold Macmillan. And Kennedy was engaging in last-minute preparations for an afternoon session with the full National Security Council.

"What was his [President Kennedy's] mood during that time, generally? How would you describe his mood?"

In 1964, James Greenfield, Assistant Secretary of State for Public Affairs, conducted an oral history interview with Donald M. Wilson who, in October 1962, had been Deputy Director of the U.S. Information Agency. On October 21, 1962, Wilson had attended the afternoon White House meeting.

Kennedy "was completely in charge," Wilson remembered in the interview. "He was very calm and he was very serious. There was no humor that I can recall, at that particular time, and everybody was working very hard. [T]he mood was somber and serious and very businesslike."

As the afternoon meeting began, Secretary Rusk ticked off a list of things the State Department had been doing: drafting resolutions, writing letters to various heads of government, wiring instructions to America's more than one hundred embassies abroad.

Then President Kennedy gave the floor to Admiral George Anderson, tall, well-built, deeply tanned, and Chief of Naval Operations. Anderson outlined the quarantine procedures. Each Soviet ship approaching the quarantine line, he stated, would be signaled to stop for boarding and inspection. If the ship made no response, a U.S. vessel would fire a shot across the bow. If there was still no response, the Navy would shoot the rudder and cripple the ship, although not sinking it.

"You're certain that can be done?" President Kennedy asked.

"Yes, sir!" Admiral Anderson replied.

Soon after this exchange, President Kennedy and Robert Lovett, one of JFK's most trusted advisers, stepped out of the Cabinet Room together. An elder statesman now, Lovett was still tough-minded and witty, a key figure in the Washington–New York foreign policy establishment, a man whose opinion counted. And the opinion Kennedy wanted, as they conversed just outside the Cabinet Room, was whether Adlai Stevenson was up to handling a United Nations debate over Cuba. Lovett was characteristically blunt—he thought Stevenson a weakling.

Kennedy agreed; and Lovett's special assignment was that of working out details of John J. McCloy's flight back from Europe.

Back in the Cabinet Room—and soon closing the meeting— JFK announced that, while America might face threats and violence in the days ahead, the "biggest danger [lies] in taking no action."

As the group disbanded, Kennedy spoke with Admiral Anderson.

"This is up to the Navy," the President said.

"Mr. President," Anderson assured, "the Navy won't let you down."

The military indeed did not let him down. Unknown even to Defense Secretary McNamara, the commander of the Strategic Air Command raised his preparedness measures to the next-to-highest level of alert; he did so, furthermore, in a clear, uncoded order, a message promptly read by Soviet intelligence. The U.S., an observer later remembered, was rubbing "the Soviets' noses in their nuclear inferiority." For Khrushchev never did put his own forces on alert: "We had a gun at his head," a U.S. Air Force general would recall, "and he didn't move a muscle."

5　　　Sunday evening found Washington, the inner Washington, the covert Washington, erupting with action and alarms.

The State Department received an urgent message from the embassy in Caracas. In a letter dated October 12, 1962, someone in Venezuela had threatened the lives of "all American citizens" living in the country if the U.S. invaded Cuba or blockaded the island.

In his massive office in the Pentagon, Defense Secretary McNamara met throughout the evening with Admiral Anderson and other top brass, approving quarantine procedures and rules of engagement. He also authorized "Air Force interceptors flying in the United States to carry nuclear weapons."

From the State Department, a message flashed to all U.S. diplomatic posts in the Western Hemisphere. "[Y]ou are instructed," the circular ordered, "to use whatever pressure tac-

tics you think will be most effective in securing prompt support" of the Latin American countries in the Organization of
American States. Diplomats were to remind hemispheric leaders
of "strong U.S. governmental and public feelings which will
exist about any country which does not support . . . solidarity
on this issue." The Kennedy administration was playing hard-
ball.

From his seat aboard *Air Force One*, Douglas Dillon, the Secretary of the Treasury, had a view of the mountain chains that
surrounded Mexico City. After landing, the presidential jet took
off again right away, off to transport congressional leaders back
to Washington. (Lawrence O'Brien, once Kennedy's campaign
manager and now White House Chief of Relations with Congress, had been working the telephone all day, asking the members, scattered nationwide as they ran for reelection, to return.)
Dillon himself proceeded to the American embassy. There, in
conference with Ambassador Thomas Mann, Dillon urged that
they tell Mexican leaders immediately of the impending blockade. Since President Adolfo López Mateos was out of the country, Dillon and Mann briefed Ortiz Mena, Mexico's finance
minister.

Aboard another Air Force jet, Dean Acheson, the former Secretary of State, was winging his way toward Europe, off to see
France's President Charles de Gaulle, but first to talk with
David K. E. Bruce, America's ambassador to Britain. When the
airplane put down at the Newbury base, west of London and
just south of Oxford, Acheson, accompanied by a CIA man who
carried photographs of the missile launchers, descended the
ramp. Darkness had fallen and a cold wind whipped over the
runway. Only one person was on hand to greet Acheson, Ambassador Bruce.

"I thought this would be a day of quietude," Bruce would
write in his diary.

> Such is not the case. I received a message from Washington early in the
> morning, asking whether I expected to be in London today and tomor-
> row [Bruce was spending the weekend in an English country house]. A
> couple of hours later, I began to get telephone calls and messages

transmitted through three separate embassy channels, indicating that something unusual was astir in Washington. Telegrams brought out to me were not especially enlightening until supplemented by a conversation with Bill Tyler in the [State] Department, who said I was to meet a military plane at twelve o'clock tonight. . . . A telegram that followed mystified me slightly by naming one of the passengers on the plane as Dean Acheson.

However mystified, Bruce did his duty. Accompanied by an aide, he drove the two-hour trip to the airfield near Newbury.

Tall and distinguished, Bruce had come from money and had married money—Mellon money—and almost by inheritance he possessed the right touch. Just for Acheson, he had brought along a bottle of scotch.

Bruce also said, "Put your hand in my pocket and see what's there."

Acheson did so, reaching his fingers into the side pocket of Bruce's overcoat. There lay a revolver.

"Why?" Acheson asked.

"I don't know," Bruce answered. "I was told by the Department of State to carry this when I went to meet you."

"There was nothing said about shooting me, was there?" Acheson quipped.

"No," Bruce retorted. "Would you think it's a good idea?"

Giving Bruce an overview of the Cuban missile crisis, Acheson passed along instructions for Bruce to see Prime Minister Macmillan the next day. Bruce was to pass along the photographs of the Soviet missile launchers. Even before Kennedy gave his speech, thus, the British Cabinet would have physical proof of the existence of danger.

Acheson then flew on to Paris. He got to bed at three in the morning.

Flying in another airplane and descending over the seemingly endless birch forest that surrounded Ottawa, Livingston Merchant reached the Canadian capital. His mission, he knew, would be sensitive. In 1957, Canada and America had joined in creating the North American Air Defense System (NORAD), a plan for linking the two countries' military forces in cases of emergency. And now was a time of emergency. But Canada's tall, curly-haired Prime Minister from the prairies out in the west, John G. Diefenbaker, was still known in Washington for his prickliness toward America in general and his distrust of John F. Kennedy in particular. Merchant knew full well that he would have to proceed with tact.

Back in Washington, the big secret was crumbling fast. "[Too] many reporters had seen too many lights," in the words of Elie Abel, "burning too late in unexpected places." Indeed, by late evening, President Kennedy realized he had no choice: he himself called Max Frankel and Phillip Graham, publishers of *The New York Times* and *The Washington Post*; and he also had Robert McNamara telephone John Hay Whitney of the *New York Herald Tribune*. All three pressmen agreed to hold the full story.

But the genie was out of the bottle—and into the next morning's top headlines.

The Miami Herald: "IS MAJOR U.S. MOVE IN STORE FOR CUBA NEXT?"

The *Chicago Tribune:* "WHITE HOUSE SILENT ON CUBA CRISIS RUMORS!"

The *San Francisco Examiner:* "A DAY OF MYSTERY IN D.C.!"

The New York Times: "CAPITAL'S CRISIS AIR HINTS AT DEVELOPMENTS ON CUBA; KENNEDY TV TALK LIKELY!"

"There was an air of crisis in the capital tonight," *The New York Times* went on, referring to the evening of October 21, 1962.

"President Kennedy and the highest administration officials have been in almost constant conference all weekend, imparting serious agitation and tension to official Washington.

"Mr. Kennedy is expected to go on television to give the country an explanation in the next day or two, but he has wrapped a tight veil of secrecy around the source of his concern so far.

"Coincidentally, the Navy and the Marine Corps were staging a powerful show of force in the Caribbean, not far from Cuba, which has been the site of a large Communist buildup in recent weeks.

"The administration denies that there is any connection between the anxious mood here and these maneuvers, which involve about 20,000 men, including 6,000 Marines.

"But the speculation in Washington was that there has been a new development in Cuba that cannot be disclosed at this point. . . ."

CHAPTER 11

Prime Time

1   *Monday, October 22, 1962*
Plowing through the morning snowdrifts, Moscow's first of the
season, a dark Volga sedan stopped in front of an apartment
building, the car's occupants racing toward the edifice. The
occupants were from the KGB. Within moments they made a
critical arrest—Red Army Colonel Oleg Penkovsky, who in fact
was a spy. Recruited by British intelligence in April 1961, Penkovsky had been passing along reams of secrets, including evidence that Soviet rocketry was far less advanced than America's.

Was Penkovsky's arrest—carried out on the day of Kennedy's
television broadcast—coincidental? We cannot know. In the
judgment of the CIA, nonetheless, the information he had
shared was of "supreme importance."

The morning skies over Florida were dark with airplanes, and
the top news item was the reports of war. The state, declared
the *Miami News*, "bristled with armed might, from Jacksonville
to Key West." Military aircraft by the scores were descending on
the air bases. Workers at the Key West airport were working
around the clock to improve the control tower. Nearly every
U.S. naval vessel was putting out to sea—so many sailors were

gone that, in the words of the *Miami Herald*, the Mardi Gras nightclub on Key West's Duval Street was as "quiet as a YMCA."

A crisis clearly was looming. In the Canal Zone, U.S. military personnel loaded transport planes with more than eighty tons of matériel, including rifles, carbines, ammunition, grenades, gas masks, and helmets, equipment then airlifted for the protection of the nation's embassies throughout Latin America. In Guantánamo, the U.S. force level was doubled, civilians and dependents racing to airplanes to fly to the safety of Norfolk. And in Washington, the Pentagon was ordering the Strategic Air Command to keep one-eighth of its B-52 force in the air at all times; those aircraft, and many others, were to be armed with nuclear bombs.

Lights came on early in the State Department and the White House windows, as reporters could plainly see. Behind those windows, officials were putting down their last-minute thoughts—and rationales.

Averell Harriman, tall, stoop-shouldered, rich, a past ambassador to Russia and a present behind-the-scenes wielder of power (someone had said of Harriman, "He's the only ambitious seventy-year-old I know"), was giving the State Department the benefit of recent experience. "There has undoubtedly been great pressure on Khrushchev for a considerable time to do something about our ring of bases, aggravated by our placing Jupiter missiles in Turkey," he wrote in a secret memorandum. "Wherever I went during my visit to the Soviet Union in June 1959, even in Central Asia and Siberia, people asked me, 'Why do you have your bases threatening to attack us? We were such close friends during the war. Why don't you want to live in peace?' . . . In my judgment, Khrushchev has been under pressure from his military and from the more aggressive group to use Cuba to counter U.S. action and to offset the humiliation [of] nuclear bases close to their borders." Thus, Harriman advised, the Kennedy administration should pin blame on the hawks in the Kremlin, allowing Khrushchev to save face. Harriman then urged a swap—missiles in Cuba for missiles in Turkey, as Adlai Stevenson also had urged.

Another official, at the White House and on a White House notepad, was scrawling these words:

> Is there a plan to brief
> and brainwash key press
> within 12 hours or so?
> —*N.Y. Times*
> —Lippmann
> —Childs
> —Alsop
> —Key bureau chiefs?

Walter Lippmann, Marquis Childs, Joseph and Stewart Alsop were prominent Washington columnists. But who had authored the note? It "may," stated a later intelligence report, "have been penned by the President himself." But the John F. Kennedy Library in Massachusetts, keeper of the note, has asserted otherwise. According to the library, the note "was written by Maj. Gen. Chester 'Ted' Clifton, who served as a military aide to President Kennedy. Clifton wrote it during a meeting of the National Security Council, left it on the table where it was picked up by Evelyn Lincoln, President Kennedy's secretary, [who] placed it in the presidential files. It was never brought to President Kennedy's attention." Perhaps not. But, clearly, *somebody* in the White House was interested in brainwashing the press.

And McGeorge Bundy, the national security adviser, was typing up another memorandum, and *this* piece of paper *did* reach Kennedy. In the hubbub of the last few days, Bundy confessed, he had "left" something "out" of the message to Prime Minister Macmillan: "if the Soviet nuclear buildup in Cuba continues, it would be a threat to the whole strategic balance of power, because really large numbers of missiles from this launch could create a first-strike temptation. Any such shift in the balance would be just as damaging to our allies as to us. The missiles that are there now do not create this hazard but a further buildup would."

America, to Bundy's thinking, could live with the missiles already in Cuba, as Russia was living with the missiles already in Turkey. So if the missiles already in Cuba—missiles JFK wanted withdrawn—were no threat to America's security, to what were they a threat? Democratic chances in the November election?

· · ·

Eleven in the morning found President Kennedy in the Oval Office, presiding over an Excomm meeting. As the participants were taking their seats, he happened to glance through the French windows and spy, out on the White House lawn, his daughter Caroline and several other children from her Washington nursery school. Rising from his desk, Kennedy suddenly strode outside and, as he sometimes did to get his daughter's attention, clapped his hands. She did not come running up, and he returned to his desk.

A moment later she dashed into the Oval Office.

"Daddy," she said. "I would have come sooner but Miss Grimes [Alice Grimes, the teacher] would not let me go."

"That's all right, Caroline," JFK said, and she scampered outside again.

Kennedy now turned his full attention to the meeting. He had just had messages sent to the U.S. missile commanders in Italy and Turkey, he said, directing that no Jupiter be fired without his explicit authorization.

But then a public relations problem cropped up. Instead of basing a blockade of Cuba on the United Nations Charter, which assured a country's right of self-defense in case of armed attack, contended State Department lawyer Abram Chayes, the President might stress the right of the Organization of American States (headquartered on Seventeenth Street, just downhill from the Old Executive Office Building) to "take collective measures to protect hemispheric security." Kennedy agreed with Chayes. But why the new justification? Was Excomm afraid that citing the U.N. Charter might be dangerous? That the Cubans would bring up their own right to self-defense? And, in the U.N., state that point for the world to hear?

And another point got settled, this one brought up by State Department lawyer Leonard Meeker: the blockade ought to be called a "quarantine." In the autumn of 1937, President Franklin D. Roosevelt had urged a "quarantine" of Nazi Germany and Imperial Japan. Now, by using the word himself, JFK could wrap his Cuba policy in the mantle of FDR.

Concerned always with image, then, Kennedy gave a last-minute directive just before the meeting adjourned. After his television address that evening, he said, he would allow photographers to record some of the Excomm sessions. So, whenever the cameras were around, everyone on the committee would have to keep his suit jacket on, his necktie up, and his demeanor serious. In the days ahead, appearances would matter.

2   So would support from the allies. The greater the accord among America's partners, the more would Kennedy's forthcoming action appear just—in the eyes of America's voters. Hence special missions to special capitals.

Bonn   In the dowdy little West German capital, a provincial town overladen with official buildings that looked like barracks, U.S. Ambassador Walter C. Dowling was closeting himself with the Chancellor of the Federal Republic, Konrad Adenauer. Once the mayor of Cologne and twice imprisoned by Hitler, Adenauer was known throughout Germany as *Der Alte*, the Old Man; eighty-six years old and stiff in posture, he looked out on the world from behind high, almost Slavic, cheekbones, and a face that looked like parchment. In all of Europe he probably was America's most loyal ally.

Dowling showed him the photographs taken from high over Cuba, as well as the text of Kennedy's forthcoming speech, and Adenauer responded with enthusiasm. If the United States "could seize [a] Soviet ship en route to Cuba with military equipment . . . ," Adenauer allowed, "it would make [an] overwhelming impression on world opinion."

London   Allowed to enter through the front door of Number 10 Downing Street, Ambassador David Bruce passed along a corridor lined with portraits of Prime Ministers past, and entered the study of the Prime Minister present, Harold Macmillan. Grandson of the London and New York publishing firm family, Macmillan had grown up with the gifts of the most privileged: French, from his nanny in nursery, as his first language; an intelligence so keen that, after schooling at Eton, he had won double firsts in mathematics and classics at Balliol College, Oxford; a fearlessness, or perhaps an upper-class–bred sense of independence, that had won the approbation of Winston S. Churchill; a suavity that, in the words of one journalist, had enabled him to "turn up in Moscow wearing an astrakhan cap, or sit cross-legged talking oil with a Middle Eastern sheik without loss of dignity." Macmillan was six feet tall, with an Edwardian mustache and brown eyes so drooping that they looked like the eyes of a basset hound. Those eyes also were attentive, as Macmillan followed every word spoken by Ambassador David Bruce.

Bruce supported his words with the photographs, and Macmillan responded with warmth. His first reaction, he confessed later, was to tell Kennedy "to seize Cuba and have done with it." So he said to Bruce, "Now the Americans will realize what we here in England have lived through [the threat of attack from abroad] for the past many years." President Kennedy, he added, could be assured of Great Britain's support.

Macmillan's perspective, however, differed from the Americans'. For, to Macmillan, Europe mattered far more than Cuba—especially since he already had received from Ambassador Ormsby-Gore in Washington a wire stating that "the missiles so far landed [in Cuba] contributed little significant military threat to the United States."

Macmillan offered to support Kennedy. But he failed to define "support."

Paris   As former Secretary of State Dean Acheson entered the Elysée Palace to see France's President, Charles de Gaulle, even he—even Acheson—must have felt trepidation. For de Gaulle, at best, was difficult.

"I remember very well the first time I met General de Gaulle," wrote Mary Borden, an English novelist and wife of a general. After the fall of France in 1940, de Gaulle, a two-star general, had escaped to London, there to establish the Free French resistance. Borden encountered him at a dinner party. "It was almost like fear," she went on. "It was certainly mingled with a painfully strong feeling of revulsion. He had brought

Madame de Gaulle to dine with us. . . . A gentle, slight timid figure, I turned to her with relief, watching de Gaulle out of the corner of my eye, not wanting to look straight at him. I watched him through the evening. His face never showed the slightest change of expression as he talked. No flicker of interest lifted his hooded eyelids. I was fascinated, the novelist came into play. I began to study him. . . . His one relief, in fact his one pleasure, was to hate. And he hated . . . most especially those who tried to be his friends. . . . To come to the British as a suppliant . . . was intolerable. The weaker his position the more arrogant he became."

Even sympathizers of the tall, gangling French general were left aghast. During his weekdays in London he lived in the Connaught Hotel, and one night invited General Edward Spears (Mary Borden's husband) and a few others to dine with him privately. "As we sat round the gas fire after dinner," Spears wrote, "de Gaulle said suddenly, following a thought unperceived by the others, 'You know, I really am Joan of Arc.' "

Harold Macmillan said of de Gaulle, in the war years: "He was never rude by mistake." President Franklin D. Roosevelt dismissed de Gaulle as a "nut."

Now, in 1962, of course, de Gaulle was the President of France. And as Dean Acheson knew full well, de Gaulle's haughtiness—and his distrust of the English-speaking world—remained unabated.

As Acheson entered de Gaulle's ornate office, the old general rose stiffly from his desk, shook hands, sat again, and said, in French of course, *"Je vous écoute"* ("I am listening to you").

Acheson handed him a letter from President Kennedy. "Dear General de Gaulle," Kennedy had written: "I have asked Mr. Dean Acheson to come to Paris to convey to you the text of a public statement which I intend to make this evening at 1900 hours Washington time. We now have unquestionable evidence, which Mr. Acheson will explain fully to you, that the Soviets, in spite of my warnings last month and of their subsequent assurances, have installed offensive nuclear missiles in Cuba. This constitutes a direct threat to the peace and to the security of this hemisphere and of the entire free world. . . .

"I need not point out to you the possible relation which this secret and dangerous Soviet move may have to the situation in

Berlin. We in the West must be prepared for a real test of our determination.

"It is of the utmost importance that we should all keep in very close touch with each other during the critical times which confront us. I will do my best to keep you fully informed of my thinking. . . ."

Putting the letter down, de Gaulle looked over at Acheson.

"Do I understand," he asked the American, "that you have come from the President to inform me of some decision taken by your President—or have you come to consult me about a decision he should take?"

Consultation! During and after the war, de Gaulle had long complained, Britain and America had sought consistently to act without consulting France—meaning, de Gaulle. Hence de Gaulle's famous tantrums: the English-speakers had treated him, and France, without honor.

So as he answered de Gaulle's question, Acheson must have taken a deep breath. For he said: "We must be very clear about this. I have come to *inform* you of a decision which he has taken."

De Gaulle raised his hand imperiously.

But then he responded: "It is exactly what I would have done. . . . You may tell your President that France will support him."

Ottawa   Late afternoon found former Ambassador Livingston Merchant meeting with Prime Minister John Diefenbaker in the great corner office by the Canadian House of Commons. The windows overlooked the Ottawa River, now starting to ice. Livingston gave Diefenbaker the letter from Kennedy. The wording was close to Kennedy's epistle to de Gaulle, except for Kennedy's saying that some of the missiles in Cuba "may already be operational."

A tall man with slightly stooped shoulders and curly gray hair, Diefenbaker had a habit of tilting his head forward and impaling adversaries with his piercing blue eyes. And Merchant, as Kennedy's representative, was an adversary. For Diefenbaker thought JFK a charlatan: even after glancing at the photographs of the missiles in Cuba, Diefenbaker wondered aloud if there was really any threat.

Diefenbaker did agree, as requested by the U.S. government, to stop any Soviet airplanes destined for Cuba from landing in Newfoundland. But he refrained from complying with the rest of Kennedy's request—that of putting Canada's armed forces on maximum alert.

Perhaps because he was "tired, harassed, and wrapped up in other things," Ambassador Merchant would remember, Diefenbaker in demeanor was decidedly chilly. Almost curtly, in fact, he asked that Kennedy, in his televised address, omit an unflattering reference to Gromyko. Then he dismissed Merchant, going home to eat dinner and to watch the President on the tube.

What Diefenbaker thought, or said, while observing the screen we do not know. In his memoirs, nonetheless, he stated that America's Cuban policy "had been an irritant in our relations . . . since my first meeting with Kennedy." The Prime Minister, furthermore, believed Kennedy had a hidden agenda. "Diefenbaker," allowed Dick Thrasher, his special assistant, thought "Kennedy was playing politics with Cuba—that he was grandstanding." "I believed," Diefenbaker himself stated,

> that the President thought he had something to prove in his personal dealing with Khrushchev after their unpleasant Vienna meeting when Khrushchev had treated him like a child, referring to him as "the boy."

To Diefenbaker, as to many Canadians, Cuba was remote, of little importance, and of interest only to Americans. Some in Canada even sympathized with Castro: *MacLean's*, Canada's weekly news magazine, saw Castro's seizures of U.S.-owned property as "legitimate efforts of a small economy to free itself from excessive foreign influence"; and Toronto's *Financial Post* called Americans' widespread demand for an invasion of Cuba a case of "irresponsibility rampant." Was Kennedy, Diefenbaker may have wondered, reflecting such "irresponsibility"?

"Our duty," Diefenbaker said that evening, as he arose from his front-row desk to address the House of Commons, "is not to fan the flames of fear but to do our part to bring about relief from the tensions, the great tensions of the hour." He then proposed that the United Nations form an inspection team—to obtain a "full and complete understanding of what is taking place in Cuba." Kennedy, Diefenbaker was implying, had not told the whole truth.

3   *Washington, 12:00 P.M.*
The White House, on Monday, October 22, 1962, had entered countdown, with seven hours remaining before Kennedy gave his speech. Precisely at noon, Press Secretary Salinger placed a telephone call to Robert Fleming, Washington bureau chief for ABC and chairman of a television network committee that handled presidential requests for air time. President Kennedy, Salinger told him, would speak on a subject of "the highest national urgency." All three networks agreed to carry the broadcast. The 12:30 news spots, nationwide, carried the announcement.

President Kennedy himself placed calls to his three living predecessors, Presidents Hoover, Truman, and Eisenhower. It was a good move: whatever JFK decided to do, Eisenhower for one declared, the President would have his support.

Up in Massachusetts, Edward M. Kennedy, busy with his senatorial campaign, called down to Washington and got Ted Sorensen, asking if he should give a dinner speech on Cuba that night, as scheduled. "No," Sorensen snapped.

Then the White House had a scare. Andrei Gromyko, the Soviet Foreign Minister, would be flying out of Washington's National Airport at 2:00 P.M. There, according to a U.S. television news correspondent who called the White House, he would be making an "important statement."

Washington, 2:00 P.M.
Outside the White House, a crowd of onlookers was clustering around the tall iron fence; inside, officials were fretting over what Gromyko might say.

Over at the airport, he did give a press conference. But he said nothing unusual.

At 2:14 P.M., U.S. military forces worldwide went on a mid-level alert. The Soviets made no overt response.

Washington, 3:00 P.M.
Taking their seats around the long, burnished table in the Cabi-

net Room, the Excomm members, their ranks expanded to include representatives of the Office of Emergency Planning, met again. Secretary Rusk had a bit of a shocker for them: over in London, the *Evening Standard* (a tabloid about the size, shape, and quality of the *National Enquirer*) had leaked the secret of the missiles in Cuba.

Entering the room, President Kennedy gave instructions about what those present should say to America's own press. From the transcript of the meeting:

"a. In September we had said we would react if certain actions were taken in Cuba. We have to carry out commitments which we had made publicly at that time.

"b. The secret deployment by the Russians of strategic missiles to Cuba was such a complete change in their previous policy of not deploying such missiles outside the U.S.S.R. that if we took no action in this case, we would convey to the Russians an impression that we would never act, no matter what they did anywhere.

"c. [sanitized].

"d. The effect in Latin America would be very harmful to our interests if, by our failure to act, we gave the Latinos the impression that the Soviets were increasing their world position while ours was decreasing."

General Taylor wanted to know what to say if reporters asked: "Are we preparing to invade?" "We should ask the press," the President responded, "not to push this line of questioning."

Washington, 4:00 P.M.
Kennedy left the Cabinet Room for a long-scheduled meeting with Milton Obote, the Prime Minister of Uganda. They sat in the Oval Office for about an hour, chatting about the problems of Africa. The appointment concluded, Kennedy personally escorted the Ugandan outside. As Obote's limousine pulled away from the West Wing, Kennedy turned back, but smiled at a clutch of reporters.

One of them called out, asking how things were going.

Pausing at the doorway, JFK responded, "It's been an interesting day."

Washington, 5:00 P.M.
Led in by two prominent Democratic senators, Richard B. Rus-

sell of Georgia and J. William Fulbright of Arkansas, more than a dozen congressional leaders, many of them rounded up by *Air Force One*, trooped into the Oval Office, mystified but alert. After they had seated themselves, Kennedy entered and, as he did so, Senator Everett McKinley Dirksen, the Illinois Republican, said with a chuckle: "That was a nice speech you gave for Sid Yates in Chicago. Too bad you caught that cold making it."

Responding quickly, Kennedy told them what had been going on—and most of them expressed support for the blockade. Senators Russell and Fulbright, however, wondered aloud if Kennedy was being tough enough: they would have favored an air strike or an invasion, they said.

Washington, 6:00 P.M.
In his massive seventh-floor office in the State Department building, Dean Rusk met with the visitor he had summoned, the big, shambling Soviet ambassador, Anatoly F. Dobrynin. The administration knew all about the missiles in Cuba, Rusk told him—the Soviet Union, Rusk said, had committed a "gross error"—and he handed over an advance copy of President Kennedy's speech. Dobrynin read the document in silence. He himself, apparently, had had no word of the missiles from Moscow. The Russian, Rusk said later, aged "ten years right in front of my eyes."

At the same time, in Moscow, U.S. Ambassador Foy Kohler delivered to the Kremlin a copy of the speech and a two-page letter from Kennedy to Khrushchev.

"Dear Mr. Chairman," the letter read;

"In our discussions and exchanges on Berlin and other international questions, the one thing that has most concerned me has been the possibility that your Government would not correctly understand the will and determination of the United States. . . .

". . . I must tell you that the United States is determined that this threat to the security of this hemisphere must be removed. At the same time I wish to point out that the action we are taking is the minimum necessary to remove the threat. . . .

". . . I hope that your Government will refrain from any action which would widen or deepen this already grave crisis and that we can agree to resume the path of peaceful negotiation."

. . .

Washington, 6:15 P.M.
In the Executive Mansion, President Kennedy was putting on a freshly pressed suit, adjusting the knot of his necktie, and combing his hair.

In the Oval Office, network technicians were removing furniture to make space for lights and cameras, laying down canvas to protect the carpet, erecting a screen to block out the French doors and to emphasize Kennedy's face, clearing the desk and covering it with brown felt to reduce the glare. They put an eight-inch-high lectern in the middle of the desk and, in Kennedy's black leather chair, they placed two pillows, designed to increase his height.

Washington, 6:40 P.M.
Kennedy returned to the Oval Office and sat behind the desk; technicians adjusted lights and focused cameras. Text of the speech in hand, JFK slipped out to the Cabinet Room for a last-minute glance at the script.

Washington, 6:59 P.M.
Kennedy came back, positioning himself in the chair. Evelyn Lincoln, his private secretary, approached with a hairbrush. He ran it through his mop of hair.

A voice said, "Thirty seconds."

Kennedy fingered the text, placed it on the rostrum. He seemed relaxed. Then the red lights came on.

4   "Good evening, my fellow citizens," Kennedy said.

"This government, as promised, has maintained the closest surveillance of the Soviet military buildup on the island of Cuba. Within the past week, unmistakable evidence has established the fact that a series of offensive missile sites is now in preparation on that imprisoned island. The purpose of these bases can be none other than to provide a nuclear strike capability against the Western Hemisphere. . . .

"The characteristics of these new missile sites indicate two distinct types of installations. Several of them include Medium Range Ballistic Missiles, capable of carrying a nuclear warhead for a distance of more than one thousand nautical miles. Each of these missiles, in short, is capable of striking Washington, D.C., the Panama Canal, Cape Canaveral, Mexico City, or any other city in the southeastern part of the United States, in Central America, or in the Caribbean area.

"Additional sites not yet completed appear to be designed for Intermediate Range Ballistic Missiles—capable of traveling more than twice as far—and thus capable of striking most of the major cities in the Western Hemisphere, ranging as far north as Hudson Bay, Canada, and as far south as Lima, Peru. In addition, jet bombers, capable of carrying nuclear weapons, are now being uncrated and assembled in Cuba, while the necessary air bases are being prepared. . . ."

In the bars along Geary Street out in San Francisco, the *Examiner* reported, afternoon drinkers had their eyes glued to the television sets, just as they had been the week before at the end of the World Series. Their faces were "grim." In Atlanta, people wearing the same grim expressions stood in silent groups around the television sets for sale in Davison's department store.

"The size of the undertaking," Kennedy continued, "makes clear that it has been planned for some months. Yet only last month, after I had made clear the distinction between any introduction of ground-to-ground missiles and the existence of defensive antiaircraft missiles, the Soviet Government publicly stated on September 11 that, and I quote, 'The armaments and military equipment sent to Cuba are designed exclusively for defensive purposes. . . .

"Only last Thursday, as evidence of [the] rapid offensive buildup was already in my hand, Soviet Foreign Minister Gromyko told me in my office that . . . Soviet assistance to Cuba . . . 'pursued solely the purpose of contributing to the defensive capabilities of Cuba. . . .' That statement was false."

In a New York hotel, wrote Ralph McGill, editor of the *Atlanta Constitution*, a "group of educators, gathered in a private dining room, . . . listened in silence, some leaning forward toward the screen."

"Neither the United States of America nor the world community of nations," Kennedy was saying, "can tolerate deliberate deception and offensive threats on the part of any nation, large or small. . . . Our own strategic missiles have never been transferred to the territory of any other nation, under a cloak of secrecy and deception; and our history, unlike that of the Soviets since the end of World War II, demonstrates that we have no desire to dominate or conquer any other nation or impose our system upon its people. . . .

"But this secret, swift and extraordinary buildup of Communist missiles—in an area well known to have a special and historical relationship to the United States . . . , in violation of Soviet assurances, and in defiance of American . . . policy—this sudden, clandestine decision to station strategic weapons for the first time outside of Soviet soil—is a deliberately provocative and unjustified change in the status quo. . . .

"The 1930s taught us a clear lesson: aggressive conduct, if allowed to grow unchecked and unchallenged, ultimately leads to war. This nation is opposed to war. We are also true to our word. Our unswerving objective . . . must be to prevent the use of these missiles against this or any other country, and to secure their withdrawal or elimination from the Western Hemisphere."

At the Secretariat of the United Nations, a tower of light that blazed above First Avenue in New York, the Ghanaian delegation was giving a cocktail party, accompanied by an African dance band, up on the fourth floor. In the ground floor auditorium of the U.S. mission across the street, however, members of the press sat in a row of folding chairs to see and hear the President on television. A *Herald Tribune* reporter described them. They were, he wrote, a "sober lot."

President Kennedy had reached the conclusion of his speech. "Acting . . . in the defense of our security and of the entire Western Hemisphere," he stated," . . . I have directed that the following initial steps be taken . . . :

"1) *First:* To halt this offensive buildup, a strict quarantine on all offensive military equipment under shipment to Cuba is being initiated. . . .

"2) *Second:* I have directed the continued and increased close surveillance of Cuba and its military buildup. . . .

"3) *Third:* It shall be the policy of this nation to regard any nuclear missile launched from Cuba against any nation in the Western Hemisphere as an attack . . . on the United States, requiring a full retaliatory response upon the Soviet Union.

"4) *Fourth:* As a necessary military precaution, I have reinforced our base at Guantánamo. . . .

"5) *Fifth:* We are calling tonight for an immediate meeting of . . . the Organization of American States, to consider this threat to hemispheric security. . . .

"6) *Sixth:* Under the Charter of the United Nations, we are asking tonight that an emergency meeting of the Security Council be convoked without delay to take action. . . .

"7) *Seventh and finally:* I call upon Chairman Khrushchev to halt and eliminate a reckless and provocative threat to world peace and to stable relations between our two nations. . . . He has an opportunity now to move the world back from the abyss of destruction—by returning to his government's own words that it had no need to station missiles outside its own territory, and withdrawing these missiles from Cuba. . . . We are prepared to discuss new proposals for the removal of tensions on both sides—including the possibilities of a genuinely independent Cuba, free to determine its own destiny. We have no wish to war with the Soviet Union—for we are a peaceful people who desire to live in peace with all other peoples. . . . Our goal is not the victory of might, but the vindication of right. . . . God willing, that goal will be achieved."

John Kennedy had finished his speech. Rolling the leather chair back a foot or two, he leaned back and glanced around at the clutter of camera, sound, and lighting gear. For almost a full minute he sat in silence, until a technician cued him that the program was over. Then he rose from his chair and left the Oval Office, heading outside.

There a friend joined him—Florida's Democratic Senator George A. Smathers, a crony from JFK's own Senate days (in 1950, Smathers had won the Democratic primary by telling voters that his opponent, incumbent Claude Pepper, had a sister who was a "thespian")—and together they walked in the night down the long promenade that led to the personal quarters.

5   The speech over, reporters for the three television networks appeared on the nation's screens, ad-libbed their summaries. What they said on the whole was bland. Even then, however, their words conveyed some questions.

Kennedy had drawn a distinction between two kinds of missiles, defensive and offensive. Yet since a missile flies from here to there whatever the sender's purposes, was not the distinction dubious?

The Soviets had failed to own up to their missile deployment, that was true, and in fact they *had* tried to deceive the Kennedy administration. Was not their placement of missiles in Cuba, nonetheless, similar to America's placement of missiles in Turkey?

Saying that America had no wish to "dominate or conquer" any other nation, Kennedy bespoke America's "special and historical relationship" with Cuba, espousing the idea of the island's independence. But had not America itself, for decades, occupied Cuba?

Kennedy said that the Soviets, for the first time, had placed nuclear missiles outside their borders, and that their doing so represented an "unjustified change in the status quo"; and he called upon Khrushchev to withdraw the missiles. But did Kennedy mean that America alone had the right to place missiles outside its borders? Did he mean that America alone had the right to make the rules?

Kennedy denounced the suddenness of the Soviet action—yet said it had been going on for months. And given the U.S. buildup of missiles in Britain, Italy, and Turkey, were suddenness and secrecy on the part of the Soviets necessarily vices?

Such questions underlay the protests of two prominent winners of the Nobel Prize. From his home in Pasadena, Cal Tech's laureat, chemist Linus Pauling, wired the White House: "Your warlike act . . . can only be described as an act of the utmost irresponsibility." And from his cottage in Wales, Britain's nonagenarian philosopher Bertrand Russell telegraphed U Thant, Secretary General of the United Nations: "I appeal to you for swift condemnation of tragic U.S. action. . . ."

Such voices, however, were lost in the cacophony of praise. The West German government welcomed Kennedy's "resolute action." The British Foreign Office saw the military buildup in Cuba as a "shock to the . . . civilized world." Leaders of both parties in Congress gave Kennedy their support. Florida Governor Farris Bryant sent JFK a telegram of congratulations. The *Chicago Tribune*, conducting interviews with people on street corners, ran quotations such as, "I feel it is a step in the right direction," "He is doing the only thing he could," and "I hope the Russians will back down." Said New York's Mayor Robert Wagner: "the President speaks and acts for a united America." Added New York's Senator Kenneth Keating: "[Kennedy] will have the 100 percent backing of every American."

In Moscow, Nikita Khrushchev responded with rage. Denouncing "the naval blockade as banditry, the folly of degenerate imperialism"—this quotation according to dissident Soviet historian Roy Medvedev—"he issued orders to captains of Soviet ships as they were approaching the blockade zone to ignore it and to hold course for the Cuban ports."

At the speed they were steaming, the Soviet ships would reach the blockade at 10:00 A.M., two days later. The U.S. ships were under orders to shoot.

Late in the night, President Kennedy telephoned Prime Minister Macmillan, in the first of a series of talks between the two men in the time of the crisis; as so often before, JFK was turning to a much older man as a sounding board. Both found their "press to speak" buttons hard to operate, and so the conversation was disjointed. But an interesting point emerged: Macmillan played the tape to his top Cabinet colleagues and, listening, they formed the distinct impression that the Prime Minister had been playing the role of keeping Kennedy calm.

Part III
Stalemate

CHAPTER 12

Back Channels

1   *Tuesday, October 23, 1962*
America by morning was a-flutter with flags. In New Orleans,
a parade of high school students trooped to the front of City Hall
and raised two dozen Stars and Stripes. In Columbia, South
Carolina, pickup trucks, adorned with hand-drawn copies of Old
Glory, drove en masse up and down in front of the State House.
And in Chicago, Kiwanians from all over the country, gathered
downtown for their annual convention, raised their arms and
waved little red-white-and-blues high over their straw-hatted
heads.

America, in fact, was almost rejoicing. Out in the land of the
big sky, from Kansas to Idaho and from Arizona to Utah, where
a reporter from *The Washington Post* was conducting a fast-as-
possible survey of public opinion, people were saying things
like, "Let's knock Castro's block off," and "We ought to send
in the Marines tomorrow." And back in the inner sanctum of
the Mayflower Hotel in Washington, in the bar, bartender Mike
Murphy, washing and drying his glassware, told another *Post*
reporter, "It's high time we did something. It had to happen,
and it's overdue."

Beyond the water's edge, reactions were more varied. From
Geneva, the World Council of Churches sent out word that
Kennedy's action had caused it "grave concern and regret." Up

in Canada, in Montreal and Toronto, young people took to the streets, brandishing placards that denounced John Kennedy. Across the Atlantic in Britain, Bertrand Russell sent a wire to Nikita Khrushchev, urging the Soviet leader to exercise restraint in the face of the "unjustified action of U.S." Russell lived in Wales, but, five hours away in London, demonstrators were marching back and forth in front of the American embassy—a blocky, then-modernistic building fronted by rows upon rows of windows that overlooked Grosvenor Square—and they were chanting slogans such as "We Want Peace," and "Hands Off Cuba."

Looking down from his top-floor office window, Ambassador David Bruce could see London policemen in their tall hats, standing in rows ten deep, as they guarded the embassy steps. Wired Bruce to Washington: "PROTESTS CLEARLY ORIGINATED FOR MOST PART FROM PROFESSED COMMUNISTS OR NUCLEAR DISARMERS." But London's *Daily Telegraph*, a right-of-center paper, was wishing that Kennedy had stated his case "to the United Nations and to the Organization of American States before, instead of after, so far-reaching a pronouncement." And *The Guardian* insisted that Britain cast its U.N. vote against Kennedy; Khrushchev had put missiles in Cuba, *The Guardian* claimed, "primarily to demonstrate to the United States and the world the meaning of American bases close to the Soviet frontier."

In America, however, the press was gunning down such thoughts. "How Our Missile Ring Is Different," ran the headline in an article released by the Pentagon and carried by the *San Francisco Examiner*. Some might ask, the paper stated, whether the Soviets are "doing any more, in establishing missile bases, than the U.S. has done around the perimeter of Russia." But "the United States deployed . . . missile bases to protect nations threatened by Russia and . . . Cuba has been under no such threat of attack."

But the *Examiner* was only reinforcing public opinion. According to a Gallup Poll, taken the morning of October 23, 1962, 84 percent of the American people favored the blockade. And, perhaps to make sure that the populace continued to favor it, Hollywood released a film entitled *We'll Bury You*. Viewers would see advertised film posters in mid-Manhattan theaters proclaiming:

Khrushchev, World Enemy #1
Castro, Bearded Betrayer
Stalin, Mass Murderer
Mao Tsetung, Red China's Tyrant
Lenin, Genius of Revolution
Trotsky, Victim of Revenge
Uncensored! Shocking! Authentic!

As the first sightseers of the morning lined up for a tour of the White House, they found the security tighter than ever. Just inside the East Gate, Secret Service agents had installed a fluoroscope in a trailer. There they X-rayed each visitor, insisting that all purses and cameras be left behind in the trailer.

Inside the Oval Office, President Kennedy was having a 10:00 A.M. meeting with Excomm, approving the wording of what would be the quarantine proclamation. JFK, nonetheless, still seemed worried about public relations. "Pres. says," goes a note written by hand by Lyndon B. Johnson, "Bobbie 2 points which cause concern—Why didn't we locate this ahead of time [Even in this Excomm meeting, JFK was upholding the fiction that he had had no previous idea of the missiles in Cuba]—why locate missiles & lock doors after horse is. . . . Low level flights in order to prove to layman existence of missiles. There will be six flights low level. . . . McCone and [George] Ball get photographs for Stevenson [at the United Nations]. Pictures. OAS. . . ."

What would happen, someone asked, if one of the low-level airplanes or, for that matter, a U-2, was shot down? Air Force bombers, Excomm members agreed, would destroy the missile site in question.

And if the Soviets kept firing at the airplanes? Then the Air Force would smash all the missile sites.

In Moscow, Nikita Khrushchev and Kremlin colleagues showed themselves in public, waddling into the Bolshoi Theater to hear a performance of *Boris Gudonov*. Singing the title role was Jerome Hines, the immense basso from the Metropolitan Opera; after the performance the Soviet leaders went to his dressing room. Khrushchev had seemed in "jolly good humor," Hines told reporters later, and had praised the singer for his good

Russian diction. Hines and Khrushchev had even exchanged toasts.

But in private, we can assume, Khrushchev had given vent to fury, as Ambassador Foy Kohler discovered, on being summoned to the Kremlin. There, from Acting Foreign Minister V. V. Kuznetsov, Kohler received a 2,500-word letter, Khrushchev's response to Kennedy's speech. Kuznetsov's attitude, Kohler cabled Washington, was "restrained." The letter was not:

> I should say frankly that measures outlined in your statement represent serious threat to peace and security of peoples. . . . We confirm that the armaments now in Cuba, regardless of the classification to which they belong, are destined exclusively for defensive purposes, in order to secure Cuban republic from attack of aggressor.

> I hope that the United States government will display wisdom and renounce the reactions pursued by you, which may lead to catastrophic consequences for world peace.

Implying he had put the missiles in Cuba to save the island from an American invasion, Khrushchev was defiant: he gave no indication at all that he would stage a withdrawal. In his letter of transmittal, nevertheless, Ambassador Kohler pointed out that Khrushchev had made no "specific threats."

Directly overlooking the Tidal Basin from the corner of Seventeenth Street and Constitution Avenue in Washington stood the headquarters of the Organization of American States. The driveway that lay before the main doors, on the morning of October 23, was filled with limousines with diplomatic license plates. Inside, past the fronds of tropical trees that ringed the fountain in the courtyard, the ambassadors from the various Latin American republics were taking their seats in the building's main assembly hall. They were buzzing with excitement. Then they went still.

Secretary of State Dean Rusk had entered—the time was precisely 10:00 A.M.—and, striding to the rostrum, was spreading out the text of a speech. He had come to lobby the OAS for its support over Cuba.

The OAS, Lyndon Johnson once remarked, "couldn't pour

piss out of a boot if the instructions were written on the heel."
Founded in 1948, the OAS was the Western Hemisphere's counterpart of the U.N., and held by many Americans, including
LBJ, in just about equal esteem. Yet the organization did have
its uses: the United States used it to legitimate Washington's
Latin American policies. With the OAS close by, three blocks
from the White House and four from State, U.S. officials had
ample opportunity to pressure the group.

And Rusk was pressuring. What he wanted from the OAS, he
stated, was a resolution approving all measures, including the
use of force, needed to eliminate the missiles positioned in
Cuba. He spoke in English, of course, and the delegates listened
through instantaneous Portuguese and Spanish translation. His
speech finished, then, Rusk walked briskly out of the chamber
and, followed by a retinue of aides, entered his waiting limousine. The OAS would vote in the afternoon.

2   *Washington, 3:00 P.M.*
Dispensing with their usual oratory, with its grand flourishes
and twists and turns of phrasing, the delegates to the Organization of American States did their duty: they gave the United
States nearly unanimous support for its proposed resolution—
that the OAS support any measures necessary to get the missiles
out of Cuba. Mexico and Brazil did hesitate somewhat; and
Emilio Oribe of Uruguay, failing to hear any instructions from
home, thought it best to abstain. But the rest of the diplomats
were 100 percent on board. "Russia," one of them said, "by
pushing things too far, has not only complicated her efforts to
aid her Cuban ally, but has finally succeeded in lining up all
Latin America behind the United States."

Sitting with the translation earphones over his head, Secretary Rusk, in the words of *The Washington Post*, was "visibly
moved." He expressed his thanks.

One can understand why. Given the history of U.S. interventions, many in the Western Hemisphere, especially the intellec-
tuals, had shown a distinct tolerance for Castro. It "is difficult,"
Juan de Onis, a *New York Times* correspondent, had reported
from Rio only a few days before, "for South American countries,
many far larger than Cuba, to see a threat in a Caribbean island

thousands of miles away." But now the OAS had voted with Washington, for which Rusk did feel relieved.

3   *New York, 4:00 P.M.*
Adlai Stevenson had got the message—and just to make sure he did not forget it, John J. McCloy, the stocky, tough, balding international lawyer, whom the White House had called back to Manhattan, was seated right behind him. They had taken their places behind the great horseshoe table of the Security Council of the United Nations. Stevenson's assignment was to give a speech and to make it tough.

Tough he was, for once. Blistering the Soviets, he called their action in Cuba "a grave threat to the Western Hemisphere and to the peace of the world." Castro's regime, Stevenson went on—knowing that, down in Washington, the President was watching the speech on television—"has aided and abetted an invasion of this hemisphere," making itself "an accomplice in the Communist enterprise of world domination. . . . If the United States and other nations of the Western Hemisphere accept this new phase of aggression, we would be delinquent in our obligations to world peace."

Some, Stevenson stated, might equate the presence of Soviet bases in Cuba with the presence of NATO bases in Turkey. But that equation would be false: it was the *Soviet* action that had created a "dangerous situation. . . . If we do not stand firm here our adversaries may think that we will stand firm nowhere."

So saying, Stevenson presented the Security Council with a draft resolution. It called for the "immediate dismantling and withdrawal" from Cuba of all "offensive" weapons.

At this point, Kennedy sent Stevenson a wire: "Dear Adlai: [Your speech] has given our cause a great start. . . . The United States is fortunate to have your advocacy. You have my warm and personal thanks."

Stevenson did not have Cuban or Soviet thanks. As soon as he had finished, Marid García-Inchaustequi, the Cuban ambassador to the U.N., grabbed a microphone. Jumping and shaking in his seat, and at one point nearly losing his voice, he shouted for action against the "North American imperialists." Spiking his speech with sarcasm, he demanded an end to the "blockade" and ridiculed the idea that Cuba presented anyone with a threat. Were "the United States," he concluded,

> able to give Cuba effective guarantees and satisfactory proof concerning the integrity of Cuban territory, and were it to cease its subversive and counter-revolutionary activities against our people, then Cuba would not have to strengthen its defenses.

At this juncture, Soviet Ambassador Valerian Zorin spoke up, or rather shouted. Stevenson's charges, he yelled, were nothing but contemptible efforts to cover up America's own aggression toward Cuba. The quarantine itself he denounced as a "new and extremely dangerous act of aggression" and "undisguised piracy"; the charge that the Soviets had placed *offensive* weapons in Cuba, he charged, was a lie.

Zorin, however, did leave a door open. He called for negotiations to end the crisis.

Ensconced in his office on the thirty-eighth floor, U Thant, the Burmese diplomat who recently had become the U.N. Secretary-General, was for the moment alone, deep in thought. The day before he had watched President Kennedy on television and, as he was to write in his memoirs, he "could scarcely believe my eyes and ears. . . . If the allegation of the *secret* installation of missiles and bomber bases in Cuba were true, then the Chairman [Khrushchev] must have been out of his mind. Everybody knew that U.S. reconnaissance planes were flying all over the world—Russia, Eastern Europe, China, and certainly Cuba. Why was Khrushchev building such bases in Cuba—bases that were fully exposed to the supersharp camera lenses of American U-2s? . . . And was the United States, the most powerful country in the world, prepared to plunge the world into a nuclear holocaust? Never before had the lives of so many millions around the world been at the mercy of two men who had the power to make the ultimate decision. I was more deeply troubled than I had ever been in my life."

But U Thant had little time to brood. Even before the sun descended behind the Manhattan skyline, he was busy trying to arrange a deal: getting Kennedy to agree to preliminary talks; getting Khrushchev to agree to a moratorium on further action.

Havana, 5:40 P.M.

Down in Havana, in the presidential palace he had taken over from Batista, Fidel Castro ordered a combat alert, putting Cuba's armed forces on their highest level of readiness. At about the same time—according to Khrushchev's memoirs—the Cuban leader spoke with Alexsandr I. Alekseyev, the Soviet ambassador. "We have incontrovertible evidence," Castro apparently told the Russian, that the U.S. was preparing within hours to launch an invasion of Cuba. Castro may have been desperate: he insisted that the Soviets—this, again, is according to Khrushchev—fire their missiles in a preemptive strike against America.

When Khrushchev read his ambassador's cable, he realized, he has stated, that Castro "had failed to understand us correctly. We had installed the missiles not for the purpose of attacking the United States, but to keep the United States from attacking Cuba."

Washington, 6:00 P.M.

Meeting in the White House press auditorium with print reporters and representatives of the networks, Pierre Salinger circulated a memorandum regarding twelve types of information the White House wanted kept out of the news. These included: "any discussion of plans for employment of [U.S.] strategic or tactical forces"; intelligence estimates of enemy plans or capabilities"; and "degree of alert of military forces." Reporters would be kept away from the quarantine zone, being allowed aboard neither the ships nor the planes.

Some of the journalists present bridled: Wes Gallagher of the Associated Press and William McAndrew of NBC demanded to know why they could not at least sail on ships bound for the blockade. After all, they pointed out, reporters had been aboard battle-bound ships in World War II. Shipboard news reports, Salinger retorted, would "inform the Russians how the blockade was operating." But World War II reports, the news people shot back, had given no aid and comfort to the enemy. Salinger left the room.

Upstairs in the White House, CIA Director McCone was telling Excomm members that intelligence had spotted Soviet submarines moving about the Caribbean. President Kennedy, according to his brother Robert, told the Navy to give "the highest priority to tracking the submarines and to put into effect the greatest possible safety measures to protect our own aircraft carriers and other vessels.''

Washington, 6:51 P.M.
President Kennedy sent a new message to Moscow. Stressing that both sides should exercise ''prudence and do nothing to allow events to make the situation more difficult to control than it already is,'' Kennedy asked Khrushchev to have the Soviet ships observe the quarantine zone: peace, according to Kennedy's telegram, was Khrushchev's responsibility.

Washington, 7:06 P.M.
President Kennedy entered the Oval Office, prepared to sign Proclamation 3504, the document that would establish the quarantine formally. Earlier in the day, his mood had been cheerful, even buoyant. Now, however, he was grim. Intelligence reports showed twenty-five Soviet ships en route to Cuba, their course down the Atlantic unchanged in the past twenty-four hours. Kennedy signed the proclamation, and left the room without a word.

"Whereas the peace of the world and the security of the United States and of all American states are endangered by reason of the establishment by the Sino-Soviet powers of an offensive military capability in Cuba . . . ,'' the proclamation began. By this point, actually, the Sino-Soviet bloc no longer existed, China and Russia being virtually divorced. And China had about two hundred technicians—but certainly no missiles—in Cuba.

"Whereas . . . the American Republics meeting in Washington on Oct. 23, 1962,'' the proclamation continued, "recommended that the member states . . . take all measures . . . to insure that the government of Cuba cannot continue to receive from the Sino-Soviet powers military material . . . which may threaten the peace . . . :

"Now, therefore, I, John F. Kennedy, President of the United States of America . . . do hereby proclaim that the forces under my command are ordered, beginning at [10:00 the following morning] to interdict . . . the delivery of offensive weapons . . . to Cuba.''

Washington, 8:00 P.M.
Defense Secretary McNamara called over to the White House, indicating that the blockade forces were now in position. All naval vessels had orders to be prepared for action, starting at 10:00 A.M.

Havana, 8:35 P.M.
Addressing the Cuban people on television, Fidel Castro accused the United States of aggression and denied that the purpose of the missiles was offensive. Calling the blockade a "pirate act," the most "dangerous adventure since the end of World War II," and Kennedy's reasons for the blockade "absolutely without foundation," he added a note that was perhaps boastful and perhaps ominous. "If continued," Castro said, JFK's action "will very soon have repercussions."

4   *Washington, 9:00 P.M.*
In through the front door of the Soviet embassy, on Sixteenth Street in Washington, a group of American officials proceeded down a long corridor—flanked on both sides with one-way mirrors—and off into a downstairs reception room. There, perhaps not coincidentally, Lieutenant General Vladimir A. Dubovik, the Soviet Army attaché, was giving a cocktail party for his Washington counterparts. He had them frightened. Through the haze of the vodka, he seemed to be saying that the captains of the Soviet ships, the two score and more vessels that were headed for Cuba, were under orders to defy the blockade.

Anatoly Dobrynin, the Soviet ambassador, joining the party, was besieged immediately by questioners: was General Dubovik, the guests all wanted to know, speaking the truth? Dobrynin had recovered his composure after his session of the previous day with Secretary Rusk. Now he answered, simply: Dubovik "is a military man, I am not. He is the one who knows what the Navy is going to do, not I."

Across the river and under the nighttime sky in Langley, the CIA was recording a warning that had just appeared in TASS, the Soviet news agency. If the Americans sank the Russian ships, went the statement, the Soviet Union would retaliate.

Washington, 9:30 P.M.

Dobrynin did not linger downstairs. A limousine had pulled into the alley behind the embassy, and a small, wiry figure, semiconcealed in an overcoat, had darted in through a back door. It was Robert Kennedy. At the President's suggestion, he had come to meet with Dobrynin in the quiet of the ambassador's top-floor office.

According to RFK's account, they sparred for a while, Dobrynin denying knowledge of missiles in Cuba and Kennedy calling Soviet statements "hypocritical, misleading, and false." But then, something else transpired. In the hush of the Soviet embassy upstairs, Robert Kennedy told Anatoly Dobrynin that the U.S. missile sites in Turkey could be dismantled.

Washington operated—and operates—as much through back channels as through regular channels. According to myth, Presidents conducted foreign policy in the open, using the regular bureaucracy to hammer out positions, and holding themselves aloof from the concerns of domestic politics. Yet the RFK-Dobrynin connection illustrated just the opposite. For reasons of domestic politics, President Kennedy did not dare acknowledge that he would compromise with Khrushchev. And his brother was just about the only person in Washington he could trust to keep his evolving position a secret.

Washington, 10:15 P.M.

Racing back to the White House, Robert Kennedy went up to the family quarters, there to find the President conversing with British Ambassador David Ormsby-Gore. Patently worried, they pressed Robert Kennedy for details of his talk with Dobrynin.

President Kennedy revealed his anxiety. As soon as his brother had finished, he raised the question of whether he and Khrushchev should arrange a summit.

Then he dismissed the thought. A summit would be useless, the President allowed, unless Khrushchev "First accepted . . . U.S. determination [over the missiles]." Khrushchev had to acknowledge defeat. Then they could talk.

Washington, 11:00 P.M.

Martin Agronsky's evening report on Channel 4 in the capital built the suspense. Using a large weather map, he pointed out four shaded triangles drawn on the ocean: from Puerto Rico up toward Cuba; from Bermuda down toward Cuba; from Jackson-ville out into the Atlantic; and from Key West over toward the Bahamas. The triangles represented the zones being watched by the U.S. Air Force—and the Navy was watching the channels between the triangles.

Agronsky carried a film clip from the Pentagon, of a press conference with McNamara. Just how far from Cuba the block-ade ships would be on patrol, the Defense Secretary refused to say. He did allow, however, that with a "stream" of Soviet vessels still on course toward Cuba, the next day might well bring a showdown.

The program ended with the favorite topic of the nation's capital, politics. Denying that Kennedy's moves had hurt the Republicans, former President Eisenhower told reporters at Get-tysburg that Americans were "free to ask . . . how we arrived at our present state, even in foreign affairs." But Democrats on Capitol Hill were gleeful. "If it turns out all right," one of them said to a reporter, "President Kennedy will be a hero."

5   *Wednesday, October 24, 1962*
As the sun rose on Wednesday, the skies from Washington to Cuba were clear. The sun was bright, the sea was sparkling, and the forces of the blockade were all in their places.

The Key West airport was civilian, ordinarily, but by now the Air Force had taken it over, operating the new control tower and sending reconnaissance planes down the runway at closely spaced intervals. Over by the naval base, a thirty-truck artillery and missile convoy rumbled into sight; military police spotted a television crew, about to photograph the trucks, and they detained the cameramen until the vehicles were out of sight behind the gate.

One piece of news that did go out from Key West was a Navy announcement that the waters around Cuba had become "dan-gerous." Heeding the warning, two steamship cruiser lines that plied the Caribbean, Holland-America and Swedish-America, rerouted their vessels, giving Cuba wide berth.

The press, too, was kept away from the blockade zone: Gene Miller, a reporter with *The Miami Herald*, chartered a seaplane, flew out of Key West, saw a U.S. destroyer swing its guns in his direction, and hightailed it back to Florida. Another reporter, Charles T. Taylor of *The Washington Post*, got farther, and before a pair of jet fighters escorted his aircraft back to land, he saw a bit of the blockade below. "Flying south from Miami . . . just offshore from the Florida Keys," he wrote,

> we saw a dozen fishing boats and freighters plying the Gulfstream sea lanes. . . . The ocean then appeared empty . . . but a few miles eastward . . . stood the first picket ship—destroyer 465. She was still in the water, without a wake, her bow turned toward Cuba. . . . About 35 miles beyond, a second destroyer picket hove to. . . . The two ships were guarding with interlocking radar the main deep-water shipping channel running southward along the Florida Keys. The two ships were sufficient for the job since beyond them to the west were the Cay Sal shallows, not deep enough to permit a large ship to pass. On the other side of the shallows were more picket ships guarding other deep-water sea lanes.

Venturing forward no more, the reporter and his pilot turned back toward Miami, radioing in a slight change in the flight plan. For the next hundred miles, the pilot had to answer questions "about his plane, his destination, and his positions. As we came in to Miami, the airport radio demanded more than an estimated course. It wanted the precise radial of the 360 degrees on the compass that the plane was using to approach. 'Man, there's never been surveillance like this,' [the] pilot said."

Far to the north, in Norfolk, the war room of the Atlantic fleet headquarters was in a hubbub. Extra Marine guards patrolled the perimeter. Sentries outside headquarters regarded anyone not in uniform with sharp suspicion. Admirals and generals, armed with bulging briefcases, paraded in and out of the war room. Inside, Admiral Robert L. Dennison, the man in charge of the blockade, and taken to sleeping when he could on a cot by his desk, was receiving up-to-the-minute reports and sending detailed directives to the ships.

Dennison was fretting. With good reason: the Canadians had stopped and inspected an Air Cubana plane, en route from Prague to Havana, and Sékou Touré, President of Guinea, had promised he would refuse the Soviets any landing rights; but

Morocco, a point on one of the air routes from Moscow to Cuba, was noncommittal. Were the Soviets going to fly in nuclear warheads?

Another worry: naval intelligence had spotted six Soviet submarines plying the waters around Cuba. Were they spying on the blockade ships? Were they planning to torpedo them? Only one thing was certain—the submarines were diesel-powered, and therefore every several hours had to surface. So word went out from Norfolk—U.S. surface vessels were to harry them until they came up, and then keep harrying them until they scattered.

Fresh U-2 photographs revealed, furthermore, that workers in Cuba were erecting new sheds around the missile sites. Herein lay the quarantine's weakness: the missiles, and possibly their warheads, were still down there, still present in Cuba.

Cuba, the news reports were indicating, had mobilized, bracing itself against imminent attack. All along the Havana waterfront, Reuters reported, "open spaces bristled with mortars and anti-aircraft guns, manned by troops, militia, or armed students. Police patrols were strengthened and more militiamen guarded every city block. A fast corvette has been on constant patrol in Havana Bay. . . . Loading and unloading continued uninterrupted at the docks. Many . . . East Europeans [are] helping with the work."

With the Cuban capital under armed guard, and facing the threat of invasion, the city's hotels and bars were nearly deserted. How different from the days of Batista!

As the Castro government rightly suspected, moreover, some of Batista's old chums, the Alpha 66 group, were doing all they could do to restore those glory days: even as President Kennedy was excoriating Khrushchev for trucking in offensive missiles, Alpha 66 was launching a new offensive against Cuba—and doing so with U.S. governmental assistance. The evidence? On Wednesday, October 24, 1962, the U.S. Air Force Intelligence Center put in the hands of Cuban "freedom fighters" a manual entitled "Special Evasion and Escape Study: Cuba." Much of the manual, now declassified, is "sanitized." Remaining pages, however, contain a checklist of what anti-Castro Cubans should tote along as they waded ashore the island. Among the items were:

—Radio equipment.
—Whistles.
—Snare or roll of wire for small game.
—Appropriate maps.
—Sunglasses.
—Snakebite kit.
—Sunburn cream.
—Contraceptives, provided free by the U.S. government.

The morning of October 24 in Moscow saw sleet, and office workers turned up their collars as they clambered down from the buses. But despite the cold, a throng of about two hundred students rode in from the university, charged the U.S. embassy, and smashed at least four bottles of ink against the shuttered, nine-storied building. Long streams of red ink stained the façade. Then, while the crowd was chanting "Viva Cuba!" and "Shame on the Yankees!," a limousine sporting two small American flags pulled up toward the embassy—and a student threw a stone against the side of the car. Inside the vehicle was Ambassador Floyd Kohler. He proceeded, unhurt.

Over in the Kremlin, William Knox, a sixty-one-year-old American and president of Westinghouse International, who had been invited for an interview, proceeded into Khrushchev's office. The room was long and narrow, with plain wooden walls and yellow curtains drawn over the windows. Khrushchev was seated behind a desk at the end of the office; when he saw Knox he got up. Accompanied by a waiting translator, they sat nearby at a baize-covered conference table.

Khrushchev had learned of Knox's presence in Moscow, and had calculated that he could use the businessman to pass a message to Kennedy. As Knox cabled them to Washington, Khrushchev's remarks were the following:

1. He was loath to think that what occurred on October 22 was done for electoral reasons. It appeared to stem from hysteria. The President was a very young man; in fact Khrushchev's own son was older. . . .
2. Except in time of war, a blockade is illegal. If the U.S. stopped and searched Soviet ships, this would be piracy.

3. Khrushchev repeated several times that Soviet ships were un-armed. . . .

4. The United States is now unable to take over Cuba.

5. To Mr. Knox's comment that the President was infuriated because he had been assured that the Soviet Union would not send offensive weapons to Cuba and found that he had been lied to, Khrushchev replied with a half-hour discussion on the distinction between offensive and defensive weapons. The U.S. said that its Turkish bases were defensive, but what was the range of the missiles there?

6. Khrushchev then stated specifically that the Soviet Union had anti-aircraft missiles in Cuba as well as ballistic missiles with . . . nuclear warheads. The Cubans were too temperamental to turn over these weapons to them; for this reason all sophisticated military equipment was under direct, 100 percent Soviet control. They would never be fired except in defense of Cuba. . . . [I]f the United States did not believe this, it should attack Cuba and it would find out the answer. Guantánamo would disappear the first day.

Knox's cable went from Moscow to U. Alexis Johnson in the State Department, thence to the White House. Khrushchev had ended the conversation with a taunt. He told a story, the cable related, "about a man who had learned to get along with a smelly goat, even though he did not like the goat. The Soviet Union had its goats in Italy, Greece, etc. [where the U.S. had military bases], and was living with them. The U.S. now had its goat in Cuba."

Flying back to Moscow, the airplane carrying Foreign Minister Gromyko back from the States put down in East Berlin. While the craft refueled, Gromyko gave a short talk on the runway. He mentioned neither West Berlin nor Cuba.

From around the world, journalists and diplomats were telephoning and telegraphing, letting America know what the world was thinking. Thoughts, of course, were varied.

Germany

West Berlin was calm, as a *Chicago Tribune* reporter, sent to test out the route from Bonn to Berlin, attested. The "Berlin-bound plane from Bonn had made its regular half-hour stop at Hanover," he wrote. "It was on the runway, ready to take off. Darkness had set in, and then, like a blanket, the fog rolled in. . . . The pilot had difficulty even taxiing the plane back to the terminal. . . . Maybe there were other ways to continue on to Berlin. Yes, there was a regular bus, which leaves . . . at midnight. . . . Every seat on the bus was taken as it slowly moved through the fog on the four-lane autobahn. . . . Despite the hour and darkness, the traffic to West Berlin was heavy. [Coming the other way] a large number of East German military vehicles was moving in the direction of the international border between East and West Germany. It was explained that this had nothing to do with the Cuban crisis. These military units were returning from east bloc maneuvers, which had just been completed."

Argentina   The government in Buenos Aires, *The New York Times* reported, was ready, as a gesture of friendship to Kennedy, to send warships to the Caribbean. The actual value of the gesture, to be sure, was limited—the Argentinian Navy would position itself in the southern reaches of the Caribbean, and the Soviet ships were steaming in from the north. The White House, nonetheless, expressed appreciation.

Japan   From Tokyo, Edwin O. Reischauer, U.S. ambassador and Harvard professor of Japanese studies, cabled the State Department: to non-Communists in Japan, JFK's action seemed "understandable but regrettable."

France   In the Norman city of Rouen, reporter Robert Allen informed *The New York Times*, people were "huddled over the papers in the cafés, and their talk was agitated." Former Premier Pierre Mendés-France called on his country to extend its support to Kennedy.

Mexico   The "recently formed National Liberation Movement, a leftist group," reported the *Los Angeles Times*, had stated that Kennedy had brought "us to the edge of a new war." Moderate and conservative newspapers in Mexico City backed Kennedy to the hilt.

Asia   India's main papers were shrill. The blockade, many claimed, was a violation of international law; some editors thought Khrushchev had been right to put the missiles in Cuba. The *People's Daily* in China excoriated the blockade as "flagrant piracy."

Great Britain   In Cardiff, some forty students demonstrated, peaceably, outside the American consulate. In Leeds, antinuclear activists lay down in the paths of newspaper trucks. In London, Ambassador Bruce spent the morning considering how best to protect the embassy: he increased the Marine guard outside, but he ordered that under no circumstances were they to fire their guns, even if they were attacked. And attacks did seem possible. In a Grosvenor Square demonstration, right in front of the embassy, young Britons tore an American flag to shreds, and others held high the peace banners of the Campaign for Nuclear Disarmament. Scuffles took place, and the police arrested more than a hundred.

From his cottage in Wales, Bertrand Russell, founder of the Campaign for Nuclear Disarmament, sent off telegrams, urging the Kremlin and the White House alike to be cautious. Khrushchev's response came quickly: "The question of war and peace," the Chairman stated, "is so vital that we should consider a top-level meeting. . . . As long as rocket nuclear weapons are not put into play it is still possible to avert war." Kennedy's answer to Russell was blunt: "I think your attention might be directed to the burglars rather than to those who have caught the burglars."

How could the Soviets be burglars, Russell asked in retort, if the Cubans had invited them in?

But Americans were supporting their President, and doing so overwhelmingly. Campaigning for the Senate in South Dakota, the Democratic candidate, a former professor, was catching up with his opponent fast, and was doing so on the basis of his expressed support for Kennedy; his name was George McGovern. In another farm state, Nebraska, reported *The New York Times,* "the long-simmering frustration over the need for some action showed through in comments by farmers, businessmen, housewives, laborers, students, and in newspaper editorials. 'President John F. Kennedy caught up with most other Americans Monday when he finally concluded that decisive steps were necessary to put a halt to the Communist buildup in Cuba,' the *Alliance Daily Times-Herald* said in western Nebraska. . . ." In Iowa, a businessman and school board member called the blockade 'long overdue. After all, Cuba's on our doorstep.' "

Here and there, as on the campuses at Indiana and Minnesota, small-scale protests did erupt. Several hundred students in Chicago were organizing an anti-blockade march in the Loop, scheduled for Saturday; a similar group, the Student Peace Union, in the Boston area, was receiving advice from Harvard history professor H. Stuart Hughes, grandson of Chief Justice Charles Evans Hughes.

In the San Francisco Bay area, however, William I. Olsen, Assistant Dean of Oakland City College, forbade demonstrations on his campus. New York Police Commissioner Michael J. Murphy barred anti-blockade marches in Times Square. District of Columbia Police Chief Robert V. Murphy announced that his 2,800-man force was on standby alert, prepared at any moment to snuff out a peace rally.

One voice of moderation was that of Walter Lippmann. Typing his column in the study of his northwest Washington home, he wrote:

It is Wednesday morning . . . , and the president's proclamation of a . . . blockade has just gone into effect. There are a number of Soviet and

Communist-bloc ships on their way to Cuba. . . . For the present, all depends upon orders [from Moscow]. We do not know whether the orders are to turn away from Cuba, to proceed and submit to search, or to proceed and to refuse to submit to search. . . .

I have lived through two world wars, and in both of them, we made the same tragic mistake. We suspended diplomacy when the guns began to shoot. In both wars as a result we achieved a great victory but we could not make peace. There is a mood in this country today which could easily cause us to make the same mistake again. We must in honor attempt to avoid it.

President Kennedy later claimed he had not read this Lippmann column. The claim was dubious—Lippmann was the nation's most influential journalist. A detached, fastidious man who appeared in public attired in gray fedoras and dark, custom-tailored suits, Lippmann's influence was based on his writing. Through his column he "commanded a loyal and powerful constituency," his biographer has written, "some ten million of the most politically active and articulate people in America. Many of these people literally did not know what they ought to think about the issues of the day until they read what Walter Lippmann had said about them. A politician could ignore that kind of power only at his own risk." Kennedy *must* have read the column.

For "there are three ways to get rid of the missiles already in Cuba," Lippmann stated:

One is to invade and occupy Cuba. The second way is to institute a total blockade, particularly of oil shipments, which would in a few months ruin the Cuban economy. The third way is to try . . . to negotiate a face-saving agreement.

But negotiate what? "The only place that is truly comparable with Cuba," Lippmann contended, "is Turkey."

This is the only place where there are strategic weapons right on the frontier of the Soviet Union. . . . There is another important similarity between Cuba and Turkey. The Soviet missile base in Cuba, like that of the U.S.-NATO base in Turkey, is of little military value. The Soviet military base in Cuba is defenseless, and the base in Turkey is all but obsolete. The two bases could be dismantled without altering the world balance of power.

The oracle of Washington, Walter Lippmann, had spoken, or rather, written, advising a trade—missiles in Turkey for missiles in Cuba. But, given the nation's clamor for action, could Kennedy accept the advice?

6   Occupying part of the sidewalk just east of the White House was a trailer bearing the logo of the Chesapeake and Potomac Telephone Company; workers had installed it to handle the vast increase of calls during the crisis. Early-morning crowds along the White House fence were unusually thick.

The White House, 9:35 A.M.
In a brief Oval Office conversation, President Kennedy told his brother Robert that he was worried. "It really looks mean, doesn't it," Robert quoted John as saying. "But then, really, there was no other choice. If they [the Soviets] get this mean in our part of the world, what will they do next?"

"I just don't think there was any choice," [Robert Kennedy quoted himself as saying], "and not only that, if you hadn't acted, you would have been impeached."

"That's what I think," the President supposedly responded, "—I would have been impeached."

The White House, 10:00 A.M.
The quarantine now went officially into effect. As it did so, President Kennedy sat again with Excomm in a meeting Robert Kennedy called "the most trying, the most difficult, and the most filled with tension." For the committee was receiving good news, and bad news. The good news was that, of the nineteen Soviet ships heading toward Cuba, only one, the tanker *Bucharest*, still seemed to be approaching the quarantine line; the rest, including five vessels with large hatches, had turned back toward the Baltic. The bad news was the possibility that the ships were regrouping, gathering into a convoy that, with a submarine escort, would try to smash through the quarantine line.

The bad news got worse. As Secretary McNamara reported a short while after the meeting had started, intelligence now had spotted two more of the ships, the *Gagarin* and the *Komiles*, still moving southward, only miles from the quarantine line. At this point, according to Robert Kennedy, the President's "hand went up to his face and covered his mouth. He opened and closed his fist. His face seemed drawn, his eyes pained, almost gray."

Hardly able to speak, JFK finally stammered, "Isn't there some way we can avoid our first exchange with a Russian submarine—almost anything but that?"

"No," McNamara replied bluntly, "there's too much danger to our ships. . . . Our commanders have been instructed to avoid hostilities if at all possible, but this is what we must be prepared for, and this is what we must expect."

The White House, 11:24 A.M.
A cable, drafted by Undersecretary of State George Ball, flashed out to Raymond Hare, the U.S. ambassador to Turkey, and to Thomas Finletter, the U.S. ambassador to NATO, letting them know that Kennedy, secretly, was considering a Turkey-for-Cuba missile-base trade. The ambassadors were to assess on-the-spot reactions, discreetly, of course.

A solution to the crisis, the cable allowed, might have to "involve dismantling and removal" of the Jupiter rockets. Yet any explicit comparison of the missiles in Turkey and the missiles in Cuba, the cable made clear, was "refutable"—the White House drafted even secret cables with an eye on public relations.

The White House, just before noon
John Kennedy called Harold Macmillan, informing the Prime Minister that some of the Soviet ships had reversed course. JFK wondered if the ships had been carrying missiles.

The White House, 1:00 P.M.
At this point the administration gave the newspapers and the television networks fourteen U-2–taken photographs of the missile sites in Cuba; the United States Information Agency soon distributed fifty thousand prints worldwide.

According to journalist Elie Abel's account, President Kennedy had been reluctant to release the pictures, and agreed to do so only through the intervention of Press Secretary Salinger, USIA Acting Director Wilson, Ambassador Bruce, and the seemingly ubiquitous Ambassador Ormsby-Gore; only their pleas led JFK to see the light. Perhaps so. Given the Kennedy family's long-standing mastery of publicity, however, Abel's version seems strange. Why would President Kennedy *not* have wanted the photos made public? Khrushchev and Castro knew full well—and Kennedy knew that they knew—of the U-2 over-flights. The distribution of the pictures, furthermore, as Pierre Salinger would remember, "was the best thing that ever happened. Those pictures played a major role in persuading foreign opinion that the President was justified in taking action."

The United Nations, 2:00 P.M.
Celebrating its seventeenth anniversary, the United Nations, for a moment, put the missile crisis aside. Paul Newman, the actor, handed out certificates to winners of a U.N. essay contest; the Leningrad Philharmonic, filling the stage of the General Assembly's main hall, played Tchaikovsky's Symphony No. 5 in E Minor. But then the international organization got down to business.

Much to the dismay of the U.S. delegation, diplomats from the nonaligned states of Asia and Africa were deeply suspicious of Kennedy's motives. The Malaysian ambassador said he thought the U.S. was in the wrong; the Ghanaian ambassador doubted that he had seen proof of "Cuba's offensive designs." Addressing assembled Asians and Africans, Valerian Zorin, the Soviet representative, maintained: "The Americans are thoroughly mistaken if they think we shall fall into their trap. We shall undertake nothing in Berlin, for action in Berlin is just what the Americans would wish." The Soviet Union, he went on, would do all it could to preserve the peace.

In the meantime, Adlai Stevenson and John McCloy were doing all they could to lobby nonaligned delegates. Stevenson reported to Washington that he had changed many of their minds.

And from his office in the Secretariat, high over the East River, U Thant was sending identical private appeals to Khrushchev and Kennedy: he urged both leaders to "refrain from any action which may aggravate the situation and bring with it the risk of war." At the request of more than forty of the nonaligned countries, he called for a deal: the Soviets to suspend arms shipments to Cuba; the U.S., for two to three weeks, to lift the quarantine.

Khrushchev's response reached U Thant at 3:30 P.M.: ". . . I welcome your initiative," the Chairman had wired. ". . . I wish to inform you that I agree to your proposal, which is in the interest of peace."

Kennedy's response, in U Thant's hands soon thereafter, was less cooperative: "I deeply appreciate the spirit which prompted your message . . . ," Kennedy, or Sorensen, had written. "As we made clear in the Security Council, the existing threat was created by the secret introduction of offensive weapons into Cuba, and the answer lies in the removal of such weapons. . . . I can assure you of our desire to reach a satisfactory and peaceful solution of this matter." So far, no deal.

The White House, 4:00 P.M.
Tall, intense, and imperious, Henry Luce, publisher of *Time, Life, Fortune,* and *Architectural Digest,* strode in through the north central door of the White House. He had come at Kennedy's invitation; JFK seemed to be leaning on the counsel of much older men. Luce thought Kennedy looked tired. In a conversation that lasted half an hour, Kennedy asked Luce repeatedly if the U.S. should invade Cuba. To judge by the tone of his publications, Luce must have responded in the affirmative.

7   *The White House, 6:30 P.M.*
After a talk with Senator Fulbright and other congressional leaders, JFK went down to the Situation Room for a news update. Were the Russian ships forming a convoy? The answer was not yet clear. But, in the midst of the clatter of the teletypes, Bundy did have a memo for Kennedy. Ormsby-Gore had been in to see Bundy, communicating what probably would be on Macmillan's mind the next time Kennedy called. The next telephone discussion, Bundy had written in the memo,

> might be framed in terms of exchange of military bases, but the Prime Minister and Lord Home [then the British Foreign Secretary] think that is not too good. It would look like a rather cynical exchange and a weak ending to the U.S. beginning. . . . Therefore Macmillan thinks the preferred course is to get discussion on disarmament, with the recognition that something about bases might come up along the way. [W]hat

is on the Prime Minister's mind is when, and in what context, conversations [between Kennedy and Khrushchev] can be started.

Macmillan, it seems plain, was worried, worried either that Kennedy would cave in, or that he would push the nuclear button. Like many others at the time, Macmillan must have wondered about the President's maturity.

The White House and Ten Downing Street, 7:00 P.M., Washington time

Macmillan already had spoken to the House of Commons, assuring the Members that Kennedy's action was not "extreme." Macmillan had declined, however, actually to endorse the blockade. Now he was talking by telephone with Kennedy.

Kennedy "told me," Macmillan wrote in his diary, "that U Thant had asked him to suspend the quarantine for two weeks, but that he could not agree to that unless the Russians agreed to stop work on the missile bases."

"I supported him in this. 'But all the same,' I added, 'I think [Khrushchev] is a bit wondering what to do, don't you?'"

Macmillan offered some advice: "You must . . . demand that there should be some inspection by the United Nations or other independent authority to stop the work on the major military installations. . . . This would enable you to say that you had in fact obtained your objectives."

Again, we sense Macmillan's concern. Did Kennedy know what he was doing? Was his leadership truly steady?

The White House, 8:00 P.M.

Going upstairs, Kennedy dined with several guests, including his old chum Charles Bartlett, the reporter. Through the candlelight, Bartlett proposed that, since most of the Soviet ships had turned around, the party should drink a toast.

Kennedy declined to do so. The game, he said, was hardly over.

He had a point. Even as they dined, the State Department was receiving, and translating, a letter from Khrushchev. Addressed to Kennedy, the epistle stated:

Just imagine, Mr. President, that we had presented you with the conditions of an ultimatum which you have presented to us by your action.

How would you have reacted to this? I think you would have been indignant. . . .

You, Mr. President, are not declaring a quarantine, but rather are setting forth an ultimatum and threatening that if we do not give in to your demands you will use force. . . .

If you coolly weigh the situation which has developed, not giving way to passions, then you will understand that the Soviet Union cannot fail to reject the arbitrary demands of the U.S.A.

Calling the blockade "an act of aggression," Khrushchev concluded by refusing to ask the Cuba-bound ships to observe the quarantine.

The White House and Ten Downing Street, 11:00 P.M., Washington time
So Kennedy called Macmillan *again*, raising what the Prime Minister dubbed the "$64,000 question":

> *Prime Minister:* Well, I'm all right. What's the news now?
> *President Kennedy:* Well, we have no more word yet on what's going to happen out there. As you have probably heard, some of the ships, the ones we're particularly interested in, have turned around. . . .

"Rather unexpectedly," then, Macmillan recorded, the "President asked me straight out the $64,000 question, 'Should he take out Cuba?' " Macmillan must have been noncommittal, for Kennedy said next: "We're going to have to make the judgment as to whether we're going to invade Cuba taking our chances or whether we hold off and use Cuba as a sort of hostage in the matter of Berlin. . . . What's your judgment . . . ?"
Macmillan was only cautionary: "I feel myself pretty sure," he said, "that we ought not to do anything in a hurry. We ought just to let this develop a day or two."
"Right, Prime Minister," Kennedy concluded. "As I say, we are mobilizing our force so that if we decide to invade we will be in a position to do so within a few more days. . . ."

The State Department, 1:45 P.M., October 25
A message flashed across the globe to Moscow. Kennedy had fired off his retort to Khrushchev.

"I regret very much," Kennedy's message began, "that you still do not appear to understand what it is that has moved us in this matter." The Soviets, Kennedy declared, had given "solemn assurances" that they would place no offensive missiles in Cuba. The facts, however,

> required the responses I have announced. . . . I hope that your government will take the necessary action to permit a restoration of the earlier situation.

CHAPTER 13

Until Hell Freezes Over

1   *Thursday morning, October 25, 1962*
The weather in Washington had turned chilly and damp, and the morning sky, overcast, had about it the gray look of winter. The mood in Washington, too, was wintry. Pre-rush-hour radio programs told worried suburbanites where they could buy tins of water; and the owner of the Surplus Sales Company on Pennsylvania Avenue, opening the store early, soon had to tell customers that he was out of what had become his best-selling item, a raisin-and-nut concentrate with four hundred calories to a pocket-sized can. As government workers parked their cars or clambered down from their buses, they greeted each other not with "How are you?" but rather with "What do you hear?"

Other questions, as well, were surfacing. In this "always skeptical capital," the *Chicago Tribune* reported, people were starting to ask "how and why the Cuban crisis developed with so little warning. How was the Soviet Union able to build missile bases, which take weeks and months for the United States to construct, without their being detected until last week . . . ? Why did a Republican senator [New York's Kenneth Keating] have 'fully confirmed' reports about the construction of the missile bases a week before the administration had 'definite' evidence? Why didn't the United States quietly inform the Soviet Union of its evidence before making it into an international issue . . . ? Did the President really have a 'cold'?" And another question, from London, carried in *The New York Times:* was Kennedy telling the truth? Neither the Ilyushin-28 bombers, with their short range, nor the missiles visible in the photographs, missiles designed to go from surface to air, contended Alun Gwynne-Jones, *The Times'* military correspondent, were "offensive," as JFK had called them. Their function, British military authorities believed, was "defensive."

Certainly the White House was on the defensive. All day long, Press Secretary Salinger and others kept talking to reporters, kept trying to deflect the doubts. And the journalists lent the White House their helping hands. No, stated the *San Francisco Examiner*, the administration had no intention of swapping missiles in Turkey for missiles in Cuba. No, stated *The New York Times*, the U.S. was not going to lift the blockade, simply because Khrushchev stopped further arms shipments. No, reported *The Washington Post*, the government was not backing down from its determination to get the missiles out of Cuba at any cost, including war. In newsrooms across the nation, the message rang clear: JFK was hanging tough!

But so were his opponents. Joining a protest outside Philadelphia's City Hall was a tall, white-haired man in his late seventies, a Christian pacifist and the elder statesman of American socialism, Norman Thomas; he was holding a placard that read NO UNILATERAL ACTION—SOLUTION THROUGH U.N." The student government at the University of Chicago echoed Thomas's sentiment, calling on Kennedy to comply with "U Thant's request that the blockade be temporarily suspended." Several thousands of miles to the east, in Prague, a mob of Czech students raced down narrow streets, swarmed up to the baroque palace that housed the U.S. embassy, smashed in half a dozen windows with stones, and chanted "Cuba si, Yankee no!" When Jack M. Fleischer, the U.S. chargé, drove up in his official limousine, they swirled around the car, shouting and waving their fists. Fleischer had to retreat.

In Moscow, *Pravda* published a poem telephoned in the day before from Cuba and penned by Yevgeny Yevtushenko. He considered himself Russia's angry young man, and perhaps he was so. Having gone to Havana to script a propaganda film, however, he was by no means out of the Kremlin's good graces. His poem was entitled "Letter to America" its first stanza:

> *America, I'm writing you from Cuba,*
> *Where the crags and the cheekbones*
> *Of rigid sentries shine anxiously tonight*
> *Awaiting the arrogant fleet . . .*

The "arrogant fleet" of which Yevtushenko had versified opened the day with a flurry of action. Shortly after dawn, just off the Florida coast, the USS *Gearing* spotted the Soviet tanker *Bucharest*, still heading for Cuba, and made contact by radio. A few other vessels had crossed the quarantine line: a British ship destined for Jamaica; a Greek tanker, Czech and Polish freighters, and the *Völkerfreundschaft*, an East German passenger liner, all of them bound for Havana. But the *Bucharest* was Russian. So the *Gearing* demanded to know what the tanker had in its hold. The answer came back in minutes: oil. Any weapons? No.

After direct consultation with the White House, the *Gearing* allowed the *Bucharest* to proceed. Explaining why he had decided to let the tanker through, President Kennedy said to advisers: "We don't want to push him [Khrushchev] to a precipitous action. I don't want to put him in a corner from which he cannot escape."

The State Department, 6:17 A.M.
At just about the time the *Bucharest* resumed course, a telegram came into Washington from the U.S. ambassador to Indonesia, Loy Henderson. Born on an Arkansas farm, Henderson had gone to law school in Denver, then in the 1920s had joined the fledgling Foreign Service. Since then he had served in virtually every continent and, cautious and even stodgy like most of his colleagues, was known to be reliable. Hence the White House's attention to his cable. The Indian and Soviet ambassadors in Jakarta had conversed, he wired. The Soviet diplomat had warned that, if Americans sank Russian ships, Moscow was sure to retaliate.

Through the Indian ambassador, nonetheless, the Soviet had passed along a hint as to how to end the crisis. The removal of the Soviet missiles in Cuba, he had indicated, just might be "negotiable."

The State Department, 9:09 A.M.
But would Turkey accept negotiations? From Ankara, Ambassador Thomas Finletter, a dignified and dispassionate New York lawyer, cabled that Turkey set "great store" by the presence of the Jupiter missiles: the Jupiters, to the Turkish government, were proof positive of an American commitment to defend the country against Russia. The very idea of a swap had left the Turks aghast.

Wanting to be a good ambassador, for he was a political appointee, Finletter may have bowed to Turkish pressures. For in his cable, he added a personal thought, a note to be passed along to Kennedy. We "must be most careful in working out any horse trade of this type," he had wired, "to be sure it does not set pattern for handling future Russian incursions in other parts of the world (perhaps in other Western Hemisphere countries)."

The White House, 10:00 A.M.
Excomm was meeting and Roger Hilsman, of the State Department, expressed a worry. "Soviet strategy," he had written in one of Washington's inevitable memoranda, "at the moment . . . is designed to gain time and flexibility for political action, designed to get the quarantine stopped while the missiles stay in Cuba."

So what to do? Excomm came up with three possible answers.

First, in a program christened Operation Bugle, U.S. airplanes would shower Cuba with leaflets. Entitled *La Verdad*, "The Truth," the pamphlets would state in Spanish that "the Russians have constructed nuclear missile bases of an offensive character in Cuba. These bases put Cuban lives and the peace of the world in danger, because Cuba now is an advanced base for Soviet aggression. . . . When these materials of war are taken out of Cuba the quarantine will be ended."

Second, as Theodore Sorensen later acknowledged, the U.S. could step up the pressure on the Soviets. Sorensen listed the options discussed: "tightening the blockade. . . . Increased low-level flights. . . . Action inside Cuba [including] ways of reaching Castro directly. . . . Air strike. Invasion. Those who had favored the last two courses the previous week now renewed their advocacy."

And third, as Sorensen hinted, the government would wink at the activities of Alpha 66, the band of Cuban exiles dedicated to killing Castro. This third option reached the press; somebody leaked it. In an article datelined Miami, the *Chicago Tribune* ran a headline, "ANTI-CASTRO CUBANS BUY U.S. WEAPONS." "Members of Alpha 66," the subsequent story related, ". . . have bought American military weapons, presumably in Miami. . . . [Antonio] Veciana [founder of the group], a meek-appearing certified public accountant, and another Alpha 66 leader, sat in a borrowed office suite and quoted the prices his group now is paying for American arms in Florida. [He] talked freely of buying arms here, but refused to give any clue as to how or with whom the group carried out clandestine purchases of government weapons intended only for use by American military forces. He and his partner would say only that 'we have the contacts to buy.' "

The United Nations, 2:26 P.M.
At the prompting of numerous nonaligned delegates, General Secretary U Thant sent a second appeal to Khrushchev and to Kennedy, urging, above all, calm. To Kennedy in particular, U Thant recommended that the U.S. "do everything possible to avoid a direct confrontation with Soviet ships in the next few days."

At about the same time, from the Ballhausplatz in Vienna, Austria's Foreign Minister Bruno Kreisky launched his own appeal for calm. His credentials for doing so were impeccable: as a blond-haired and chunky youth, and Jewish, Kreisky in the early 1930s had suffered imprisonment for his socialist activities; then, released and a law student at the time of the Nazi annexation, he had fled to the safety of Sweden. Now he saw himself as a perfect go-between, especially since his Austria was neutral. Like Walter Lippmann, he proposed a trade of missiles in Turkey and Cuba.

2   So far at least, the appeals had made little difference. It "is self-evident," Pierre Salinger said in a White House press conference, "that as long as Soviet ships continue to sail toward Cuba with unknown cargoes, the blockade by United States naval forces will continue." The Kennedy administration still looked tough.

As if to emphasize its toughness, or at least to whip up a war scare, the White House let the newspapers carry photographs of military dependents returning from Guantánamo to Norfolk. As tugboats nudged four Navy transports into their berths off the James River, fireboats sent streams of water arching over the mile-long dock, and a service band played "Sailing, Sailing, Over the Bounding Main." More than two thousand women and children, suntanned but shivering in the late October wind, wended their way down the gangplanks. Volunteers greeted them with warm garments, donated by the local Sears, Roebuck; and reporters conducted pierside interviews, and many wives expressed fears for their husbands still in "Gitmo."

The press also revealed—again with White House approval—that strict security measures had gone into effect in the eight-state region, from Raleigh to New Orleans and from Memphis to Key West, the part of the country closest to the missiles in Cuba. Louisiana's Air National Guard had stepped up patrols; Florida's National Guard was on a twenty-four-hour alert; and in all of the southeastern states, commercial aircraft were operating under stringent regulations imposed by the Federal Aviation Agency. And in Key West, a string of Pullman train cars disgorged a thousand new Army infantry-men. To house them, the Army took over motels, guest homes, and the 167-room Casa Marina, the island's largest hotel. Up and down the 150-mile stretch of the Florida Keys, anti-sabotage units, heavily armed, were on round-the-clock patrol.

But Cuba, too, was defending itself. Defiantly, the government newspaper, *Revolución*, announced the arrival of a twenty-two-nation "international combat brigade" from countries as diverse as Algeria, Peru, South Africa, and North Vietnam. Scattered along the island's coastline, these units, joining Cuban regulars, militia, and students, stood guard in the wind and rain for the invasion they said would surely come. How effective the international brigade could be, no one in Washington was sure.

What the CIA was sure about, however, was that the military buildup in Cuba was continuing apace. Cuban militia had fended off an Alpha 66 attack at the Matahambre copper mine. At the town of Remedios, low-level reconnaissance flights revealed the presence of a mobile, heavily armored Soviet regiment—it consisted of four combat teams, each with about 2,500 men and 100 tanks. And as U-2 photographs showed, work on the missile sites was still moving ahead. These facts did not reach the American press, the last thing the White House wanted in the papers was the allegation that Russia had deterred America.

Nosing around the Pentagon and the State Department, however, John G. Norris, a *Washington Post* reporter, learned from sources that the Soviets may well have deterred the Americans. Cuba's true "order of battle," Norris wrote, went as follows:

—22 anti-aircraft guided missile bases already operational and two more under construction. [O]ne Cuban base [has] three missiles on launchers and another 12 missiles stacked up in reserve.

—Surface-to-surface "cruise" missiles somewhat similar to the U.S. Air Force Mace and Matador air-breathing missiles [are now evident].

—Some 100 MIG-21s [are] operational on Cuban airfields. The MIG-21 is comparable to the latest service-type U.S. fighters.

—More than 20 IL-28 light jet bombers, which can deliver either conventional or nuclear weapons [are present].

—High-speed Komar-class Russian PT boats carrying guided missiles with a range of 10 to 15 miles designed for attacks on approaching warships [also are in evidence].

Such an array of weaponry had led to disquietude. While by "no means making invasion [of Cuba] impossible," Norris concluded, Soviet defensive power on the island "could make any such assault costly in lives. It is a factor well appreciated by U.S. strategy planners."

The Soviets were deterring an American invasion of Cuba, and that invasion would have been the largest of all the U.S. invasions in the Caribbean in the history of the twentieth century.

3   *The United Nations, 4:00 P.M.*

Adlai Stevenson continued his new tough stance. The Soviets

had called the Americans warmongers, but "this is the first time," the U.S. ambassador said to the Security Council, reiterating Dean Acheson's earlier line, "that I have ever heard it said that the crime is not the burglary but the discovery of the burglar."

Valerian Zorin, Soviet ambassador to the United Nations and president pro tem of the Security Council, was unimpressed: he challenged Stevenson to prove that Soviet missiles were present in Cuba. Stevenson was ready for that one:

Stevenson: Well, let me say something to you, Mr. Ambassador: we do have the evidence. We have it, and it is clear and incontrovertible. And let me say something else: These weapons must be taken out of Cuba. . . . Sir, let me ask you one simple question. Do you, Ambassador Zorin, deny that the U.S.S.R. has placed and is placing medium- and intermediate-range missiles and sites in Cuba? *Yes* or *no?* Don't wait for the translation, yes or no?

Zorin: I am not in an American courtroom, sir, and therefore I do not wish to answer a question that is put to me in a fashion in which a prosecutor puts questions. . . .

Stevenson: You are in the courtroom of world opinion right now and you can answer *yes* or *no.* You have denied that they exist and I want to know whether I have understood you correctly.

Zorin: Continue with your statement. You will have your answer in due course.

Stevenson: I am prepared to wait for my answer until hell freezes over. . . .

Never, in all his career in politics, had Adlai Stevenson assumed so popular a stance! And he had done so on television! By the time the evening news was over he was a hero, even to country-club Republicans back in Lake Forest, Illinois; some Chicago friends thought he should make another bid for the White House. For old Adlai, at last, had stood up to the Russians.

In its logic, however, the "hell freezes over" speech was flawed. Waiting until hell froze over was precisely what John F. Kennedy was not prepared to do.

Washington, nighttime
During the evening, Kennedy talked with Macmillan who, speaking that day before the House of Commons, had termed Khrushchev's move in Cuba a "deliberate adventure." But he also prompted Kennedy to avoid confrontation.

The State Department received a new epistle from Khrushchev, a message addressed to Kennedy. The chairman was almost patronizing. "Let us therefore display statesmanlike wisdom," he had written:

> I propose: we for our part will declare that our ships bound for Cuba are not carrying any armaments. You will declare that the United States will not invade Cuba with its troops and will not support any other forces which might intend to invade Cuba. Then the necessity for the presence of our military specialists in Cuba will be obviated.

Khrushchev's proposal may have caught the White House off guard. He was suggesting, not missiles in Cuba for missiles in Turkey, but rather no *more* missiles in Cuba for no *more* invasion attempts.

The chairman's gambit was clever, and one senses that the administration was worried. "I am increasingly disturbed over indications," analyst Raymond L. Garthoff wrote at some point in the day to Walt W. Rostow, head of the State Department's policy planning board, "that in all of our planning for the development of the Cuban crisis we have *to our peril* [emphasis added] neglected one particular contingency: that the Soviets would react mildly and with great caution."

What if Khrushchev did little, perhaps even backed down? What if Khrushchev, in his crude, coarse way, gave peace a chance? Then what? Would not, Garthoff asked, America's alliances cease to have reason for being?

4   *Friday, October 26, 1962*
In the predawn darkness of the Caribbean, the Russian tanker *Vinnitsa* slipped into the Havana harbor. A U.S. destroyer had hailed it and, on the captain's assurance that he was hauling no weaponry (and with White House approval), had waved it through the blockade line. Now, despite a heavy rain, a huge

crowd was present at the pier to give the ship a welcome: people sang, cheered, shined their flashlights up toward the deck. Anders Soler of Cuba's longshoremen's union gave a dockside speech, praising "the courage of the sailors who had crashed the blockade."

Not far away, Vern Haugland, a reporter with the *Chicago Tribune*, witnessed an incident at sea. Chartering a light airplane out of Puerto Rico, he flew around the Dominican Republic toward the Bahamas, noticed the ships strung out across the sea lanes to Cuba—and then detected a flurry of action. In a sudden rush, one of the U.S. destroyers left its position and intercepted an oncoming foreign tanker. From the airplane, Haugland reported, "we saw the destroyer bearing down from the northeast on a collision course. The wake of the two ships—clear in the blue water—plainly indicated that an interception was in prospect. We circled the area [just off Great Inagua Sound] for almost half an hour, waiting for the encounter."

The encounter never came. When the destroyer, #148, the *Brough*, was "some distance away," Haugland's article continued, "its blinkers started signaling the tanker [*Mylla*, a Norwegian tramp steamer] furiously. We were unable to see the *Mylla*'s return signals. The tanker had big cargo crates on the decks; its hatches were boarded over and it appeared more likely to be carrying grain or other bulk cargo than oil. A few crew members were visible. The two ships were only a few hundred yards apart when the destroyer turned sharply, allowing the tanker to proceed southward."

The *Chicago Tribune* also reprinted from its files a photograph of U.S. destroyer #850, the *Joseph P. Kennedy, Jr.* (a picture taken of the *Kennedy* in the Chicago River in July 1959, during an official visit to the city). The *Kennedy* was involved in the only blockade incident that remotely resembled an encounter. The incident took place at 6:51 A.M., October 26, 1962. The ship involved was called the *Marucla*.

Built in Baltimore as a World War II liberty ship, the *Marucla* had become, by 1962, a tramp steamer flying the flag of Lebanon, a country hardly in a position to mount a major international protest. So the *Marucla* was safe for a boarding—especially since her cargo of industrial goods such as emery powder, lathes, asbestos, trucks, and spare parts for trucks, had been picked up in Latvia and was destined for Cuba. Intelligence planes had been trailing the *Marucla;* Washington had pieced together details of the ship's background. So when, late in the afternoon of October 25, 1962, the vessel lumbered up close to the quarantine line, the U.S. Navy was ready to act, to show to all the world President Kennedy's determination to enforce the blockade.

Just off Bermuda, the destroyer USS *John R. Pierce* pulled alongside the *Marucla* and radioed the White House for instructions. Officers from the *Pierce* could have boarded the steamer, but President Kennedy ordered the action postponed until the morning: he wanted the boarding carried out by the *Joseph P. Kennedy, Jr.*, and, as darkness fell, the *Kennedy* was quite some miles away.

"I suppose," the President complained soon thereafter, "that I sent the *Kennedy* in there deliberately to give our family some publicity."

During the night, the *Kennedy* caught up with the *Pierce*, keeping exact pace with the *Marucla;* and as soon as the sky began to lighten, the *Kennedy* raised signal flags that spelled out, in international code, OSCAR NOVEMBER, or "Stop." The *Marucla* kept on going. With a blinking light, then, the *Kennedy* flashed out a warning: REQUEST YOU STOP. I INTEND TO BOARD YOU. REQUEST YOU ADVISE WHEN YOUR SEA LADDER IS READY. Now the *Marucla* did stop, signaling back that the ladder was ready. The ships stood due east of the Kennedy estate in West Palm Beach.

As the *Kennedy* lowered a launch to the water, a Russian-language translator and three officers dressed in Navy whites clambered down, set out across the sea—they carried no weapons—and climbed to the *Marucla*'s deck. There, escorted by Georgios Condorrigas, the captain, they poked around, skimmed the ship's manifest, squinted down into the hold, saw boxes stenciled in Cyrillic script, and did no more. They did not climb down to the hold. At about 9:00 A.M., they signaled the *Kennedy* that the *Marucla* could proceed, and they returned to their destroyer.

The incident played well in the press. *The New York Times* presented it as scary and dramatic.

5   Elsewhere, too, the Kennedy administration was flaunting its toughness.

In Norfolk, Admiral Robert L. Dennison told reporters that, despite its lack of natural defenses, the U.S. could safeguard the Guantánamo base. "You must remember," he stated, "that we are not dependent on just the forces there."

Out in the Pacific, thirty to forty miles over Johnson Island, the U.S. government detonated a nuclear device. The blast was so powerful that it was visible even in Hawaii, where observers said they saw a flash that turned from red to green to gray-blue. The explosion had been scheduled, but for later. A source in Washington told *The Washington Post* that the explosion had been moved up because of the missile crisis—to frighten the Russians.

Down in Key West, officials announced, the U.S. military buildup was still going on. On the islandlike spit of land three miles east of the downtown area, trucks were hauling long cigar-shaped objects marked "Explosives," and taking them behind a protective mound of earth about thirty feet high; late in the afternoon of October 26, soldiers, working in open view on the beach, were busy erecting target-finding radar units. The Pentagon was equipping Key West with anti-airplane missiles.

And in Washington, in the State Department auditorium, press officer Lincoln White "underlined" President Kennedy's point in the Monday night television address—that, if the "offensive military preparations [in Cuba] continue . . . further action will be justified." White's statement had reporters hopping up with questions: was White saying that Kennedy was going to bomb the missile sites? The response was only: "As to specific further steps, that is not my function here. I simply cite to you the gravity of the situation."

How grave *was* the situation? In the 10:00 A.M. Excomm meeting, President Kennedy allowed that the quarantine alone was

never going to get the missiles out. Only an invasion, he said, would do the job—or some sort of trade.

Invasion was clearly an option: thousands of Marines now were present in Guantánamo, albeit huddling in their ponchos under torrents of rain; 25,000 more Marines were in ships that were positioned all around Cuba; 100,000 more soldiers were stationed in Florida, poised to board more ships. Two aircraft carriers, the *Enterprise* and the *Independence*, were approaching Cuba fast; and officers aboard U.S. cruisers had received instructions about where, along the Cuban coast, they could first fire their guns.

As he heard these facts recited in the Cabinet Room, however, Defense Secretary McNamara must have blanched. Pentagon studies, he informed Excomm, were showing that an invasion of Cuba would lead to heavy casualties. President Kennedy himself then conceded that any invasion would be a "very bloody fight."

But if not an invasion, then what? Shutting off petroleum products? That might work, the group opined, but would do so slowly, and President Kennedy wanted results fast. Bombing Cuba? The Air Force was ready to launch three massive strikes a day, on the first day alone sending down nearly two thousand bombing sorties. Kennedy, however, was hesitant. Would that kind of bombing, he wanted to know, in the end simply outrage the American people?

As Excomm adjourned, at about 11:00 A.M., JFK seemed to feel boxed in. About all he could do to secure the removal of the missiles from Cuba was to keep on keeping on, maintaining the quarantine and putting on a show of force—and, in the shadows, working out a deal. And a deal was in the works.

6   A balding, owlish man of medium height, John A. Scali, diplomatic correspondent for ABC news, was having a busy day; for lunch on October 26, he was reduced to bolting down a bologna sandwich in his State Department press room cubicle. At about 1:30 P.M., however, his telephone rang. The caller was Alexander S. Fomin, a "counselor" in the Soviet embassy and an acquaintance with whom Scali had had lunch

before. Fomin wanted to have lunch again, that very afternoon, right then.

Scali protested. There was no way he could get away, he said.

Fomin, however, persisted. "It's very important," he responded. "Meet me at the Occidental in ten minutes."

The restaurant was not far from the State Department, just up on Pennsylvania Avenue. Suspecting that Fomin was KGB and thus knowledgeable about the Soviet side of the crisis, Scali went. When he walked into the restaurant, he saw that Fomin already was seated, occupying a small table by a wall. Noticing Scali, he rose. Stocky and blond, Fomin usually looked robust. Now he seemed pale. A waiter came, took orders, left. Fomin spoke, in a whisper.

"The situation is very serious," he said. "Something must be done." He wanted to use Scali as an intermediary between the Soviet embassy and the State Department.

The waiter brought the food and left again.

Fomin murmured. He thought he knew a way out of the crisis, he said, a way based on a U.N. speech made several weeks earlier by Cuba's President Osvaldo Dorticós. A trade—Cuba's dismantling its weaponry in exchange for Kennedy's making a noninvasion pledge—Dorticós had contended, might defuse the Caribbean's tensions. Kennedy, at the time, had ignored the suggestion. But now?

Fomin put down his utensils, and looked at Scali intently. Would the U.S. government be interested in a settlement? Fomin queried. He had three specific proposals; together they might comprise a deal.

1. Under U.N. supervision, the Soviet Union would dismantle its missiles in Cuba and ship them back home.
2. Castro would pledge that, in the future, he would accept no offensive weapons.
3. Kennedy would pledge that, in the future, he would not invade Cuba.

Newsmen, Scali hastened to explain, did not necessarily speak for the government. Fomin understood; he only wanted Scali to present the proposal to the proper sources, the higher the better. Scali said he would do his best and Fomin gave him two telephone numbers, one at his flat and the other at his embassy desk. Scali could get back to him at any time.

Returning straightaway to the State Department, Scali typed up a record of the conversation, then hurried upstairs to see Roger Hilsman, the brisk, energetic head of Intelligence and Research. Hilsman read what Scali had typed, and hurried Scali in turn to see Rusk.

Rusk read Scali's piece of paper. From a desk drawer, he extracted another sheet, wrote on it, handed it over to Scali, and said, "I want you to go back to this man and tell him this":

I have reason to believe [Rusk had scrawled] that the U.S.G. [United States Government] sees real possibilities in this and supposes that representatives of the two governments [Soviet and American] could work this matter out with U Thant and with each other. My impression is, however, that time is very urgent.

Rusk, however, was not finished. Wanting to clear the message with Kennedy, he raced with Scali into the basement garage, and together they went by limousine to the West Wing of the White House.

While they waited outside the Oval Office, they encountered Pierre Salinger who, all week, had been trying to keep reporters at bay. "What the hell are you doing here?" he bellowed at Scali.

Rusk reassured him. "It's all right, Pierre. I brought him here."

Once seated with Kennedy, Rusk described Scali's encounter with Fomin, showing the President what he had written out for the Russian. Kennedy glanced at it, nodded, and agreed that Rusk's note was useful. Scali should inform Fomin of the message as soon as possible. "But don't," Kennedy said, "use my name."

After a telephone call to Fomin, Scali proceeded by taxi to the Statler Hotel, where he met the Russian in the lobby; they repaired to the coffee shop. With Rusk's note memorized and tucked into a pocket, Scali recited: "I believe that the U.S.G. sees real possibilities. . . ."

Fomin cut in. Did Scali's words, he insisted upon knowing, come from the highest sources?

Yes, Scali assured him.

At this point, Fomin threw a new element into the pot. According to Scali's notes, Fomin wanted to know if

> it would be possible to have United Nations inspectors . . . check the American military bases in Florida to make sure that there would be no invasion of Cuba. He also asked whether it would be possible to inspect surrounding Caribbean countries.

Scali allowed that Fomin's new request was a "terrible complication at a period when time was of the essence in settling the Cuban problem." He promised nonetheless to pass the word along. Twenty minutes after they had entered the coffee shop, they were both off, Fomin to the Soviet embassy and Scali to the State Department.

7   Time indeed was of the essence. Kennedy's opponents had smelled blood, and were moving in for the kill.

From its Capitol Hill headquarters the Republican party's Congressional Campaign Committee issued a newsletter, claiming that JFK had timed his blockade proclamation to maximize votes in the November election and that, in dealing with Castro, he had shown a "reluctance to crack down hard." The newsletter listed specific charges against the President:

Seventy-two hours after the President's announcement of the blockade, the U.S. Navy still had turned back no Soviet vessels.

In his blockade proclamation, Kennedy had failed to order the search of vessels bearing offensive weapons to Cuba, merely authorizing the Secretary of Defense to do so.

Defense Secretary McNamara in turn had passed the buck, turning that authorization over to Chief of Naval Operations Admiral George W. Anderson, Jr.; word had been "leaked" that the Navy would really not halt all ships bound for Cuba, but instead would select one vessel as a test. The newsletter did not elaborate on the source of the "leak."

Washington, in fact, was leaking like a sieve. The Soviets were keeping up work on the missile sites, reporters learned, and indeed were trying to camouflage their efforts. Reconnaissance planes, furthermore, had spotted a new Soviet submarine, northwest of the Dominican Republic and inside the quarantine zone. Someone in the Pentagon, finally, had put in the hands of the press new facts about the Soviet forces in Cuba. They had:

Twenty-five anti-aircraft missile bases.
About one hundred MIG jet fighters.
At least thirty-nine MIG-21s, comparable to the latest U.S. Air Force fighters; the thirty-nine were lined up at the sides of a a Cuban airstrip.

So what was emerging in Washington was political pressure, pressure from the Republicans, the Pentagon, and the press alike, pressure on Kennedy to end the missile crisis, to end it fast, and to end it with a victory. Kennedy had to produce.

Plenty of proposals were in the works.

From Brazil, Ambassador Lincoln Gordon, a calm, chunkily-built man who was fluent in Portuguese, forwarded a top-secret suggestion. If Washington was willing, Gordon's cable made clear, Luis Batian Pinto, Brazil's ambassador in Cuba, would make an offer to Castro. Castro would have to ask the Soviets to take the missiles away. And if he did so, Brazil would make sure that the Organization of American States would condemn a U.S. invasion of Cuba. The U.S. "would not risk upsetting hemispheric solidarity by invading a Cuba clearly committed to a peaceful course." If Castro behaved himself, Kennedy would have to do so too.

In his office high over the East River, U.N. Secretary General Thant also was trying to find a way out of the crisis. In a letter forwarded to Havana, he reminded Castro (as Fomin had reminded John Scali) of the words spoken by Osvaldo Dorticós: "Were the United States to give us any proof . . . that it would not carry our aggression against our country . . . our weapons would be redundant. . . ." If U Thant could secure such proof, the letter asked, would Castro halt the missile buildup?

Khrushchev himself laid out a proposal. In a long, emotional letter that reached Washington in separate parts throughout the evening, Khrushchev wrote to Kennedy:

[Y]ou and I should not now pull on the ends of the rope in which you have tied a knot of war, because the harder you and I pull, the tighter the knot will become. And a time may come when this knot is tied so tight that the person who tied it is no longer capable of untying it, and then the knot will have to be cut. What that would mean I need not explain to you, because you yourself understand perfectly what dread forces our two countries possess.

Then, having used the Scali-Fomin channel to make sure he was on solid ground, Khrushchev tendered an offer. "I propose," he signaled, that

we, for our part, will declare that our ships bound for Cuba are not carrying any armaments. You will declare that the United States will not invade Cuba with its troops and will not support any other forces which might intend to invade Cuba. Then the necessity of the presence of our military specialists in Cuba will disappear.

Emphasizing his point, Khrushchev, while this letter was being transmitted to Washington, ordered all Soviet shipping to stay away from the quarantine zone. The Chairman's letter itself was almost paternalistic: we will do what is right, he was saying to Kennedy, and *you* will do what is right.

Just what Kennedy thought about Khrushchev's letter we do not know. But Roger Hilsman of the State Department, it is clear, immediately saw a way out of the crisis.

A 1943 graduate of West Point, Hilsman was a Kennedy favorite, unafraid to raise challenges. An example: in a 1961 White House briefing on Vietnam, General Lyman Lemnitzer had lumbered up to a map, pointed with his swagger stick to an Asiatic river system, and identified it as Indochina's Mekong Valley. But Hilsman, bespectacled, intense, and knowledgeable, had arisen, taken the pointer from his superior officer, moved the tip southward along the map, and said that *this* is the Mekong Valley. Lemnitzer had been pointing to China's Yangtze Valley. Now, in a 10:00 P.M. Excomm meeting, Hilsman was equally decisive.

Why not, he urged, put Scali's notes from his meeting with Fomin side-by-side with the text of Khrushchev's letter, and see where we stood?

Excomm did so. In the two documents they saw an offer they dared not refuse.

CHAPTER 14

Those Frigging Missiles

1 *Late Friday afternoon, October 26, 1962*
Carried by courier in a military airplane, a classified document, drafted in the White House, soon was on its way to Stevenson and McCloy at the United Nations in New York:

SECRET

NATURE OF THE DEAL

1. Soviet agreement to pull missiles and bomber aircraft out of Cuba, under U.N. inspection.
2. Cuban agreement never again to permit offensive weapons on its soil.
3. U.S. government to respect the territorial integrity and political independence of Cuba (no commitment to prop up Castro government).
4. Cuban agreement to restrict its subversive activities in Latin America (perhaps this could take the form of a Cuban guarantee of the territorial integrity and political independence of other Latin American states).

Even before this document had reached New York, Robert Kennedy was off in the night by limousine, slipping through the rear door of the Soviet embassy to see Dobrynin. Ritualistically, the Soviet ambassador defended his country's placement of missiles in Cuba, but he also made mention of the missiles in

Turkey. At this point, Robert Kennedy bolted out of Dobrynin's office to telephone the White House. When he returned, he informed Dobrynin: "The President said that we are ready to consider the question of Turkey, to examine favorably the question of Turkey."

Having thus tendered his own offer to the Soviets, Kennedy looked for sustenance, talking far into the night with Prime Minister Macmillan. The Britisher had a suggestion: "Would it be worthwhile our undertaking to immobilize the missiles [the Thors] which are here in England during a time of negotiation?" Kennedy was hesitant.

> *President Kennedy:* I think that the prospect of a trade of these missiles is still . . . vague. . . . Maybe by tomorrow evening at this time I'll know better.
>
> *Prime Minister:* Yes, because of course at this stage any movement by you could produce a result in Berlin which would be very bad for us all. That's the danger now.
>
> *President Kennedy:* Well, we are not going to have any problems because he [Khrushchev] is keeping his ships out of there. . . . On the other hand, if at the end of 48 hours we are getting no place and the missile sites continue to be constructed, then we are going to be faced with some hard decisions. . . .

So problems still loomed, and nothing seemed more problematical than whether Fidel Castro would accept a deal. The odds of his doing so were unfavorable, for his embassy in London had just denounced the blockade as "an act of war." We also know now that, ensconced in a Havana bomb shelter, Castro had written a letter to Khrushchev. "Dear Chairman Khrushchev," the epistle began:

> From an analysis of the situation and the reports in our possession, I consider that aggression is almost imminent within the next 24 or 72 hours.
>
> There are two possible variants: the first and likeliest one is an air attack against certain targets with the limited objective of destroying

them; the second, less probable although possible, is invasion. . . . You can rest absolutely that we will firmly and resolutely resist attack, whatever it might be. . . .

If the second variant is implemented and the imperialists invade Cuba with the goal of occupying it, the danger that that aggressive policy poses for humanity is so great that following that event the Soviet Union must never allow the circumstances in which the imperialists could launch the first nuclear strike. . . .

Castro *seemed* to be asking Khrushchev to consider starting a nuclear war. He *certainly* took a provocative step of his own, over the pleas of the Soviet ambassador, ordering Cuban artillery units to fire on U.S. aircraft flying over the island. Castro was in no mood to accept any deal.

At some point during the day of Friday, October 26, 1962, Arthur Schlesinger gave JFK a copy of a letter just in from John Bartlow Martin, U.S. ambassador in the Dominican Republic. "Dear Arthur," Martin had written,

I thought you and the President might enjoy knowing that the day after the President's speech on Cuba, the leftist-inspired rumors in the streets of Santo Domingo were a) that I had been assassinated and b) that there had been a coup in Washington and Kennedy was no longer President.

This will give you some idea of what this kookie place is like.

Passing the letter along to President Kennedy, Schlesinger appended a note:

I have asked John Martin to supply the missing element in this story—i.e., who took over after the coup in Washington?

And also at some point in the day, or in the evening, JFK, discussing the Jupiter missiles in Turkey, lost his cool. According to several accounts, he stormed about the Oval Office, screaming, "Get those frigging missiles off the board!"

2   *Saturday morning, October 27, 1962*

Well before dawn, Washington time, a near-riot erupted in Moscow. Hurling stones, bricks, and bottles, about two thousand Soviet citizens jeered and whistled in front of the fence that guarded the U.S. embassy. Some of the demonstrators, workmen, held up placards that demanded "HANDS OFF CUBA" and "AWAY WITH THE BLOCKADE". Others, some of them young women, used pocket mirrors to divert the sun's rays and to blind embassy employees who were looking down from the windows. An American reporter moved into the throng. No one harmed him, but they did ask sharp questions: "What is this blockade all about?" people insisted on knowing. "Why don't you leave Cuba alone? Who gives you the right to stop ships on the high seas?"

One person, a student, admitted to the reporter that Russia might have missiles in Cuba. But "just suppose," the youth added, "there *are* a few Soviet bases off the United States. Look at all the United States bases that ring the Soviet Union. Are we not justified in starting a blockade of our own?"

The demonstration went on for four hours. Only then, using loudspeakers, did the police appeal for order.

In his Kremlin office not far away, Chairman Khrushchev sat closeted with his generals, poring over maps and deliberating their next move. Hammering out what they would do, Khrushchev wrote, they decided to "remove the rockets and warheads if the President would give public assurances . . ." that America's "armed forces would not invade Cuba." "We believed," Khrushchev went on,

> that Kennedy could incite one of the Latin-American countries under U.S. influence to attack Cuba. What difference does it make who attacks? They could accumulate a relatively big force to outnumber the armed forces of Fidel Castro.

With that fear in mind, apparently, Khrushchev cabled Ambassador Dobrynin in Washington, instructing him to renew contact with Robert Kennedy. For Khrushchev, RFK was "the basic intermediary."

3   As Khrushchev and comrades were putting their heads together, a U.S. military transport plane was rising from the runway at Berlin's Templehof Airport. Hardly had the plane finished its ascent than two Soviet MIG fighters appeared from the east. High over the Autobahn, they made three passes at the American aircraft.

Notified soon thereafter of the incident, Pentagon officials became worried. Were the Soviets, they pondered, planning further to harass air traffic in and out of Berlin?

In the center of London, thousands of people took advantage of clear Saturday weather to line the streets around Trafalgar Square. The government had refused permission for a demonstration there, and the base of the Nelson Monument was ringed with barricades and uniformed policemen, their truncheons at the ready as they surveyed the crowds in the side streets. Organized by the Committee for Nuclear Disarmament, the demonstrators stood in silence, awaiting their signal. It came: at 3:00 P.M. (10:00 A.M. Washington time), Big Ben began to toll. And almost as one person, the mob, yelling "Hands Off Cuba!," pushed into the famous square.

Police grappled with demonstrators, demonstrators swung back with fists, policemen threw their own blows, and only the arrival of more policemen, on horseback, prevented a riot. Many of the demonstrators were arrested, but many others slipped away, shouting "Grosvenor Square! Grosvenor Square!" A column started on the long trek to the American embassy.

There, more policemen still were on hand. Fists flew. More persons were arrested, many shrieking, "Up Fidel! Kennedy to hell!" Then the demonstration began to peter out.

The storm system that for a time had socked in over Cuba and southern Florida had cleared; the breezes were soft for the moment, and the sky hardly contained a cloud. So in a secret base in the interior of Florida, Major Rudolph Anderson, Jr., the CIA pilot, climbed into his U-2 again. It was Anderson's U-2 photographs that, on October 16, 1962, McGeorge Bundy had taken to President Kennedy.

Anderson, this time, was heading for eastern Cuba, roughly over Guantánamo. For the CIA had thought that, there, the Soviets might be building a submarine base. This time, however, he would not return with photographs. In fact, he would not return.

Washington's weather, too, was clear, and the morning sunshine glittered in the trees. To officials in the White House, however, this particular day—Saturday, October 27, 1962—promised to be long and dreary.

"It was generally agreed," Pierre Salinger was to recall, "that we couldn't go beyond Sunday without a further decision."

Robert McNamara agreed: "The air strike was ready to go in forty-eight hours," he stated; "if pressed we could have done it in thirty hours."

4 A thousand or more pickets marched up and down the sidewalk in front of the White House—some were for Kennedy, but most were against, and three Cuban exiles who lived in Washington threw eggs and tomatoes on one group of dissenters. Heaving themselves into their chairs inside the mansion, Excomm members at 10:00 A.M. sat down to a day of marathon discussion.

Entering the Cabinet Room, Robert Kennedy was in a most somber mood. He had just received word from FBI Director J. Edgar Hoover that the Soviet mission at the United Nations was preparing to burn its papers, a step usually associated with diplomatic rupture, even with war. Was Hoover's information correct? Was war coming? Having no sure answers, Robert Kennedy took his seat, glaring around the polished table.

Fifteen others were present: Rusk, McNamara, and Bundy, along with Salinger and Lyndon Johnson. Then Douglas Dillon from Treasury; George Ball and U. Alexis Johnson, Latin American specialist Edward Martin and Llewellyn Thompson, all from State. From Defense, Maxwell Taylor, Roswell Gilpatric, and Paul Nitze. Theodore Sorensen sat with pencil and paper, ready to take notes. McCone sat with hands folded over the report he soon would deliver. They all, RFK noted, were as hushed as in church.

Then President Kennedy, clothed in a dark suit and with his hair freshly brushed, entered the room. The meeting began.

McCone led off, flipping past the title page of his latest report, and cited the latest intelligence. As of 6:00 A.M., he stated, six missile sites in Cuba seemed to be fully operational.

That piece of news was bad enough. But, then, Secretary McNamara informed the group that one Soviet tanker, the *Grozny*, seemed still heading for Cuba; at the moment the vessel was about six hundred miles from the quarantine line. Perhaps, interjected George Ball, the Soviets did not know how far the quarantine line extended—someone ought to tell U Thant, he recommended, and the Secretary General could tell the Russians.

President Kennedy accepted the recommendation. But a question remained: should the U.S. board the *Grozny?*

Now the news turned even worse. At some point between 10:15 and 11:00 A.M., Washington time, a U-2 pilot out of Alaska drifted into Siberian airspace, realized where he was, and radioed for a fighter escort to get him back in safety. Even before the escort—aircraft armed with air-to-air nuclear missiles— could take off from Alaska, however, Soviet MIGs were climbing to intercept the U-2.

The U-2 did get away in time. Before word of its escape reached the White House, nonetheless, McNamara lost control. He "turned absolutely white," remembered one of the Excomm members, "and yelled hysterically (seeming to have lost touch with his senses), 'This means war with the Soviet Union!' "

President Kennedy remained quieter, referring to the U-2 pilot, "There is always some son of a bitch," he said, "who doesn't get the word."

And *then* a new letter from Khrushchev flashed into the Situation Room. The time was 11:03 A.M. Stated Khrushchev:

You are disturbed over Cuba. You say that this disturbs you because it is 90 miles by sea from the coast of the United States. But . . . [Y]ou have placed destructive rocket weapons, which you call offensive, in Turkey, literally right next to us. . . .

I therefore make this proposal: We are willing to remove from Cuba the means which you regard as offensive. . . . Your representatives will make a declaration to the effect that the United States . . . will remove its analogous means from Turkey . . . and after that, persons entrusted by the United Nations Security Council could inspect on the spot the fulfillment of the pledges made. . . .

[We] will make a statement within the framework of the Security Council to the effect that the Soviet government gives a solemn promise to respect the inviolability of the borders and sovereignty of Turkey, not to make available our territory as a bridgehead for such an invasion, and that it would also restrain those who contemplate committing aggression against Turkey. . . . The United States government will make a similar statement within the framework of the Security Council regarding Cuba. . . .

As copies of Khrushchev's newest proposal were passed around the Cabinet table, a few of the Excomm members expressed outrage. Some were puzzled, others just thoughtful. For Khrushchev now had toughened his terms—his previous proposal had not mentioned Turkey.

Why did he do so now? Someone in the Cabinet Room suggested that Khrushchev actually had fallen from power and that top Soviet generals had written the letter; someone else thought that Khrushchev might be trying to buy time, sowing confusion until he could get all his missiles in place.

We now know the truth: Khrushchev could propose the Turkish-Cuban missile trade because, the day before, Robert Kennedy had told Anatoly Dobrynin that JFK would "examine" the Turkish issue "favorably." And the Kennedy brothers had kept this offer secret—even from the members of Excomm.

Why the secrecy?

Leaks. Washington was awash with leaks. Someone had leaked the presence of missiles in Cuba to Senator Keating. Lyndon Johnson had leaked the possibility of an invasion of Cuba to the Dallas newspaper. Someone in the Pentagon had leaked information about the true strength of Cuba's defenses to the national papers. And even in Excomm, the President was confronted with real or potential enemies—Vice President Johnson, Director McCone, possibly even General Taylor; and from NATO headquarters near Paris, General Lauris Norstad had cabled the White House, denouncing the idea that "missiles in

Cuba [are] on the same basis as those in Turkey." Had Excomm realized that Kennedy had offered the Turkey deal, any one of these personnages might have gone straight to the press, destroying his career.

You can sense the President squirming, even in the transcript of the Excomm tape:

> *JFK:* He's [Khrushchev] got us in a pretty good spot here, because most people will regard this [the new letter] as not an unreasonable proposal, I'll just tell you that. In fact, in many ways—
>
> *Bundy* [challenging his own boss]: But *what* most people, Mr. President?
>
> *JFK:* I think you're going to find it very difficult to explain why we are going to take hostile military action in Cuba, against those sites—what we've been thinking about—the thing that he's saying is, "If you'll get yours out of Turkey, we'll get ours out of Cuba." I think we've got a very tough one here.

A tough one indeed. Kennedy could not move backward: he could not tolerate the presence of the missiles in Cuba, not that and remain President. But he could not move forward: so strong were Cuba's defenses that, now, he could hit the island only at the cost of many American lives. So he could only move sideways: he had to give the public the impression that he had won a great victory, but agree in private to Khrushchev's terms, and hope that his political enemies did not find out.

Part IV
Endgame

Endgame

CHAPTER 15

The Brink

1   *Noon, October 27, 1962*

Lunchtime in the White House brought a shock: on the order probably of two Soviet generals in Cuba (Stepan N. Grechko and Leonid S. Garbuz), a Soviet rocket crew fired off a missile and shot down Major Rudolph Anderson and his U-2 spy plane; it crashed in the jungle over eastern Cuba. He must have died immediately.

No one in the White House knew who had given the order to fire. But President Kennedy did allow that "we are in an entirely new ball game." And the Joint Chiefs, who had been clamoring for permission to bomb Cuba, saw their opening. No "later than Monday morning, the 29th, unless there is irrefutable evidence . . . that the offensive weapons [in Cuba] are being dismantled and rendered inoperable," insisted General Maxwell Taylor, the U.S. should start blasting away at Cuba.

Soon after lunchtime, Roger Hilsman, who had been at the State Department, rode over to the White House with a message for McGeorge Bundy. As his limousine passed through the Pennsylvania Avenue gate, he noticed a few hundred demonstrators marching up and down the sidewalk. The males in the group wore crewcuts, the females bouffant hairdos. They were members of a collegiate group, Young Americans for Freedom, and they were holding up signs that said, simply, "INVADE!"

2   *Afternoon*

War seemed to be closing in fast. A Pentagon press officer announced the loss of the U-2 over Cuba. Then, out of Florida, six more U.S. airplanes, low-level reconnaissance aircraft, took off for the island. Two developed engine trouble, returning to base. The remaining four, reaching Cuba's shoreline, ran into antiaircraft fire. One plane was hit, barely managing to return to the States.

Moving fast, Dean Rusk, who at lunchtime had returned to the State Department, called in John Scali again, giving the reporter a new message for Fomin. Scali did Rusk's bidding. Meeting Fomin at a table in an empty ballroom of the Statler Hotel, Scali exploded.

Why, Scali demanded, had Khrushchev in his newest epistle put the Jupiter deal in writing? Fomin's response was vague, and Scali allowed himself to become even more angry. Shouting at the Russian, Scali denounced Khrushchev's latest condition as a "stinking double-cross." An "invasion of Cuba," Scali declared—and here he may have been going beyond his instructions from Rusk—"is only a matter of hours away." Frightfully upset in his turn, Fomin denied any double-cross, and he urged Scali so to inform the State Department.

Scali, calmer now, agreed to do so. His memo reached the 4:00 P.M. Excomm meeting.

Excomm had reconvened in a sense of urgency, President Kennedy seeming desperate for a way to resolve the crisis. He ordered a message sent to New York: U.S. officials at the U.N. were to ask U Thant to find out if the Soviets, in return for negotiations, temporarily would stop work on the missile bases. Hardly had JFK given this order, however, than the Defense Department people around the table turned the discussion to the U-2 shoot-down. Four days before, they reminded the President, Excomm had agreed that, in the event of a U-2 downing, the U.S. would take "immediate retaliation upon the most likely [missile] site involved." So now, according to Robert Kennedy's memoir, there "was almost unanimous agreement that we had to attack early the next morning . . . and destroy the sites."

President Kennedy held back. If ground fire from Cuba hit any more U.S. planes, he agreed, then he would order air strikes. Yet for the moment he would order no reprisal.

But if Kennedy ordered air strikes, then Khrushchev could trigger his missiles. Khrushchev was in the commanding position.

Much of the afternoon meeting, however, focused on Khrushchev's latest letter, and pitted Kennedy against most of his advisers. For to the horror of the majority around the table, Kennedy seemed willing to accept Khrushchev's terms, trading missiles in Cuba for missiles in Turkey. Various Excomm members presented counter-suggestions. Some of the State Department people were for rejecting Khrushchev's letter altogether. McNamara thought the Jupiters could come out of Turkey, but only as a prelude to an invasion of Cuba. General Taylor wanted to bomb Cuba and invade the place, then and there.

In the end, Kennedy and his advisers compromised. They would not go to war, not yet; but the U.S. would respond only to Khrushchev's letter of the previous day, making no mention of Turkey.

Sorensen and Robert Kennedy left the Cabinet Room to draft such a response. When they returned, President Kennedy glanced over the text, made a few changes, had it typed, and added his signature. Excomm adjourned until the evening.

JFK's private response to Khrushchev, went, in part:

> As I read your letter, the key elements of your proposals . . . are as follows: 1) You would agree to remove these weapons systems from Cuba under appropriate United Nations observation and supervision; and undertake, with suitable safeguards, to halt the further introduction of such weapon systems into Cuba. 2) We, on our part, would agree—upon the establishment of adequate arrangements through the United Nations—to ensure the carrying out and continuation of these commitments (a) to remove promptly the quarantine measures now in effect and (b) to give assurances against the invasion of Cuba.

So Khrushchev had realized part of what he wanted—he had deterred an American takeover of Cuba. But, as his second letter had emphasized, he wanted more, and sensed he could get it.

For as the Excomm members drifted off for dinner, President Kennedy whisked a few—McNamara, Bundy, Rusk, Llewellyn

Thompson, Sorensen, and Robert Kennedy, but not General Taylor—into the privacy of the Oval Office. There, behind closed doors, they agreed quickly that Robert Kennedy would talk again with Dobrynin, threatening military action if the missiles remained in Cuba—and also promising to pull the Jupiters out of Turkey.

3   *Evening, October 27, 1962*

Fidel Castro was full of defiance. Any further warplanes that violated Cuban airspace, he proclaimed in one of his marathon broadcasts, would do so "at their own risk." Announcing that he had stretcher-bearer teams in every neighborhood and work center, he declared that "Cuban forces are in a state of maximum alert . . . , disposed to defend the sacred rights of the fatherland."

But Castro, too, perhaps fearing now that Khrushchev would desert him, was looking for a deal. If the U.S. lifted the blockade, he wrote U Thant at around 9:00 P.M., he would order work on the missile sites to cease. He also invited the Secretary General to visit the island.

At about the time Castro was writing, Anatoly Dobrynin was closeting himself with Robert Kennedy in the attorney general's office. Outside the Justice Department, the street lamps were on, and Pennsylvania Avenue looked deserted. Of this particularly secretive rendezvous, we have conflicting accounts.

In his memoirs (edited by Theodore Sorensen), Robert Kennedy remembered telling Dobrynin that:

> We had to have a commitment by tomorrow that [the missile] bases would be removed. I was not giving them an ultimatum but a statement of fact. He should understand that if they did not remove those bases, we would remove them. . . .
>
> He asked me about what offer the United States was making, and I told him of the letter that President Kennedy had just transmitted to Khrushchev. He raised the question of our removing the missiles from Turkey. I said that there could be no quid pro quo or any arrangement made under this kind of threat or pressure. . . . However, I said, President Kennedy had been anxious to remove those missiles from

Turkey and Italy for a long period of time. He had ordered their removal some time ago, and it was our judgment that, within a short time after this crisis was over, those missiles would be gone. . . . Time was running out. We had only a few more hours—we needed an answer immediately from the Soviet Union. I said we must have it the next day. . . .

Dobrynin, however, told the story differently. According to the former ambassador, (1) Robert Kennedy in fact threatened no military action, and (2) the attorney general said nothing at all of an earlier order for the removal of the Jupiters. In Dobrynin's version, RFK suggested an explicit deal—missiles in Cuba for missiles in Turkey.

Who was speaking the truth? We have no smoking gun. It is significant nonetheless that Robert Kennedy did meet with Dobrynin. Why would he have done so, other than to add something missing from President Kennedy's letter to Khrushchev?

4   Slicing through the darkness of the late October night, the headlights of official limousines illuminated the fence in front of the White House, and pulled up in a long row as they parked by the North Portico. By 9:00 P.M., the Excomm members were in their brass-studded leather chairs again, groggily trying to attend to the latest revelations. A CIA study showed that a blockade of petroleum products would bring "the Cuban economy to a halt"; President Kennedy read aloud General Lauris Norstad's denunciation of any Turkey-for-Cuba missile swap. And as the meeting ended, McNamara turned to Robert Kennedy, exclaiming that the U.S. had better be "dammed sure" it had "two things ready, a government for Cuba, because we're going to need one"—someone had suggested that Robert Kennedy serve as mayor of Havana—"and secondly, plans for how to respond to the Soviet Union in Europe, because sure as hell they're going to do something there."

Yet something here, in Washington, in the White House, in the Cabinet Room, was surreal. Rusk was absent from the Excomm session, at President Kennedy's instructions telephoning Andrew Cordier, a Canton, Ohio–born U.S. diplomat who had been a U.N. undersecretary. At the time, Cordier was president of Columbia University. But Rusk wanted him to go back across Manhattan, talk with U Thant, and tell the Secretary General that JFK would agree to a Cuba-Turkey missile swap.

Rusk's telephone call was in secret. And as Excomm adjourned for the night, President Kennedy said, "That's the trouble with all that we're doing. Once we walk out of this room, people can start to be killed."

CHAPTER 16

Finale

1   *Predawn, Sunday, October 28, 1962*
During the middle of the night, Washington-time, but just before dawn, Moscow-time, Nikita Khrushchev awoke—he was in his dacha just outside the Soviet capital—lumbered out of bed, breakfasted, and went to his desk to compose the first of two letters. It was to Fidel Castro. "I would like to recommend to you now," Khrushchev penned, obviously trying to keep the Cuban leader calm,

at this moment of change in the crisis, not to be carried away by sentiment and to show firmness. I must say that I understand your feelings of indignation toward the aggressive actions and violations of elementary norms of international law on the part of the United States.

But now, rather than law, what prevails is the senselessness of the militarists in the Pentagon. Now that an agreement is in sight, the Pentagon is searching for a pretext to frustrate this agreement. This is why it is organizing the provocative flights. Yesterday you shot down one of these, while earlier you didn't shoot them down when they overflew your territory. The aggressors will take advantage of such a step for their own purposes.

Therefore, I would like to advise you in a friendly manner to show patience, firmness, and even more firmness. . . . On our part, we will do everything possible to stabilize the situation in Cuba, [to] defend

Cuba against invasion. . . . I send you greetings, extensive to all your leadership group.

2   *Daybreak, Sunday, October 28, 1962*
As the morning sun reached the Western Hemisphere, very little presaged peace. Quite the opposite indeed.

Down in Venezuela, early morning explosions in Lake Maracaibo ripped through electrical substations of the U.S.-owned Creole Corporation. According to a CIA report cabled to Washington, Venezuelan Communists "had been listening to Radio Havana, and had acted on a call for the destruction of 'any kind of Yankee property.' "

In Washington, the CIA's daily 6:00 A.M. report to the President seemed ominous. By dawn on October 28, 1962, the update stated, Soviet technicians had made all missile sites in Cuba fully operational.

Moments after receiving this report, President Kennedy went to mass. He went by himself—Mrs. Kennedy and the children had repaired to their estate in Virginia's horse country for the weekend—and as he left the press was on his trail. As he entered the church of St. Stephen the Martyr, on Pennsylvania Avenue, a photographer caught him unawares: bareheaded and dressed in a pin-striped suit, he was carrying his hat. He was walking alone.

A bit more than two miles to the north, in the Washington Cathedral, the Very Rev. Francis B. Sayre, Jr., dean of the cathedral and grandson of President Woodrow Wilson, mounted the pulpit. Surely, he told his congregants, as he spoke of the President,

> we must all pray that he will restrain any contemplated invasion [of Cuba], at least until every avenue of negotiation has been patiently explored.

At the end of the service, he read a statement signed by theologians Reinhold Niebuhr and Paul Tillich, as well as by the deans of the Union, Harvard, and Chicago seminaries:

> We stand responsible before God and man to exercise care that every possible avenue for resolution of this dilemma be properly explored. We

should take no new military steps until it is abundantly clear that we cannot achieve our goals through negotiation.

Whether the priest at St. Stephen's Catholic Church on Pennsylvania Avenue made any such remarks in the presence of John Kennedy, we have no record. We have only news photographs, pictures of President Kennedy reentering his limousine and starting off again for the White House. He reached the mansion just before 9:00 A.M.

At just about that time, Michael V. Forrestal (a senior staffer on the National Security Council and son of the late Defense Secretary James Forrestal), who was watch officer on duty in the Situation Room, received a start: a bulletin of considerable importance had just flashed in on the teletype. He notified Andrew T. Hatcher, associate White House press secretary, immediately, and Hatcher without delay telephoned the Oval Office.

President Kennedy was not yet available.

In a few moments Hatcher tried again.

This time JFK came on the line.

Hatcher delivered the message. Radio Moscow was about to broadcast a statement by Khrushchev.

3 *Just after 9:00 A.M., October 28, 1962*

Khrushchev's words, translated simultaneously, fed directly into the Oval Office. "I have received your message of October 27," Khrushchev was saying—and his words would have been seen in Moscow as a reprimand to Kennedy:

In 1960, we shot down your U-2 aircraft. . . . [D]uring the period of your tenure of office as President, a second instance of the violation of our frontier by an American U-2 aircraft took place in the Sakhalin area. We wrote you about this violation on August 30. You replied that this violation had taken place as the result of bad weather and gave an assurance that it would not be repeated. We gave credence to your assurance because there was indeed bad weather in that area at that time. However, if your aircraft did not have the task of flying near our territory, then even bad weather could not cause an American aircraft to enter our airspace. . . .

An even more dangerous case occurred on October 28 [Far Eastern time] when your reconnaissance aircraft intruded into the territory of the

Soviet Union in the north, in the area of the Chukotka Peninsula, and flew over our territory.

One asks, Mr. President, how should we regard this? What is it? A provocation?

As Kennedy and his advisers listened to these words, they may have sensed danger: JFK soon apologized publicly for the U-2 overflight. But they also must have wondered what Khrushchev was going to say about Cuba and the missiles. They found out soon: "I regard with respect and trust the statement you made in your message of October 27," Khrushchev continued,

that there would be no attack, no invasion of Cuba, and not only on the part of the United States, but also of other nations of the Western Hemisphere, as you said in your message. Then do the motives which induced us to render assistance of such a kind to Cuba disappear?

The Oval Office must have been dead still. Was Khrushchev going to close the deal? Was he truly going to withdraw the missiles?

The translator paused, stumbled over a word. Then Khrushchev's intent came through loud and clear:

. . . the Soviet government, in addition to earlier instructions on the discontinuance of further work on the construction sites, has given a new order to dismantle the arms which you describe as offensive, and to crate them and return them to the Soviet Union. . . .

President Kennedy's response was almost immediate, and beamed toward Moscow via the Voice of America:

I welcome Chairman Khrushchev's statesmanlike decision to stop building bases in Cuba, dismantling offensive weapons and returning them to the Soviet Union. . . . This is an important and constructive contribution to peace.

4   *The rest of the day, October 28, 1962*
Positively beaming, Ambassador Dobrynin showed up at the

Justice Department at 11:00 A.M. Sitting down with Robert Kennedy, he conveyed Khrushchev's personal regards to the attorney general and to the President. Excomm at the same time agreed for the moment to discontinue intelligence flights over Cuba and to avoid any action against Soviet bloc ships.

At an early afternoon State Department press conference, Secretary Rusk cautioned reporters against gloating: "If there is a debate, a rivalry, a contest going on in the Kremlin over how to play this situation," Rusk said, "we don't want . . . to strengthen the hands of those in Moscow who wanted to play this another way." After telephoning former Presidents Hoover, Truman, and Eisenhower, President Kennedy took off by helicopter—a United Press photographer snapped a picture of the chopper as it rose in front of the columns of the South Portico—and lunched with his wife and children at their estate in Virginia. When he returned in the late afternoon, he walked away from the helicopter pad with a very light step.

At about 6:00 P.M., Defense Secretary McNamara motored from his office in the Pentagon to his big brick home in northwest Washington. He had not slept in his own bed for a week.

In Cuba, an outraged Fidel Castro went on the radio, denouncing the Khrushchev-Kennedy settlement. A true agreement, he contended, would have to include five more points: (1) an end to the economic blockade against Cuba; (2) an end to all guerrilla raids carried out from Florida against Cuba; (3) a halt to all attacks on Cuba carried out from bases in Puerto Rico; (4) a cessation of reconnaissance flights over Cuba and its territorial waters; and (5) the return of Guantánamo to Cuba.

Key West reacted to news of the agreement with restraint, many of the locals being in church when the bulletins reached the radio stations. But, for the first time in a week, residents in the afternoon left their homes for the beaches, or drove up to the smaller Keys for picnics.

New Yorkers were relieved, and skeptical. A Northport, Long Island, physician thought the news was "tremendous," according to *The New York Times;* a Times Square sight-seeing tour guide opined that the "Russians never live up to their promises."

In London, Harold Macmillan, who had not gone to bed for two nights, collapsed in a chair by the ticker-tape machine in Admiralty House. He felt, he quipped, as if he were attending the aftermath of a wedding, "when there is nothing to do but drink the champagne and go to sleep."

In Ankara, Feridon Cemal Erkin, the Turkish foreign minister, reacted to reports of Khrushchev's decision by saying, "That's wonderful news, if true!" In a press conference, he added: "Missiles in Turkey are entirely defensive. Turkey cannot be the subject of bargaining in this matter." Little did he realize, then, that Turkey and Cuba were in the same boat— both subjects of bargaining.

Washington itself lost little time returning to normality. On Sunday afternoon, television viewers watched their beloved Washington Redskins up in Yankee Stadium, receiving a 49 to 34 shellacking at the hands of quarterback Y. A. Tittle and the New York Giants. Movie theaters in the evening were crowded again: filmgoers could see Marcello Mastroianni in *Divorce Italian Style* and Shelley Winters in *A Place in the Sun*.

In their time-honored fashion, District socialites turned out for a reception at the National Gallery. A few, such as Mrs. Sargent Shriver and Mrs. Stephen Smith, sisters of the President, glanced at the collection of 114 drawings by old masters, owned by the Duke of Devonshire and now placed on exhibit. Most of the Americans, dressed in their finest, gawked at the eleventh duke and his duchess.

The Leningrad Symphony that evening performed Shostakovich and Tchaikovsky in Constitution Hall. The brass section, reported *The Washington Post*, "played with thrilling sonority" and the audience rose to its feet in applause.

But across the river in the Pentagon, the Joint Chiefs ordered the Atlantic naval headquarters in Norfolk to work further on plans for an invasion of Cuba. The Chiefs wanted to know specifically if, in the event of an invasion, U.S. forces should use tactical nuclear weapons.

Had President Kennedy lived past November 22, 1963, would he have reneged on his deal with Khrushchev? We shall, of course, never know.

Epilogue

Washington's weather had turned autumnal, by Tuesday, October 29, 1962; the high was going to be in the fifties only, and throughout most of the morning, downtown was drizzly and cold. But people were feeling a sense of relief. The cooling of the Cuban crisis had sent the financial markets positively sailing; and just after noontime, President Kennedy did what he did best, exercising the art of greeting. In lieu of his wife, who had signaled that she was "unavoidably detained" at their Virginia estate, he showed up in the State Dining Room to welcome members of the International Council of the Museum of Modern Art, convened in Washington to sponsor an exhibit at the Corcoran, just down on Seventeenth Street. JFK made the rounds, exuding his usual charm, and then while the guests sipped sherry and toured the Rose Garden, he returned to the Oval Office.

While the crisis had eased, it was hardly over. Wanting further intelligence, he ordered eight low-level reconnaissance flights over the missile sites; and learning, angrily, that CIA sabotage missions into Cuba were still going on, he told Director McCone point-blank to terminate operations. And he instructed Secretary McNamara to start pulling the Jupiters out of Turkey. Said John McNaughton, one of McNamara's civilian aides, to a task force of admirals and generals, who were resisting the Turkey part of the deal: "Those missiles are going to be out of there [Turkey] by April 1 if we have to shoot them out."

The Jupiters nonetheless left the Kennedys nervous. Holing

up again with Ambassador Dobrynin, who had brought along a letter from Khrushchev—the epistle reiterated the terms of the agreement and included RFK's pledge that the Jupiters would come out of Turkey—Robert Kennedy read the document, then spirited it away to the White House. When he saw Dobrynin the next day, October 30, 1962, the attorney general insisted that the letter be kept private. The notes RFK wrote out to prepare for his Dobrynin session went as follows:

> Read letter—Studied it over night. . . . You asked me about the missile bases in Turkey. I told you [they would be out]—four to five months. That still holds. . . . You have my word on this & that is sufficient. Take back your letter—Reconsider it & if you feel it is necessary to write letters, then we will also write one which you cannot enjoy. Also, if you should publish any document indicating a deal, then it is off. . . .

Early November brought President Kennedy good news: according to the reconnaissance photographs, workers in Cuba were bulldozing the missile sites and trucks were hauling missile equipment into the ports. On November 5, 1962, nevertheless, President Kennedy handed Secretary McNamara a short memorandum, expressing concern that U.S. plans for an invasion of Cuba seemed "thin." McNamara in turn told the Joint Chiefs that the Army might need more divisions for an invasion.

Despite the deal with Khrushchev, then, Kennedy still at least was contemplating an invasion; certainly many of the U.S. forces that before and during the crisis had gathered around the Caribbean had remained in place. That fact may explain why, early in November 1962, the Soviets granted Castro's wish for the stationing of a Russian combat brigade on the island indefinitely.

In the crisp air of the Massachusetts morning, President Kennedy on November 6, 1962, pulled up before the Joy Street police station on Boston's Beacon Hill, near the apartment he still retained as his legal residence, ducked inside, and voted. He was in and out of the polling booth in less than a minute. He had flown up the night before, and he spent the rest of the day with his father on Cape Cod. In the evening, he turned on the television to watch the election reports.

The results were gratifying. The Democrats did lose four seats in the House, and two of Kennedy's choice candidates, Sidney Yates in Illinois and Robert Morgenthau in New York, failed to win. But in the Senate, the Democrats picked up their biggest majority in twenty years and, clearly, much of Kennedy's campaigning had paid off: Abraham Ribicoff won in Connecticut; Birch Bayh triumphed in Indiana; Gaylord Nelson scored in Wisconsin; and, in Massachusetts, brother Edward M. Kennedy swept into the Senate on a landslide. Yet JFK must have viewed California's gubernatorial race with especial relish—incumbent Edmund Brown sent challenger Richard Nixon to ignominious defeat. Said Nixon in his soon-to-be-infamous press conference in Beverly Hills:

> Now that all the members of the press are so delighted I lost, I'd like to make a statement. . . . [In sixteen years] you've had a lot of opportunity to attack me, and I think I've given as good as I've taken. . . . [But] just think how much you'll be missing. You won't have Nixon to kick around anymore. Because this is my last press conference.

So at least one harsh critic of Kennedy's Cuba policy was finished—for the moment. Yet one news item dimmed the Democrats' rejoicing: on November 7, 1962, hospitalized in Manhattan, Eleanor Roosevelt passed away. Her body was taken for burial to the Roosevelt estate at Hyde Park, New York, and laid in the rose garden there beside the grave of her husband.

With the approach of Thanksgiving, 1962, the Cuban problem seemed to be winding down. Most of the missiles, along with their trailers and erectors, were aboard Soviet ships, steaming back to the Baltic. President Kennedy in response lifted the quarantine. Then, on Christmas Eve, 1962, James Donovan's efforts to negotiate the release of the Bay of Pigs prisoners bore fruit, Castro agreeing to let them go in return for $54 million worth of baby food and medical supplies. In January 1963, Italy and Turkey announced the phase-out of the Jupiters. And late in January 1963, the White House (despite the outrage of Goldwater Republicans and Cubans in Miami) abolished Operation Mongoose.

Just before the turn of the year, however, on December 29, 1962, President Kennedy had flown to the Orange Bowl in Miami to greet the Bay of Pigs veterans. Holding their flag aloft, he had promised—as was widely reported in the news—that they would see their banner fly in "a free Havana."

And soon attacks on Cuba began anew. In March 1963, Alpha 66 units attacked a Soviet freighter, as it lay anchored off the port of Isabela de Sagua, sank another as it was taking on a load of Cuban sugar, and raided a Soviet infantry camp on the island, wounding twelve Russians. Those raids, according to a counter-insurgency specialist with the Joint Chiefs of Staff, were "planned and conducted under the supervision of the CIA . . . from bases in southern Florida." On April 3, 1963, then, President Kennedy approved a new set of Mongoose-like operations, scheduled to get under way on June 19, 1963.

Kennedy, to be sure, moved as well along another track: 1963 saw the establishment of the "hotline," the direct teletype link between the White House and the Kremlin, and the signing in Moscow of the Limited Nuclear Test Ban Treaty. And on June 10, 1963, speaking at American University, President Kennedy seemed to call for improved relations with the Soviet Union. "Above all," he declared,

> while defending our own vital interests, nuclear powers must avert those confrontations which bring an adversary to a choice of either humiliating retreat or nuclear war.

Yet nine days later JFK renewed his okay of the fresh program of sabotage against Cuba. The program's objective:

> to nourish a spirit of resistance and disaffection [in Cuba] which could lead to significant defections and other by-products of unrest.

So in preparation for the fall season, the CIA would prepare numerous raids on Cuba's factories, mines, and ports. Whether Castro himself was a target is uncertain.

Sweeping in over the suburban sprawl of Dallas–Fort Worth, *Air Force One* aligned itself with the main runway of Carswell Air

Force Base, descended and landed, and taxied along the tarmac toward the apron in front of the giant General Dynamics plant. There, pulling to a stop before a crowd of hundreds of cheering workers, the pilot allowed the engines to whine down into silence. Then, as soon as the boarding steps were in place, the plane's main door swung open—and President Kennedy, waving, appeared at the top of the ramp.

Just a year before—shortly after the resolution of the Cuban missile crisis—the Kennedy administration had awarded the contract for the TFX fighter plane not to Boeing of Seattle but rather to General Dynamics of Connecticut, Long Island, California, and Texas; the plane was to be assembled in the Fort Worth plant. Led by Henry Jackson, the Democrat from Washington State, however, a U.S. Senate committee had investigated the award process—and had turned up the following incriminating points:

1. The military services had favored Boeing, on grounds of quality and price alike, and had done so unanimously.

2. The one—and only—Pentagon document that had purported to justify the award to General Dynamics was chock-full of errors, including a miscalculation of $32 million.

3. One Pentagon Vice Admiral, Robert Pirie, had raised questions about the worth of the General Dynamics deal; McNamara had shunted him off to early retirement.

4. When McNamara's office had learned that the Senate investigation was pending, it had panicked: two teams of officials had worked around the clock to produce "authentic" records.

5. As Secretary of the Navy, Fred Korth had retained $160,-000 of stock in his Fort Worth bank (General Dynamics' banker); and when he finished his tour of duty in Washington, he intended fully to return to the bank.

6. As General Dynamics' own records showed, Deputy Secretary of Defense Gilpatric, while still a private attorney, had served on the company's board of directors, recruited retiring Air Force personnel to work for the company, and had done legal work for the company billed at more than $100,000. During his Senate confirmation hearings, to be sure, Gilpatric stated that he had quit his Wall Street law firm and cut all ties with General Dynamics. But had he done so in truth? Correspondence between Cravath, Swaine & Moore, in which he had been a partner, and its insurance company referred to Gilpatric's time in

Washington as a "leave of absence." When he went to Washington, investigators also learned, Gilpatric arranged for another partner, M. T. ("Tex") Moore to take over the General Dynamics account; and in the very week of the TFX contract award, Moore had joined the General Dynamics board.

The Senate subcommittee was scheduled to make these findings public late in November 1963. To be sure of reelection, President Kennedy had to gloss over the scandal.

So, a year after the contract award, he flew to Texas, landing on the tarmac by the General Dynamics plant. Smiling and waving, he descended the ramp to the microphones. Mrs. Kennedy, beautiful and dark-haired, stood beside him. The TFX, President Kennedy declared, justifying the contract, was the "best fighter system in the world." As in the missile crisis, JFK was playing politics to the end.

The wind was chilly and the sun was bright, and soon President and Mrs. Kennedy left Fort Worth for downtown Dallas. The date was November 22, 1963.

"It can be said" of Kennedy, eulogized one editorialist, shortly after the funeral,

> that he did not fear the weather, and did not trim his sail, but instead challenged the wind itself, to improve its direction and cause it to blow more softly and more kindly over the world and its people.

To that editorialist, as to much of "the world and its people," Kennedy's greatest challenge to the wind had come during the Cuban missile crisis; indeed the crisis had assumed mythic proportion. According to that legend, the Soviet Union, ever intent on burying America, had engineered Castro's revolution, turning Cuba into a Communist satellite, then treacherously and without just cause introducing missiles with which they intended to bring the U.S. to its knees. The legend continued: although caught by surprise by photos of the missiles, President Kennedy kept his cool. Assembling a team of advisers, he quickly devised the best strategy for getting the missiles out of Cuba. Succumbing neither to appeasement nor belligerence, he (1) kept all planning before his October 22 speech a secret, thereby avoiding any chance that the Soviets would be tipped off; then (2) he presented the Kremlin with a quarantine, an implied threat of force, and the face-saving device of a U.S. noninvasion pledge; and (3) he thereby induced Khrushchev to back down.

Having thus realized his overriding goal, the return of the global strategic balance to the status quo ante, Kennedy turned his attention to the cause of world peace. Abroad he became a good neighbor; at home he became a statesman.

Thus the myth. The reality was different.

Had Kennedy, becoming a statesman, ceased to be a politician? The TFX story alone suggests otherwise.

Had he become a good neighbor? The 1963 son-of-Mongoose doings were hardly neighborly. Nor was what happened in Canada, soon after Prime Minister Diefenbaker publicly questioned JFK's veracity, and *then* said, as was leaked to the press, that he thought Kennedy "perfectly capable of taking the world to the brink of thermonuclear destruction to prove himself the man for our times." Two months later, Diefenbaker fell from office. In his memoirs, he charged that the Kennedy administration had conspired with Opposition Leader Lester Pearson and Defense Minister Douglas Harkness (who, behind Diefenbaker's back, had put Canada on a midlevel alert) to throw him out—as if Canada were a "banana republic."

Was he right? Did he fall from office? Or was he pushed, by America?

After the Cuban missile crisis was over, the issue of nuclear weapons still marred U.S.-Canadian relations: the Kennedy administration still wanted nuclear weapons under its exclusive control at U.S. bases in Argentina, Newfoundland, and Goose Bay, Labrador; and Diefenbaker still resisted what he saw as a threat to Canadian rights. From behind the scenes, however, Minister Harkness was undermining Diefenbaker further. Early in January 1963, the tall, blond, Nordic-looking U.S. General Lauris Norstad, the newly retired commander of NATO, passed through Ottawa; and for him Harkness's Defense Ministry organized a press conference. Under questioning from reporters, he publicly chastised Prime Minister Diefenbaker, stating forcefully that if Canada continued to refuse nuclear weapons, it would be betraying its obligations to NATO.

Five days later, in Washington, Norstad went further. If Canada failed to fulfill its nuclear commitment, he told a reporter, NATO "would suffer a great loss." The implication was blunt: if Diefenbaker stayed in power, Canada might be out of NATO.

Angered, Diefenbaker virtually cut off communications with Washington, hoping to stall on the nuclear issue, call a new election, and return to power with a strong majority government. Enter the State Department. In a January 30, 1963, press release, a document prepared by W. Walton Butterworth, the U.S. ambassador in Ottawa, the State Department challenged Canada's own Prime Minister. The document declared that the Soviet nuclear bombing fleet remained a threat, that Diefenbaker had denied the reality of that threat, and that he was undercutting an "effective continental defense." Some Canadians flared back. "To put it in the bluntest terms," wrote one Ottawa paper, "the State Department publicly called Prime Minister Diefenbaker a liar. . . . President Kennedy was being called a 'bully,' among other things. . . . The immediate and general reaction was that Washington had gone too far." And on the floor of the House, Diefenbaker noted a "striking resemblance" between the State Department's press release and earlier statements by Pearson, the Opposition leader, who *did* favor nuclear weapons for Canada. Diefenbaker asked him "when he was going back [to Washington] for further instructions."

Then Defense Minister Harkness resigned, breaking up the Diefenbaker Cabinet; and on the evening of February 5, 1963, in the House, Diefenbaker lost a no-confidence vote, and resigned. On April 22, 1963, Pearson won election as Canada's Prime Minister—and, three weeks later, flew to Hyannis Port for a conference with Kennedy. Pearson's government accepted the nuclear weapons.

Through a press conference and a press release—and through an implicit threat to cast Canada out of the North Atlantic community—the Kennedy administration intervened in the internal affairs of another country, helping to bring Diefenbaker down and avenging the Prime Minister's refusal to play along with the White House.

"Kennedy wanted to control us," said a Diefenbaker aide:

The whole American dream is to control all countries around the United States. . . . [I]t was Kennedy's dream, too.

Had Kennedy, as he developed his missile crisis strategy, then risen above concern with his own political interest in being reelected President? No. When meeting with Excomm, of course, he was shrewd enough to stay off the subject of politics—the last thing he needed was to have John McCone or Lyndon Johnson leaking word that JFK had cooked up the whole thing for his own advantage. But McNamara understood. "I'll be quite frank," he said on October 16, 1962. "I don't think there is a military problem here. . . . This is a domestic political problem." For domestic political reasons, Kennedy simply *had* to stand up to Khrushchev.

Had he indeed stood up to Khrushchev? Only in part. Kennedy was able to realize a compromise, trading the noninvasion pledge for the Cuban missile withdrawal, but *then* having to throw in the Turkish missile withdrawal. No wonder Robert Kennedy was so anxious to suppress written evidence of the Jupiter deal!

Had Kennedy, before October 15, 1962, had no idea of the presence of the missiles in Cuba? He would have had to be blind, deaf, and dumb not to know. McCone had shown him the intelligence reports.

Had the Soviets deceived JFK about the presence of the missiles? Yes and no. They had promised not to introduce "offensive" missiles but had left open the option of deploying "defensive" ones; so the Kremlin did shade the truth. But Khrushchev had made clear, emphatically clear, that he intended to defend Cuba with missiles.

Had the Soviet deployment of missiles to Cuba been without just cause? And had Khrushchev intended, with those missiles, to bring the U.S. to its knees? If protecting an ally against invasion was a just cause, then Khrushchev had justice on his side. If Khrushchev wanted to bring the U.S. to its knees, he could have done so just as well from missiles in the Soviet bloc countries as from Cuba.

Had Kennedy truly been on the verge of invading Cuba? Nowhere do we find a document bearing his signature and saying, "Invade." What we do find in the archives, however, are plans for an invasion, massive proof of the buildup of an invasion, statements by top-ranking officials that they wanted to provoke Castro into providing a pretext (as with a strike at Guantánamo), and the fact that Operation Mongoose was to give Castro no choice but to provide that pretext. Late in the summer and early in the fall, 1962, we know, the Kennedy brothers were practically violent in their insistence that the Mongoose chieftains get moving.

So why the wish to invade Cuba? We might proceed, to use a term much employed in the Kennedy White House, along three "tracks."

First, the Kennedy track. As character molded the JFK presidential campaign, with Joseph Kennedy in the background, intent on victory at all costs and striving to master all relevant factors, so did the campaign mold the Kennedy presidency, with its effort above all else to portray JFK as a leader who could stand up to the Russians. The Kennedy White House, in today's parlance, tried to control the spin, the story line. But reality intruded. The Bay of Pigs was a failure. Laos was a failure. Vienna was a failure. JFK needed a victory, desperately. He had to regain control: he had to oust Castro.

Second, the worldwide track. From Hiroshima and Nagasaki onward, two American administrations, those of Presidents Truman and Eisenhower, had sought to perpetuate America's de facto postwar global empire: herein lay the meaning of the Truman Doctrine, NSC-68, the containment policy, and John Foster Dulles's threat of massive retaliation. Kennedy inherited this legacy of worldwide (or nearly worldwide) dominance—and he had no intention of letting that dominance go to pieces on his watch. So, like his predecessors, he believed that U.S. forces were required, and could prevail, wherever U.S. interests seemed to be threatened, or might be advanced. And down here was Castro, eluding that grasp.

Third, the Cuban track. In the imagination of Americans, Cuba throughout the century had been little more than an extension of Florida: the U.S.—so we believed—had liberated Cuba from Spain, had preserved the right (granted by God, or by the Platt Amendment, which amounted to the same thing) to intervene in Cuba (for Cuba's own good, of course), had brought to Cuba the benefits of baseball, tourism, and dollars. And all Cuba had had to do in return was to accept America's de facto control. But Fidel Castro had refused to accept such control. He thus was an outlaw. And, as in the old cowboy movies, you do

not negotiate with outlaws. You shoot them down in front of
the town saloon. Until the next week's episode, you have
brought the bad guys under control.

Each of these "tracks" helps explain why Kennedy's Cuban
policy (which grew out of Eisenhower's Cuban policy, which
grew out of Eisenhower's Guatemalan policy) evolved into a
full-blown effort to invade the island. But the Cuban-American
relationship, in the real world, was hardly a B-grade Hollywood
cowboy flick. Or, if it was, then Nikita Khrushchev waddled
into the theater, pushed his way up to the projection booth, and
with a toss of one of his beefy hands, hurled the projector to the
floor. The movie—the illusion of control—was over.

For Khrushchev had got away with doing the unthinkable: he
had deterred American aggression. How? In the background of
the Cuban missile crisis, always, was the one element of international affairs consistently beyond American control: Berlin.
Had Khrushchev made a grab at Berlin, the U.S. could have
done little to stop him; or the cost at least would have been
sky-high. And, recognizing Khrushchev's advantage at Berlin,
Kennedy, to get the Soviet missiles out of Cuba, caved in over
the U.S. missiles in Turkey.

Kennedy's court historians have pretended otherwise, denying that the Jupiters were part of the deal. But they have lost
control of the evidence. And the evidence exists in Washington.
The National Security Archive, housed in a building next door
to the Brookings Institution, just off Dupont Circle on Massachusetts Avenue, has collected all the documents, so far declassified, on the Cuban missile crisis. The documents are available
for all to see. What they show is this: Khrushchev beat Kennedy
in Vienna. And he beat him again in Cuba.

In the end, therefore, we confront the "lessons" of the Cuban
missile crisis. These "lessons" fall into two groups, those
"learned" by the Kennedy administration and those "learned"
by America ever since.

As the officials of the Kennedy administration rested, then
returned to their duties, they shifted their attention from Cuba
to Vietnam. To Southeast Asia they applied four principles they
had gleaned from the Caribbean: (1) that success in an international crisis was "largely a matter of national guts"; (2) that the

"opponent would yield to superior force"; (3) that presidential control of force can be "suitable, selective, swift, effective, and responsive" to the situation's demands; and (4) that "crisis management and execution are too dangerous and events move too rapidly for anything but the tightest secrecy." Framed, as it were, as plaques on the walls of the Oval Office, these "lessons" underlay President Johnson's bombing of Hanoi in 1965 and President Nixon's bombing of Cambodia in 1973.

Nearly two decades later, in the winter of 1990–1991, the United States entered the Persian Gulf War. Justifying that belligerency, Les Alpin, Democratic Representative from Wisconsin and chairman of the House Committee on Armed Services, wrote in *The Washington Post*:

> The model [for President Bush to follow] is the Cuban missile crisis of 1962. In that crisis, as in this one, the United States sought to restore the status quo ante—no Soviet missiles capable of reaching the United States in Cuba.
>
> Then, as now, there was no backing down on the basic demand. The missiles had to go then, and Iraq has to leave Kuwait now.

For three decades then the "lesson" of the Cuban missile crisis has persisted in the textbooks of our minds: when confronted by aggression, you hang tough, stay cool, show flexibility over minor points, but never yield on major ones; plan to operate with surgical precision, but keep the bludgeon conveniently nearby.

Yet are the "lessons" valid? The Cuban missile crisis hardly culminated in a grand victory; as a triumph for Kennedy it was, at best, ambiguous. And at worst? The Cuban missile crisis was the direct result, as the Soviets have reminded us repeatedly, of the American desire to overrun Cuba—to restore the status quo ante, the status quo of the "glory days" of Fulgencio Batista or even of Teddy Roosevelt.

The more appropriate lesson of the missile crisis might be in the ancient idea of hubris, pride, arrogance, and that these qualities lead to a fall. As sure that they could control the Caribbean and indeed the world as they had controlled their own campaign, the Kennedys found themselves, in the end, faced down by that stubby little peasant, Nikita Khrushchev.

President Kennedy had often turned for guidance to a book by Professor Richard Nedstadt, entitled *Presidential Power.* But he also might have pondered a book by Eric Ambler, the English novelist. The book was called *A Coffin for Demetrios.* In it Ambler wrote:

> The situation in which a person, imagining fondly that he is in charge of his own destiny, is, in fact, the sport of circumstances beyond his control, is always fascinating. It is the essential element in most good theater. . . .

But the ultimate lesson of the Cuban missile crisis is what you see, nowadays, when you fly into the Havana airport. As your airplane lowers over the Caribbean, you look out the cabin window. You see the sky, you see the sea, you feel the aircraft touch down; and then, as it seems to rush by the window, you see it. It is mounted on a pile of what looks like cement blocks. Its substructure is a jumble of girders and cables, and from its bottom extend what resembles four fins. It is cylindrical and long, about sixty feet high. It stands aloft, at a slight angle, and the conical tip seems to be pointed toward the United States of America.

As your airplane reaches the Havana terminal, you realize what you have just seen—a Soviet missile, one of Khrushchev's rockets that did *not* come out. It seems to have no military significance. It does symbolize, though, the real meaning of the Cuban missile crisis. True to his upbringing and indeed to the creed of the American nation, President Kennedy had been sure he could do anything—he could conquer the White House, he could vanquish Castro, he could control the risks. Yet in the end it was Castro who survived.

Notes

Note: sources are given in full in the Bibliography.

Prologue

11. Anderson's flight: Burrows, *Deep Black*, pp. 122–23.

Chapter 1. The Cold Warriors

22. Lewis quotation: Laurence, *Dawn Over Zero*, p. 221. "Greatest thing in history": Mee, *Meeting at Potsdam*, p. 242. Truman to Byrnes: Ibid., p. 242.
22. "prime weapon of destruction": John Nichols, "Dollar Strength as a Liability in United States Diplomacy", John M. Carroll and George Harring, eds. *Modern American Diplomacy*, p. 47.
24. Acheson's speech: Isaacson and Thomas, *The Wise Men*, p. 339.
24. Kennan telegram: Jensen, ed., *Origins of the Cold War*.
25. Kennan: Kennan, *Memoirs*, p. 294.
25. *Time* quotation: *Time*, February 15, 1946.
27. "Scare hell": quoted in LaFeber, *The American Age*, p. 453. Fulbright quotation: Fulbright, *The Crippled Giant*, p. 24.
28. Honey Fitz's toast: Davis, *The Kennedys*, p. 47.
29. The wardheelers' threat: Ibid., p. 41.
30. Costello quotation: Ibid., p. 57.
30. The Kennedy children: Ibid., p. 57.
32. Joseph Kennedy quotation: Harris, "The Senator Is in a Hurry."
32. Lasky letter: Franklin D. Roosevelt Library.
34. Lippmann passages: Lippmann, *The Cold War*, pp. 41–51.
34. CIA powers: Treverton, "Covert Action and Open Society."
35. Lucius Clay: Howard, "Governor-General of Germany."

36. McCarthy speech: Reeves, *The Life and Times of Joe McCarthy*, p. 224.
36. NSC-68: U.S. Department of State, *Foreign Relations of the United States, 1950*, pp. 234–92.
37. "The grim oligarchy": Ibid.
38. Call to Alsop: Goulden, *Korea: The Untold Story of the War*, p. 47.
38. Acheson to Truman: Isaacson and Thomas, *The Wise Men*, p. 505.
40. Lawrence O'Brien: O'Brien, *No Final Victories*, pp. 27–30.
41. The Senate campaign: Davis, *The Kennedys*, pp. 174–76.
42. Description of Batista: Black, *The Good Neighbor*, p. 95.
43. NSC-141: Modern Military Branch Reference Section, U.S. National Archives.

Chapter 2. Peace, Prosperity, and Progress.

44. The Truman quotation: Neustadt, *Presidential Power*, p. 22.
46. "Line to the Almighty": Isaacson and Thomas, *The Wise Men*, p. 560.
46. "Positive loyalty": Paterson, *Kennedy's Quest for Victory*, p. 485. The purge: Hoopes, *The Devil and John Foster Dulles*, p. 158. The Communists: Latham, *The Communist Controversy in Washington*, p. 338.
47. Views of McCarthy: Reeves, *The Life and Times of Joe McCarthy*, p. 563. Bohlen quotation: Isaacson and Thomas, *The Wise Men*, p. 96.
47. Bohlen quotation: Reeves, *The Life and Times of Joe McCarthy*, p. 469.
48. Macmillan on Khrushchev: Beschloss, *May Day: The U-2 Affair*, pp. 103–4.
49. Eisenhower quotation: U.S. Government, *Public Papers of the Presidents: Dwight D. Eisenhower, 1953*, p. 147.
50. Acheson's sympathy: Acheson, *Present at the Creation*, pp. 652–59.
51. Press conference: U.S. Government, *Public Papers: Eisenhower*, pp. 382–84.
53. "Salvation or seduction": Hunt, *Ideology and U.S. Foreign Policy*, p. 60.
54. Good Neighborism: Black, *The Good Neighbor*, p. 61.
55. "Don't try to consume": Ibid., p. 64.
56. "Rich Cubans": Ibid., p. 96.
56. Stimson to McCloy: Ibid., p. 87.
57. United Fruit and Eisenhower administration: Immerman, *The CIA in Guatemala*, pp. 124–25.
59. Bernays on Dulles: Black, *The Good Neighbor*, p. 98.
59. NSC-5412: Cook, *The Declassified Eisenhower*, pp. 182–83.
60. One historian: Ibid., p. 183.
60. Peurifoy: Immerman, *The CIA in Guatemala*, p. 137.
61. PBSUCCESS: Rabe, "The Clues Didn't Check Out."
61. "My God": Immerman, *The CIA in Guatemala*, p. 155. "There's no school": Rabe, "The Clues Didn't Check Out."
62. The "danger": Ibid.

62. The doggerel: Black, *The Good Neighbor*, p. 100. "New and glorious": LaFeber, *The American Age*, p. 519.
63. "First instance": Black, *The Good Neighbor*, p. 101.
63. "Covert Action": Immerman, *The CIA in Guatemala*, p. 194.
64. Communism in Guatemala: Rabe, "The Clues Didn't Check Out," p. 88.
64. Doolittle report: Ranelagh, *The Agency*, p. 277.
65. Berlin tunnel: Beschloss, *May Day*, pp. 114–15.
66. Secret speech, Paterson, *Kennedy's Quest for Victory*, p. 491.
67. *Profiles:* Davis, *The Kennedys*, pp. 272–73.
68. Eisenhower on the U-2s: Dwight D. Eisenhower Library, Diary, October 15, 1956.
69. "Name of God": Hughes, *The Ordeal of Power*, p. 228.
69. "Damnedest business": Cooper, *The Lion's Last Roar*, pp. 181–82. Eisenhower on the Hungarians: Alexander, *Holding the Line*, p. 180.
69. Angel Castro: Thomas, *Cuba*, p. 804.
70. Castro as student: Ibid., pp. 810–11.
70. Moncada barracks: Ibid., p. 837.
71. The trial: Ibid., p. 848.
72. Judgment: Ibid., p. 1055.
73. Castro's ambitions: Ibid., pp. 1057–59.

Chapter 3. Fidel

74. "Why, these people": Healy, *The United States in Cuba*, p. 34.
75. Leonard Wood: Library of Congress, Leonard Wood Papers, October 28, 1901.
76. Commerce Department: Langley, *The Cuban Policy of the United States*, p. 168. Canasta playing: Thomas, *Cuba*, p. 791.
76. Robert Alden: Black, *The Good Neighbor*, p. 96.
78. Matthews: Thomas, *Cuba*, p. 919.
79. Joseph Kennedy: Whalen, *The Founding Father*, pp. 433–34.
80. Publicity: *The Founding Father*. Acheson on Kennan: Isaacson and Thomas, *The Wise Men*, p. 580. "Us versus Them": LaFeber, *The American Age*, p. 541.
81. Announcer: Beschloss, *May Day*, p. 148.
81. Gaither Report: Donovan, *The Cold Warriors*, pp. 130–49.
82. JFK in Havana: Smith, *The Fourth Floor*, p. 222.
82. Acheson and JFK: Isaacson and Thomas, *The Wise Men*, pp. 590–91.
83. "Sons of bitches": Nixon, *Six Crises*, p. 219. "A national defeat": Rippy, "The Hazards of Dale Carnegie Diplomacy."
83. Nixon's recommendations: Nixon, *Six Crises*, pp. 229–30.
84. "Larger than life": Black, *The Good Neighbor*, p. 104.
84. "The Miami matter": Beschloss, *The Crisis Years*, p. 94.

85. "Did not drink": Thomas, *Cuba*, p. 1033.

85. American woman: Ibid., p. 1033.

86. Bonsal quotation: Bonsal, *Cuba, Castro, and the United States*, p. 38.

86. Nixon on Castro: Safford, "The Nixon-Castro Meeting of 19 April 1959." Bonsal: Thomas, *Cuba*, p. 1207.

87. "Program of Covert Action": Dwight D. Eisenhower Library, March 16, 1960.

90. Arms race: *U.S. News & World Report*, July 18, 1960.

92. JFK in Wisconsin: Davis, *The Kennedys*, p. 282.

92. Judith Campbell on JFK: Judith Exner, *My Story*, pp. 89–94.

93. Scapegoats: Black, *The Good Neighbor*, p. 145.

94. Mikoyan: Thomas, *Cuba*, pp. 1264–66.

Chapter 4. Ninety Miles Off Our Shore

96. Anti-Catholic pamphlets: Davis, *The Kennedys*, pp. 285–86.

99. Khrushchev's alarm, Clissold, ed., *Soviet Relations with Latin America*, pp. 255–57. Hanson Baldwin, *The New York Times*, July 7, 1960.

99. Fay and Sidey, Davis, *The Kennedys*, p. 291.

99. JFK's manner, Davis, *The Kennedys*, pp. 293–94.

101. JFK on Cuba, Thomas, *Cuba*, p. 1297.

102. Goodwin's statement: *The New York Times*, October 20, 1960.

102. *Hispanic American Report:* Thomas, *Cuba*, p. 1301.

102. Reportage: Davis, *The Kennedys*, p. 302.

103. Kennedy's victory: Davis, *The Kennedys*, p. 309.

105. Schlesinger on euphoria: Schlesinger, *A Thousand Days*, p. 259.

105. Halberstam's comment: Halberstam, *The Best and the Brightest*, p. 122.

107. Dennison's outrage: Wyden, *The Bay of Pigs*, p. 79.

107. Khrushchev's alarm: Abel, *The Missile Crisis*, p. 15. Castro vulnerable: Wyden, *The Bay of Pigs*, pp. 109–10.

108. Eisenhower-Kennedy: Paterson, *Kennedy's Quest for Victory*, p. 228.

108. Castro's demobilization: Higgins, *The Perfect Failure*, pp. 79–80.

109. War of national liberation: Rostow, *The Diffusion of Power*, p. 52. State of the Union: Wicker, *JFK and LBJ*, p. 31.

110. JFK's speech: *The New York Times*, January 31, 1961.

111. House scene: Wicker, *JFK and LBJ*, pp. 27–131.

113. McNamara's admission: *The New York Times*, February 7, 1961.

114. Fulbright's objection: Higgins, *The Perfect Failure*, p. 106.

114. Schlesinger's misgivings: Wyden, *The Bay of Pigs*, pp. 151–52.

115. Acheson interview: Walton, *Cold War and Counterrevolution*, p. 44.

116. Bundy: Beschloss, *The Crisis Years*, p. 107.

116. JFK to Salinger: Wyden, *The Bay of Pigs*, p. 155.

117. Press conference: *The New York Times*, April 13, 1961.

Chapter 5. Bay of Pigs

119. Castro on the CIA: Ibid., p. 295.
119. Schlesinger to JFK: Ibid., p. 291. JFK to Schlesinger: Paterson, *Kennedy's Quest for Victory*, p. 132.
120. Nixon: Hinckle and Turner, *The Fish Is Red*, p. 97. Eisenhower and Kennedy: Beschloss, *The Crisis Years*, pp. 144–45.
121. Press conference: *The New York Times*, April 21, 1961.
121. Taylor report: Beschloss, *The Crisis Years*, p. 148.
122. "Available assets": National Security Archive (hereafter NSA) 03320.
123. Kennedy on Vietnam: Davis, *The Kennedys*, p. 360.
124. Diefenbaker's gifts: *Ottawa Citizen*, December 7, 1956.
124. The welcome in Ottawa: *The Washington Post*, May 17, 1961.
125. JFK eyeing the girls: Nash, *Kennedy and Diefenbaker*, p. 112.
125. Diefenbaker and Kennedy: Robinson, *Diefenbaker's World*, p. 201.
125. Diefenbaker-Kennedy conversation: Nash, *Kennedy and Diefenbaker*, p. 114.
126. The Rostow document: Ibid., pp. 206–7.
126. Diefenbaker's excoriation: Ibid., p. 120.
127. Kennedy and Pearson: Ibid., p. 128.
127. Kennedy on Diefenbaker and Sorensen on Kennedy: Ibid., p. 131.
128. Judith Campbell: Judith Exner, *My Story*, p. 220.
128. Telephone logs: Davis, *The Kennedys*, p. 389.
129. Rusk on missiles: Beschloss, *The Crisis Years*, p. 147.
129. Khrushchev's letter: Dinerstein, *The Making of a Missile Crisis*, p. 130. JFK's reaction: Higgins, *The Perfect Failure*, p. 145.
131. Rusk's assassination fear: *The New York Times*, July 23, 1975.
132. De Gaulle's advice: de Gaulle, *Memoirs of Hope*, p. 256.
132. Kennedy and Khrushchev: *Time*, June 9, 1962, and Schick, *The Berlin Crisis*, p. 141.
133. "The testicles": Detzer, *The Brink*, p. 154. Khrushchev's admission: LaFeber, *The American Age*, p. 565.
133. JFK's speech: *The New York Times*, June 7, 1961.
134. Nuclear first strike: LaFeber, *The American Age*, p. 566. Khrushchev's complaint: *The New York Times*, October 14, 1987.
134. Smather's statement: Walton, *Cold War and Counterrevolution*, p. 48.
135. Memorandum #100: NSA 03272, p. 136.
135. Board of National Estimates: Ibid., pp. 136–37.
135. Fletcher Knebel: *Look*, December 18, 1962.
135. The Cuba Project: NSA 00178.
136. Castro's speech: Thomas, *Cuba*, p. 1373.
137. The chauffeur's statement: *The New York Times*, June 27, 1963.

137. RFK on overthrow: Davis, *The Kennedys,* pp. 395–96. Ray Cline: NSA: 03309. Final chapter: NSA 03272, p. 141.
138. Lansdale on American revolution: NSA 00174. Lansdale on military intervention: NSA 00187.

Chapter 6. Mongoose

139. *Pravda,* February 19, 1962.
140. Lansdale description: Halberstam, *The Best and the Brightest,* pp. 124–25.
140. Six-phase plan: NSA 00178 and 03272.
140. Lansdale's belief: NSA, "Memorandum for members, Caribbean Survey Group," January 20, 1962.
141. The JFK-Campbell-Rosselli connection: Davis, *The Kennedys,* pp. 400–402.
142. Lansdale's new schedule: NSA 00178. Mongoose plans: Hershberg, "Before 'The Missiles of October,' " p. 175.
142. Mongoose guidelines: NSA 00187, 03272.
142. Castro's support: NSA 00188. Cuban militarization: NSA 00192.
143. JFK's threat: *The Saturday Evening Post,* March 27, 1962.
143. Jupiters ready: NSA 00252. Leak: *The Wall Street Journal,* April 20, 1962.
144. Malinovsky: Beschless, *The Crisis Years,* p. 381.
145. Lansdale memo: NSA 00215.
145. Lansdale's worry: NSA 00215.
145. CIA in Miami: Hinkle and Turner, *The Fish Is Red,* pp. 113–17.
146. "Whiplash": NSA 00217. Press coverage: *The New York Times,* April 10, 14, 15, 25, and 29, 1962.
146. Counterforce: NSA 00213.
147. U.S. into Thailand: Hilsman, *To Move a Nation,* pp. 144–45.
148. Macmillan's wisecrack: *The Washington Post,* November 28, 1980. Vietnam description: Sheehan, *A Bright Shining Lie,* p. 44.
148. The troops will march in: LaFeber, *The American Age,* p. 563.
149. U.S. imperial attitude: Sheehan, *A Bright Shining Lie,* p. 131.
151. The Jackson-Gilpatric conversation: Franklin, *The Defenders,* p. 198.
155. Cuban demonstrations: Thomas, *Cuba,* p. 1386.
155. The troubles: Ibid., p. 1386.
155. Castro to French journalist: Ibid., p. 1392.
156. Interview with Matthews: Ibid., p. 1392.
156. "Special Group" memo: NSA 00236. Lansdale's memos: NSA 00238.
157. Khrushchev's speech: *The New York Times,* July 12, 1962.
157. High in the water: NSA 03130.
157. Lansdale's memo: NSA 00246.
158. Castro's speech: Thomas, *Cuba,* p. 1176.

158. Acheson on JFK: Beschloss, *The Crisis Years*, p. 410. Lansdale's July 31 memo: NSA 00253.
159. The Senate study: NSA 03272.

Chapter 7. Provocation

161. The de Vosjoli mission: Prados, *Presidents' Secret Wars*, pp. 132–33.
162. "Swift Strike II": NSA 03198. B-26 attacks: NSA 00269.
162. Stepped-up course B: NSA 00268. Occupation: NSA 00266. McCone's belief: NSA 02638.
163. Deletion of the four words: NSA 00277.
163. Ships to Cuba: *The New York Times*, August 25, 1962. McCone to JFK and Taylor: NSA 03272. NSAM# 181: NSA 00295, 03383, 02638.
163. "seek to provoke": Hershberg, "Before 'The Missiles of October,' " p. 184.
164. Attacks at Havana: NSA 03029.
164. CIA study: NSA 00688.
164. Press conference: NSA 00315.
164. Keating's speech: NSA 00322.
165. JFK's September 4 declaration: NSA 00340. The MIGs: NSA 03102, 03130.
165. Khrushchev's message: Sorensen, *Kennedy*, pp. 666–67.
166. Khrushchev to Udall: NSA 00363.
166. Destruction of Cuban air force: Hershberg, "Before 'The Missiles of October,' " p. 184.
168. The *Omsk:* NSA 03087. Castro's speech: *The New York Times*, September 12, 1962. Soviet warning: *The New York Times*, September 12, 1962. Kennedy's worry: Schlesinger, *A Thousand Days*, p. 505.
168. JFK's September 13 press conference: NSA 00408.
169. *Poltava* to Mariel: NSA 03130. Nixon's statement: *The New York Times*, September 16, 1962.
169. Nixon and GOP senators: *The New York Times*, September 19, 1962.
169. Simulated bombing of Cuba: NSA 03087.
170. Castro's pilot's boast: NSA 00425.
170. Red Star: *The New York Times*, September 21, 1962.
170. JFK's new instructions: Hershberg, "Before 'The Missiles of October,' " p. 185. Fishing port: *The Philadelphia Inquirer*, September 26, 1962.
171. U-2 spotting Komar: NSA 03087, 03336.
171. House resolution: *The New York Times*, September 27, 1962. View from Mexico: NSA 00469. LeMay: NSA 02811. IL-28 bombers: NSA 03130, 03102, 02972.
172. McNamara's directive to Dennison: NSA 03164, 02925.
172. The six conditions: NSA 03087.

172. "Wargame the effectiveness": Hershberg, "Before 'The Missiles of October,' " p. 188. McNamara's assurance: Ibid., pp. 188–89.
173. The Robert Kennedy–McCone exchange: NSA 03272, 00520.
173. British connection: NSA 00571.
174. Lippmann: *The Washington Post*, October 9, 1962.
174. JFK in Baltimore: *The Washington Post*, October 11, 1962. Keating's speech, Ibid.
175. JFK in Newark: *The Washington Post*, October 13, 1962.
176. JFK's directive to McCone: NSA 03154. Operation and logistic plans: Hershberg, "Before 'The Missiles of October,' " p. 191.
176. JFK in Kentucky: *The Washington Post*, October 14, 1962. Alpha 66 boast: NSA 00605.
177. Bundy: *The New York Times*, October 15, 1962.

Chapter 8. The Autumn Campaign

187. Excomm transcript: NSA, October 16, 1962, folder.
197. The de Gaulle memo: NSA, Berlin crisis files, folder forSeptember 1962.
198. O'Donnell to Bohlen: Abel, *The Missile Crisis*, p. 56.
198. Bohlen's notes: NSA 00645.
199. Stevenson's letter: NSA 00652.
200. Abel, *The Missile Crisis*, p. 57.
200. Blur of meetings: NSA 01867. Acheson versus Stevenson: Abel, *The Missile Crisis*, pp. 57–58.
201. McNamara for blockade: National Security Archive, *Cuban Missile Crisis*, I, *Chronology*, p. 55.
201. Acheson for invasion: Ibid., p. 55. Air strike preparations: NSA 01867.
202. The campaign trail: *The Chicago Tribune* and *San Francisco Examiner*, October 18, 1962.
205. Sorensen at Andrews: Sorensen, *Kennedy*, p. 686.
207. Southeastern military buildup: Detzer, *The Brink*, p. 146.
207. Cosmos X.: Burrows, William E. Burrows, *Deep Black*, pp. 131–32.

Chapter 9. Politics as Usual

208. News reports: *The New York Times*, *San Francisco Examiner*, and *Christian Science Monitor*, October 18, 1962.
209. On Ormsby-Gore: Abel, *The Missile Crisis*, pp. 73–74.
211. On Floyd Odlum: Franklin, *The Defenders*, p. 129.
212. Cuba memo: NSA 00662.
215. "This is the week": Abel, *The Missile Crisis*, p. 67. A "crock": *The New York Times*, November 15, 1990.

215. Report on Komars: NSA 03130, 03087.

216. On Gromyko: Gromyko, *1036 Dnei*, p. 218.

216. Sorensen's account: Sorensen, *Kennedy*, pp. 688–89.

217. Nixon campaigning: *The New York Times*, October 19, 1962. Goldwater: *New York Journal American*, October 14, 1962.

217. Note to Sorensen: NSA 00674.

218. On Gromyko: *Current Biography*, 1958.

219. Gromyko with JFK: Sorensen, *Kennedy*, p. 690.

220. "Sitting in back": Kennedy, *Thirteen Days*, p. 43.

221. Meeker's advice: NSA 00668.

221. The LBJ leak: *Washington Times*, October 26, 1987.

223. Khrushchev on Gromyko and Rusk: Khrushchev, *Khrushchev Remembers*, pp. 174–75.

223. Telegram from Cuba: Ibid., pp. 176–77. Radio Moscow: NSA 03130.

224. The news reports: *Chicago Tribune* and *Tampa Tribune*, October 20, 1962.

225. JFK to Dryfoos: Schlesinger, *A Thousand Days*, pp. 740–41. Leaks: Detzer, *The Brink*, pp. 147–48.

225. Ormsby-Gore: Nunnerley, *President Kennedy and Britain*, pp. 77–78.

226. Pressure on Kennedy: NSA 03154, 01867.

226. Katzenbach's argument: NSA 00699.

226. Hilsman's memo: NSA 00682.

227. Lausche: *Time*, February 20, 1956.

228. Reporter in Cleveland: *The Washington Post*, October 20, 1962.

229. Springfield: *Chicago Tribune*, October 20, 1962.

232. Salinger with press: Salinger, *With Kennedy*, p. 251.

233. Sorensen's draft: Sorensen, *Kennedy*, p. 692.

233. Sorensen's draft: NSA 00696, 00681.

234. Question in *The Washington Post*: *The Washington Post*, October 20, 1962.

Chapter 10. Air of Crisis

235. On Donovan: *Current Biography*, 1962; *The New York Times*, October 21, 1962.

236-7. White House's boy: New York *Daily News*, October 11, 1962. Bay of Pigs cover-up: Hoover Institution, Donovan Papers, "Secret Negotiating Instructions," Box 48, file 3.

237. The prisoners' fund: *The New York Times* and New York *Daily News*, October 11, 1962.

238. Salinger: Salinger, *With Kennedy*, p. 252

239. Misleading the press: *The New York Times*, October 21, 1962.

240. McCone and Gilpatric: Allison, *The Essence of Decision*, p. 208.

240. Stevenson: Ibid., p. 209.
241-2. "Adlai wanted": *Newsweek*, December 17, 1962. Aftertastes: Allison, *The Essence of Decision*, p. 209.
242. JFK's admiration: Detzer, *The Brink*, p. 159.
243. Alpha 66: *New York Herald Tribune*, October 21, 1962.
243. CIA report: NSA 00721.
245. Lippmann: Steel, *Walter Lippmann and the American Century*, p. 534.
245. On Salinger: Salinger, *With Kennedy*, p. 253.
247. Alpha 66 threat: *The New York Times*, October 22, 1962. Bundy to Salinger: Salinger, *With Kennedy*, pp. 253–54.
247. Bundy to Salinger: Salinger, *With Kennedy*, p. 257. U.S. case: NSA 00766.
248. U.S. justification: NSA 00737.
249. "90 percent": NSA 00738.
249. McNamara's memo: NSA 00738.
250. Wilson oral interview: NSA 03215.
250. JFK-Anderson exchange: Medland, *The Cuban Missile Crisis of 1962*, p. 8.
251. JFK and Anderson: NSA 03154, 02925. Soviets' noses: LaFeber, *The American Age*, p. 569.
251. "All American citizens": NSA 00735. Air Force interceptors: Abel, *The Missile Crisis*, p. 108. "You are instructed": NSA 00744.
252. O'Brien to Congress: Abel, *The Missile Crisis*, p. 107.
252. David Bruce's comment: JFK Library, David Bruce diary, p. 5.
253. Bruce-Acheson exchange: Detzer, *The Brink*, pp. 170–71.
254. "Crumbling fast": Abel, *The Missile Crisis*, pp. 101–2.

Chapter 11. Prime Time

256. On Penkovsky: Horne, *Harold Macmillan*, pp. 369–70. Florida armed: *Miami Herald*, October 23, 1962.
257. Harriman's memo: NSA 00816.
258. "Brainwash press": JFK Library, POF, Box 115.
258. The brainwasher: NSA, Cuban Missile Crisis Document Set, Record #4956.
258. Bundy's memo: NSA 00842.
259. Scene with Caroline: Detzer, *The Brink*, p. 178.
259. No Jupiters fired: NSA 03154. Chayes' advice: NSA 02780.
259. Meeker's advice: NSA 02780.
260. Jackets on: *The Washington Post*, August 26, 1990.
260. Adenauer's advice: NSA 00863
260-1. On Macmillan: *Current Biography*, 1955. Bruce with Macmillan: NSA 00880. Missiles so far: Detzer, *The Brink*, p. 177.

261. Message to de Gaulle: NSA 00797. De Gaulle to Acheson: Detzer, *The Brink*, p. 175.

262. De Gaulle to Acheson: NSA 00741. Letter to Diefenbaker: NSA 00796.

263-4. Diefenbaker's position: Abel, *The Missile Crisis*, p. 113. Merchant on Diefenbaker: Ghent, "Canada, the United States, and the Cuban Missile Crisis."

264. Dick Thrasher: Nash, *Kennedy and Diefenbaker*, p. 186. The press: *Macleans*, April 21, 1962, *Financial Post*, September 22, 1962.

265. Salinger to Fleming: Salinger, *With Kennedy*, p. 262. JFK to Eisenhower: Dwight D. Eisenhower Library, Post-Presidential Files, Box 10, Cuba. Edward Kennedy: Detzer, *The Brink*, p. 178.

265. "Important statement": NSA 03154.

266. JFK's instructions: NSA 00840.

266. JFK with press: Detzer, *The Brink*, p. 179.

267. NSA 03154.

267. JFK to Khrushchev: NSA 00806, 03323.

269. *San Francisco Examiner*, October 23, 1962.

269. Ralph McGill: *Atlanta Constitution*, October 23, 1962.

270. United Nations: *New York Herald Tribune*, October 23, 1991.

271. Kennedy finishes: *Miami Herald*, October 23, 1962.

272. Linus Pauling: *Chicago Tribune*, October 23, 1962. Bertrand Russell: NSA 00767. British Foreign Office: *The Washington Post*, October 23, 1962.

273. Farris Bryant: *Miami Herald*, October 23, 1962. Chicago reactions: *Chicago Tribune*, October 23, 1962. New York reactions: *New York Herald Tribune*, October 23, 1962. Khrushchev's rage: Blight and Welch, *On the Brink*, p. 306. JFK and Macmillan: Horne, *Harold Macmillan*, p. 367.

Chapter 12. Back Channels

277. New Orleans: *Times-Picayune*, October 24, 1962. Chicago: *Chicago Tribune*, October 24, 1962. Mayflower: *The Washington Post*, October 24, 1962.

277-8. "Grave concern": NSA, Cuban missile crisis, Box 3. Bertrand Russell: *The New York Times*, October 24, 1962. Grosvenor Square: *The Times*, October 24, 1962. Bruce's wire: NSA, Cuban missile crisis, Box 3.

278. Soviet frontier: Nunnerly, *President Kennedy and Britain*, p. 72. Our missile ring: *San Francisco Examiner*, October 24, 1962. Gallup poll: Detzer, *The Brink*, p. 192. *We'll Bury You: The New York Times*, October 24, 1962.

279. LBJ's note: Lyndon B. Johnson Library, LBJ handwritten notes, Box 8, Vice Presidential Security.

279. Destroy the missile site: NSA 00966.

279-80. Boris Gudonov: *Atlanta Constitution*, October 24, 1962. 2,500-word letter: NSA, Cuban missile crisis, Box 3, October 23, 1962, folder.

280. Specific threats: NSA 00896.

280. "Couldn't pour piss": Black, *The Good Neighbor*, p. 114.

281. Rusk's pressure: NSA 03154, pp. 113–14.

281. Rusk's success: NSA 00893. De Onis: *The New York Times*, October 22, 1962.

282. Stevenson's speech: Martin, *Adlai Stevenson and His World*, p. 225.

282. JFK to Stevenson: Ibid., p. 728.

282-3. García and Zorin speeches: Ibid., p. 728.

283. U Thant's comment: U Thant, *View from the U.N.*, pp. 156–57.

284. Cable to Khrushchev: Khrushchev, *Khrushchev Remembers*, pp. 176–77.

284. Out of the news: NSA, Cuban missile crisis, October 24, 1962, Folder C.

284. Confrontation with press: Salinger, *With Kennedy*, p. 389. "Highest priority": NSA 00965.

285. JFK to Khrushchev: NSA 00965.

286. Castro on Kennedy: *The Washington Post*, October 24, 1962.

286. Dubovik's comment: NSA 03130, p. 50. TASS's warning: Abel, *The Missile Crisis*, p. 134.

287. RFK on Dobrynin: Kennedy, *Thirteen Days*, pp. 65–66. JFK and Ormsby-Gore: Wills, *The Kennedy Imprisonment*, p. 269.

287. "First accepted": NSA 02616.

288. Key West: *Miami Herald*, October 25, 1962.

289. Admiral Dennison: *Chicago Tribune*, October 25, 1962.

290. Word from Norfolk: NSA 01289. A fast corvette: *The New York Times*, October 25, 1962.

290. Items for Alpha 66: NSA, Cuban Missile Crisis, October 24, 1962, Folder C.

291-2. Khrushchev and Knox: *Chicago Tribune*, October 25, 1962.

292. Khrushchev's message: NSA 01421, October 26, 1962, Folder B.

292. Gromyko in East Berlin: NSA 01289, 01172.

292. *Tribune* report: *Chicago Tribune*, October 25, 1962.

293. Argentina: *The New York Times*, October 25, 1962.

293-4. Reischauer: Abel, *The Missile Crisis*, p. 145. Robert Allen: *The New York Times*, October 25, 1962. Mexico: *The Washington Post*, October 25, 1962.

294. "Flagrant piracy": Abel, *The Missile Crisis*, p. 145. Demonstrations in Britain: *The Washington Post*, October 25, 1962; *The New York*

Times, October 25, 1962. Khrushchev's response: Detzer, *The Brink,* p. 203.

295. Russell's retort: Detzer, *The Brink,* p. 204. McGovern: *The Washington Post,* October 25, 1962. "Long overdue": *The New York Times,* October 25, 1962.

295. U.S. protests: *San Francisco Examiner* and *The New York Times,* October 25, 1962.

295. Lippmann: *The Washington Post,* October 25, 1962.

296. Lippmann description: Steel, *Walter Lippmann and the American Century,* p. xv.

297. JFK and RFK: Kennedy, *Thirteen Days,* p. 67.

297. Excomm: NSA, Cuban Missile Crisis Chronology, p. 65. Ships regrouping: NSA 02972. JFK: Reeves, *A Question of Character,* p. 381

298. McNamara's reply: NSA 01336. The Jupiters: NSA 01138. JFK and Macmillan: Macmillan, *At the End of the Day,* p. 199.

298. Journalist's account: Abel, *The Missile Crisis,* p. 148.

299. Leningrad Philharmonic: *The New York Times,* October 27, 1962. Zorin: NSA 01494, 01184.

299. U Thant's appeals: NSA 01110.

299-300. Khrushchev to U Thant: Thant, *View from the U.N.,* p. 165. Kennedy to U Thant: Ibid., p. 166. Luce: Kennedy Library, Henry Luce Oral History.

300. Bundy's memo: NSA, October 24, 1962, Folder B.

301. Macmillan in the Commons: NSA 03154. Macmillan's advice: NSA, October 24, 1962, Folder B.

301. Khrushchev's letter: NSA 01105, 03154.

302. Kennedy and Macmillan: Horne, *Harold Macmillan,* pp. 370–72.

303. JFK to Khrushchev: NSA 01346.

Chapter 13. Until Hell Freezes Over

304. Chicago: *Chicago Tribune,* October 26, 1962.

305. Alun Gwynne-Jones: *The Times,* October 26, 1962.

305. Norman Thomas: *The New York Times,* October 26, 1962. University of Chicago: *Chicago Tribune,* October 26, 1962.

306. "Letter to America": Abel, *The Missile Crisis,* pp. 164–65.

306. Tanker incident: Detzer, *The Brink,* p. 228.

306. Henderson's cable: NSA 03130, 01358. "Great store": NSA 01328.

307. Hilsman's worry: NSA, October 25, 1962, Folder B. *La Verdad:* NSA, October 27, Folder A.

307. Sorensen's acknowledgment: Sorensen, *Kennedy,* p. 711. Alpha 66: *Chicago Tribune,* October 26, 1962.

308. U Thant to JFK: NSA 01286. Salinger in press conference: *The New York Times*, October 26, 1962.

309. Security measures: *The New York Times*, October 26, 1962.

309. Cuba's defense: *Chicago Tribune*, October 26, 1962. Soviet regiment: Garthoff, *Reflections on the Cuban Missile Crisis* (1987), p. 78, and NSA 01289.

310. Cuba's battle order: *The Washington Post*, October 26, 1962.

311. Stevenson's speech: *The New York Times*, October 26, 1962.

311-2. Stevenson popular: Martin, *Adlai Stevenson and His World*, p. 735. "Deliberate adventure": Horne, *Harold Macmillan*, p. 373.

312. Khrushchev to Kennedy: Pope, *Soviet Views on the Cuban Missile Crisis*, p. 48.

312. Garthoff's fear: NSA, October 25, 1962, Folder B.

312. The *Vinnitsa: The New York Times*, October 27, 1962.

313. Haugland's report: *Chicago Tribune*, October 27, 1962.

314. "Some publicity": Detzer, *The Brink*, p. 230. *Marucla* incident: Ibid., p. 231.

315. Dennison: *Chicago Tribune*, October 27, 1962. "Frighten the Russians": *The Washington Post*, October 27, 1962.

315. "Offensive military preparations": *The Washington Post*, October 27, 1962. Guantánamo scene: Detzer, *The Brink*, p. 233.

316. Heavy casualties: NSA 03087. JFK's hesitation: NSA 02811.

317. "Very serious": Abel, *The Missile Crisis*, p. 177.

317-8. Fomin's proposals: Ibid., p. 178. Rusk's message: Ibid., p. 179. Rusk, Scali, and Salinger: Detzer, *The Brink*, p. 238.

319. Fomin's new element: NSA 01382.

319. GOP newsletter: *The Washington Post*, October 27, 1962.

319. Leaks: NSA 01454, 02935; *The New York Times*, October 27, 1962.

320. Gordon's cable: NSA 01376. U Thant to Castro: NSA 01391.

320. Khrushchev to JFK: NSA 01388.

321. Khrushchev's order to ships: *The Washington Post*, October 27, 1962.

321. Hilsman description: Halberstam, *The Best and the Brightest*, p. 255.

Chapter 14. Those Frigging Missiles

322. Secret deal: NSA 01424.

322-3. RFK and Dobrynin: Garthoff, *Reflections* (1989). JFK and Macmillan: Horne, *Harold Macmillan*, p. 374.

323. "Act of war": *Chicago Tribune*, October 27, 1962. Castro's letter to Khrushchev: *Granma*, December 2, 1990.

323-4. Castro's order: NSA 00323.

324. Bartlow to Schlesinger: NSA, October 27, 1962, Folder B.

324. "Frigging missiles": Kennedy, *Thirteen Days*, p. 95.

325. Riot in Moscow: *Chicago Tribune* and *The New York Times*, October 28, 1962.

325. The Soviet decision: Khrushchev, *Khrushchev Remembers*, pp. 177–78.

326. Trafalgar Square: *The New York Times*, October 28, 1962.

327. Salinger and McNamara: Abel, *The Missile Crisis*, pp. 194–95.

327. White House pickets: *Chicago Tribune*, October 28, 1962.

328. McCone's report: NSA 01492. McNamara's information: NSA 03328.

328. The U-2 episode: NSA 01490, 01867, 03268, 02655.

328. Khrushchev's message: NSA 03328, 01538, 01488.

329-30. Norstad's protest: NSA 01486.

Chapter 15. The Brink

333. U-2 shootdown: NSA 01867, 01575. Taylor's demand: Beschloss, *The Crisis Years*, p. 530.

334. Scali's anger: Garthoff, *Reflections* (1989), p. 90. "Immediate retaliation": Kennedy, *Thirteen Days*, pp. 98–102.

335. The counter-suggestions: NSA 01544.

335. JFK's letter to Khrushchev: NSA 01552.

336. Oval Office conversation: NSA 03322. Fidel's defiance: *The New York Times*, October 28, 1962. Castro to U Thant: NSA 01485.

336-7. RFK's account: Kennedy, *Thirteen Days*, pp. 108–9. Dobrynin's account: Allyn et al., "Essence of Revision: Moscow, Havana, and the Cuban Missile Crisis."

337-8. Evening revelations: NSA 01544, 01318, 01486. Rusk to Cordier: NSA 03322. "Be killed": Salinger, *With Kennedy*, p. 273.

Chapter 16. Finale

339. Khrushchev to Castro: *Granma*, December 2, 1990.

340. Venezuelan Communists: NSA 01633.

340. Sayre's sermon: *The Washington Post*, October 29, 1962.

341. Forrestal to Hatcher: *The Washington Post*, October 29, 1962.

341. Khrushchev's broadcast: *The New York Times*, October 29, 1962.

342. JFK's apology: *The New York Times*, October 29, 1962.

343. Rusk's statement: NSA 01589. McNamara home: *The New York Times*, October 29, 1962.

343-4. Macmillan's reaction: Horne, *Harold Macmillan*, pp. 377–78.

344. Turkish reaction: *The New York Times*, October 29, 1962.

344. Further plans: NSA 01664.

Epilogue

345. "Unavoidably detained": *The Washington Post*, October 30, 1962. Reconnaissance flights: NSA 01642, 02780. Directive to McCone: NSA 03272.

345-6. McNaughton to the brass: NSA 03307. RFK and Dobrynin: Schlesinger, *A Thousand Days*, pp. 522–23.

346. RFK's notes: Ibid., p. 523.

346. Reconnaissance photos: NSA 03130, 02075. JFK to McNamara: NSA 02819. Soviet brigade: Khrushchev, *Khrushchev Remembers*, p. 500.

347. Nixon's press conference: *The Washington Post*, November 7, 1962.

348. Alpha 66 attacks: NSA 03029. JFK's approval of new operations: NSA 03272.

348. American University speech: NSA 03125. Objective of new program: NSA 03272.

349. TFX: Mollenhoff, *The Pentagon: Politics, Profits, and Plunder*, pp. 314–15.

350. Eulogizing comment: Paterson, *Kennedy's Quest for Victory*, p. 3.

351. Diefenbaker: Ghent, "Canada, the United States, and the Cuban Missile Crisis."

352. Diefenbaker's fall: Ghent, "Did He Fall or Was He Pushed?"

355-6. The four principles: Lebow, "Domestic Politics and the Cuban Missile Crisis."

356. Les Aspin: *The Washington Post*, January 8, 1991.

356. Opening to Cuba: JFK Library, William Attwood, Oral History, November 8, 1965.

Bibliography

Archives

Dwight D. Eisenhower Library
Hoover Institution
John F. Kennedy Library
Library of Congress
National Archives
National Security Archive (NSA), (Washington, D.C.)
Franklin D. Roosevelt Library

Reference Work
Current Biography

Collections of Documents

Stephen Clissold, ed., *Soviet Relations with Latin America, 1918–1968: A Documentary Survey* (London: 1970).
Kenneth M. Jensen, ed., *Origins of the Cold War: The Novikov, Kennan, and Roberts Long Telegrams of 1946* (Washington: 1991).
U.S. Department of State, *Foreign Relations of the United States.*
U.S. Government, *Public Papers of the Presidents.*

Newspapers and Journals

Atlanta Constitution
Chicago Tribune
Christian Science Monitor
Financial Post

Granma
The Philadelphia Inquirer
Maclean's
Miami Herald
Newsweek
New York Herald Tribune
New York Journal American
New York Daily News
The New York Times
Pravda
San Francisco Examiner
The Saturday Evening Post
Tampa Tribune
The Times
Time
U.S. News & World Report
The Wall Street Journal
The Washington Post

Articles

Allison, Graham T., "Cuban Missiles and Kennedy Macho: New Evidence to Dispel the Myth," Washington Monthly, October 1975.

Allyn, Bruce J., "Essence of Revision: Moscow, Havana, and the Cuban Missile Crisis," International Security, Winter 1989–90.

Anderson, George W., Jr., "The Cuban Blockade: An Admiral's Memoir," Washington Quarterly, Autumn 1982.

Armstrong, Scott and Philip Brenner, "Putting Cuba Back in the Cuban Missile Crisis," in Philip Brenner, ed., The Cuba Reader: The Making of a Revolutionary Society (New York: 1988).

Ascoli, Max, "Escalation from the Bay of Pigs," Reporter, November 8, 1962.

Aynesworth, Hugh, "LBJ Leaked to Dallas Paper Cuban Missile Crisis Options," Washington Times, October 26, 1987.

Bernstein, Barton J., "The Cuban Missile Crisis: Trading the Jupiters in Turkey?" Political Science Quarterly, Spring 1980.

———— and Roger Hagan, "Military Value of Missiles in Cuba," Bulletin of Atomic Scientists, February 1963.

Blight, James G., Joseph Nye, and David Welch, "The Cuban Missile Crisis Revisited," Foreign Affairs, Fall 1987.

Branch, Taylor and George Crile, "The Kennedy Vendetta: How the CIA Waged a Silent War against Castro," Harpers, August 1975.

Brenner, Philip, "Cuba and the Missile Crisis," Journal of Latin American Studies, February 1990.

Cline, Ray, "A CIA Reminiscence," *Washington Quarterly*, Autumn 1982.

Garthoff, Raymond L., "The Cuban 'Contras' Caper: Did CIA Squads Threaten JFK Handling of the Missile Crisis?" *The Washington Post*, October 25, 1987.

Ghent, Jocelyn Maynard, "Canada, the United States, and the Cuban Missile Crisis," *Pacific Historical Review*, May 1979.

——, "Did He Fall or Was He Pushed? The Kennedy Administration and the Collapse of the Diefenbaker Government," *International History Review*, April 1979.

Haffner, Donald L., "Those Frigging Missiles: JFK, Cuba, and U.S. Missiles in Turkey," *Orbis*, Summer 1977.

Eleanor Harris, "The Senator Is in a Hurry," *McCall's*, August 1957.

Hershberg, James G., "Before 'The Missiles of October,' " *Diplomatic History*, Spring 1990.

Howard, Michael, "Governor-General of Germany," *Times Literary Supplement*, August 29, 1973.

Keating, Kenneth, "My Advance View of the Cuban Crisis," *Look*, November 3, 1964.

Knox, William E., "Close-up of Khrushchev during a Crisis," *The New York Times Magazine*, November 18, 1962.

Lebow, Richard Ned, "The Cuban Missile Crisis: Reading the Lessons Correctly," *Political Science Quarterly*, Fall 1982.

——, "Domestic Politics and the Cuban Missile Crisis," *Diplomatic History*, Fall 1990.

——, "Provocative Deterrence: A New Look at the Cuban Missile Crisis, *Arms Control Today*, July–August 1988.

Nichols, Jeanette P., "Dollar Strength as a Liability in United States Diplomacy," Proceedings of the *American Philosophical Society*, February 17, 1967.

Paterson, Thomas G., "The Historian as Detective: Senator Kenneth Keating, the Missiles in Cuba, and His Mysterious Sources," *Diplomatic History*, Winter 1987.

Rabe, Stephen G., "The Clues Didn't Check Out: Commentary of 'The CIA and Castillo Armas,' " *Diplomatic History*, Winter 1990.

Rippy, J. Fred, "The Hazards of Dale Carnegie Diplomacy," *Inter-American Economic Affairs*, Summer 1958.

Rovere, Richard, "Letter from Washington," *The New Yorker*, March 2, 1963.

Safford, Jeffrey J., "The Nixon-Castro Meeting of 19 April 1959," *Diplomatic History*, Fall 1980.

Scali, John, "I Was the Secret Go-Between in the Cuban Crisis," *Family Weekly*, October 25, 1964.

Sissman, L. E., "Innocent By-Stander," *Atlantic Monthly*, October 1973.

Steele, John L., "The Adlai Stevenson Affair," *Life*, December 14, 1962.

Trachtenberg, Marc, "White House Tapes and Minutes of the Cuban Missile Crisis: Introduction to Documents," *International Security*, Summer 1985.

Treverton, Gregory F., "Covert Action and Open Society," *Foreign Affairs*, Summer 1987.

Welch, David A. and James G. Blight, "The Eleventh Hour of the Cuban Missile Crisis: An Introduction to the Excomm Transcripts," *International Security*, Winter 1987/1988.

Welch, Richard E., "Lippmann, Berle, and the U.S. Response to the Cuban Revolution," *Diplomatic History*, Spring 1982.

Books

Abel, Elie, *The Missile Crisis* (Philadelphia: 1966).

Acheson, Dean, *Present at the Creation; My Years in the State Department* (New York: 1969).

Alexander, Charles C., *Holding the Line: The Eisenhower Era, 1952–1961* (Bloomington, IN: 1975).

Aliano, Richard A., *American Defense Policy from Eisenhower to Kennedy: The Politics of Changing Military Requirements, 1957–1961* (Athens, OH: 1975).

Allison, Graham T., *The Essence of Decision* (Boston: 1971).

Armacost, Michael, *The Politics of Weapons Innovation: The Thor-Jupiter Controversy* (New York: 1965).

Ball, George, *The Past Has Another Pattern* (New York: 1982).

Barnet, Richard J., *The Rockets' Red Glare; War, Politics, and the American Presidency* (New York: 1990).

Beschloss, Michael R., *May Day; The U-2 Affair* (New York: 1968).

———, *The Crisis Years; Kennedy and Khrushchev* (New York: 1991).

Black, George, *The Good Neighbor* (New York: 1988).

Blaiser, Cole, *The Giant's Rival: The U.S.S.R. in Latin America* (Pittsburgh: 1983).

Blight, James G. and David A. Welch, *On the Brink: Americans and Soviets Reexamine the Cuban Missile Crisis* (New York: 1989).

Blight, James G., *The Shattered Crystal Ball: Fear and Loathing in the Cuban Missile Crisis* (Totowa, NJ: 1989).

Bohlen, Charles, *Witness to History, 1929–1969* (New York: 1973).

Bonsal, Philip W., *Cuba, Castro, and the United States* (Pittsburgh: 1971).

Bradlee, Benjamin C., *Conversations with Kennedy* (New York: 1975).

Burrows, William E., *Deep Black: Space Espionage and National Security* (New York: 1986).

Chayes, Abram, *The Cuban Missile Crisis: International Crisis and the Role of Law* (New York: 1974).

Cook, Blanche Wiesen, *The Declassified Eisenhower; A Divided Legacy* (Garden City, NY: 1981).

Cooper, Chester L., *The Lion's Last Roar* (New York: 1978).

Davis, John H., *The Kennedys* (New York: 1984).

Davis, Kenneth S., *The Politics of Honor* (New York: 1967).

Detzer, David, *The Brink: Cuban Missile Crisis, 1962* (New York: 1979).

Dinerstein, Herbert S., *The Making of a Missile Crisis* (Baltimore: 1976).

Donovan, John C., *The Cold Warriors: A Policymaking Elite* (Lexington, MA: 1974).

Draper, Theodore, *Castroism: Theory and Practice* (New York: 1965).

Dunne, Finley Peter, *Dissertations of Mr. Dooley* (New York: 1906).

Exner, Judith, *My Story* (New York: 1977).

Fairlie, Henry, *The Kennedy Promise: The Politics of Expectation* (London: 1973).

Foner, Philip, *A History of Cuba* (New York: 1963).

Franklin, Roger, *The Defender: The Story of General Dynamics* (New York: 1986).

Fulbright, J. William, *The Crippled Giant* (New York: 1972).

Garthoff, Raymond L., *Reflections on the Cuban Missile Crisis* (Washington: 1987).

———, *Reflections on the Cuban Missile Crisis* (Washington, 1989).

Gaulle, Charles de, *Memoirs of Hope* (New York: 1971).

Goulden, Joseph C., *Korea: The Untold Story of the War* (New York: 1982).

Green, David, *The Containment of Latin America: A History of the Myths and Realities of the Good Neighbor Policy* (Chicago: 1971).

Gromyko, Anatoly, *1036 Dnei Presidenta Kennedi* (Moscow: 1971).

Halberstam, David, *The Best and the Brightest* (New York: 1972).

Harris, George, *Troubled Alliance: Turkish-American Problems in Historical Perspective, 1945–1971* (Washington: 1972).

Healy, David F., *The United States in Cuba, 1898–1902* (Madison: 1963).

Higgins, Trumbull, *The Perfect Failure: Kennedy, Eisenhower, and the Bay of Pigs* (New York: 1987).

Hilsman, Roger, *To Move a Nation* (New York: 1967).

Hinkle, Warren and William Turner, *The Fish Is Red: The Story of the Secret War Against Castro* (New York: 1981).

Hoopes, Townsend, *The Devil and John Foster Dulles* (New York: 1973).

Horne, Alistair, *Harold Macmillan*, vol. II (New York: 1989).

Hughes, Emmet John, *The Ordeal of Power: A Political Memoir of the Eisenhower Administration* (New York: 1963).

Hunt, Michael H., *Ideology and U.S. Foreign Policy* (New Haven: 1987).

Immerman, Richard H., *The CIA in Guatemala: The Foreign Policy of Intervention* (Austin: 1982).

Isaacson, Walter and Evan Thomas, *The Wise Men* (New York: 1986).

Kennan, George F., *Memoirs, 1925–1950* (Boston: 1967).

Kennedy, Robert F., *Thirteen Days: A Memoir of the Cuban Missile Crisis* (New York: 1969).

Kern, Montague, Patricia W. Levering, and Ralph Levering, *The Kennedy Crises: The Press, the Presidency, and Foreign Policy* (Chapel Hill, NC: 1983).

Kesaris, Paul L., *Operation Zapata: The "Ultrasensitive" Report and Testimony of the Board of Inquiry on the Bay of Pigs* (Frederick, MD: 1981).

Khrushchev, Nikita, *Khrushchev Remembers* (Boston: 1970).

———, *Khrushchev Remembers; The Glasnost Tapes* (Boston: 1990).

LaFeber, Walter, *The American Age* (New York: 1989).

Langley, Lester D., *The Banana Wars: An Inner History of the American Empire, 1900–1934* (Lexington, KY: 1983).

———, *The Cuban Policy of the United States* (New York: 1968).

———, *The United States and the Caribbean in the 20th Century* (Athens, GA: 1982).

Latham, Earl, *The Communist Controversy in Washington* (New York: 1969).

Laurence, William L., *Dawn Over Zero: The Story of the Atomic Bomb* (New York: 1946).

Lebow, Richard Ned, *Between Peace and War: The Nature of International Crisis* (Baltimore: 1981).

Lippmann, Walter, *The Cold War* (New York: 1947).

Lyon, Peyton V., *Canada in World Affairs* (Toronto: 1968).

McDougall, Walter A., *The Heavens and the Earth; A Political History of the Space Age* (New York: 1985).

Macmillan, Harold, *At the End of the Day, 1961–1963* (New York: 1973).

Martin, John Bartlow, *Adlai Stevenson and His World* (New York: 1977).

Matthews, Herbert L., *Fidel Castro* (New York: 1969).

Mecham, J. Lloyd, *A Survey of United States–Latin American Relations* (Boston: 1965).

Medland, William J., *The Cuban Missile Crisis of 1962; Needless or Necessary?* (Westport, CT: 1988).

Mee, Charles L., Jr., *Meeting at Potsdam* (New York: 1975).

Mollenhoff, Clark R., *The Pentagon: Politics, Profits, and Plunder* (New York: 1967).

Morley, Morris H., *Imperial State and Revolution; The United States and Cuba, 1952–1986* (Cambridge: 1987).

Nash, Knowlton, *Kennedy and Diefenbaker; Fear and Loathing Across the Undefended Border* (Toronto: 1990).

Neustadt, Richard E., *Presidential Power* (New York: 1960).

Nixon, Richard M., *Six Crises* (Garden City, NY: 1962).

Nunnerly, David, *President Kennedy and Britain* (New York: 1972).

O'Brien, Lawrence, *No Final Victories* (Garden City, NY: 1974).

Paterson, Thomas G., *Kennedy's Quest for Victory: American Foreign Policy, 1961–1963* (New York: 1989).

Penkovsky, Oleg, *The Penkovsky Papers* (Garden City, NY: 1965).

Pérez, Louis A., Jr., *Cuba Under the Platt Amendment, 1902–1934* (Pittsburgh: 1986).

———, *Intervention, Revolution, and Politics in Cuba, 1913–1921* (Pittsburgh: 1978).

Pope, Ronald R., *Soviet Views on the Cuban Missile Crisis: Myth and Reality in Foreign Policy Analysis* (Lanham, MD: 1982).

Prados, John, *Presidents' Secret Wars* (New York: 1986).

Rabe, Stephen G., *Eisenhower and Latin America: the Foreign Policy of Anti-Communism* (Chapel Hill, NC: 1988).

Ranelagh, John, *The Agency: The Rise and Decline of the CIA* (New York: 1987).

Reeves, Thomas C., *The Life and Times of Joe McCarthy* (New York: 1982).

———, *A Question of Character: A Life of John F. Kennedy* (New York: 1991).

Robinson, H. Basil, *Diefenbaker's World: A Populist in World Affairs* (Toronto: 1989).

Rostow, W. W., *The Diffusion of Power* (New York: 1972).

———, *View from the Seventh Floor* (New York: 1964).

Royko, Mike, *Boss: Richard J. Daley of Chicago* (New York: 1971).

Russell, Bertrand, *Unarmed Victory* (New York: 1963).

Salinger, Pierre, *With Kennedy* (Garden City, NY: 1966).

Schick, Jack M., *The Berlin Crisis, 1958–1962* (Philadelphia: 1971).

Schlesinger, Arthur M., Jr., *A Thousand Days: JFK in the White House* (Boston: 1965).

Sheehan, Neil, *A Bright Shining Lie* (New York: 1988).

Slater, Jerome, *The OAS and U.S. Foreign Policy* (Columbus, OH: 1967).

Slusser, Robert M., *The Berlin Crisis of 1961* (Baltimore: 1973).

Smith, Earl E. T., *The Fourth Floor* (New York: 1962).

Smith, Wayne S., *The Closest of Enemies: A Personal and Diplomatic Account of U.S.-Cuban Relations Since 1957* (New York: 1987).

Sorensen, Theodore, *Kennedy* (New York: 1965).

Steel, Ronald, *Walter Lippmann and the American Century* (New York: 1980).

Stone, I. F., *Time of Torment* (New York: 1967).

Suarez, Andres, *Cuba: Castroism and Communism, 1959–1966* (Cambridge, MA: 1967).

Szulc, Tad, *Fidel: A Critical Portrait* (New York: 1986).

Thant, U, *View from the U.N.* (Garden City, NY: 1978).

Thomas, Hugh, *Cuba: The Pursuit of Freedom* (New York: 1971).

Vosjoli, P. L. Thyraude de, *Lamia* (Boston: 1970).

Walker, Samuel, *In Defense of American Liberties: A History of the ACLU* (New York: 1990).

Walton, Richard J., *Cold War and Counterrevolution: The Foreign Policy of John F. Kennedy* (New York: 1972).

Welch, Richard E., Jr., *Response to Revolution: The United States and the Cuban Revolution, 1959–1961* (Chapel Hill, NC: 1985).

Whalen, Richard, *The Founding Father* (New York: 1964).

Wicker, Tom, *JFK and LBJ; The Influence of Personality Upon Politics* (Baltimore: 1968).

Wills, Garry, *The Kennedy Imprisonment* (Boston: 1982).

Wise, David and Thomas B. Ross, *The Invisible Government* (New York: 1964).

Wyden, Peter, *The Bay of Pigs: The Untold Story* (New York: 1980).

Index

PHOTO CREDITS

WL3000005528

973.922
T

Thompson, Robert
Smith.

The missiles of
October.

DATE DUE	
OCT - 9 1993	MAR 2 5 2000
MAY 5 1995	MAY 0 6 2000
JUN 2 0 1995	FEB 1 8 2001
OCT 22 1995	MAR 1 0 2001
	JUN - 5 2001
	APR 2 3 2002
NOV 1 3 1995	
DEC 23 1995	
FEB 17 1996	JUN 1 8 2002
MAY 8 1996	MAY 1 0 2003
	MAR 2 0 2004
NOV 1 2 1996	JAN 0 8 2006
JAN 27 1997	MAY 1 4 2006
	10/26/07
FEB 24 1997	
APR -2 1998	
APR -2 1998	
MAY 1 8 1998	
MAY 2 0 1999	
GAYLORD	PRINTED IN U.S.A.

BAKER & TAYLOR BOOKS